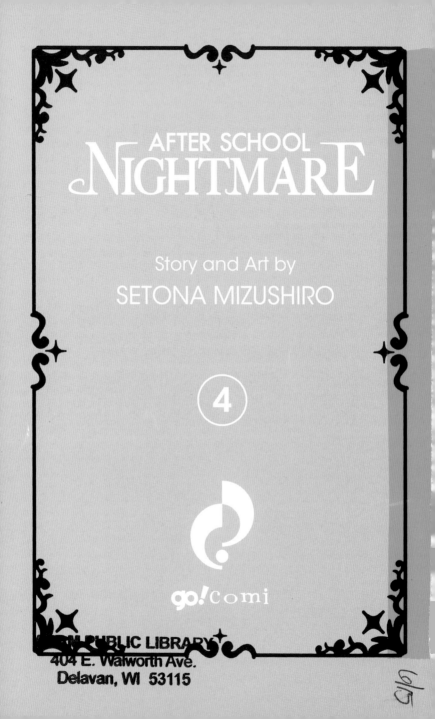

AFTER SCHOOL NIGHTMARE

Story and Art by
SETONA MIZUSHIRO

4

go!comi

Translation – Christine Schilling
Adaptation – Mallory Reaves
Lettering & Retouch – Eva Han
Production Manager – James Dashiell
Editor – Brynne Chandler

A Go! Comi manga

Published by Go! Media Entertainment, LLC

Houkago Hokenshitsu Volume 4
© SETONA MIZUSHIRO 2006
Originally published in Japan in 2006 by Akita Publishing Co., Ltd., Tokyo.
English translation rights arranged with Akita Publishing Co., Ltd.
through TOHAN CORPORATION, Tokyo.

Visit us online at www.gocomi.com
e-mail: info@gocomi.com

ISBN 978-1-933617-33-6

First printed in July 2007

2   3   4   5   6   7   8   9

Manufactured in the United States of America.

Koukoku Senior High School

Table of contents

AFTER SCHOOL NIGHTMARE

Our Story So Far

Mashiro Ichijo is a high school student whose body is half female, and half male. One day, he's called down to a secret infirmary to participate in a special "class" he needs to graduate. He learns from another student, Kureha, that each person takes on their true form in this class. When each person reaches their personal goal, their most heart-felt dream will come true. Mashiro decides to use this class to become a true male.

But, when another dreamer – a merciless knight – exposes Mashiro's secret, and everyone witnesses Kureha's tragic past, Mashiro begins to hate these "classes" that so cruelly open the wounds in people's hearts, and vows that he'll protect the weaker students, like Kureha.

Who is the real person behind the character who exposed his body's secret? He is trying to identify the other dreamers, when suddenly a guy student he's never gotten along with tells him "You're a girl!" and forces a kiss on him! How does Sou know the secret behind Mashiro's body? Could it be that Sou is another dreamer?

The newest member of the "class" is a giraffe who can see through everyone's dream-form! The student behind the giraffe, Shinonome, suddenly confronts Mashiro in school. He promises to identify the true person behind the knight – for a price... But Mashiro decides to discover these secrets on his own.

Especially – who is the knight? Mashiro suspects Sou. He prepares to face Sou straight on about it – not knowing that Sou's kiss was witnessed by his friend, Shinbashi...

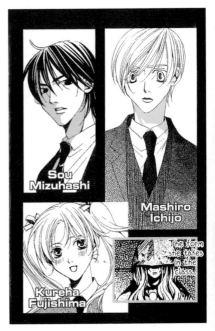

Mashiro Ichijo
Sou Mizuhashi
The form she takes in the class...
Kureha Fujishima

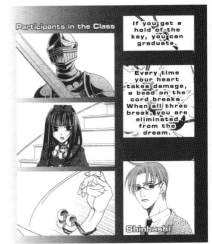

Participants in the Class
If you get a hold of the key, you can graduate.
Every time your heart takes damage, a bead on the cord breaks. When all three break, you are eliminated from the dream.
Shinbashi

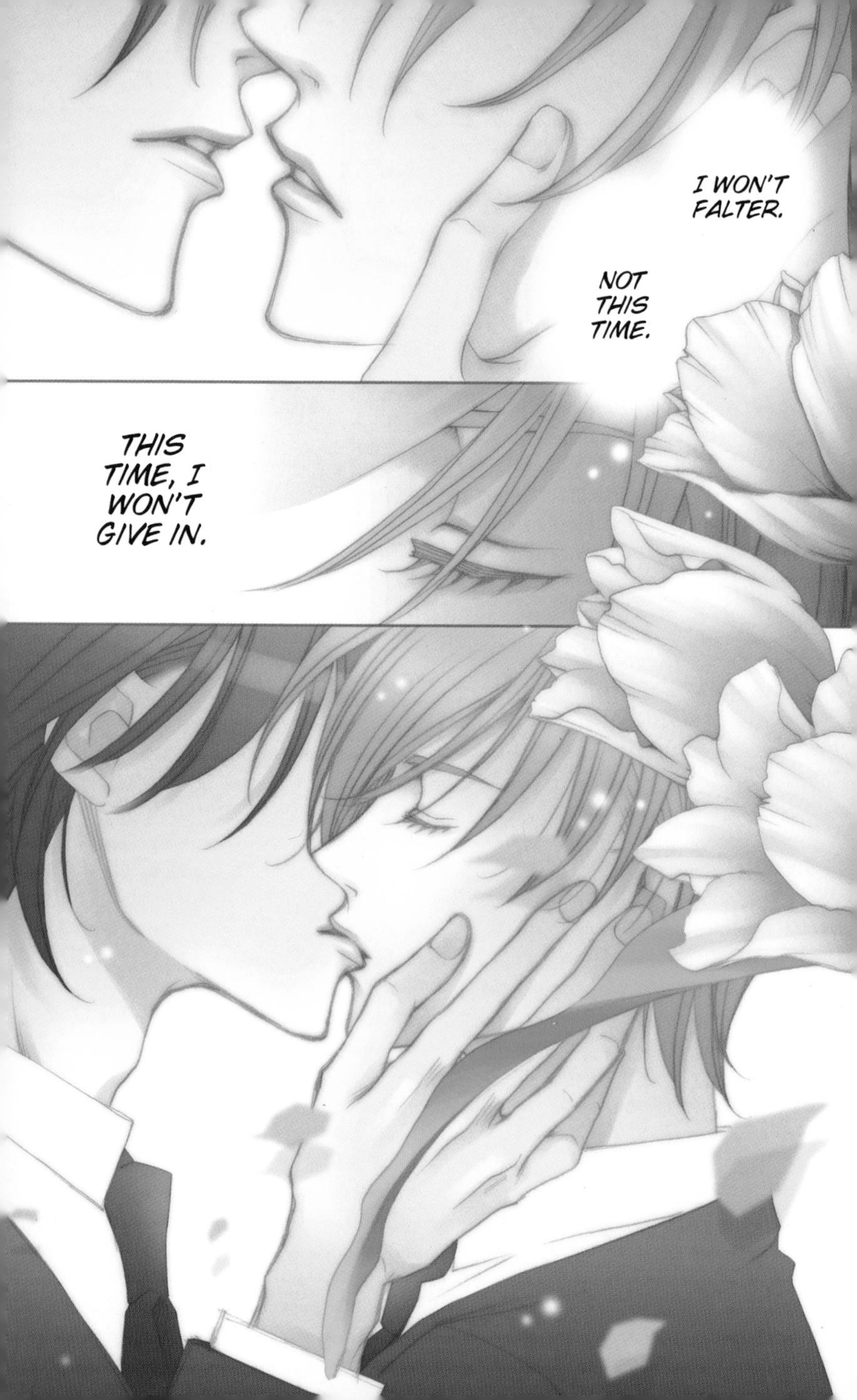
I WON'T FALTER.
NOT THIS TIME.
THIS TIME, I WON'T GIVE IN.

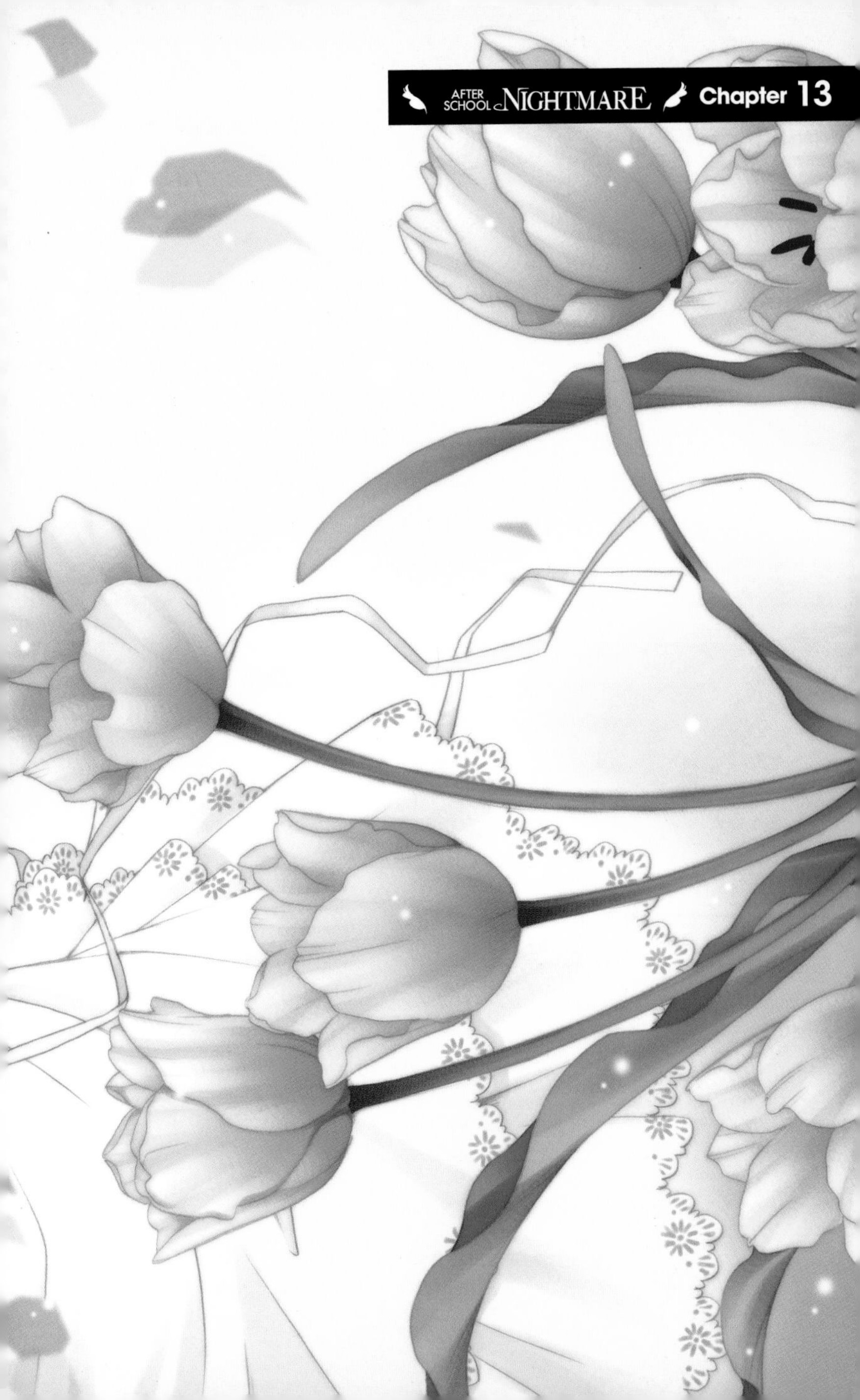
AFTER SCHOOL NIGHTMARE Chapter 13

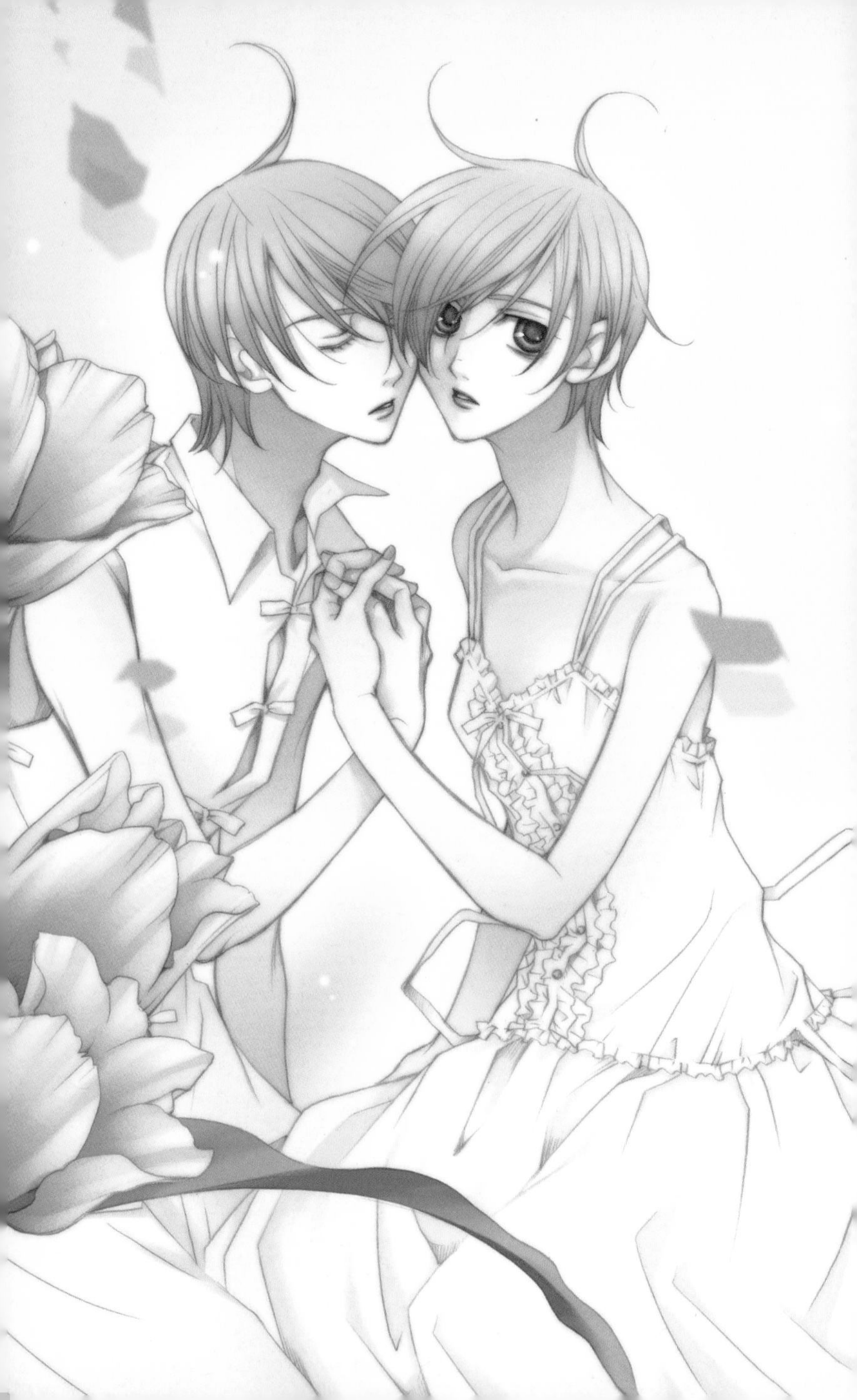

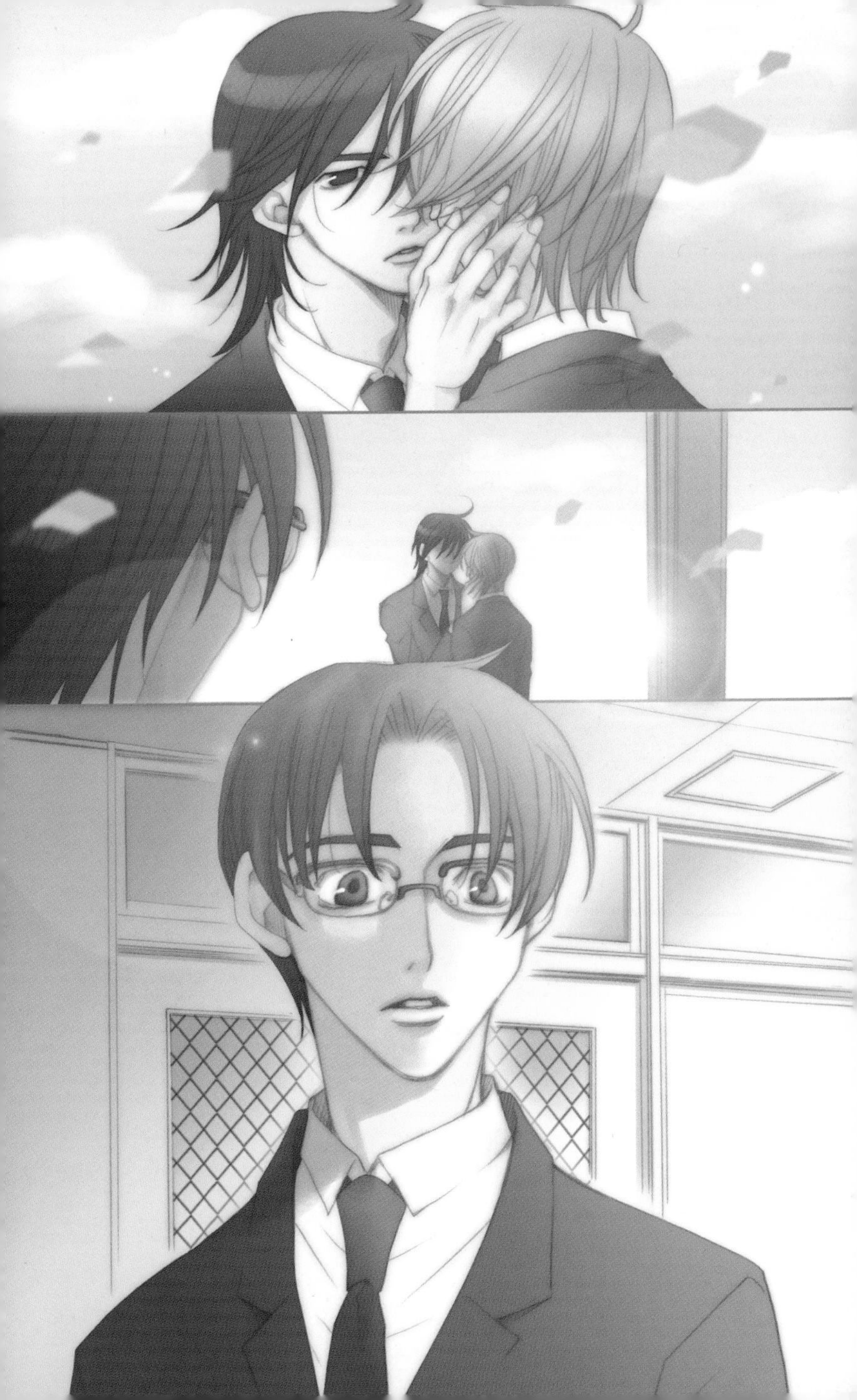

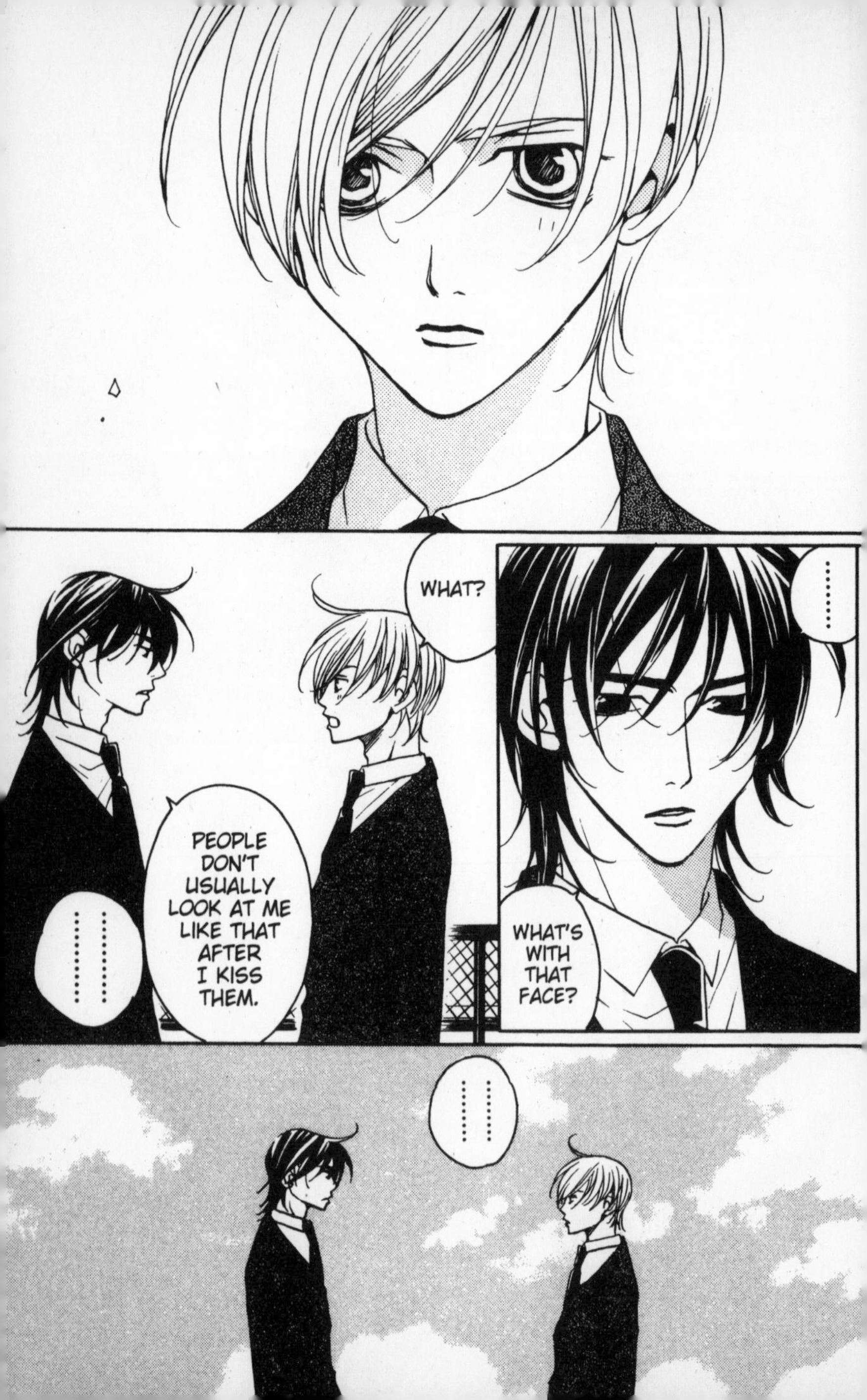
......
WHAT'S WITH THAT FACE?
WHAT?
PEOPLE DON'T USUALLY LOOK AT ME LIKE THAT AFTER I KISS THEM.
......
......

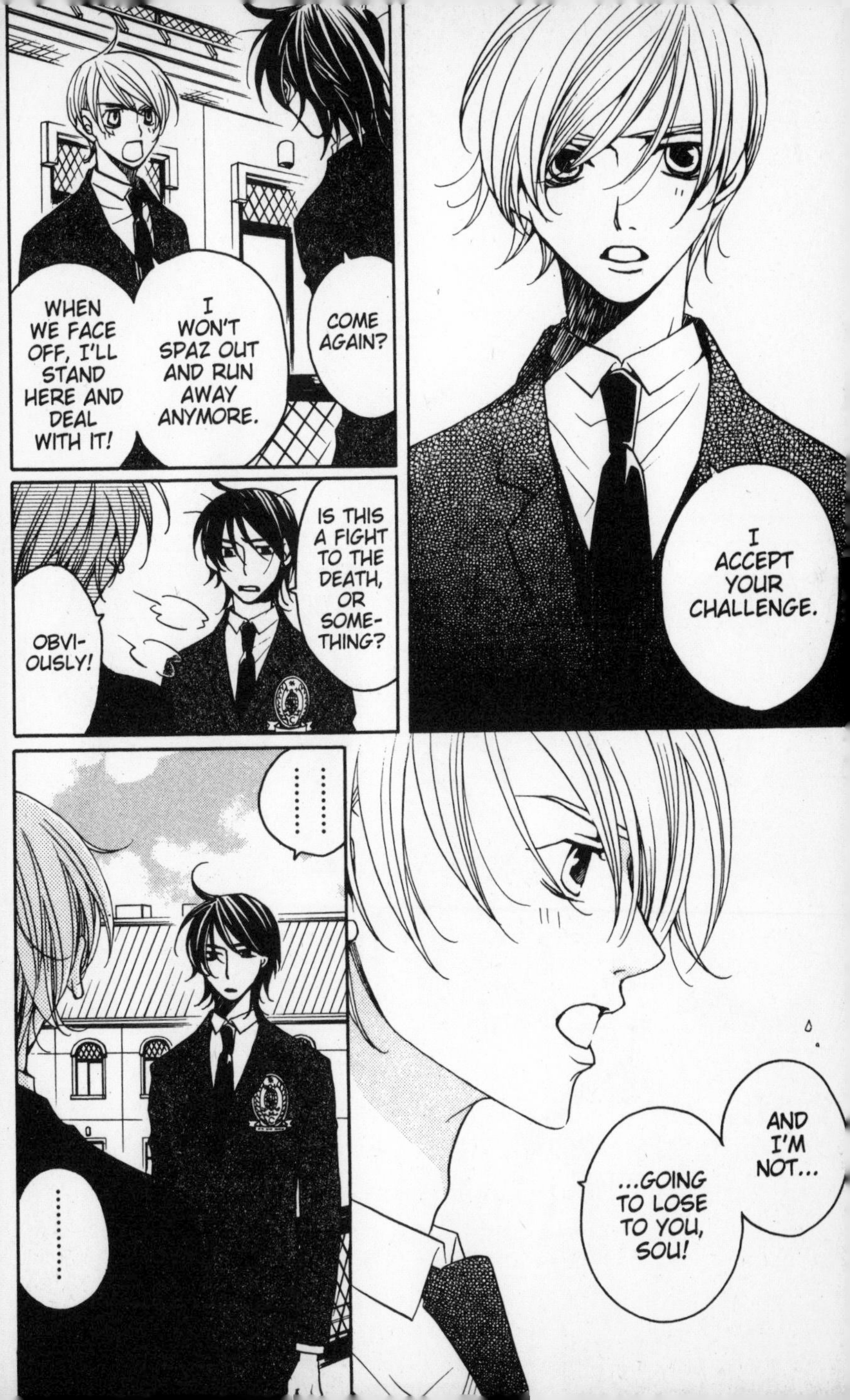
I ACCEPT YOUR CHALLENGE.
COME AGAIN?
I WON'T SPAZ OUT AND RUN AWAY ANYMORE.
WHEN WE FACE OFF, I'LL STAND HERE AND DEAL WITH IT!
IS THIS A FIGHT TO THE DEATH, OR SOME-THING?
OBVI-OUSLY!
AND I'M NOT...
...GOING TO LOSE TO YOU, SOU!
......
......

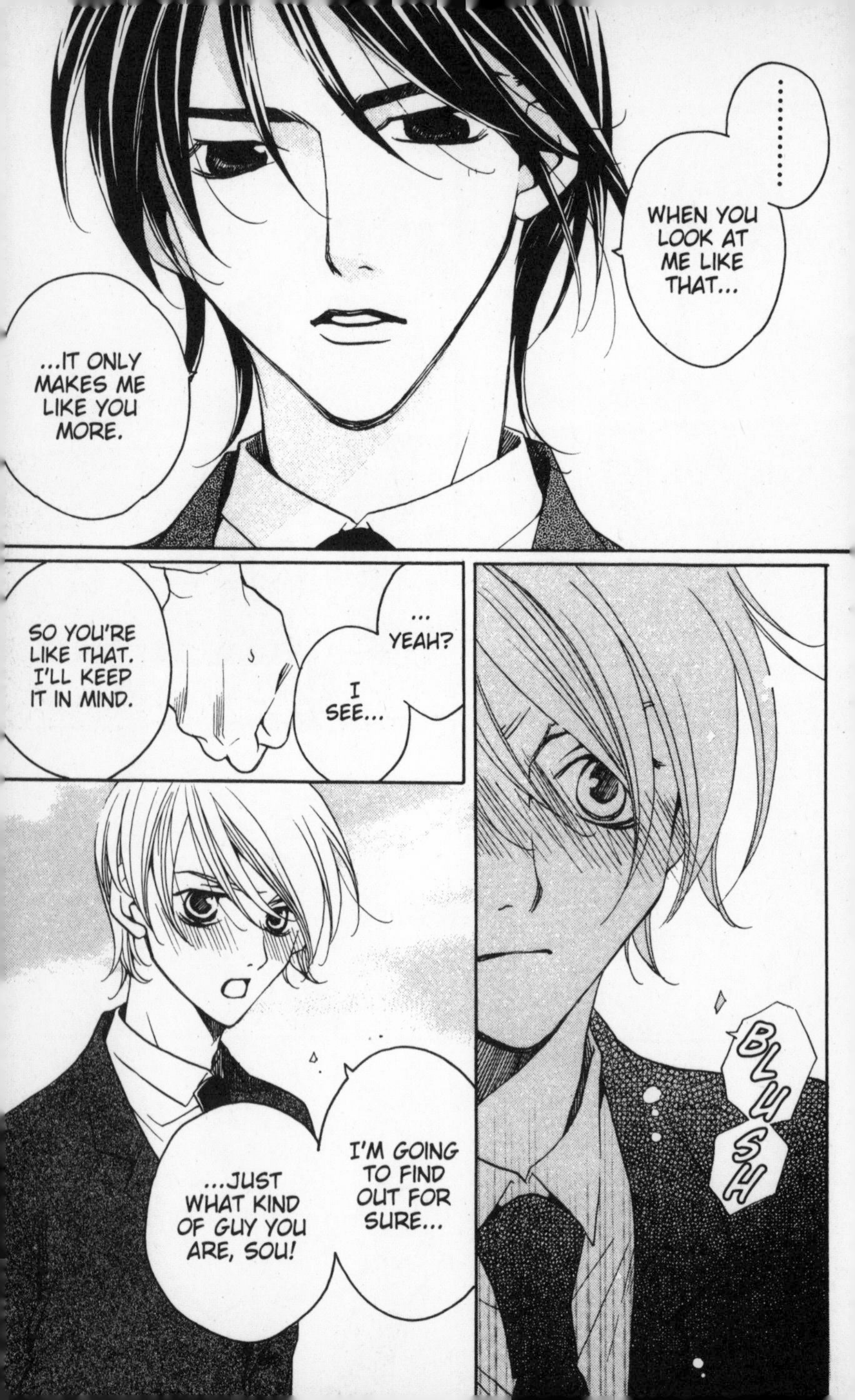
......
WHEN YOU LOOK AT ME LIKE THAT...
...IT ONLY MAKES ME LIKE YOU MORE.
BLUSH
... YEAH?
I SEE...
SO YOU'RE LIKE THAT. I'LL KEEP IT IN MIND.
I'M GOING TO FIND OUT FOR SURE...
...JUST WHAT KIND OF GUY YOU ARE, SOU!

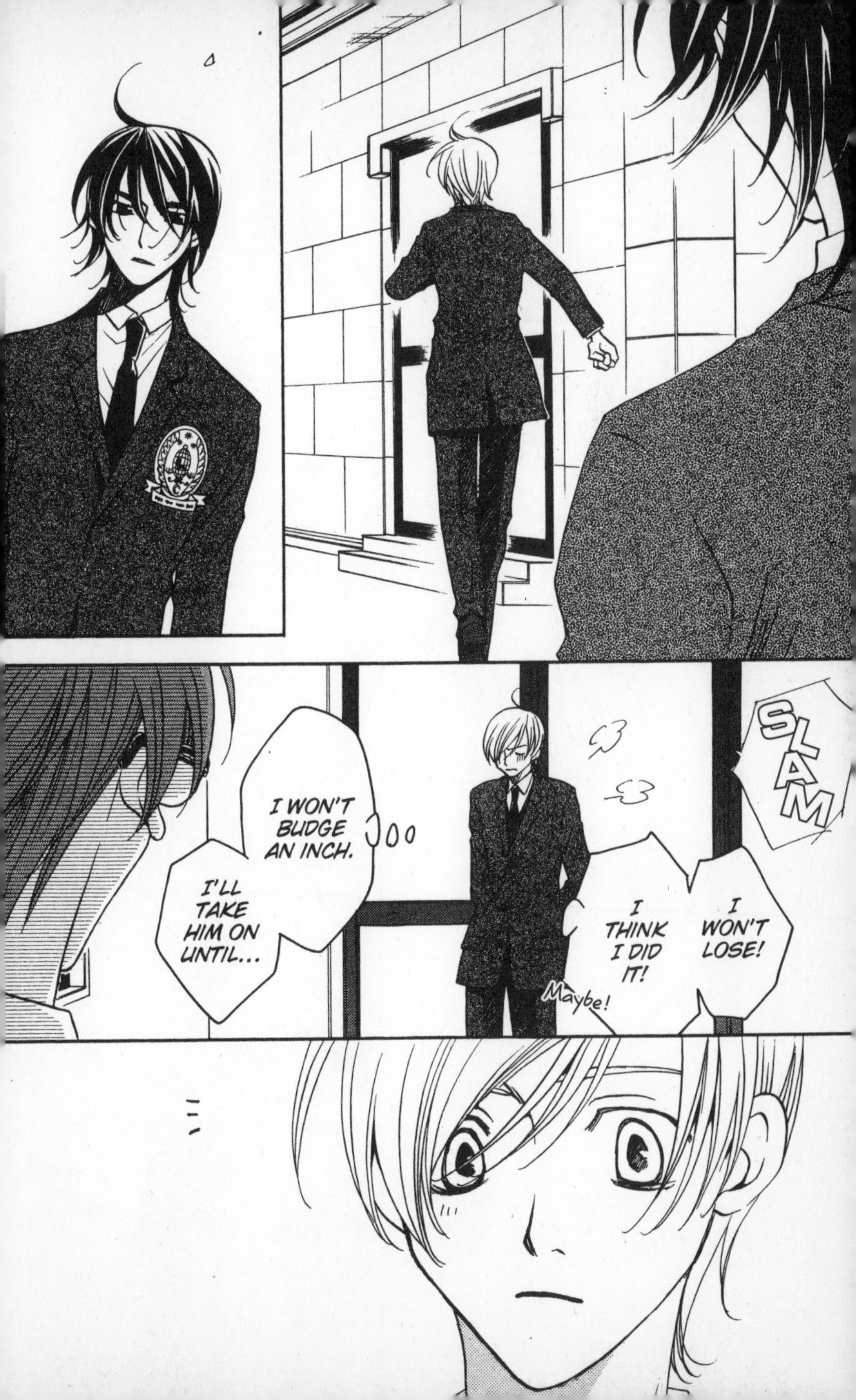
SLAM
I WON'T LOSE!
I THINK I DID IT!
Maybe!
I WON'T BUDGE AN INCH.
I'LL TAKE HIM ON UNTIL...

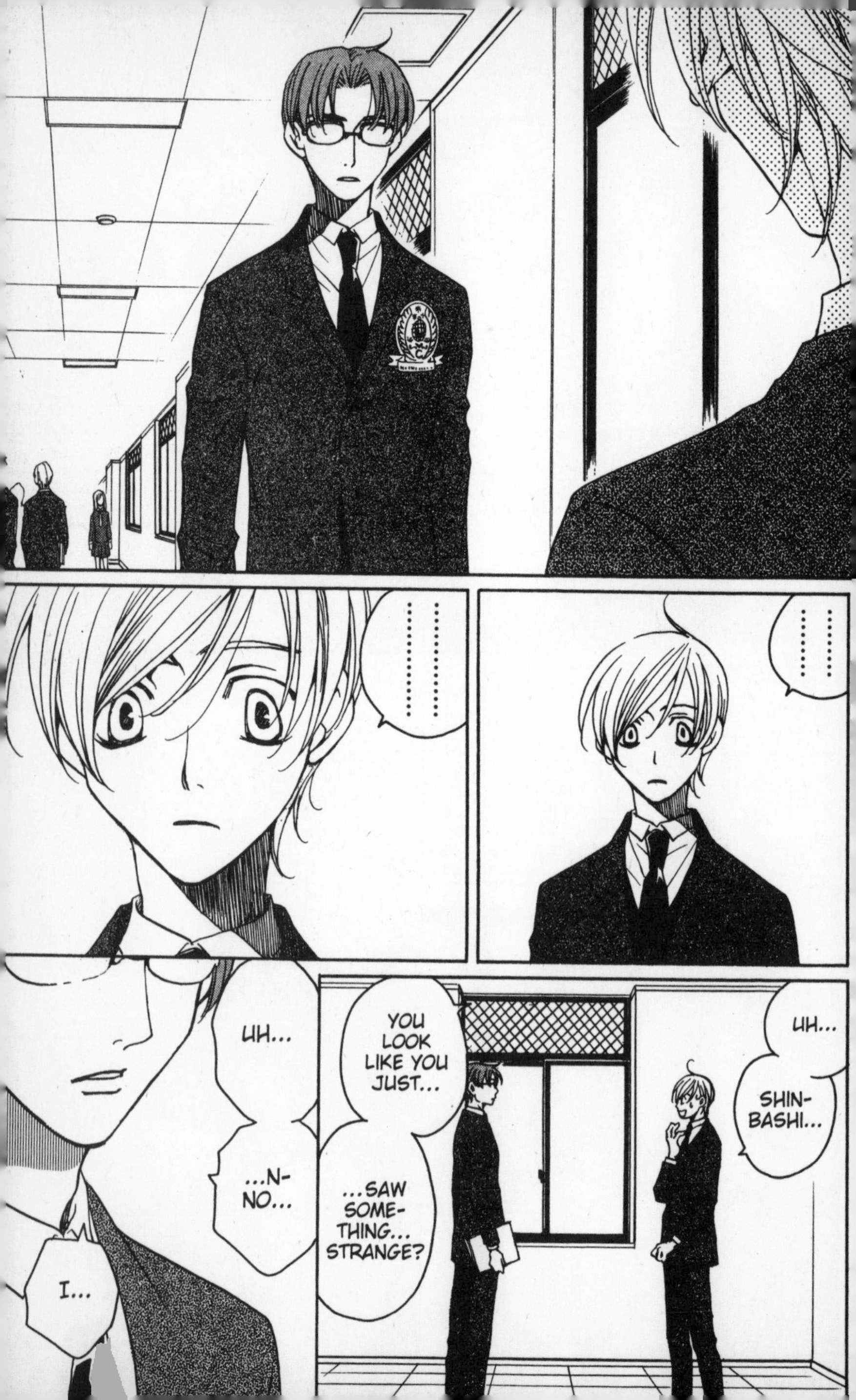
……
……
UH... SHIN-BASHI...
YOU LOOK LIKE YOU JUST...
...SAW SOMETHING... STRANGE?
UH...
...N-NO...
I...

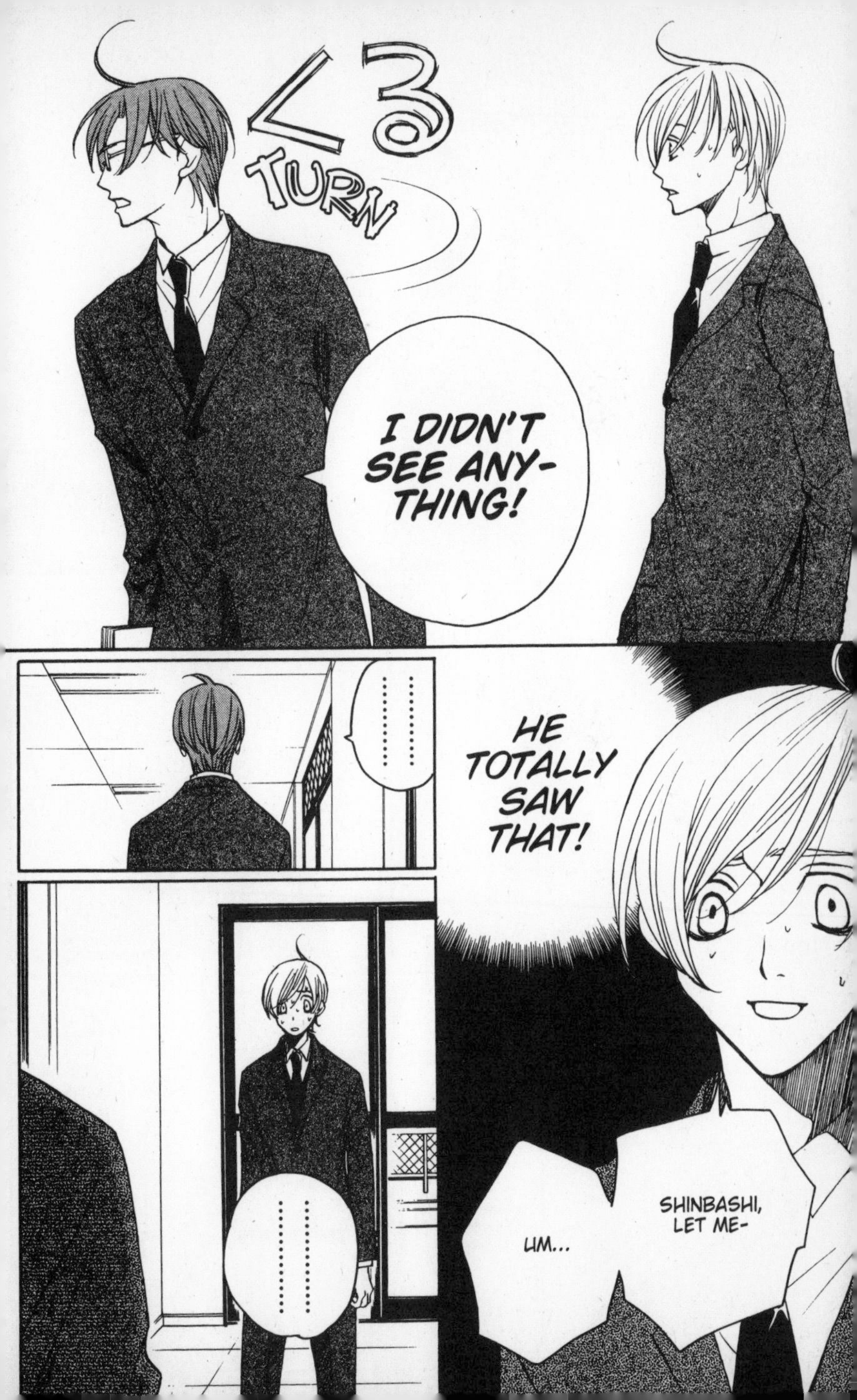
くる
TURN
I DIDN'T SEE ANY-THING!
HE TOTALLY SAW THAT!
SHINBASHI, LET ME-
UM...
......
......

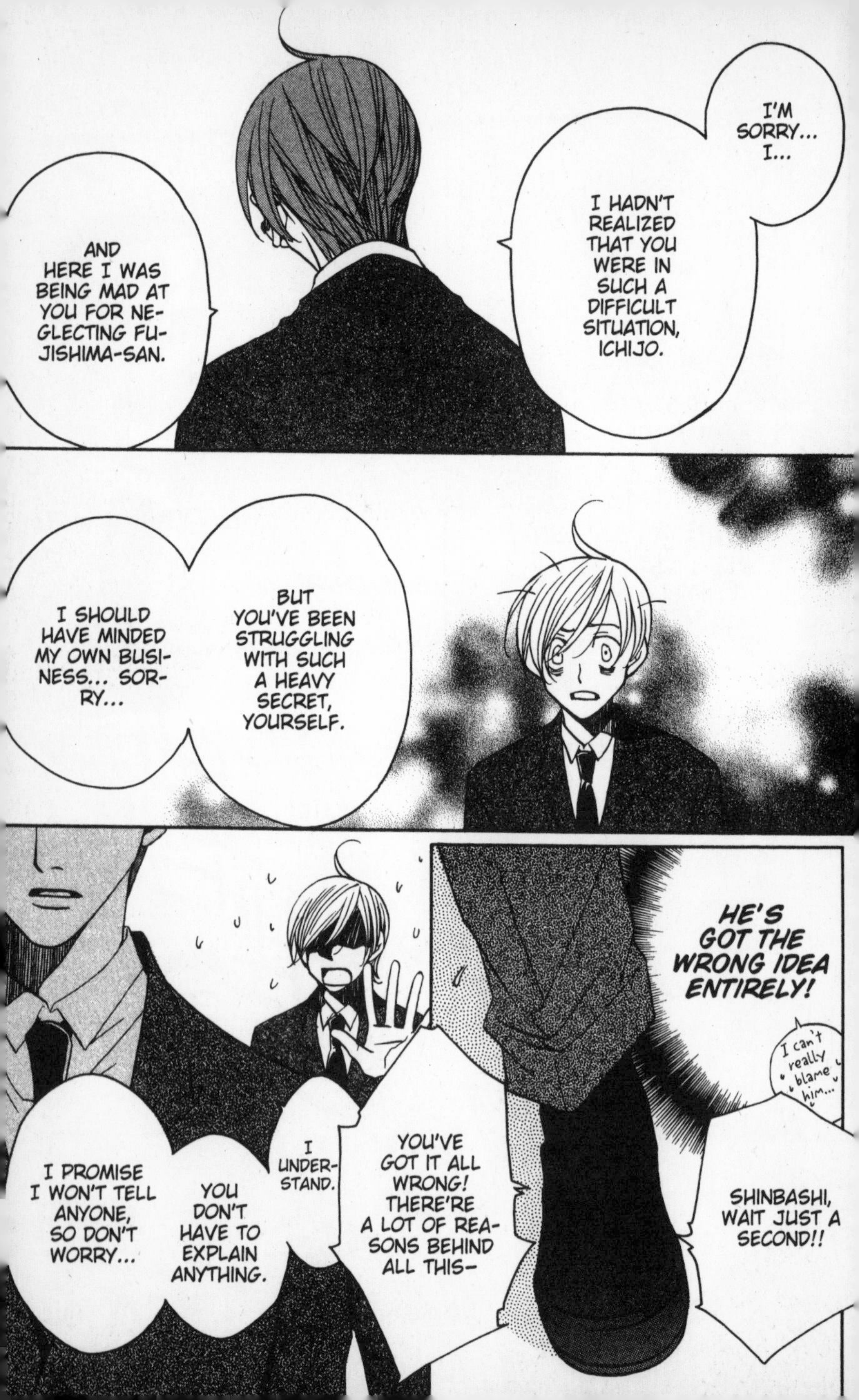
I'M SORRY... I...
I HADN'T REALIZED THAT YOU WERE IN SUCH A DIFFICULT SITUATION, ICHIJO.
AND HERE I WAS BEING MAD AT YOU FOR NE-GLECTING FU-JISHIMA-SAN.
BUT YOU'VE BEEN STRUGGLING WITH SUCH A HEAVY SECRET, YOURSELF.
I SHOULD HAVE MINDED MY OWN BUSI-NESS... SOR-RY...
HE'S GOT THE WRONG IDEA ENTIRELY!
I can't really blame him...
SHINBASHI, WAIT JUST A SECOND!!
YOU'VE GOT IT ALL WRONG! THERE'RE A LOT OF REA-SONS BEHIND ALL THIS-
I UNDER-STAND.
YOU DON'T HAVE TO EXPLAIN ANYTHING.
I PROMISE I WON'T TELL ANYONE, SO DON'T WORRY...

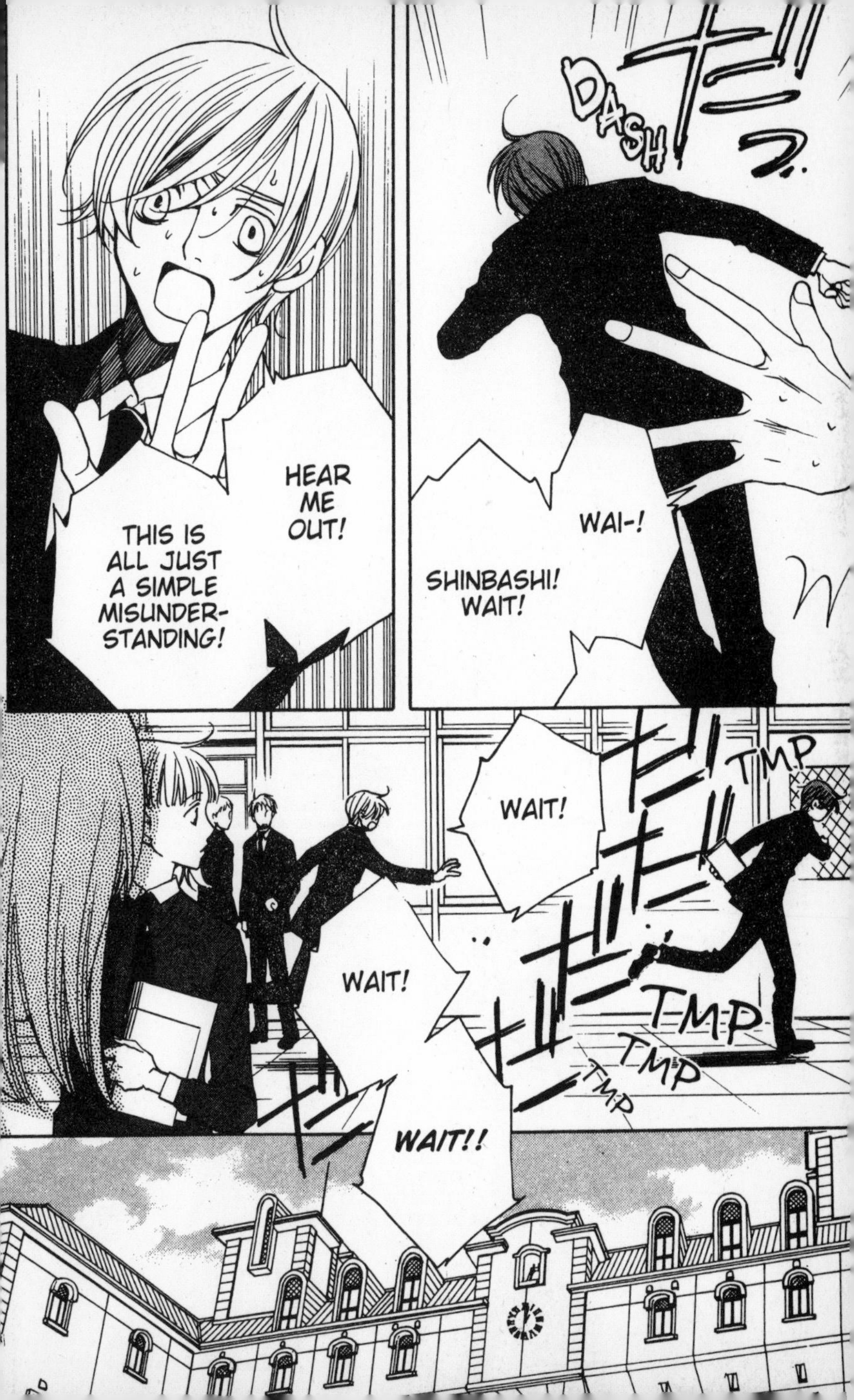
DASH
WAI-!
SHINBASHI! WAIT!
HEAR ME OUT!
THIS IS ALL JUST A SIMPLE MISUNDER-STANDING!
TMP
WAIT!
TMP
TMP
TMP
WAIT!
WAIT!!

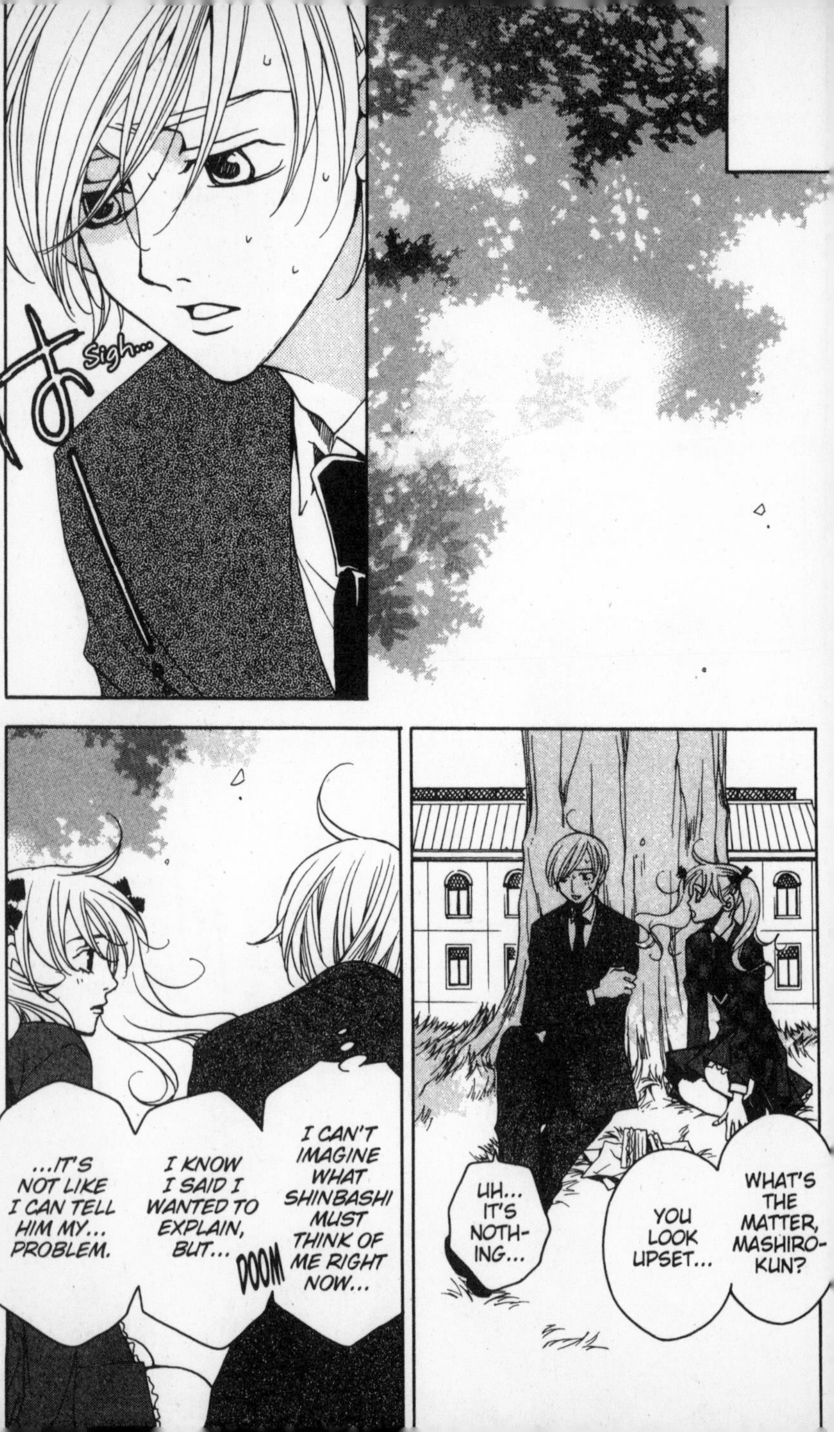
Sigh...
WHAT'S THE MATTER, MASHIRO-KUN?
YOU LOOK UPSET...
UH... IT'S NOTHING...
I CAN'T IMAGINE WHAT SHINBASHI MUST THINK OF ME RIGHT NOW...
I KNOW I SAID I WANTED TO EXPLAIN, BUT...
DOOM
...IT'S NOT LIKE I CAN TELL HIM MY... PROBLEM.

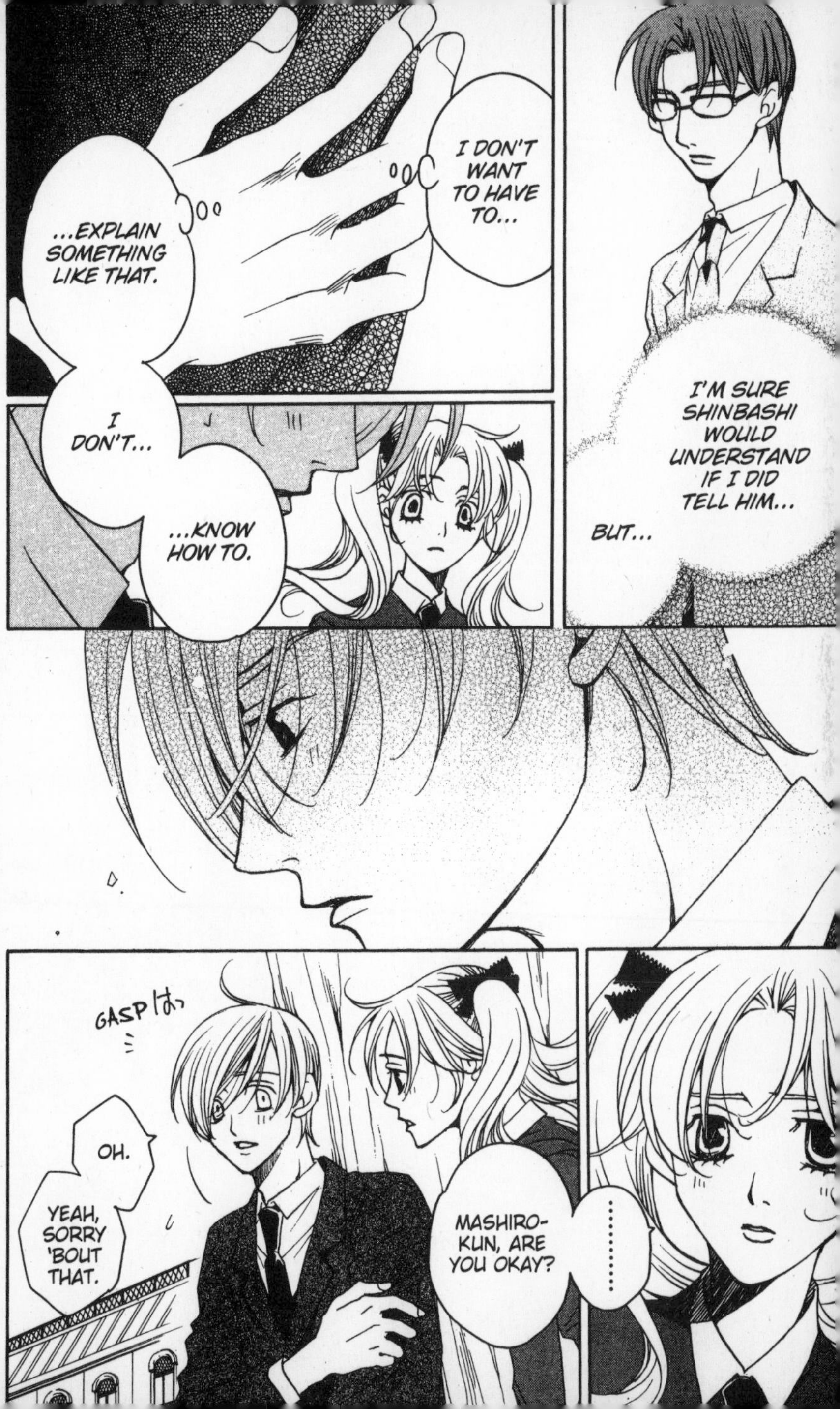
I'M SURE SHINBASHI WOULD UNDERSTAND IF I DID TELL HIM...
BUT...
I DON'T WANT TO HAVE TO...
...EXPLAIN SOMETHING LIKE THAT.
I DON'T...
...KNOW HOW TO.
......
MASHIRO-KUN, ARE YOU OKAY?
GASP はっ
OH.
YEAH, SORRY 'BOUT THAT.

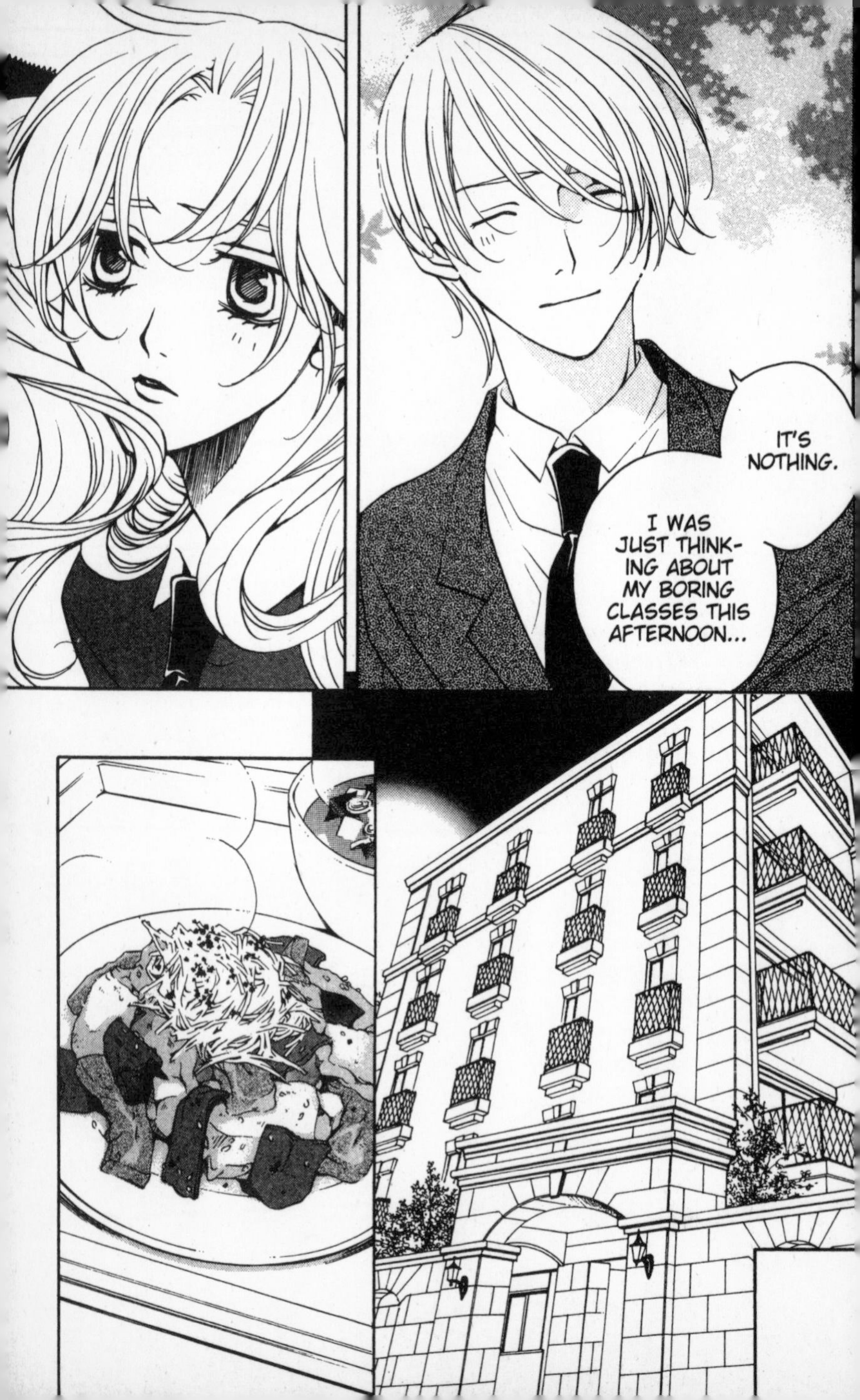
IT'S NOTHING.
I WAS JUST THINKING ABOUT MY BORING CLASSES THIS AFTERNOON...

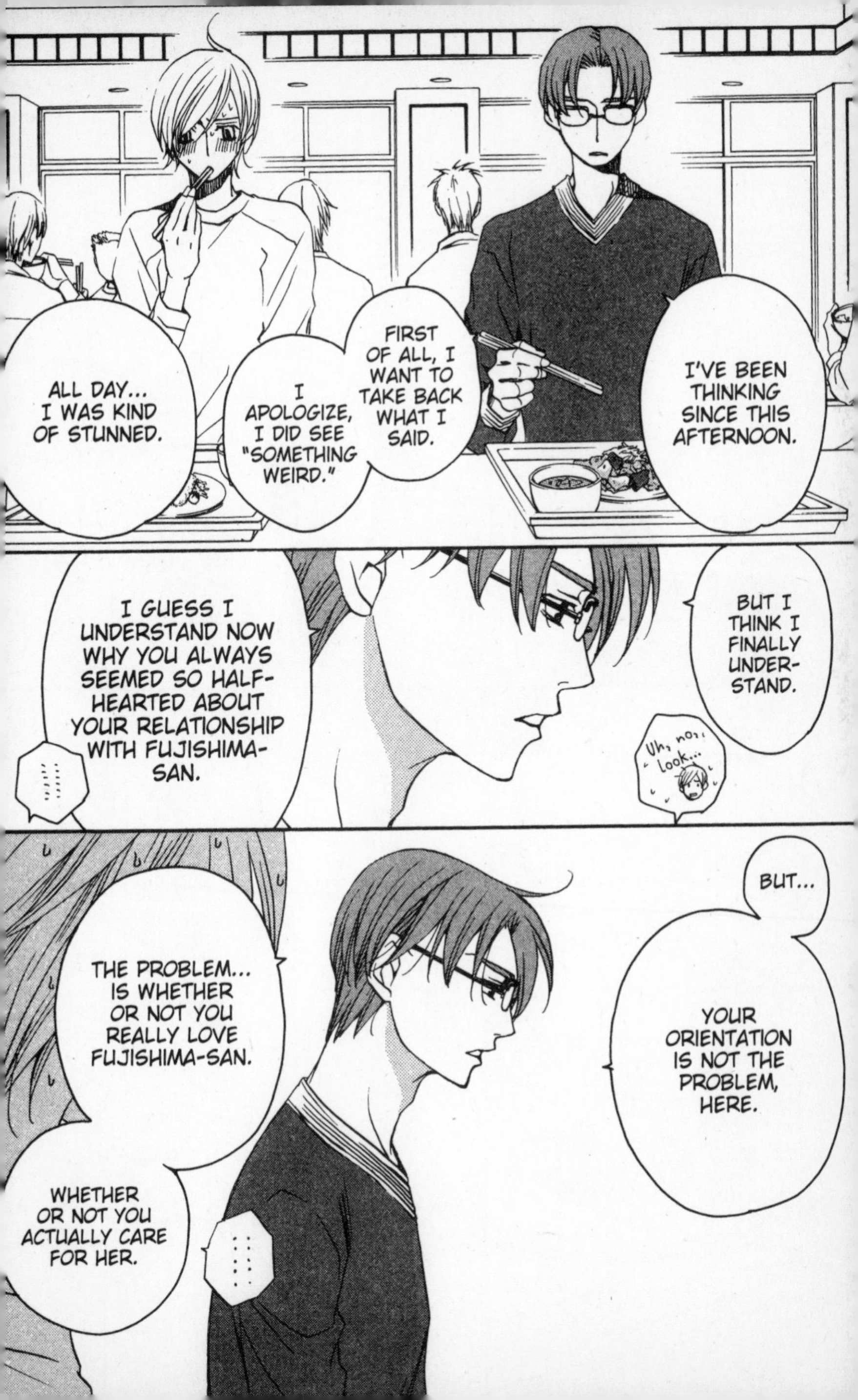
I'VE BEEN THINKING SINCE THIS AFTERNOON.
FIRST OF ALL, I WANT TO TAKE BACK WHAT I SAID.
I APOLOGIZE, I DID SEE "SOMETHING WEIRD."
ALL DAY... I WAS KIND OF STUNNED.
BUT I THINK I FINALLY UNDER-STAND.
Uh, no, look...
I GUESS I UNDERSTAND NOW WHY YOU ALWAYS SEEMED SO HALF-HEARTED ABOUT YOUR RELATIONSHIP WITH FUJISHIMA-SAN.
......
BUT...
YOUR ORIENTATION IS NOT THE PROBLEM, HERE.
THE PROBLEM... IS WHETHER OR NOT YOU REALLY LOVE FUJISHIMA-SAN.
WHETHER OR NOT YOU ACTUALLY CARE FOR HER.
......

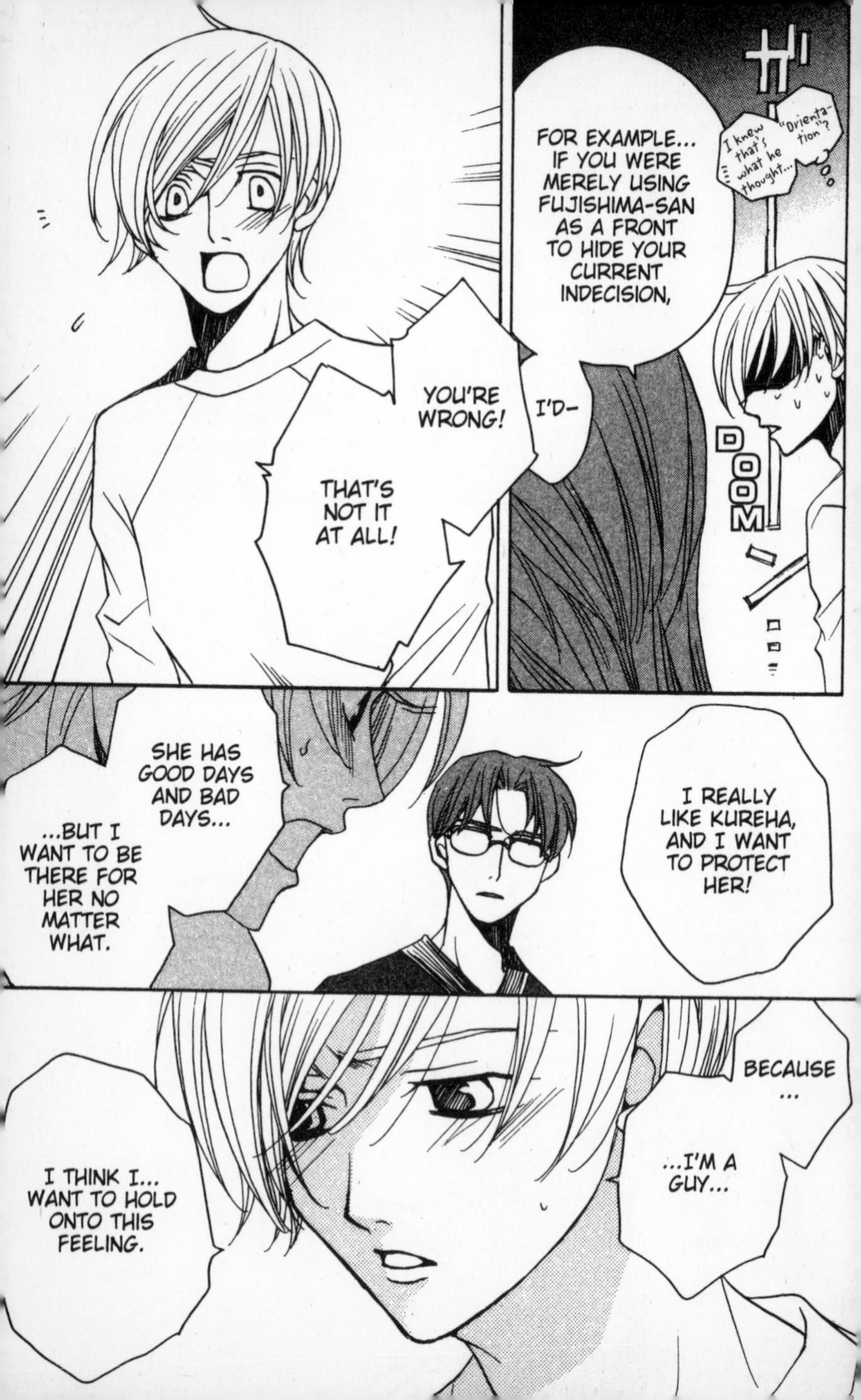
"Orientation"?
I knew that's what he thought...
FOR EXAMPLE... IF YOU WERE MERELY USING FUJISHIMA-SAN AS A FRONT TO HIDE YOUR CURRENT INDECISION,
DOOM
I'D-
YOU'RE WRONG!
THAT'S NOT IT AT ALL!
I REALLY LIKE KUREHA, AND I WANT TO PROTECT HER!
SHE HAS GOOD DAYS AND BAD DAYS...
...BUT I WANT TO BE THERE FOR HER NO MATTER WHAT.
BECAUSE ...
...I'M A GUY...
I THINK I... WANT TO HOLD ONTO THIS FEELING.

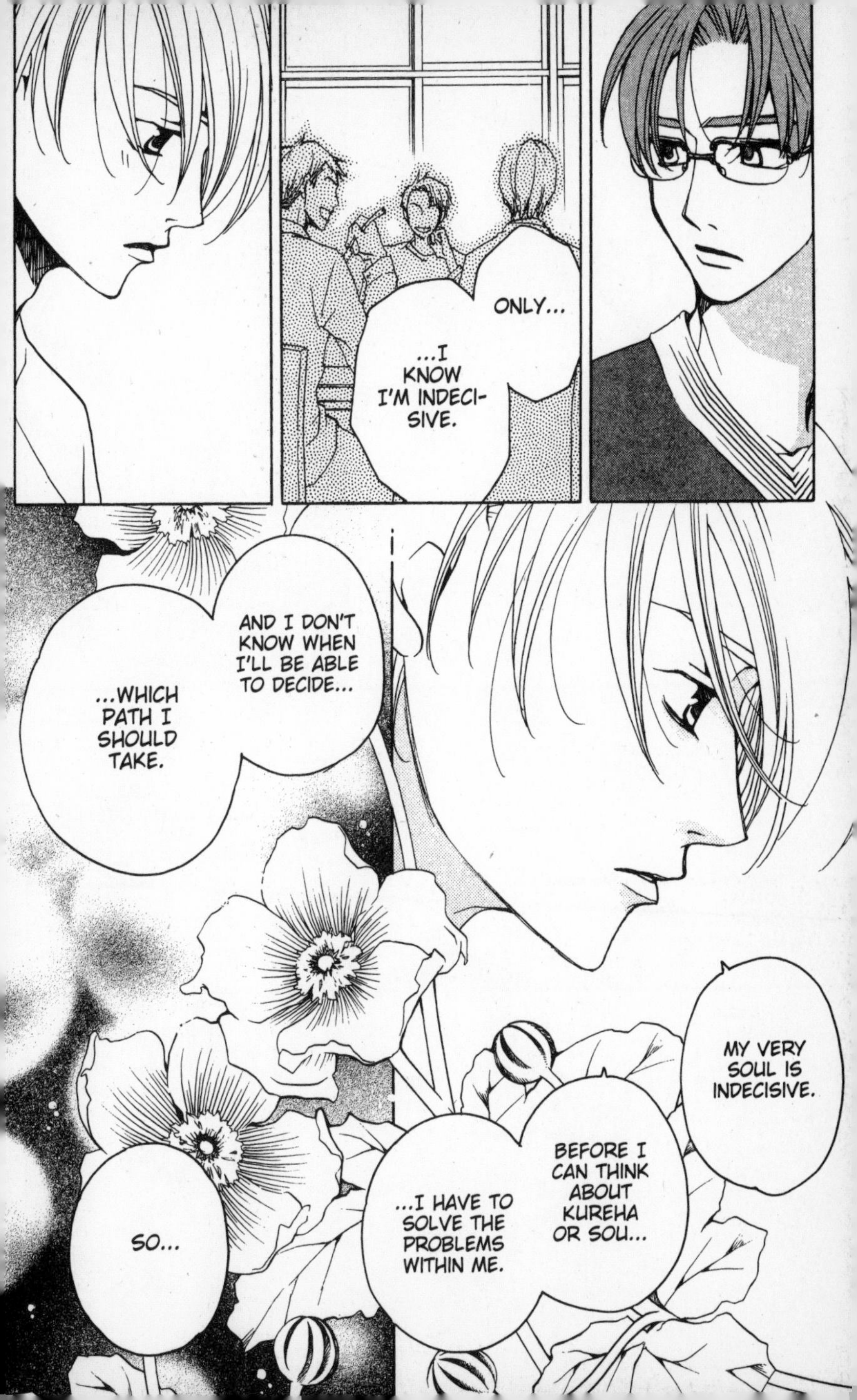
ONLY...
...I KNOW I'M INDECISIVE.
MY VERY SOUL IS INDECISIVE.
BEFORE I CAN THINK ABOUT KUREHA OR SOU...
...I HAVE TO SOLVE THE PROBLEMS WITHIN ME.
AND I DON'T KNOW WHEN I'LL BE ABLE TO DECIDE...
...WHICH PATH I SHOULD TAKE.
SO...

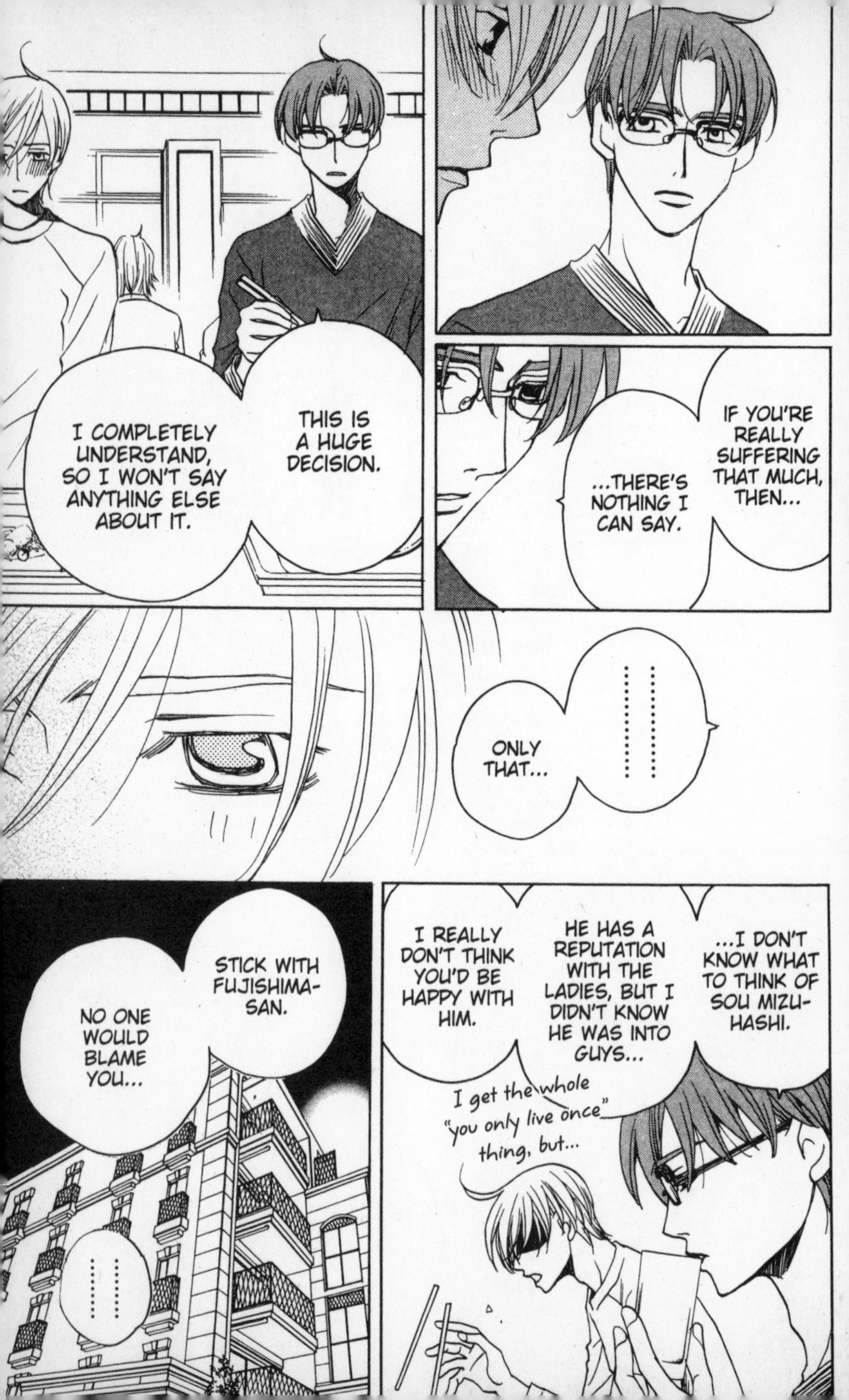
IF YOU'RE REALLY SUFFERING THAT MUCH, THEN...
...THERE'S NOTHING I CAN SAY.
THIS IS A HUGE DECISION.
I COMPLETELY UNDERSTAND, SO I WON'T SAY ANYTHING ELSE ABOUT IT.
......
ONLY THAT...
...I DON'T KNOW WHAT TO THINK OF SOU MIZU-HASHI.
HE HAS A REPUTATION WITH THE LADIES, BUT I DIDN'T KNOW HE WAS INTO GUYS...
I REALLY DON'T THINK YOU'D BE HAPPY WITH HIM.
I get the whole "you only live once" thing, but...
STICK WITH FUJISHIMA-SAN.
NO ONE WOULD BLAME YOU...
......

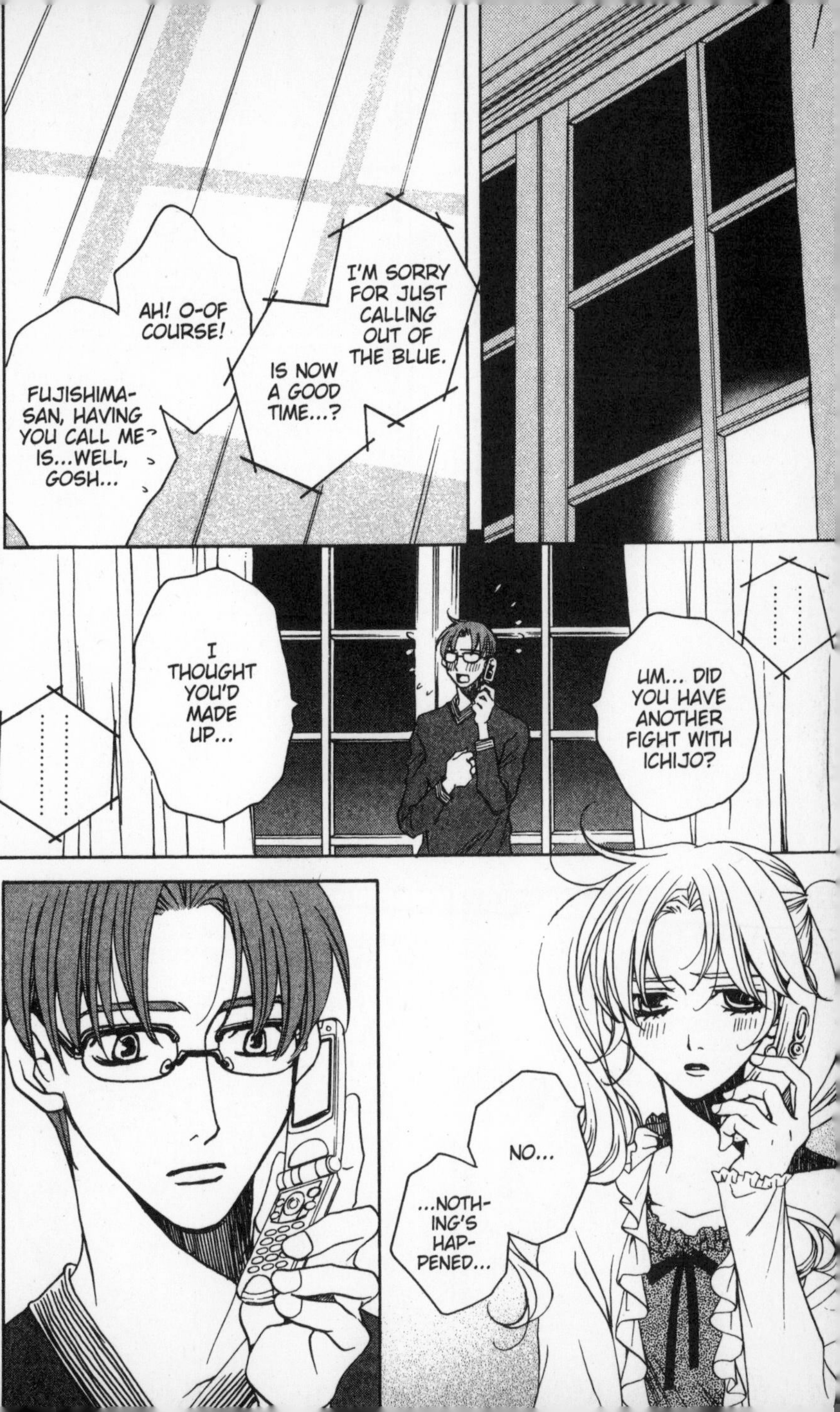
I'M SORRY FOR JUST CALLING OUT OF THE BLUE.
IS NOW A GOOD TIME...?
AH! O-OF COURSE!
FUJISHIMA-SAN, HAVING YOU CALL ME IS...WELL, GOSH...
......
UM... DID YOU HAVE ANOTHER FIGHT WITH ICHIJO?
I THOUGHT YOU'D MADE UP...
......
NO...
...NOTHING'S HAPPENED...

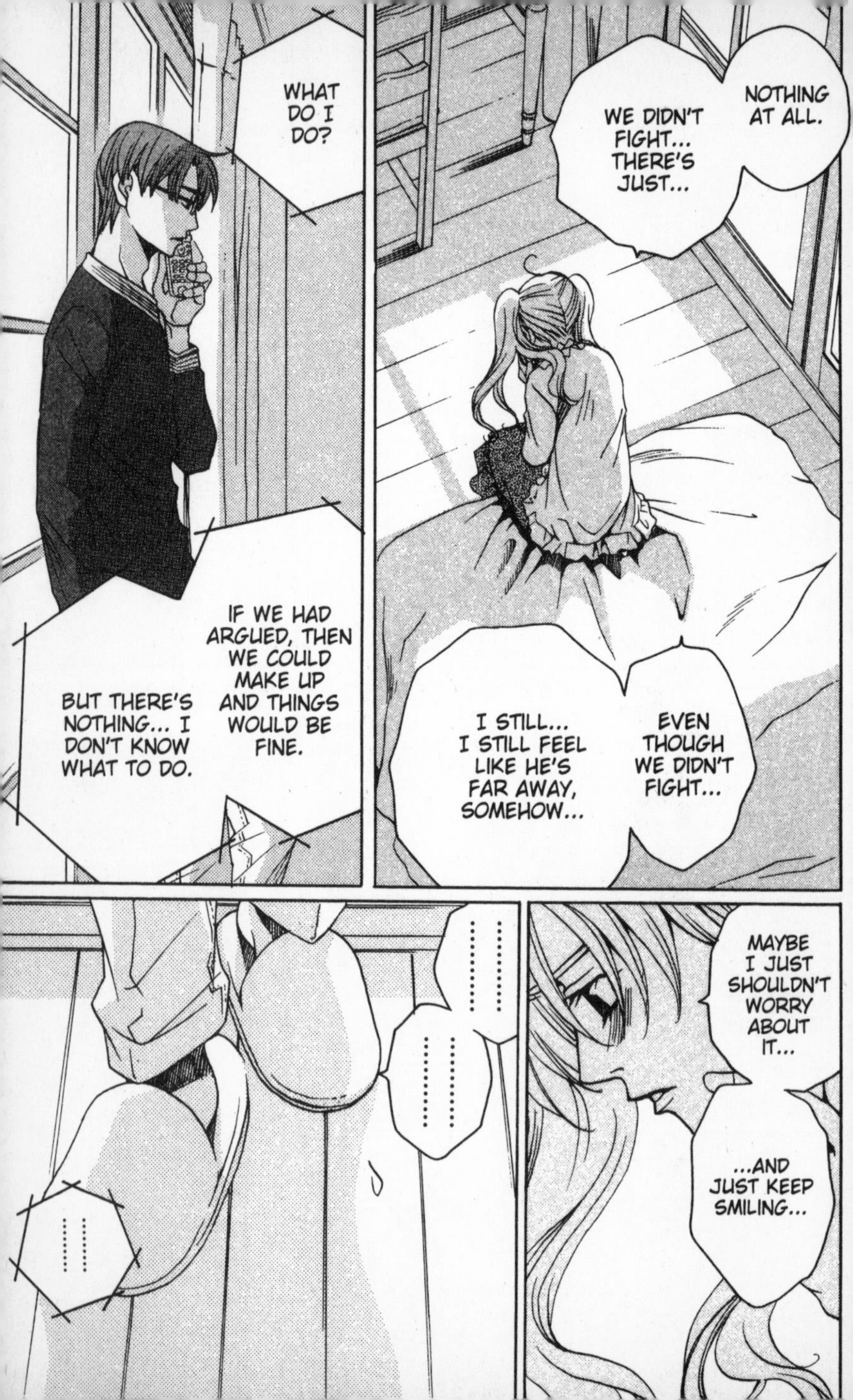
NOTHING AT ALL.
WE DIDN'T FIGHT... THERE'S JUST...
EVEN THOUGH WE DIDN'T FIGHT...
I STILL... I STILL FEEL LIKE HE'S FAR AWAY, SOMEHOW...
WHAT DO I DO?
IF WE HAD ARGUED, THEN WE COULD MAKE UP AND THINGS WOULD BE FINE.
BUT THERE'S NOTHING... I DON'T KNOW WHAT TO DO.
MAYBE I JUST SHOULDN'T WORRY ABOUT IT...
...AND JUST KEEP SMILING...
......
......
......

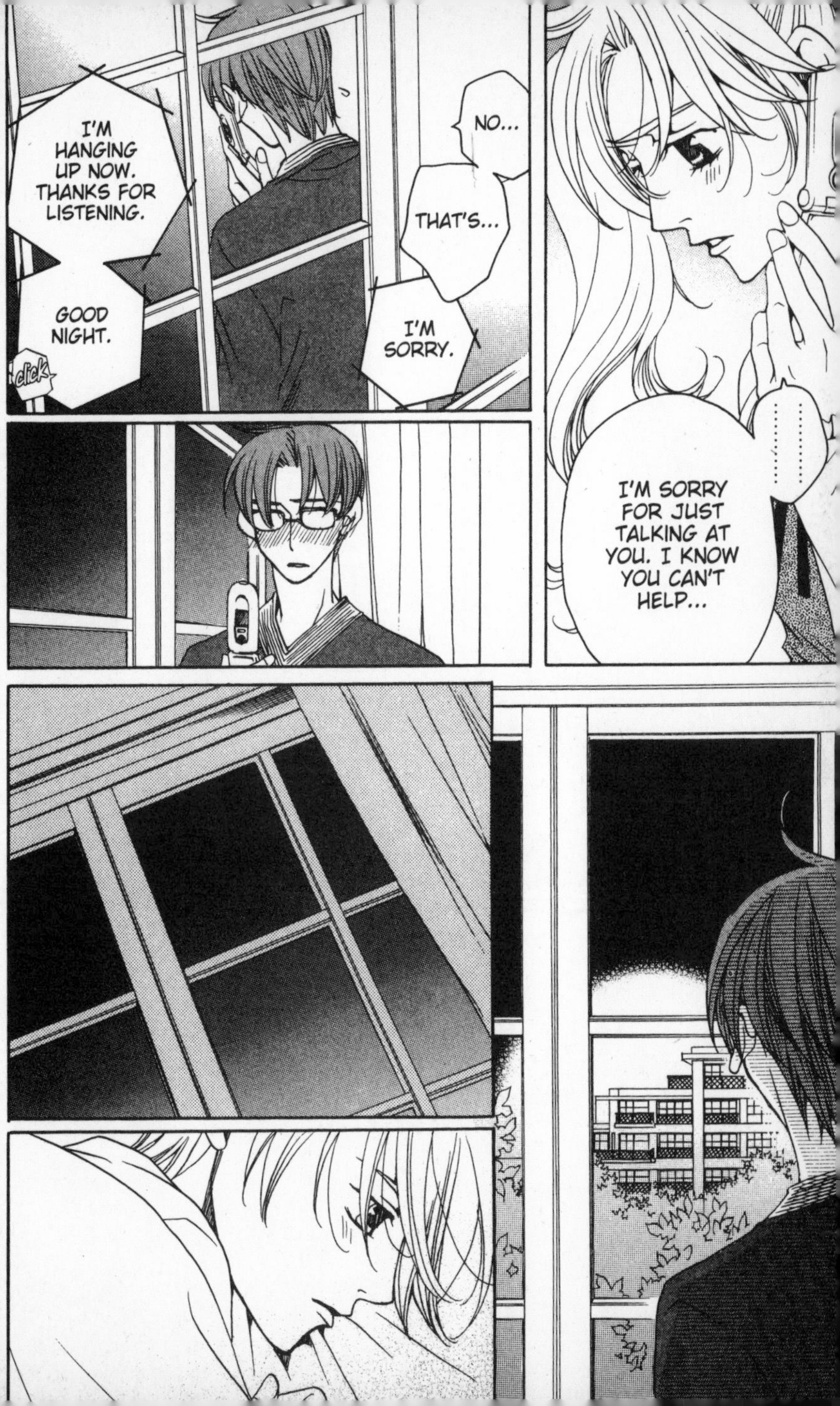
I'M SORRY FOR JUST TALKING AT YOU. I KNOW YOU CAN'T HELP...
NO...
THAT'S...
I'M SORRY.
I'M HANGING UP NOW. THANKS FOR LISTENING.
GOOD NIGHT.
click

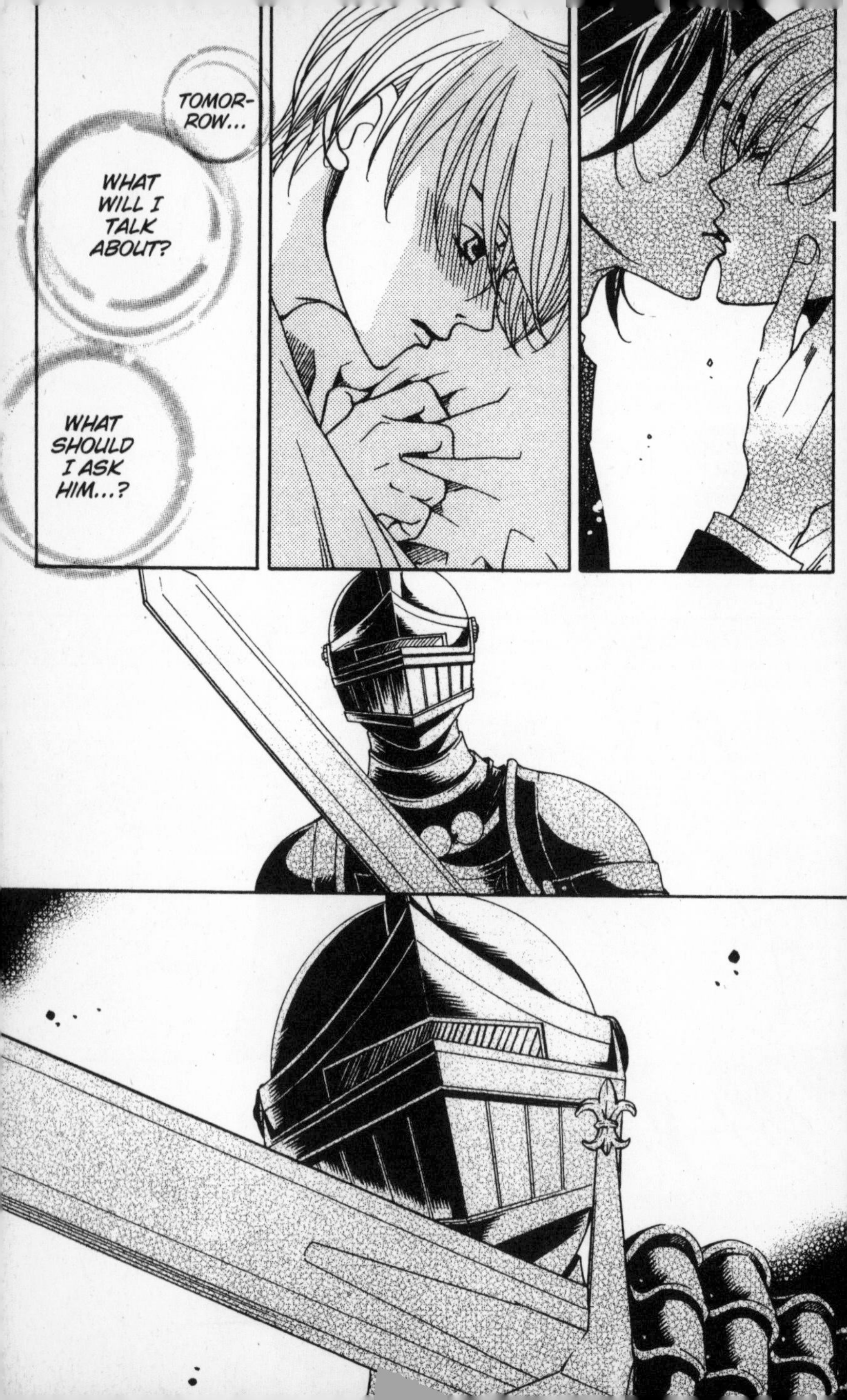
TOMOR-
ROW...
WHAT WILL I TALK ABOUT?
WHAT SHOULD I ASK HIM...?

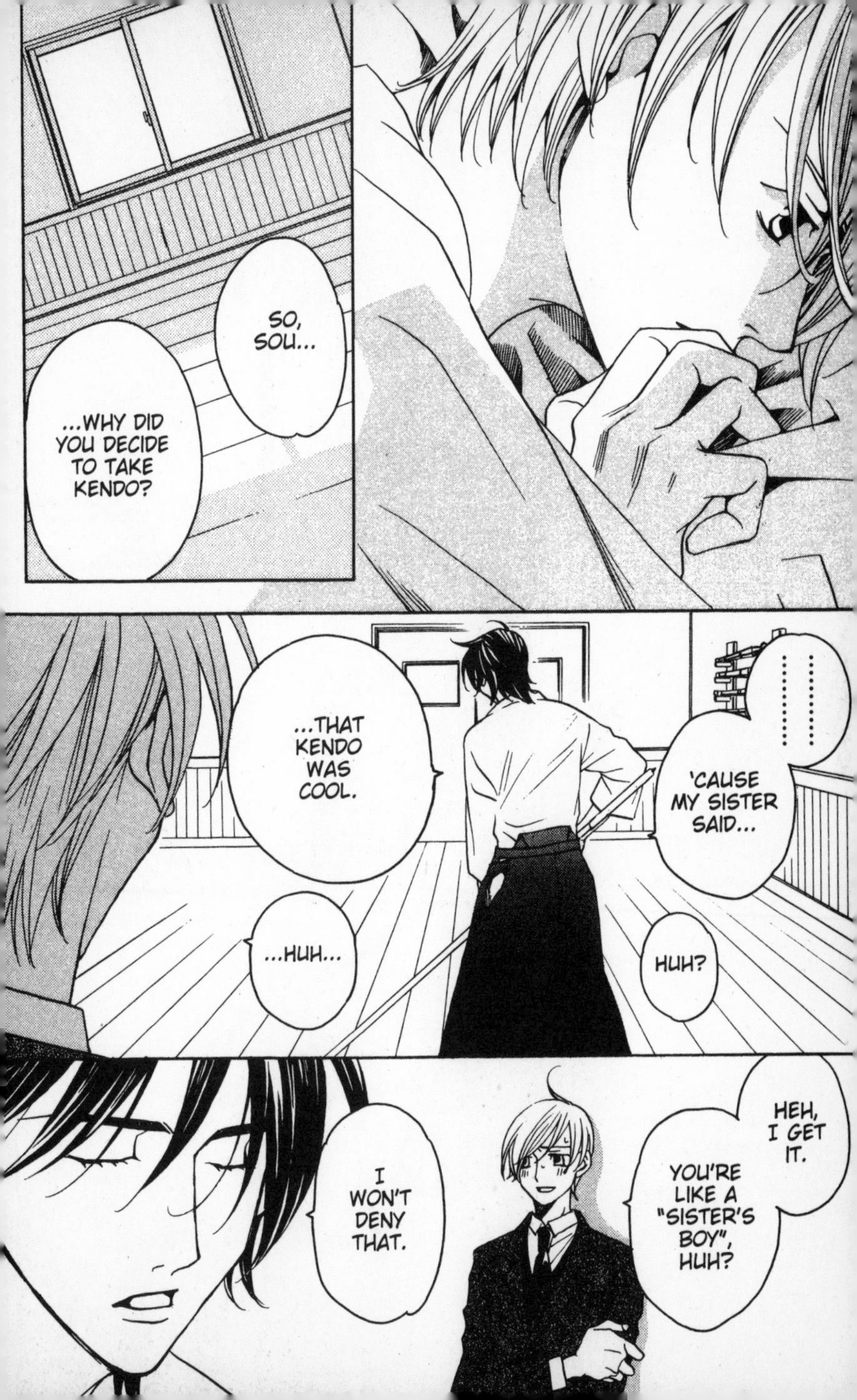
SO, SOU...
...WHY DID YOU DECIDE TO TAKE KENDO?
......
'CAUSE MY SISTER SAID...
...THAT KENDO WAS COOL.
HUH?
...HUH...
HEH, I GET IT.
YOU'RE LIKE A "SISTER'S BOY", HUH?
I WON'T DENY THAT.

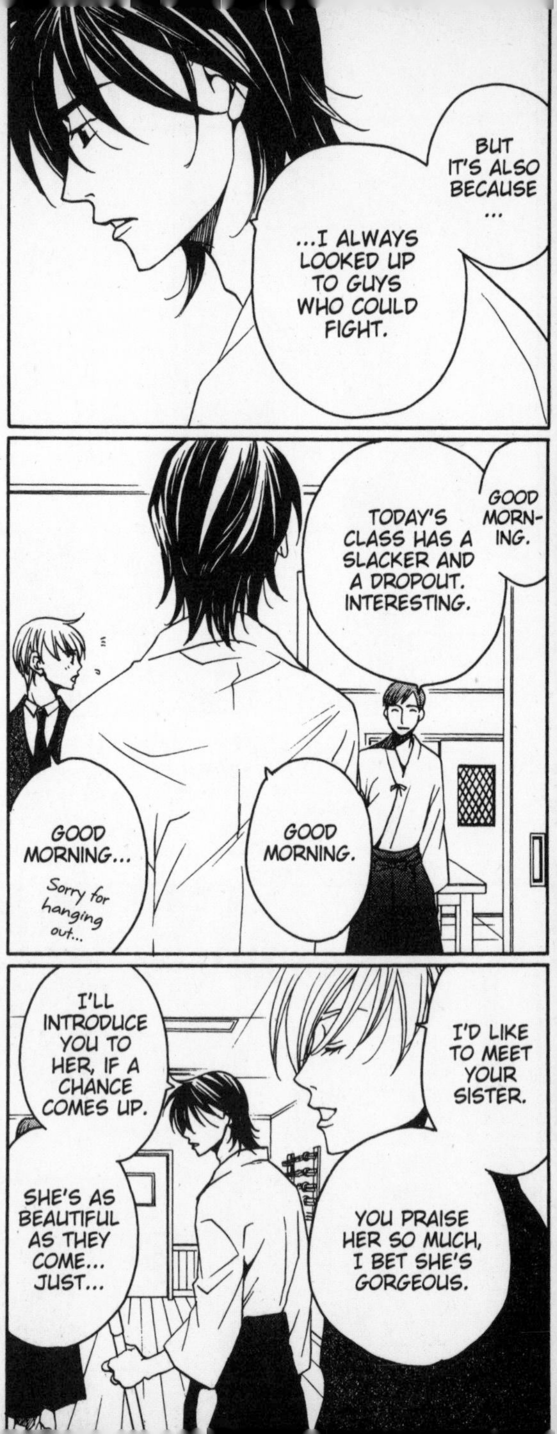
BUT IT'S ALSO BECAUSE ...
...I ALWAYS LOOKED UP TO GUYS WHO COULD FIGHT.
GOOD MORNING.
TODAY'S CLASS HAS A SLACKER AND A DROPOUT. INTERESTING.
GOOD MORNING.
GOOD MORNING...
Sorry for hanging out...
I'D LIKE TO MEET YOUR SISTER.
I'LL INTRODUCE YOU TO HER, IF A CHANCE COMES UP.
YOU PRAISE HER SO MUCH, I BET SHE'S GORGEOUS.
SHE'S AS BEAUTIFUL AS THEY COME... JUST...

The Bead Cord

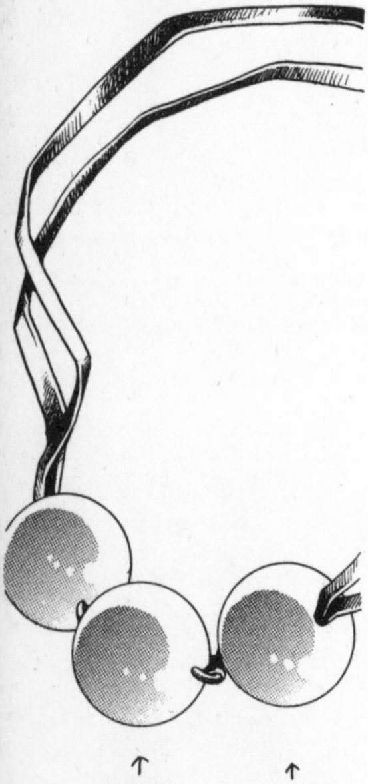
When the middle bead breaks, the cord disconnects.
The bead nearest the heart is the first to break.

I thought of various designs for the bead cord so that "when the three beads break, it comes apart" but in the end I just went with this...

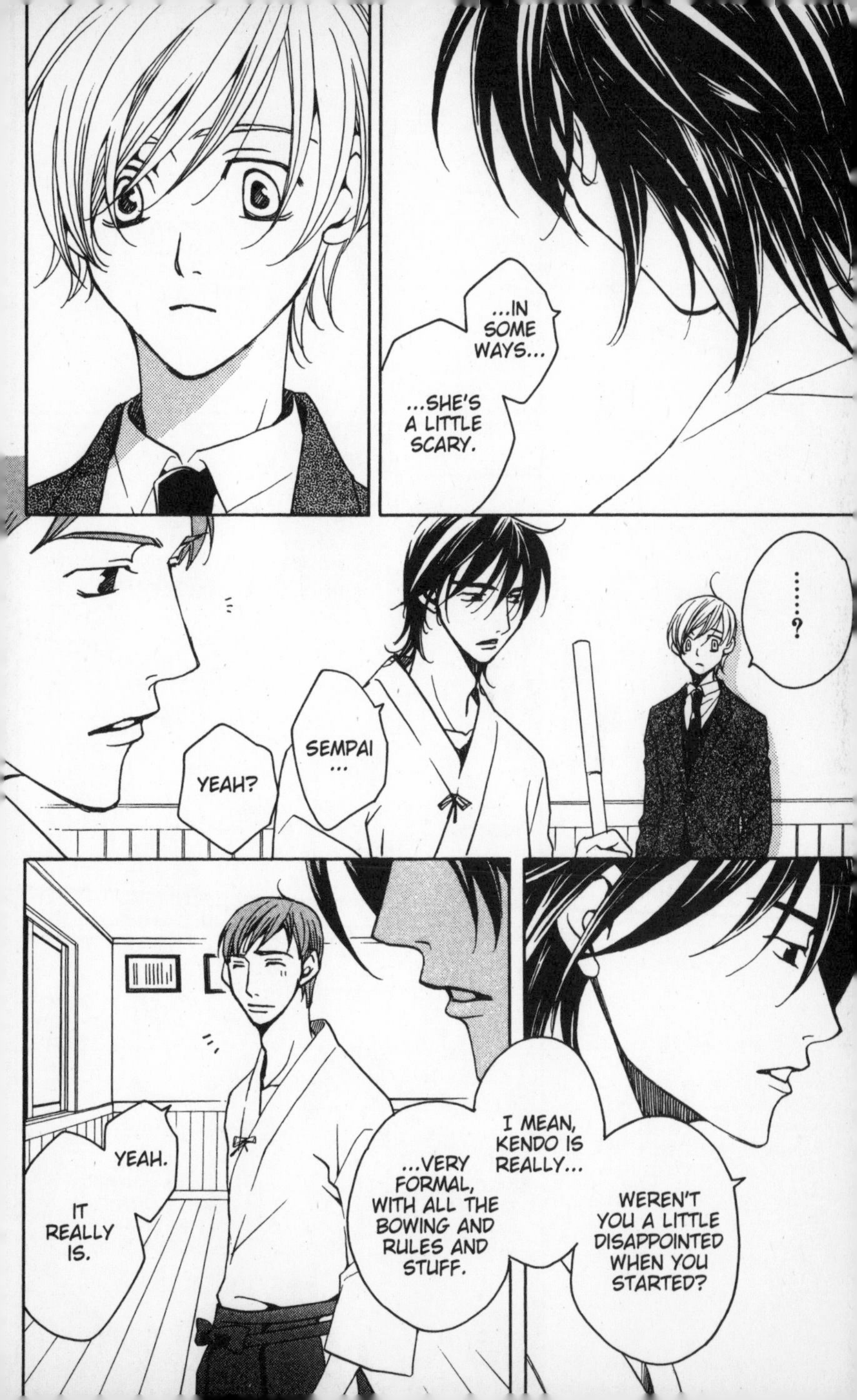
...IN SOME WAYS...
...SHE'S A LITTLE SCARY.
......?
SEMPAI...
YEAH?
WEREN'T YOU A LITTLE DISAPPOINTED WHEN YOU STARTED?
I MEAN, KENDO IS REALLY...
...VERY FORMAL, WITH ALL THE BOWING AND RULES AND STUFF.
YEAH.
IT REALLY IS.

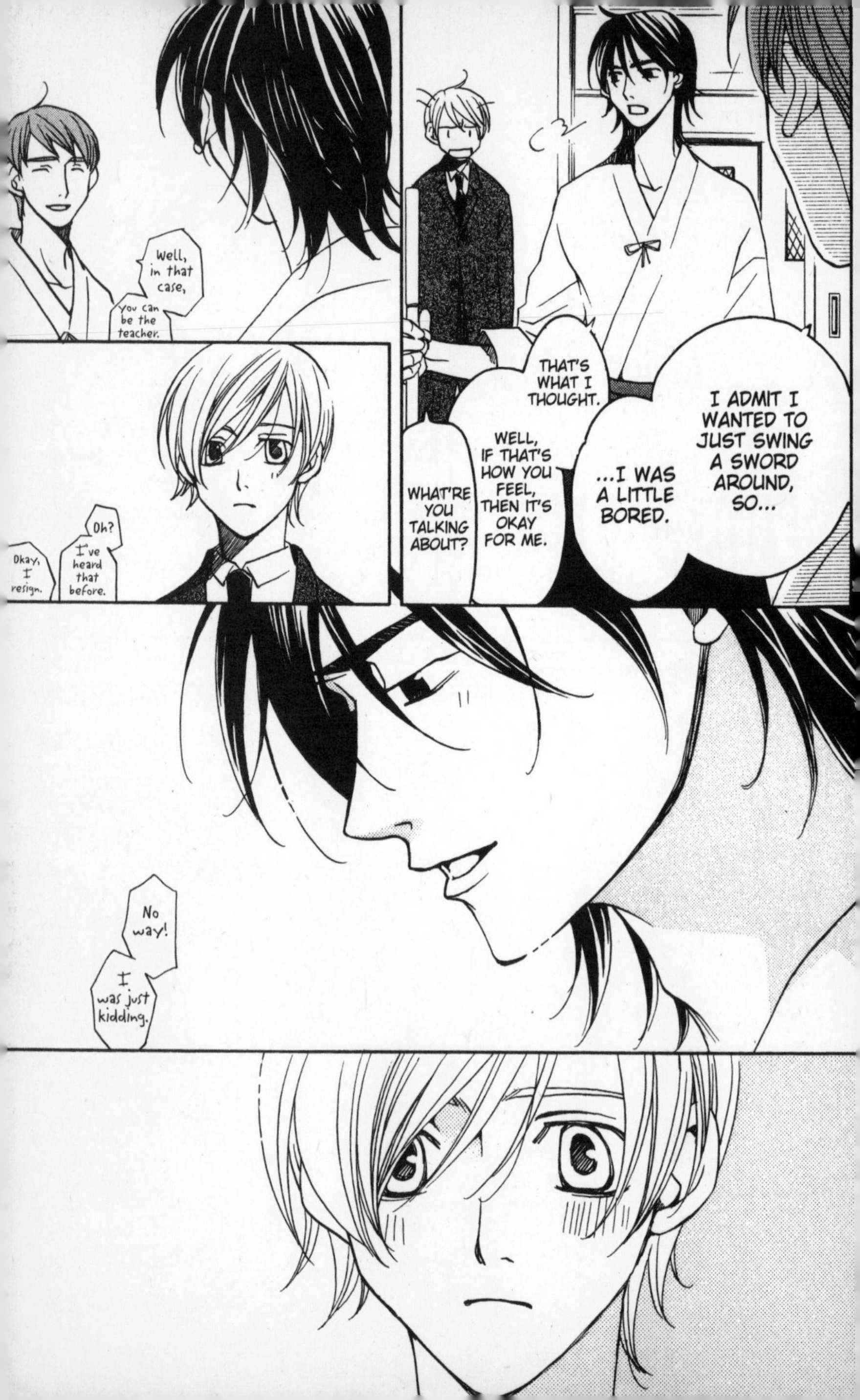
I ADMIT I WANTED TO JUST SWING A SWORD AROUND, SO...
...I WAS A LITTLE BORED.
THAT'S WHAT I THOUGHT.
WELL, IF THAT'S HOW YOU FEEL, THEN IT'S OKAY FOR ME.
WHAT'RE YOU TALKING ABOUT?
Well, in that case,
You can be the teacher.
Oh?
I've heard that before.
Okay, I resign.
No way!
I was just kidding.

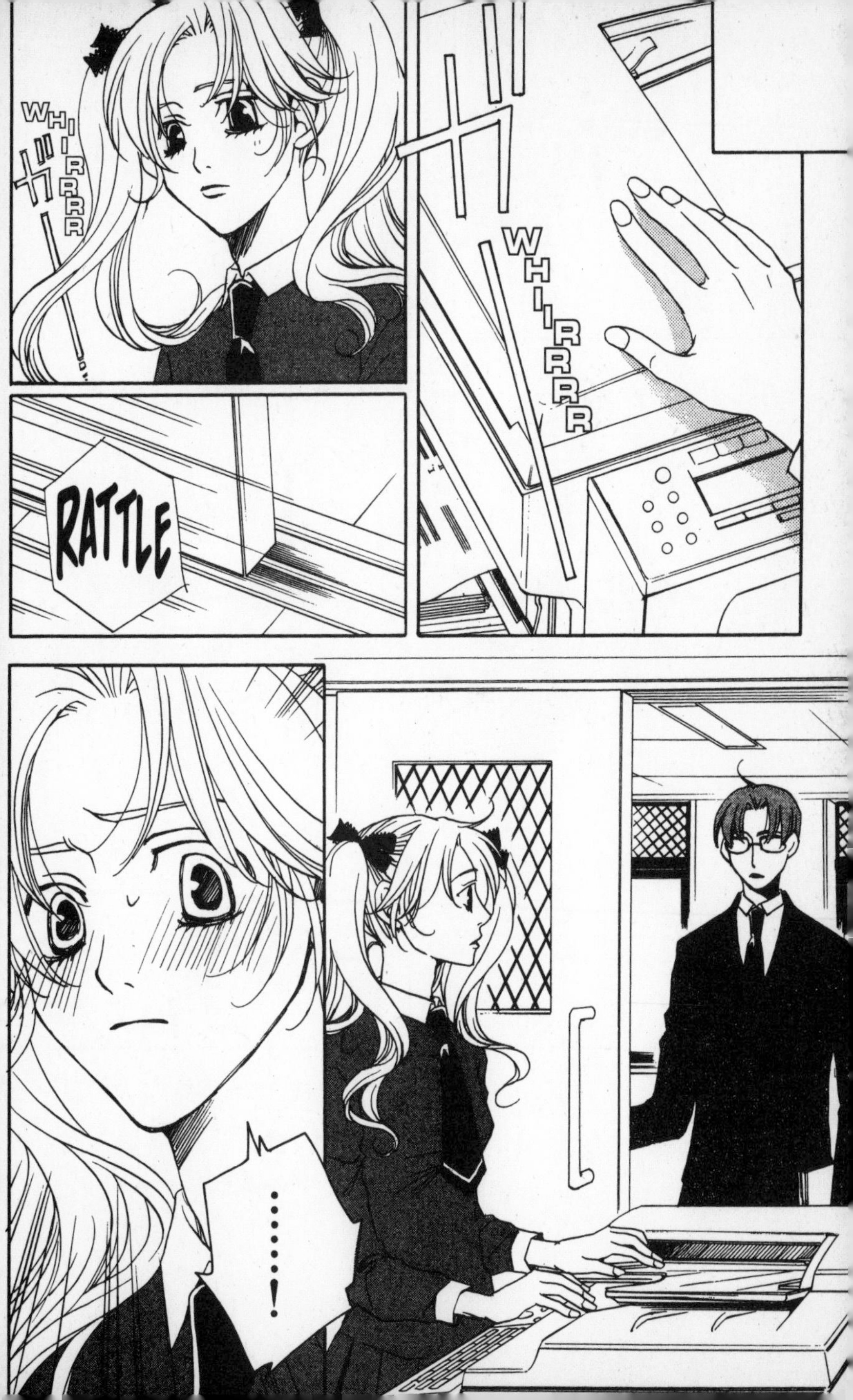
WHIIRRRR
WHIIRRRR
RATTLE
......!

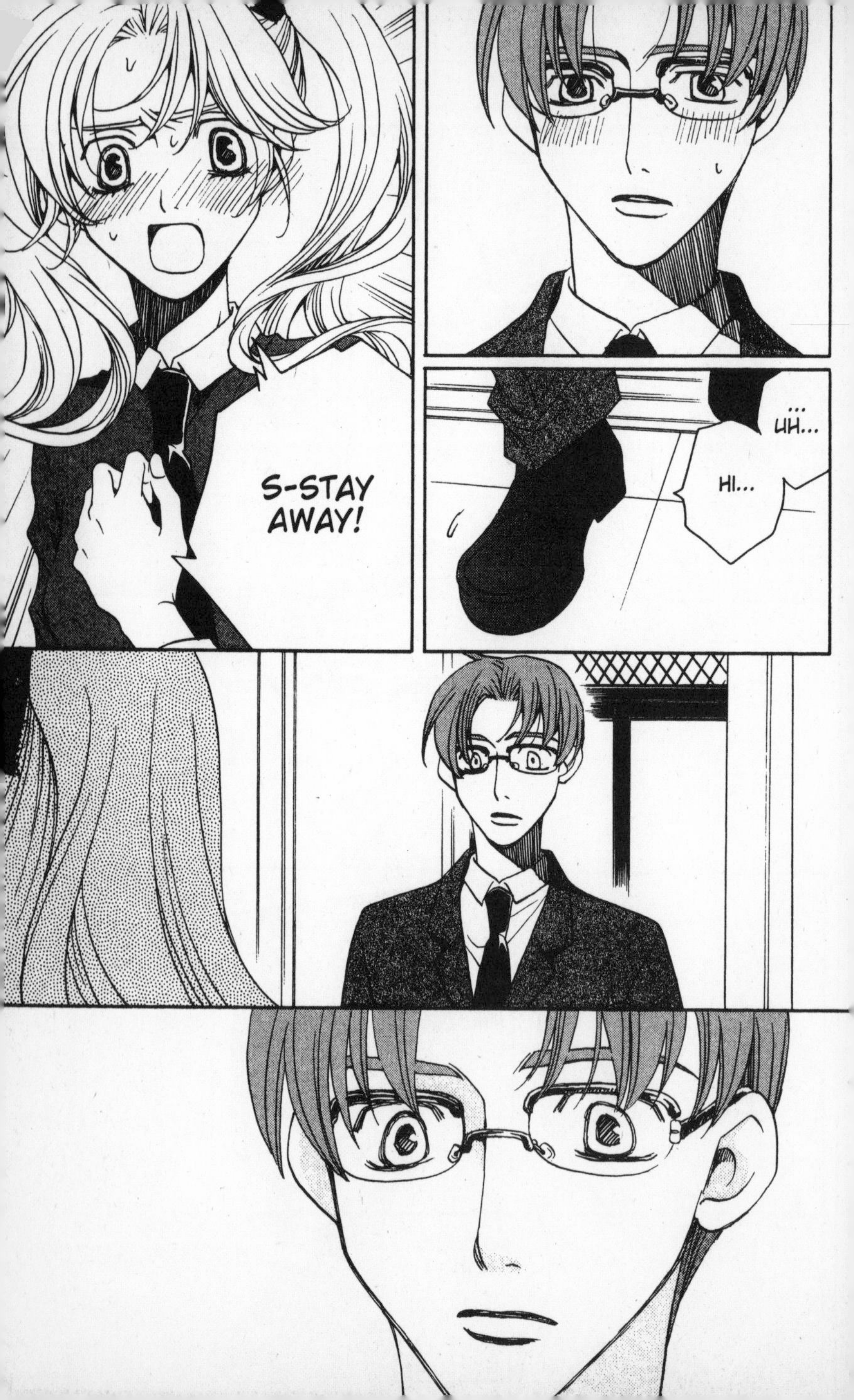
... UH...
HI...
S-STAY AWAY!

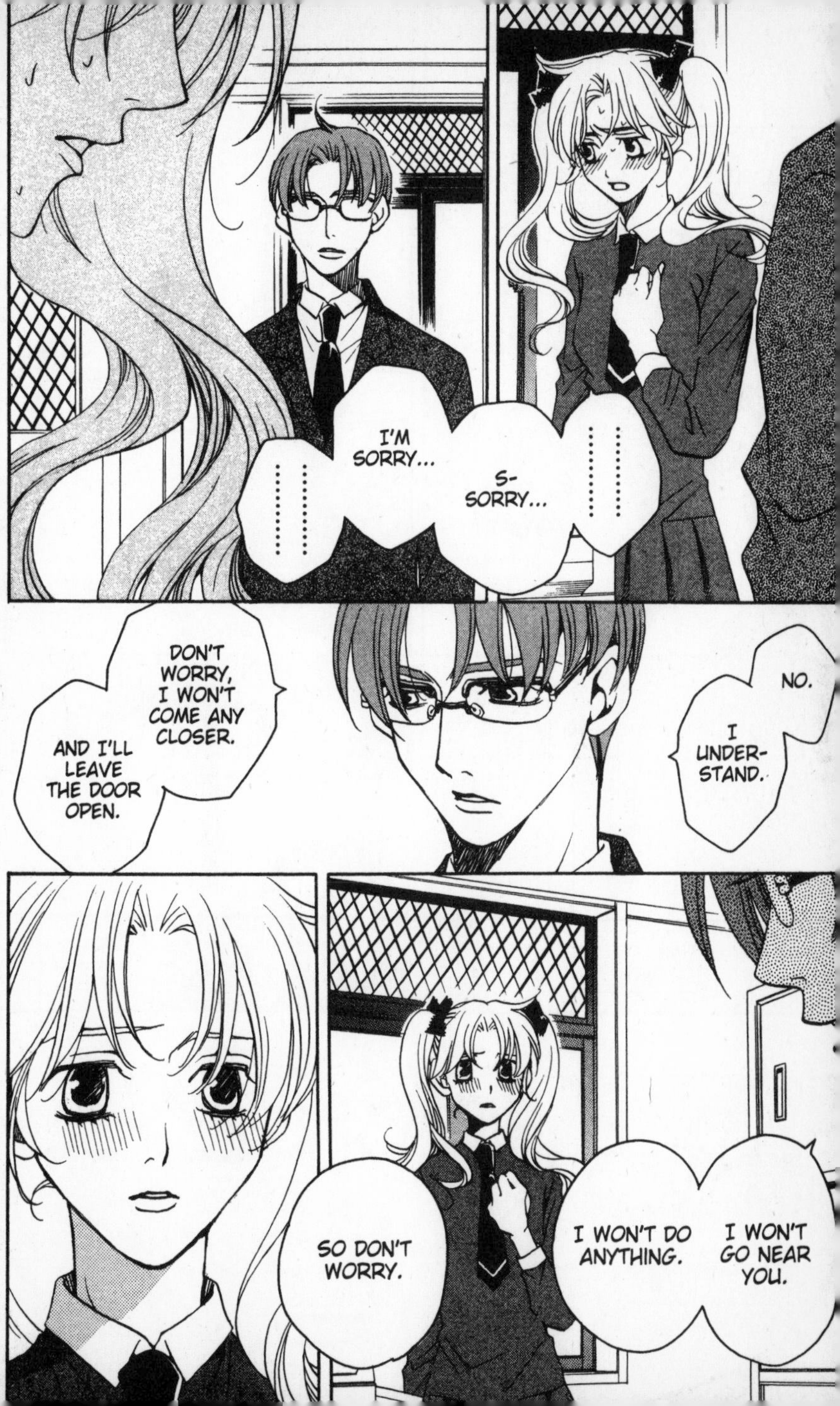
......
S-SORRY...
I'M SORRY...
......
NO.
I UNDERSTAND.
DON'T WORRY, I WON'T COME ANY CLOSER.
AND I'LL LEAVE THE DOOR OPEN.
I WON'T GO NEAR YOU.
I WON'T DO ANYTHING.
SO DON'T WORRY.

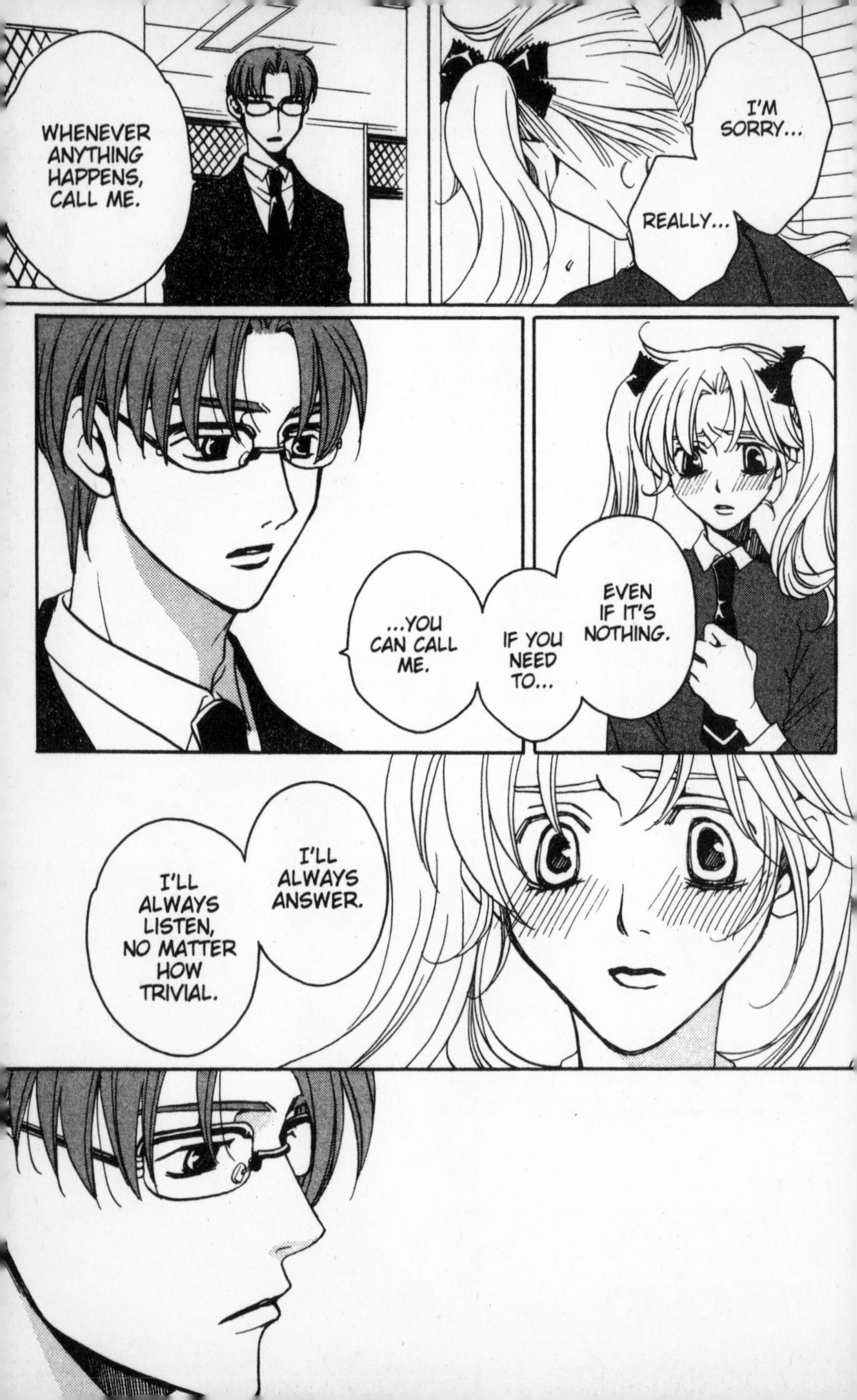
I'M SORRY...
REALLY...
WHENEVER ANYTHING HAPPENS, CALL ME.
EVEN IF IT'S NOTHING.
IF YOU NEED TO...
...YOU CAN CALL ME.
I'LL ALWAYS ANSWER.
I'LL ALWAYS LISTEN, NO MATTER HOW TRIVIAL.

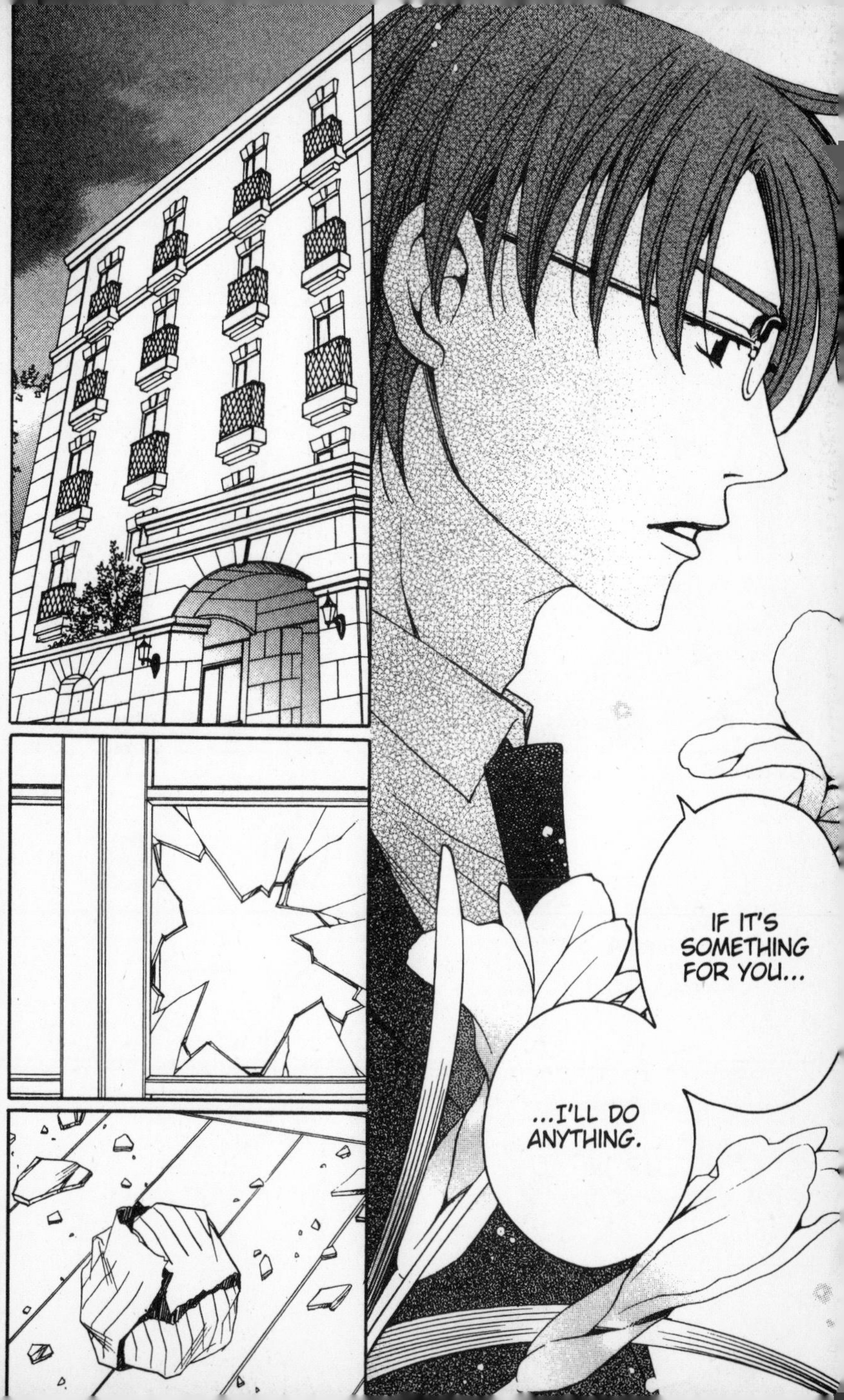
IF IT'S SOMETHING FOR YOU...
...I'LL DO ANYTHING.

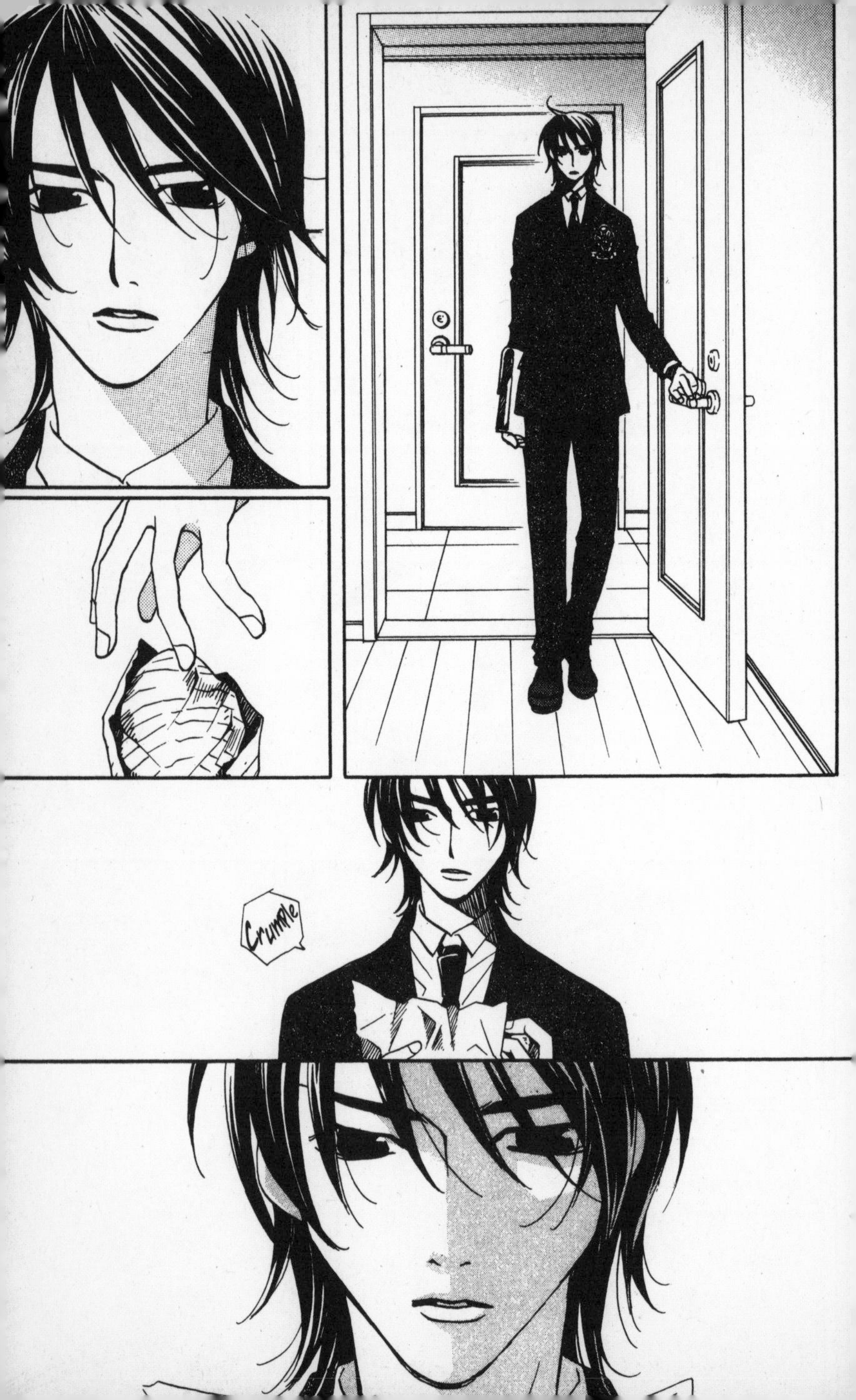
Crumple

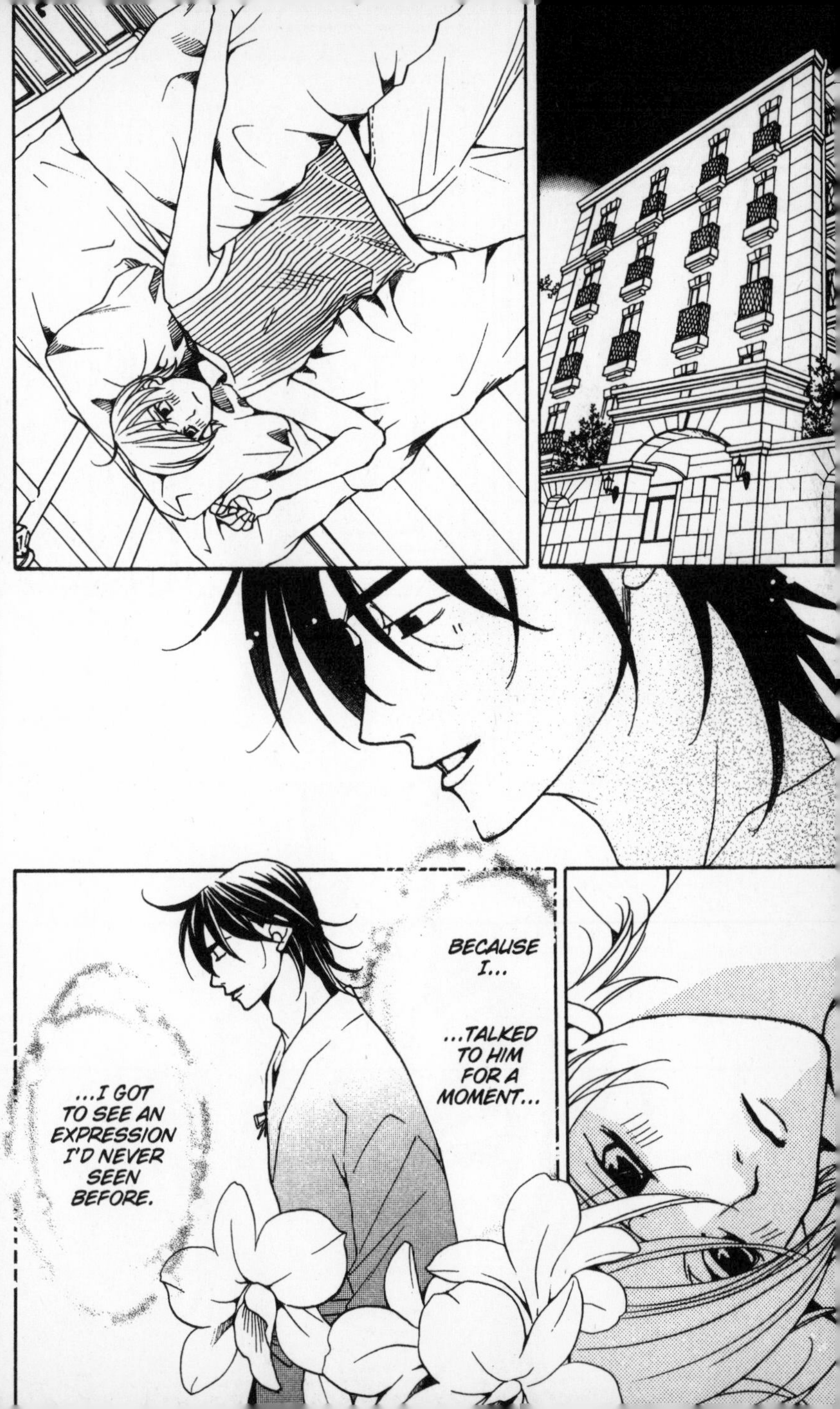
BECAUSE I...
...TALKED TO HIM FOR A MOMENT...
...I GOT TO SEE AN EXPRESSION I'D NEVER SEEN BEFORE.

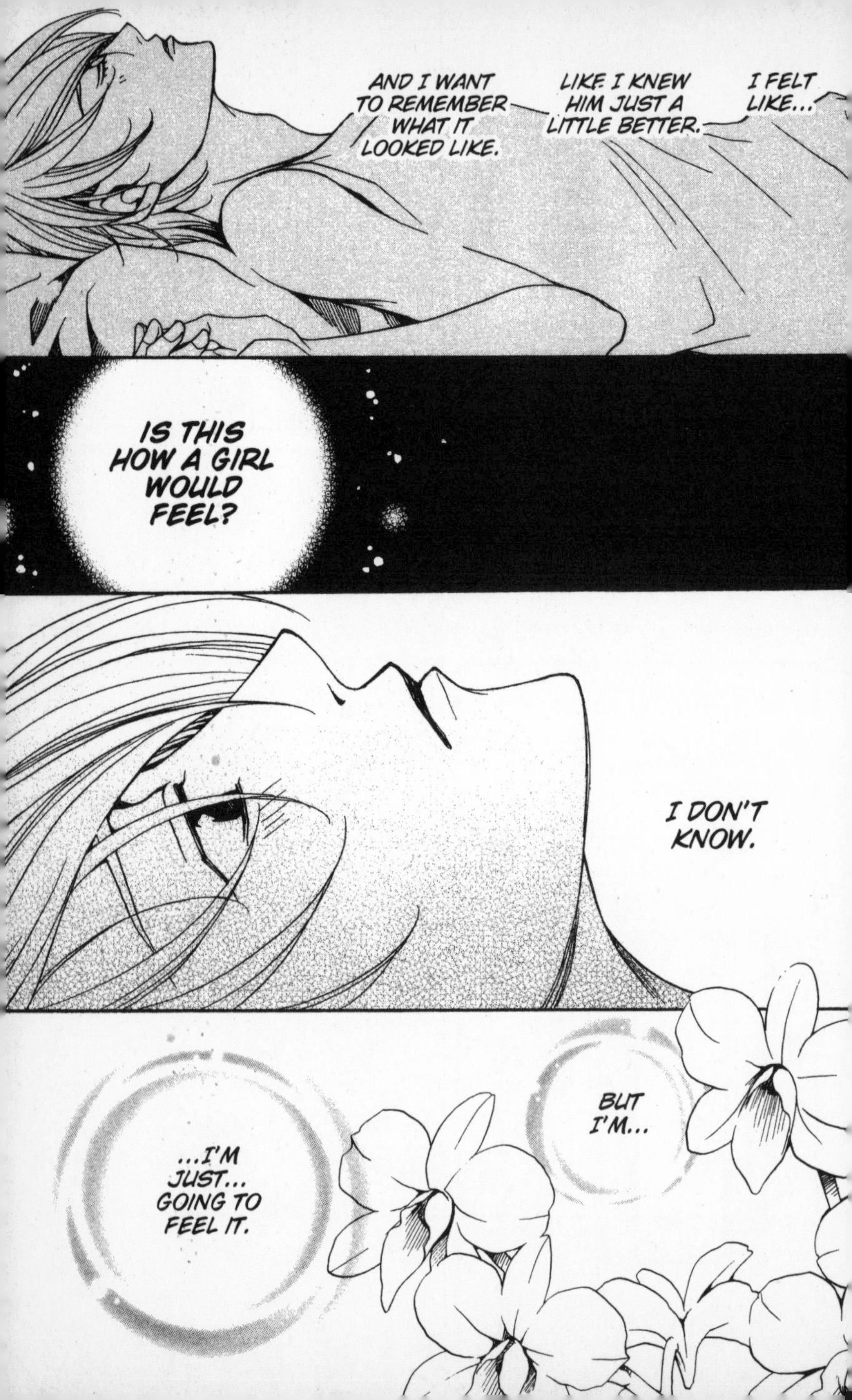
I FELT LIKE...
LIKE I KNEW HIM JUST A LITTLE BETTER.
AND I WANT TO REMEMBER WHAT IT LOOKED LIKE.
IS THIS HOW A GIRL WOULD FEEL?
I DON'T KNOW.
BUT I'M...
...I'M JUST... GOING TO FEEL IT.

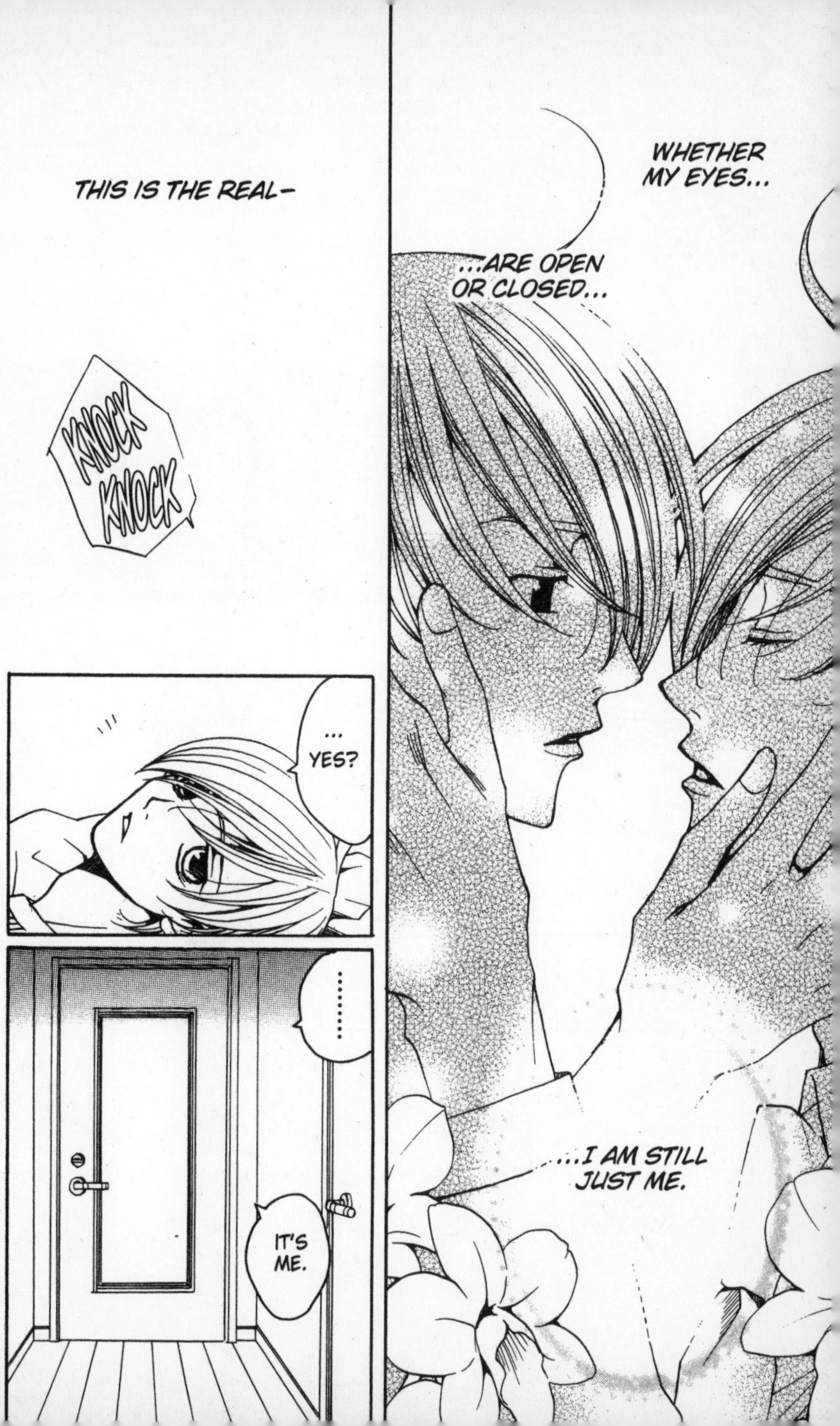
WHETHER MY EYES...
...ARE OPEN OR CLOSED...
...I AM STILL JUST ME.
THIS IS THE REAL–
KNOCK KNOCK
... YES?
....
IT'S ME.

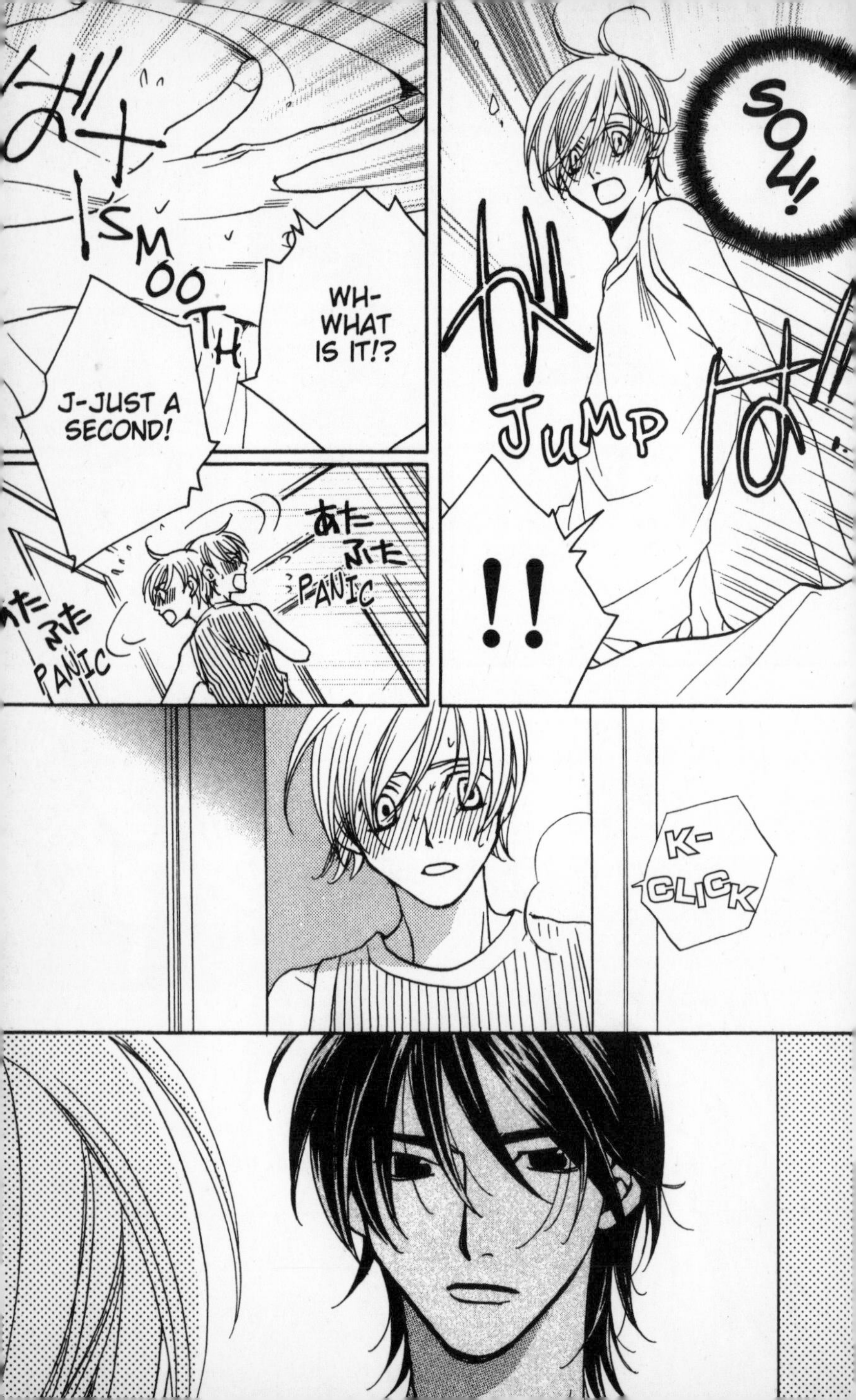
SOU!!
JUMP
!!
WH- WHAT IS IT!?
SMOOTH
J-JUST A SECOND!
あたふた PANIC
あたふた PANIC
K- CLICK

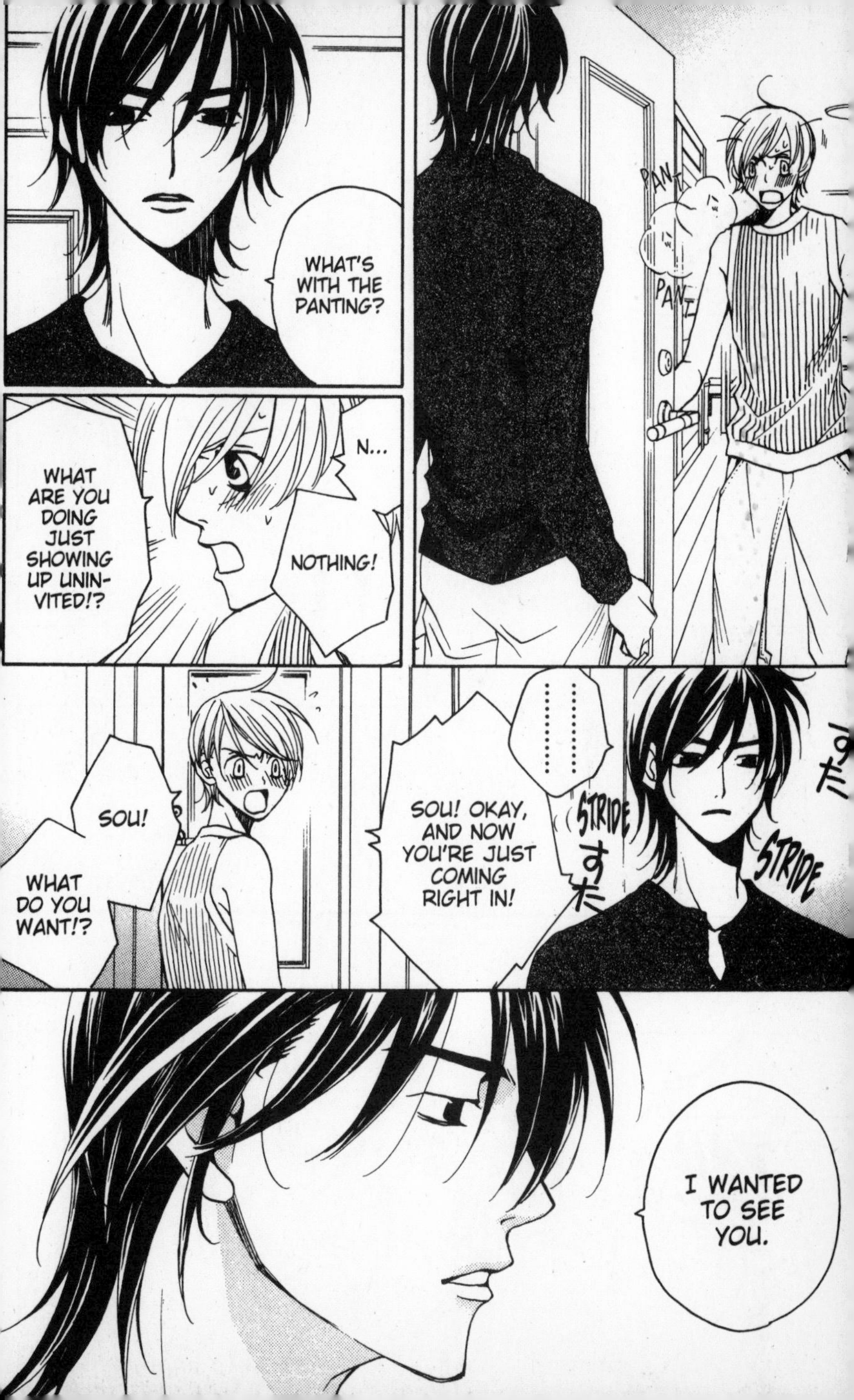
PANT
PANT
WHAT'S WITH THE PANTING?
N...
NOTHING!
WHAT ARE YOU DOING JUST SHOWING UP UNIN-VITED!?
すた
STRIDE
......
STRIDE
すた
SOU! OKAY, AND NOW YOU'RE JUST COMING RIGHT IN!
SOU!
WHAT DO YOU WANT!?
I WANTED TO SEE YOU.

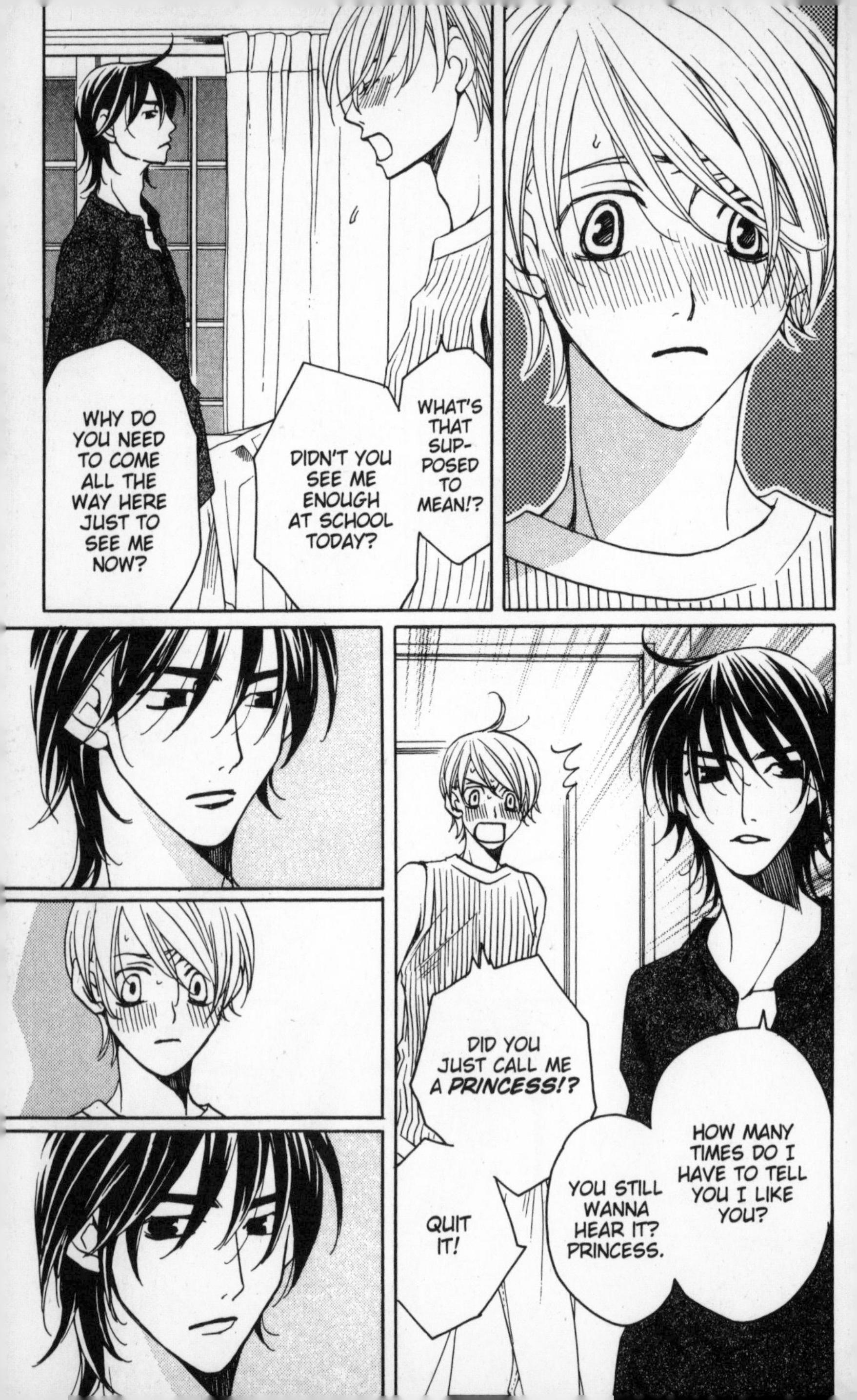
WHAT'S THAT SUP-POSED TO MEAN!?
DIDN'T YOU SEE ME ENOUGH AT SCHOOL TODAY?
WHY DO YOU NEED TO COME ALL THE WAY HERE JUST TO SEE ME NOW?
HOW MANY TIMES DO I HAVE TO TELL YOU I LIKE YOU?
YOU STILL WANNA HEAR IT? PRINCESS.
DID YOU JUST CALL ME A *PRINCESS!?*
QUIT IT!

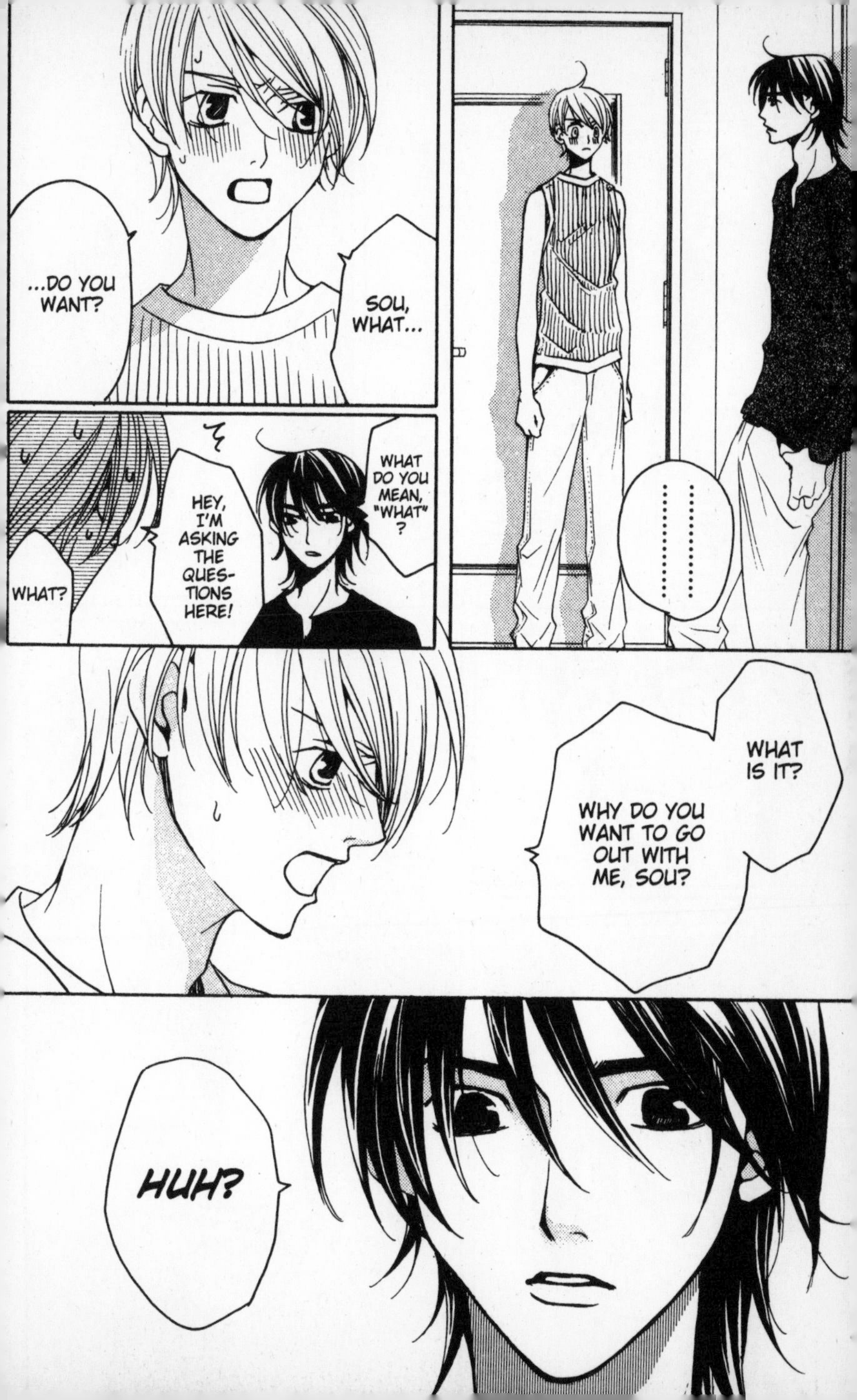
......
SOU, WHAT...
...DO YOU WANT?
WHAT DO YOU MEAN, "WHAT"?
HEY, I'M ASKING THE QUES-TIONS HERE!
WHAT?
WHAT IS IT?
WHY DO YOU WANT TO GO OUT WITH ME, SOU?
HUH?

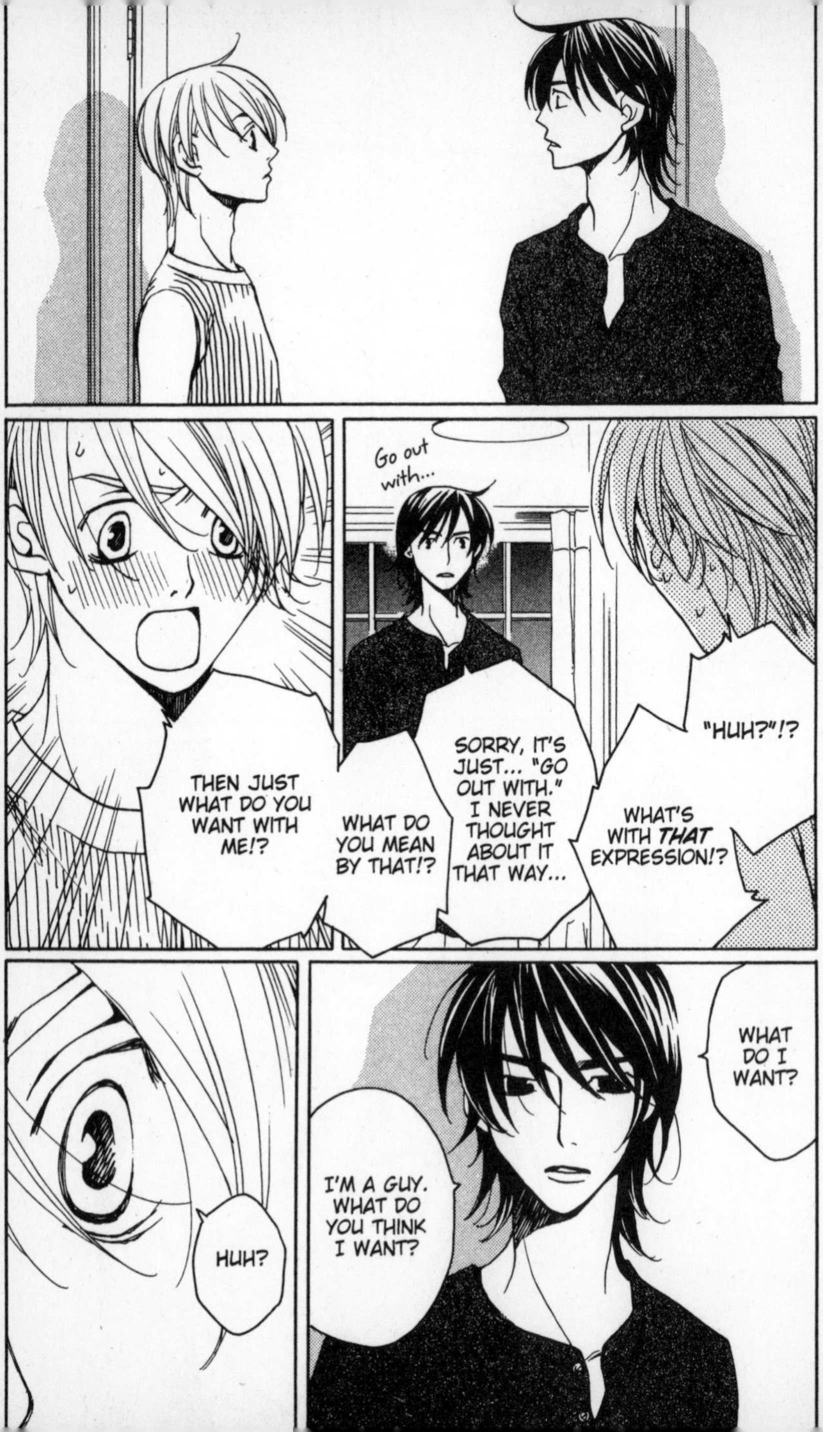

Go out with...
"HUH?"!?
WHAT'S WITH *THAT* EXPRESSION!?
SORRY, IT'S JUST... "GO OUT WITH." I NEVER THOUGHT ABOUT IT THAT WAY...
WHAT DO YOU MEAN BY THAT!?
THEN JUST WHAT DO YOU WANT WITH ME!?
WHAT DO I WANT?
I'M A GUY. WHAT DO YOU THINK I WANT?
HUH?

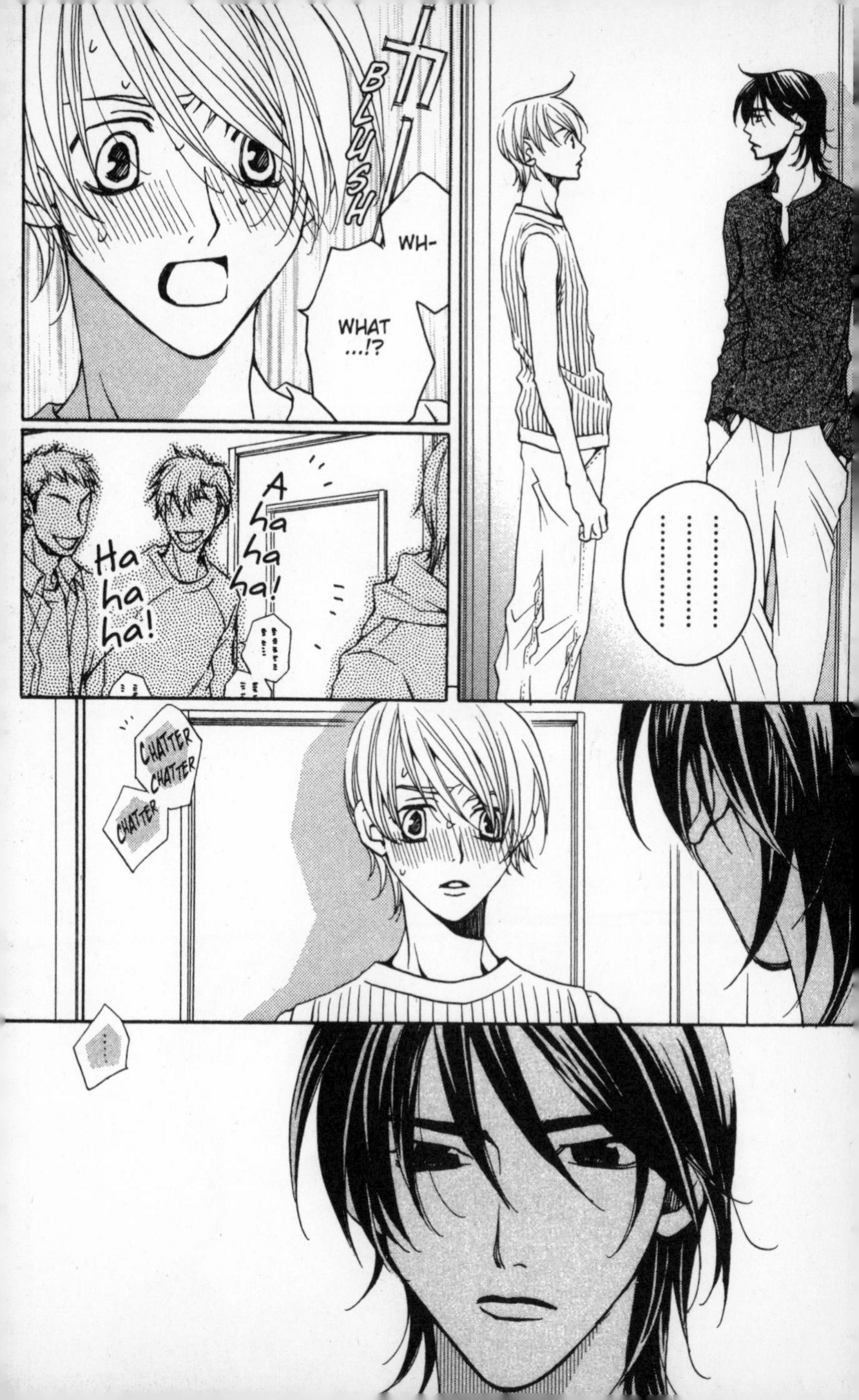
......
BLUSH
WH-
WHAT ...!?
A ha ha ha!
Ha ha ha!
CHATTER CHATTER
CHATTER
...

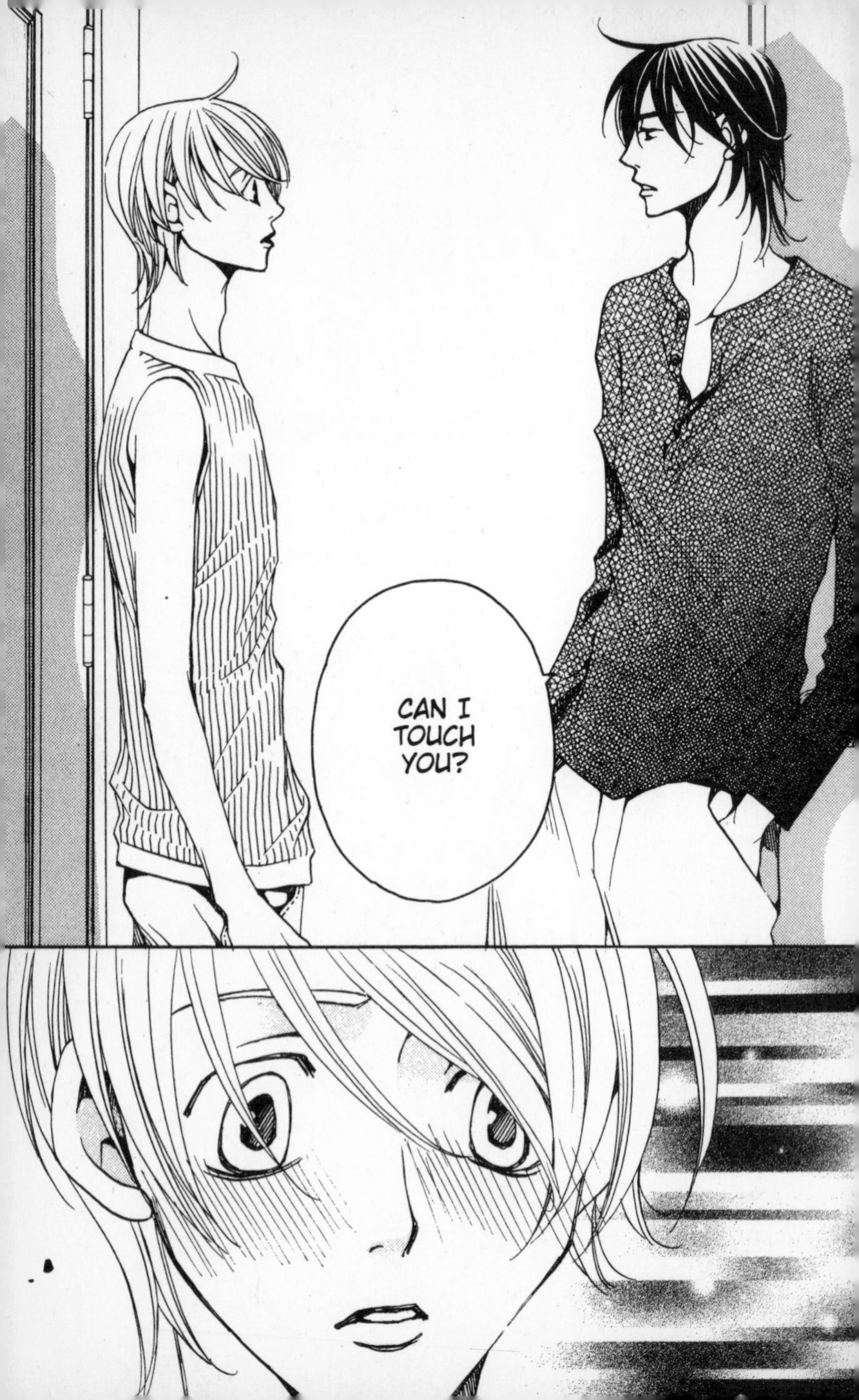
CAN I TOUCH YOU?

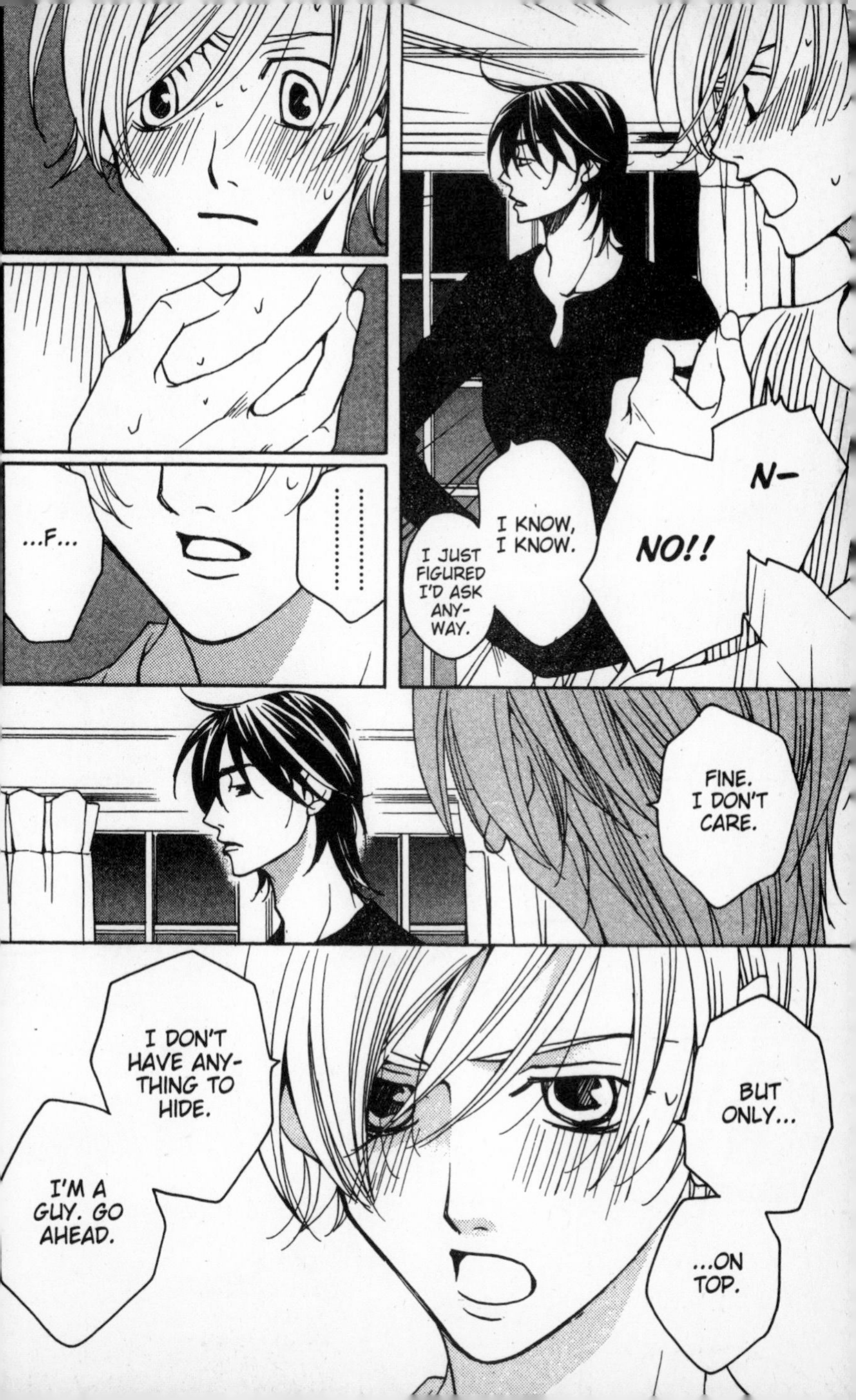

N-
NO!!
I KNOW, I KNOW.
I JUST FIGURED I'D ASK ANY-WAY.
......
...F...
FINE. I DON'T CARE.
I DON'T HAVE ANY-THING TO HIDE.
I'M A GUY. GO AHEAD.
BUT ONLY...
...ON TOP.

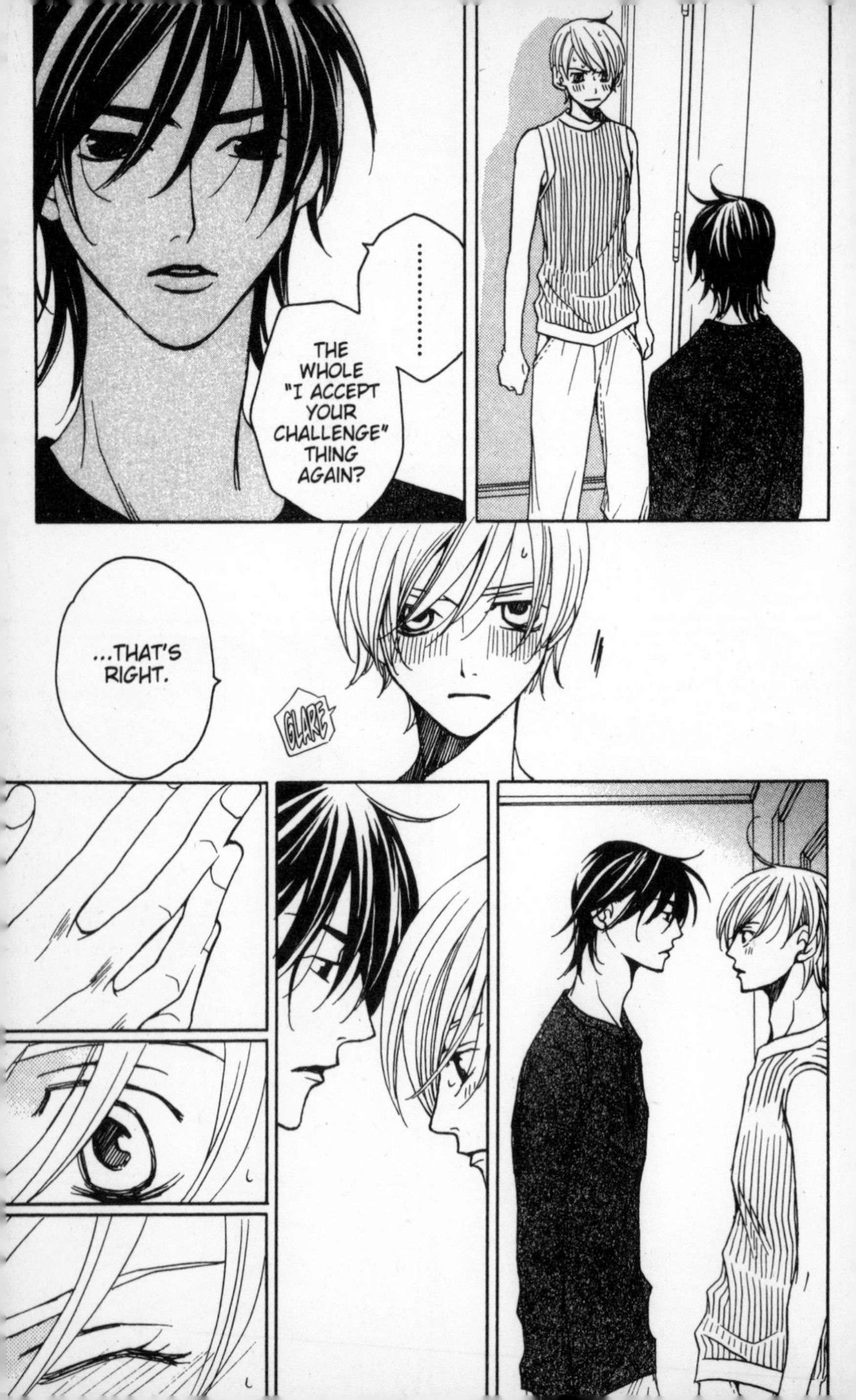
......
THE WHOLE "I ACCEPT YOUR CHALLENGE" THING AGAIN?
...THAT'S RIGHT.
GLARE

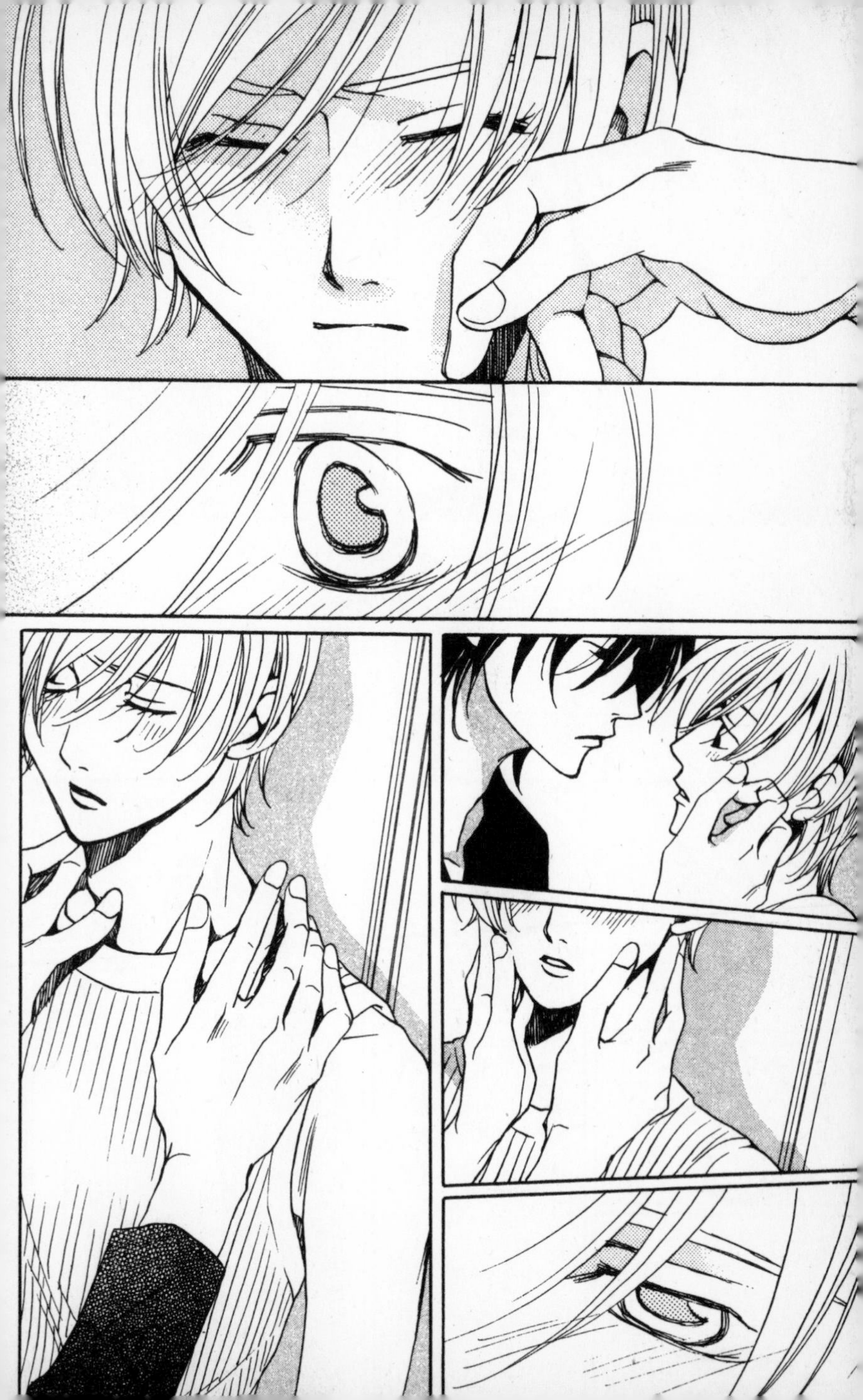

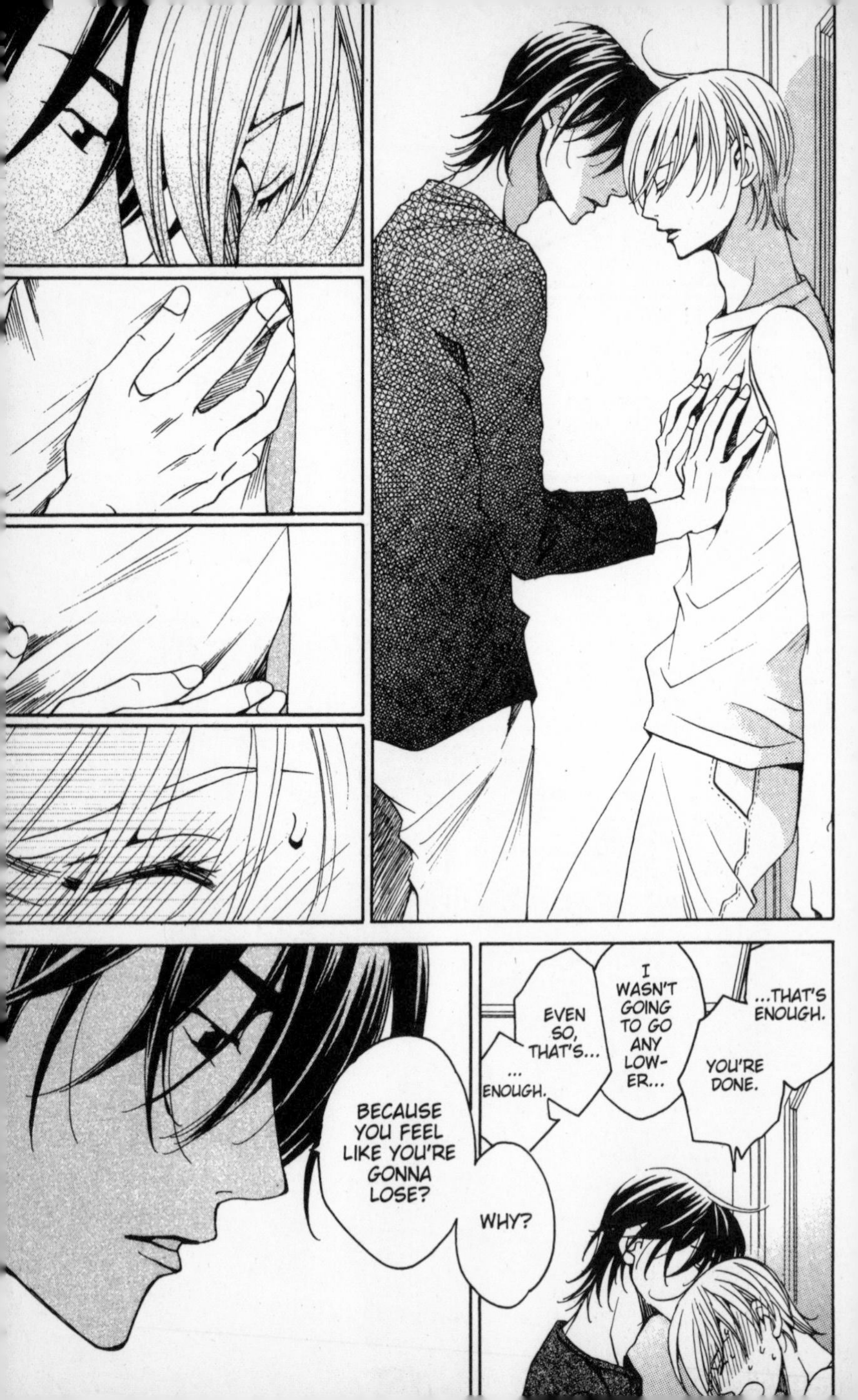
...THAT'S ENOUGH.
YOU'RE DONE.
I WASN'T GOING TO GO ANY LOW-ER...
EVEN SO, THAT'S...
... ENOUGH.
WHY?
BECAUSE YOU FEEL LIKE YOU'RE GONNA LOSE?

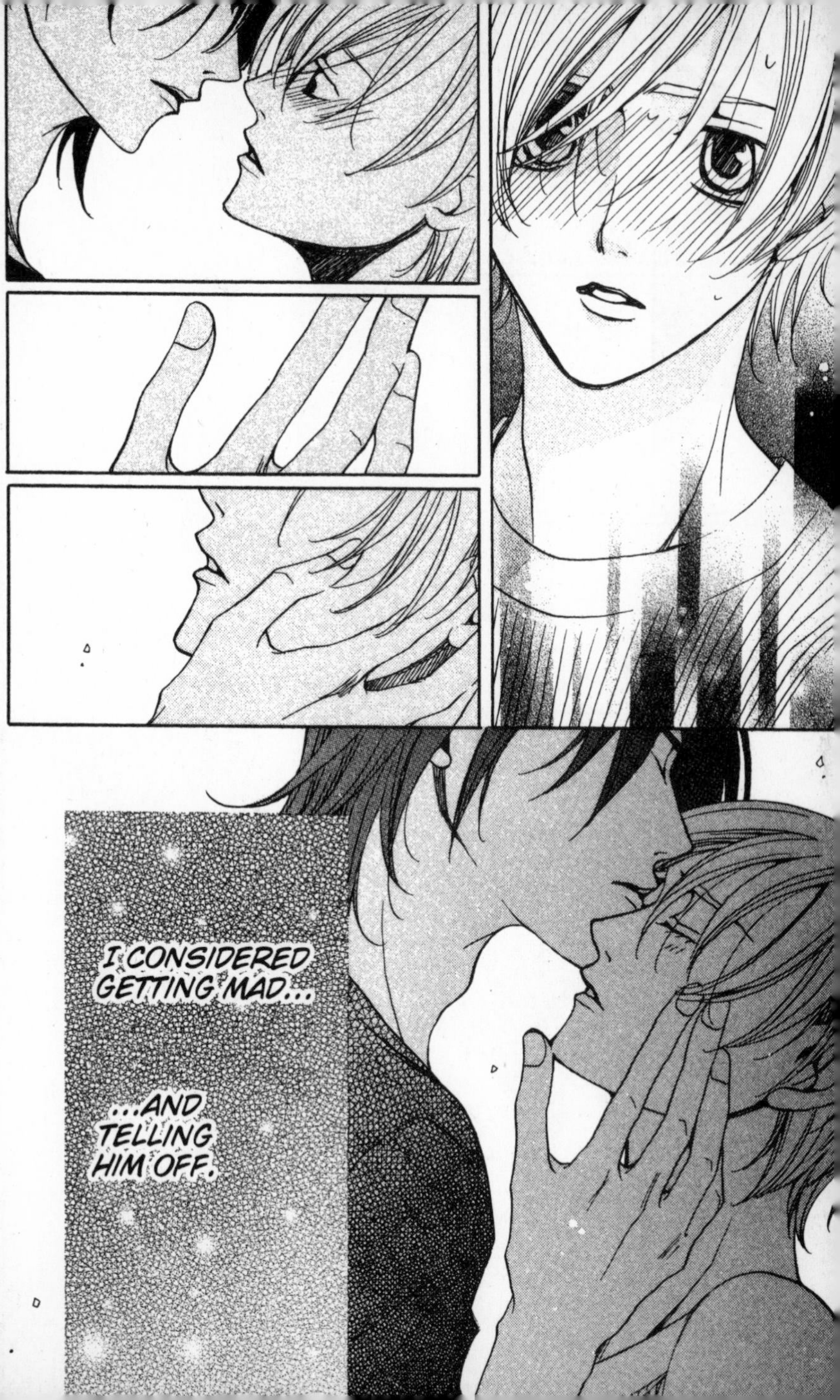
I CONSIDERED GETTING MAD...
...AND TELLING HIM OFF.

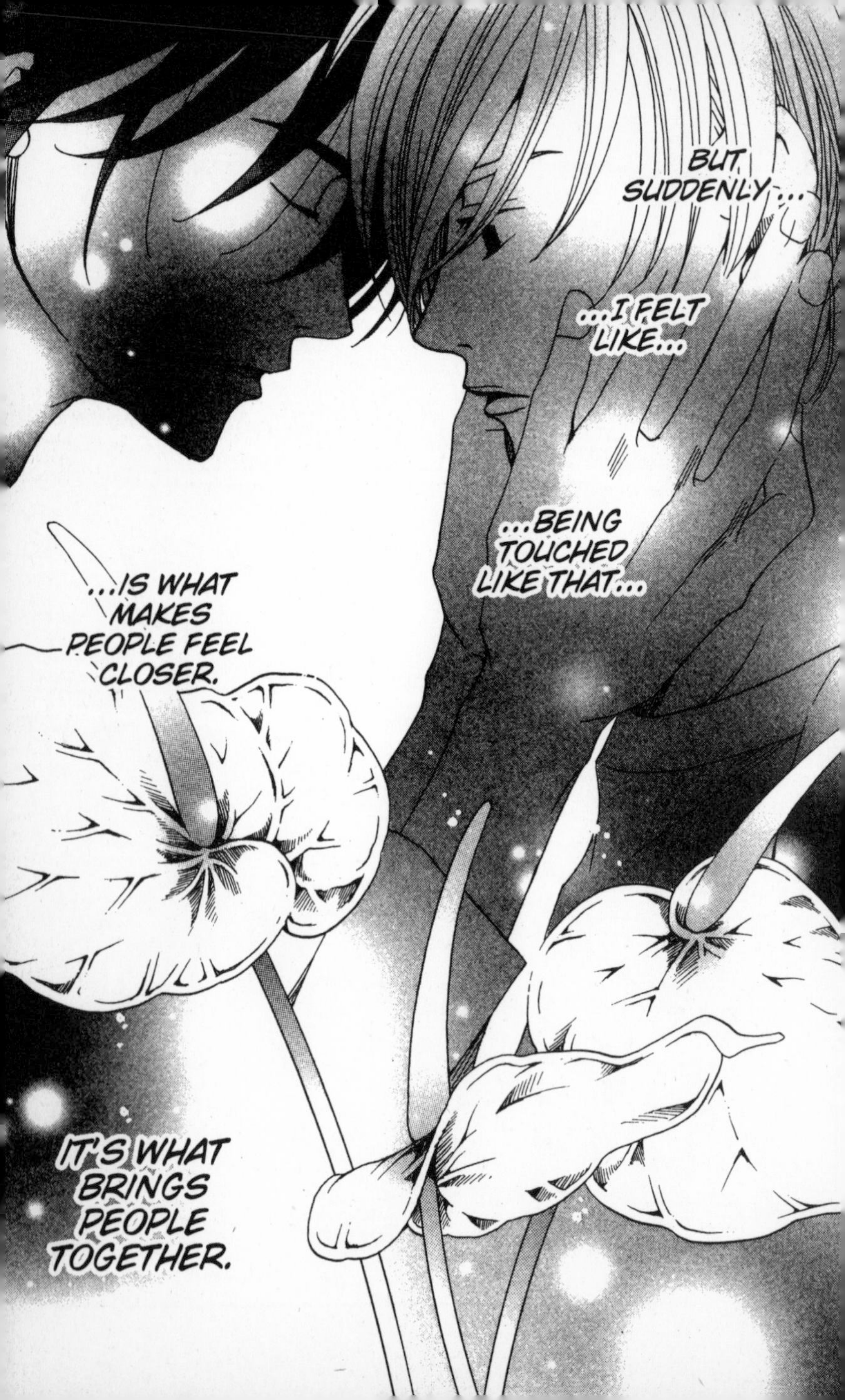
BUT SUDDENLY...
...I FELT LIKE...
...BEING TOUCHED LIKE THAT...
...IS WHAT MAKES PEOPLE FEEL CLOSER.
IT'S WHAT BRINGS PEOPLE TOGETHER.

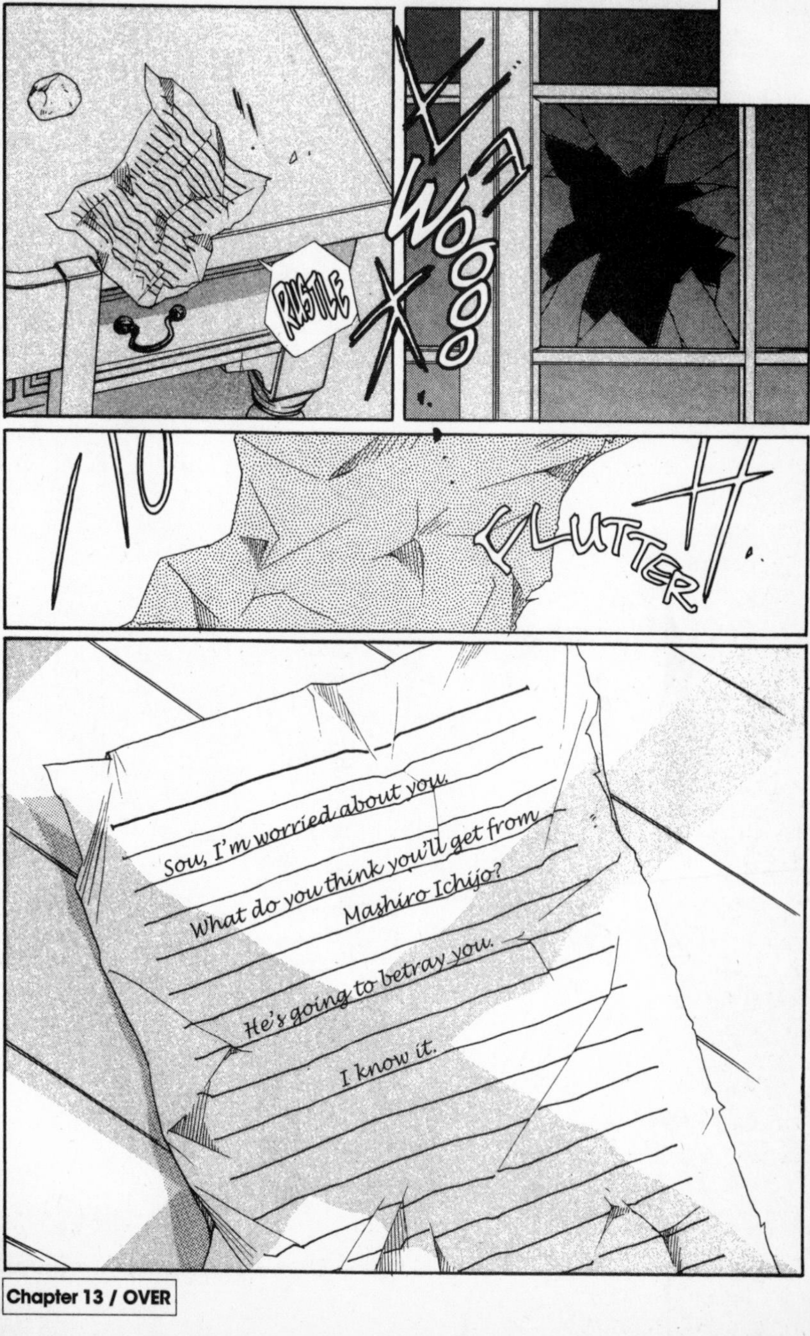
RUSTLE
FLUTTER
Sou, I'm worried about you.
What do you think you'll get from
Mashiro Ichijo?
He's going to betray you.
I know it.

Chapter 13 / OVER

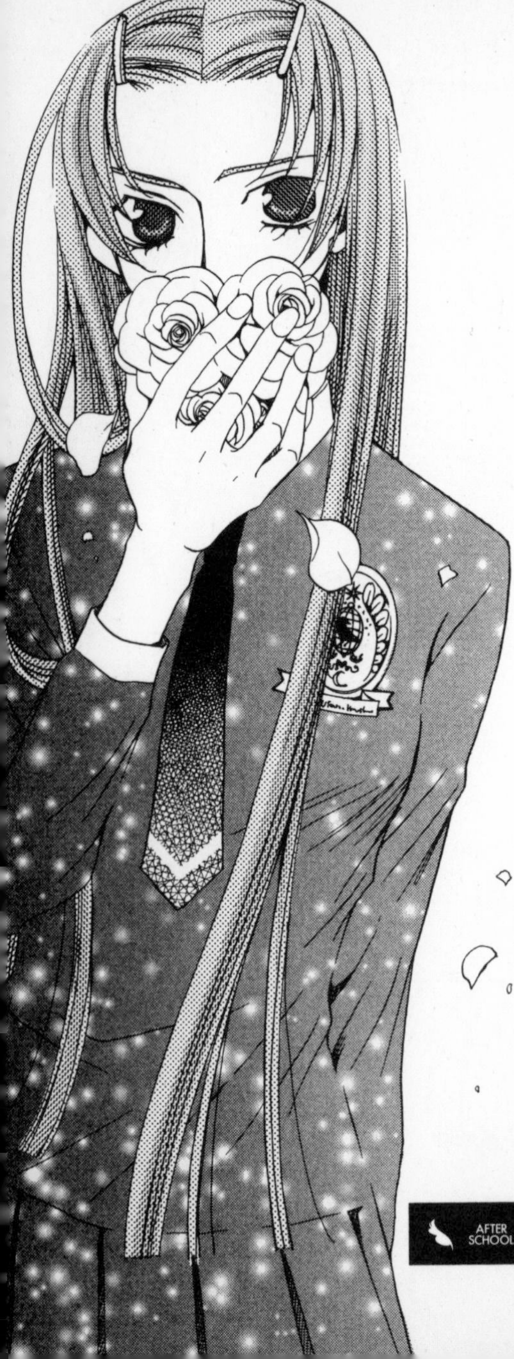

AFTER SCHOOL NIGHTMARE Chapter 14

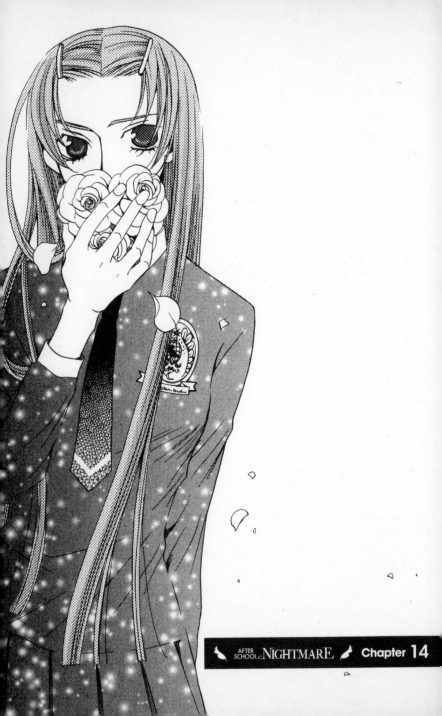

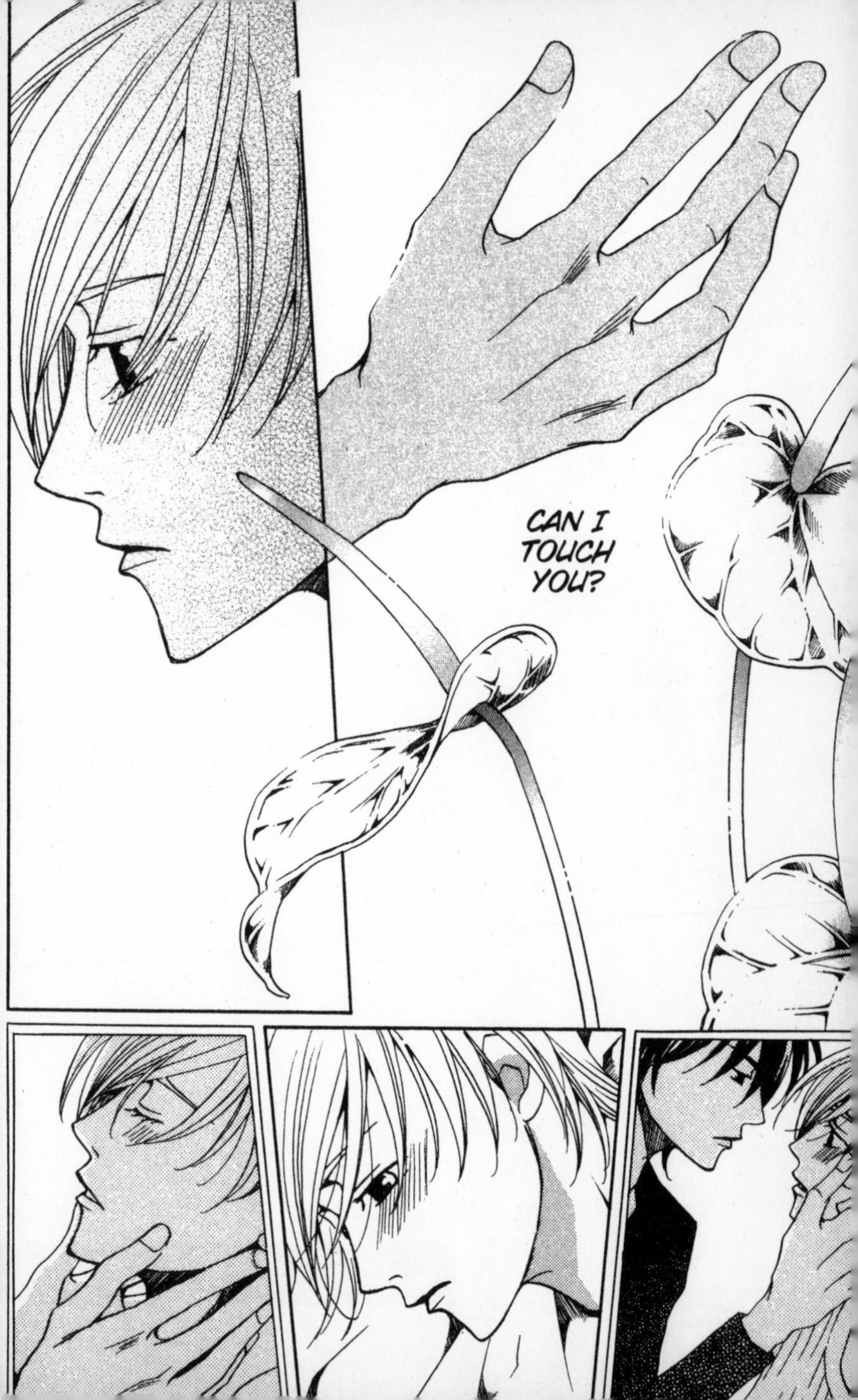
CAN I TOUCH YOU?

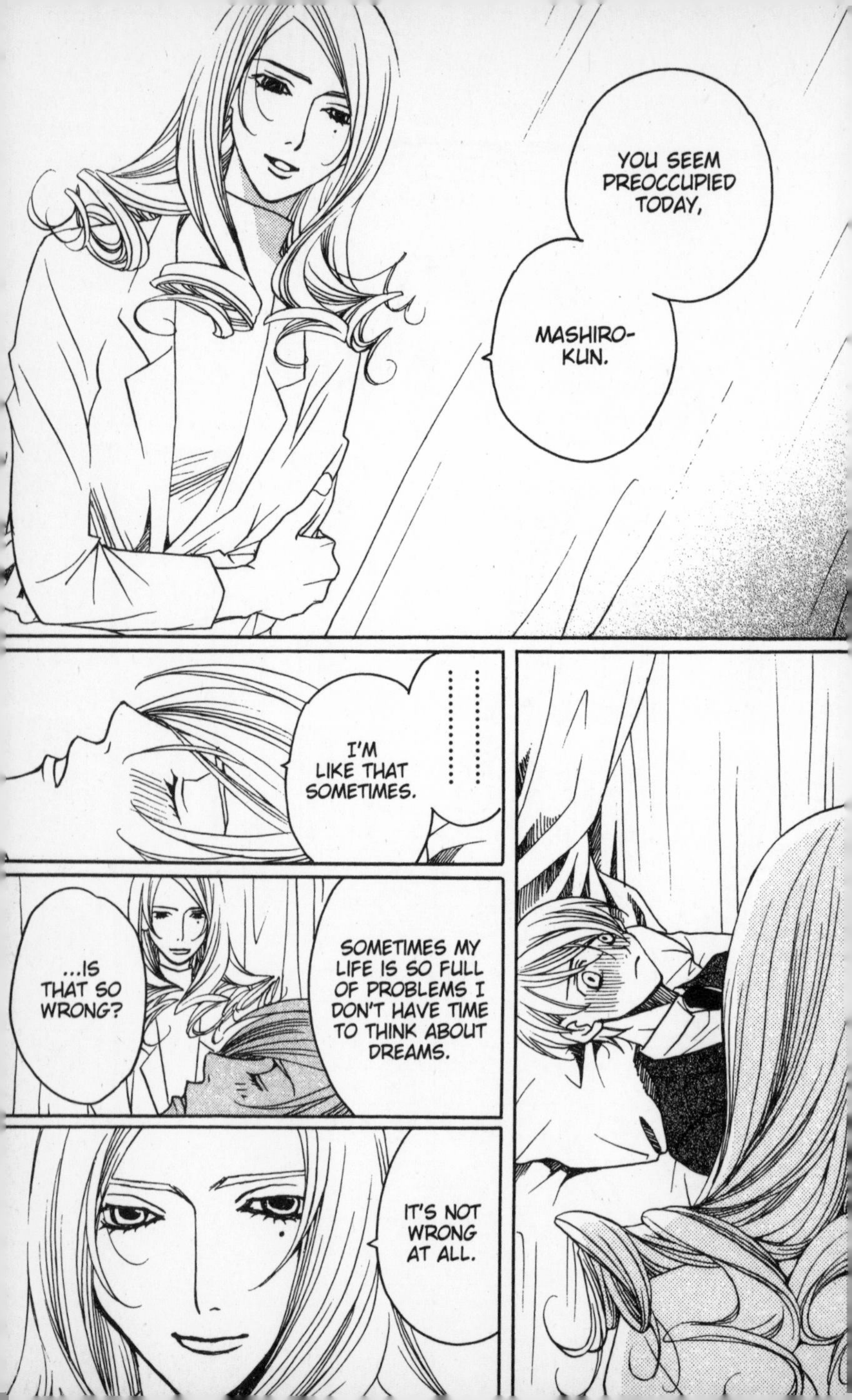

YOU SEEM PREOCCUPIED TODAY,
MASHIRO-KUN.
......
I'M LIKE THAT SOMETIMES.
SOMETIMES MY LIFE IS SO FULL OF PROBLEMS I DON'T HAVE TIME TO THINK ABOUT DREAMS.
...IS THAT SO WRONG?
IT'S NOT WRONG AT ALL.

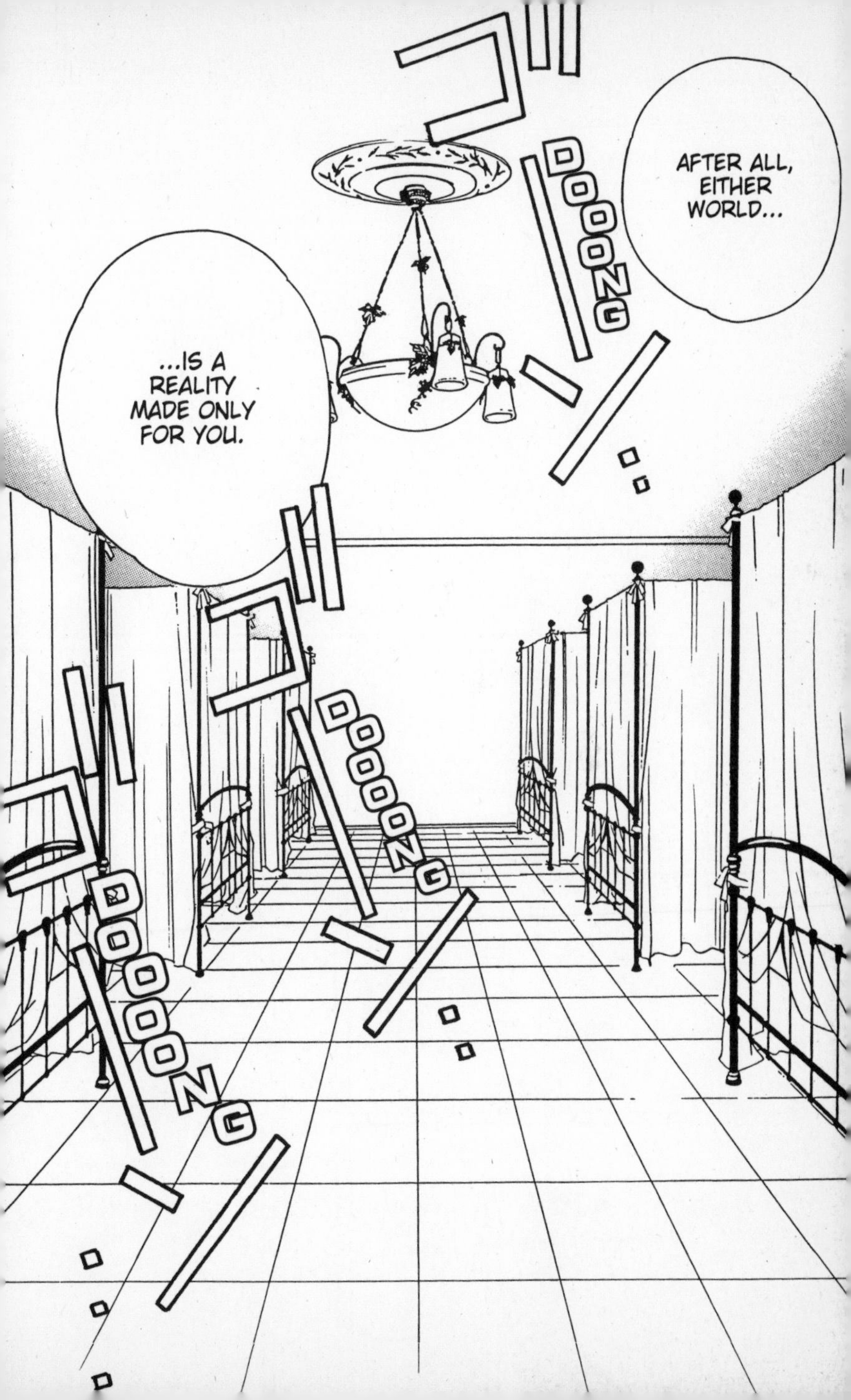
AFTER ALL, EITHER WORLD...
DOOONG
...IS A REALITY MADE ONLY FOR YOU.
DOOOONG
DOOOONG

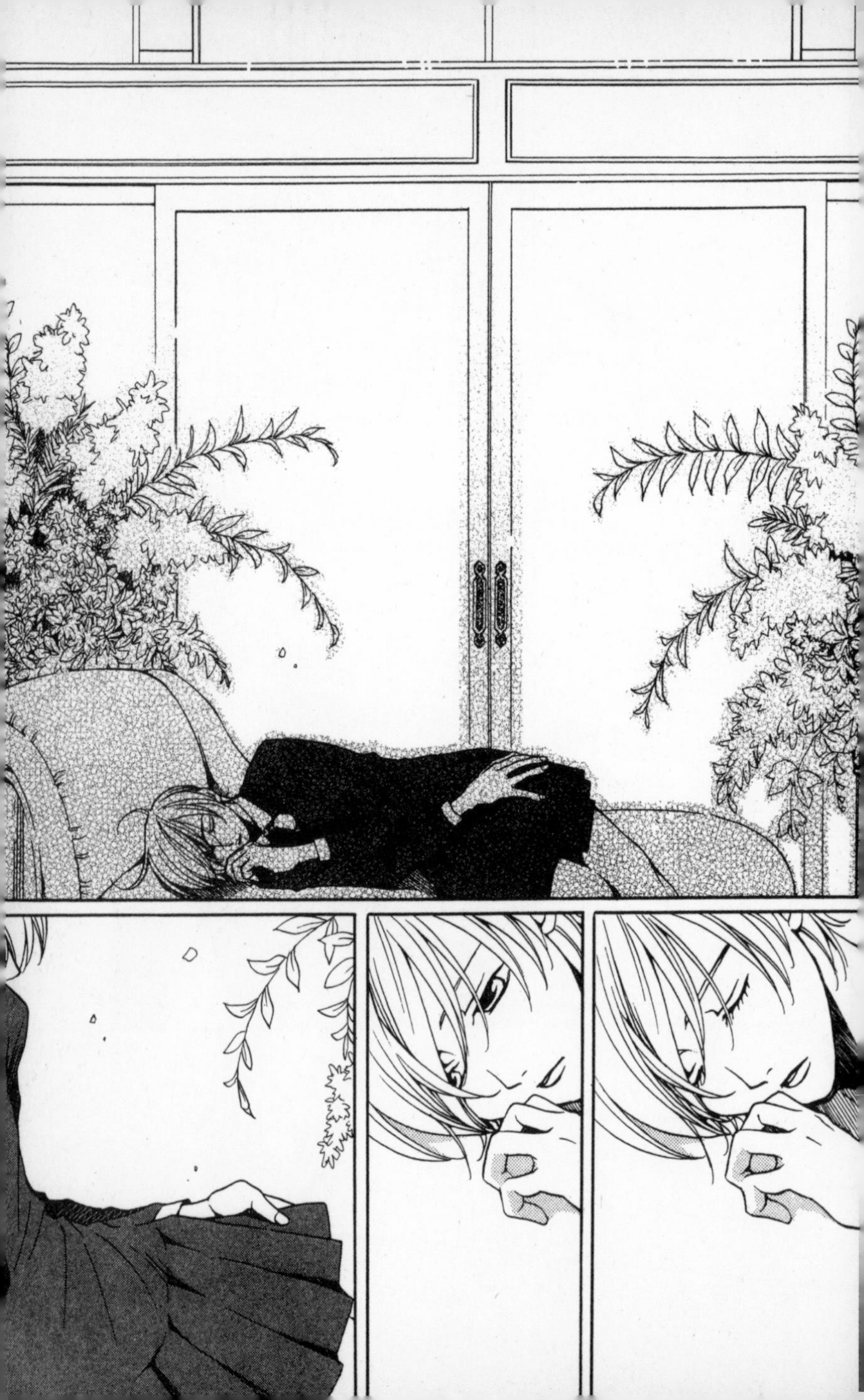

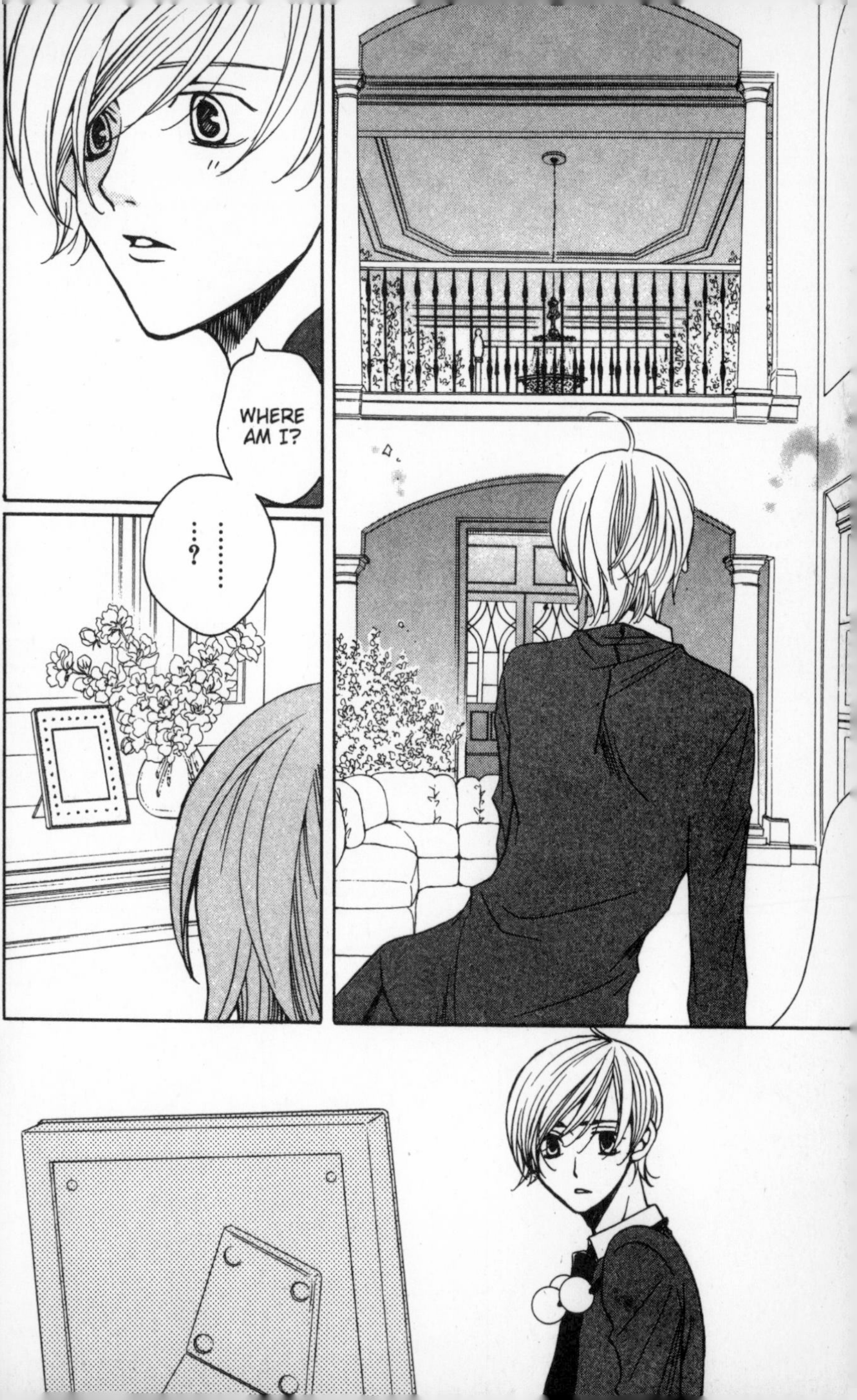
WHERE AM I?
......?

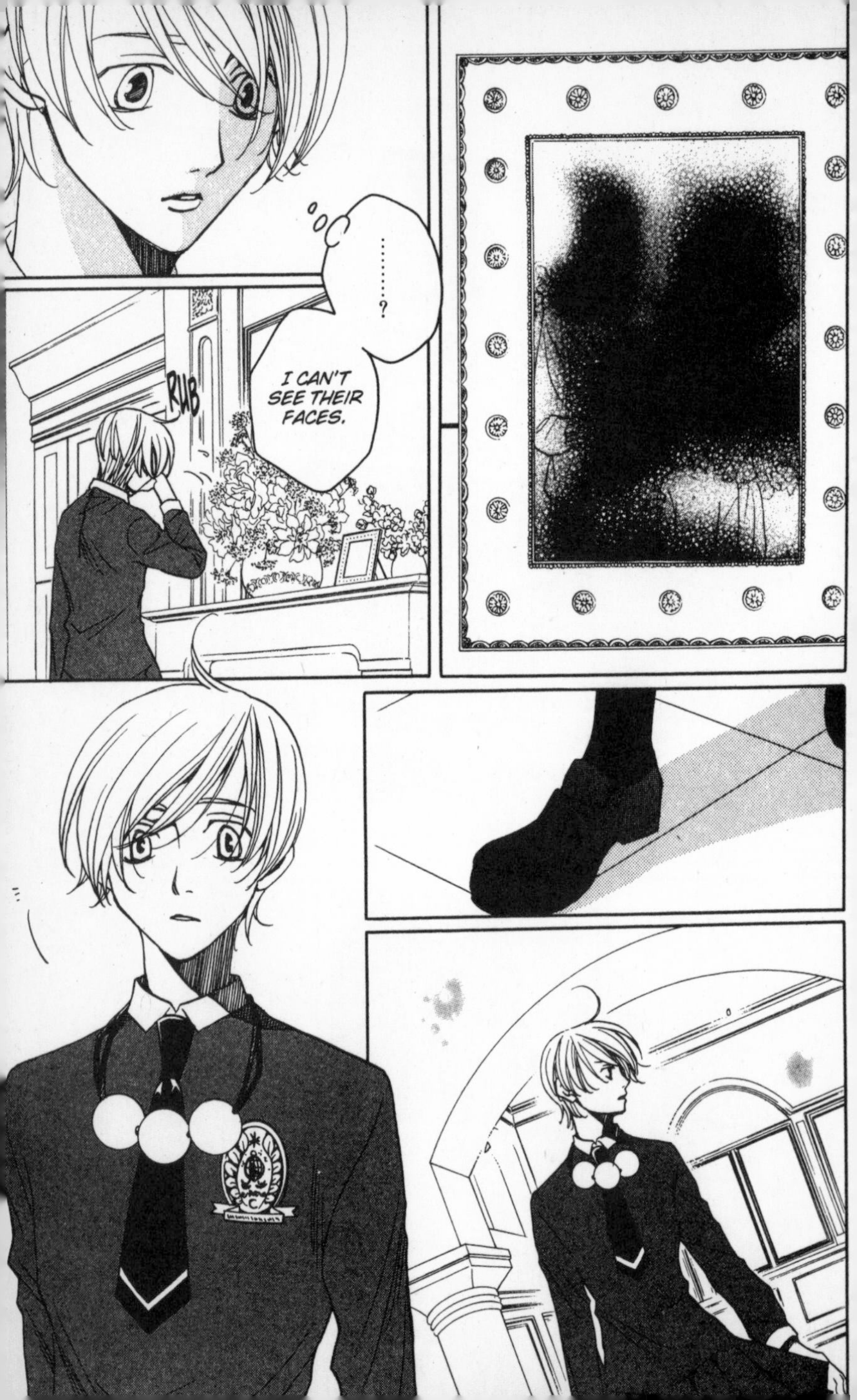

......?
RUB
I CAN'T SEE THEIR FACES.

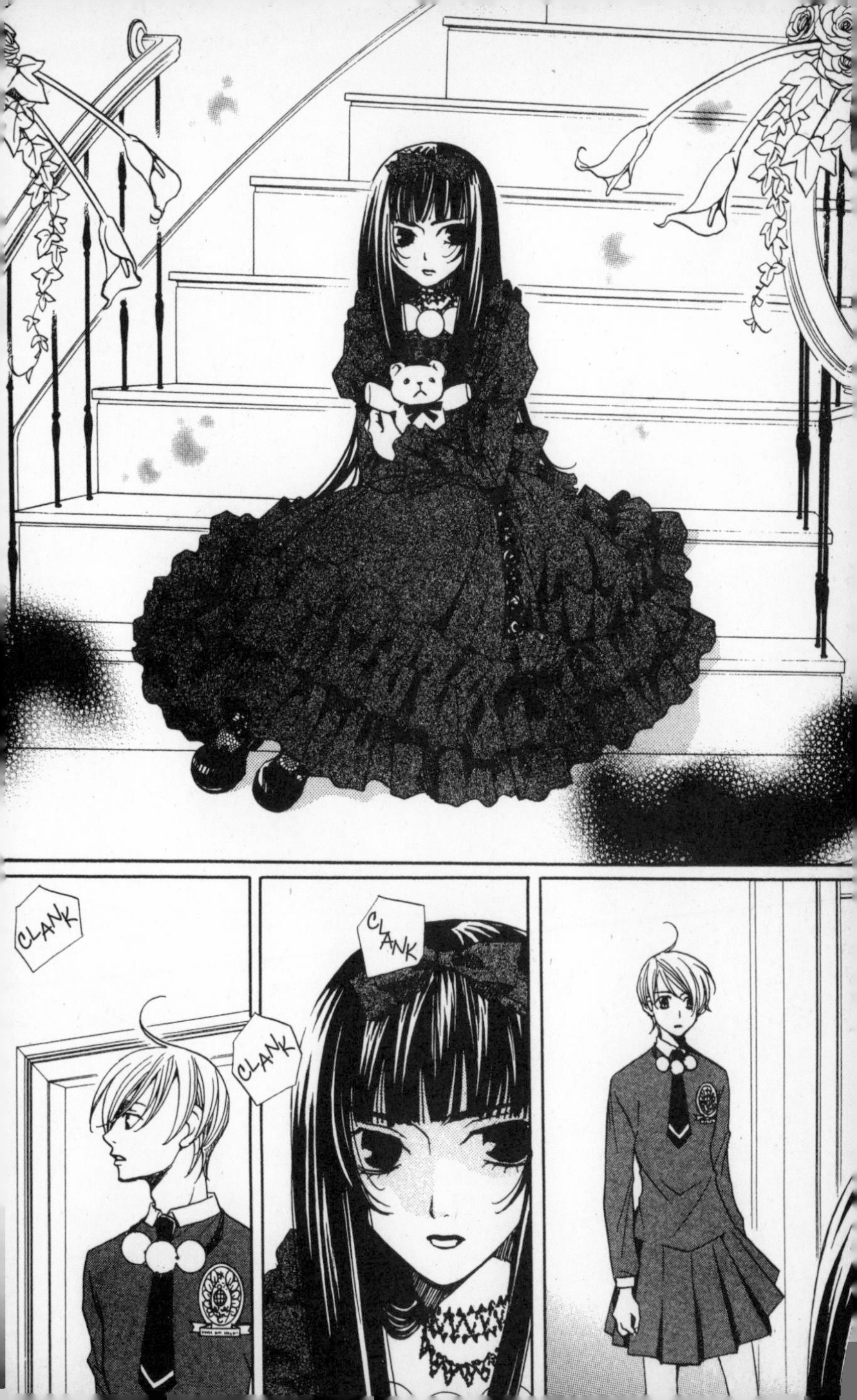
CLANK
CLANK
CLANK

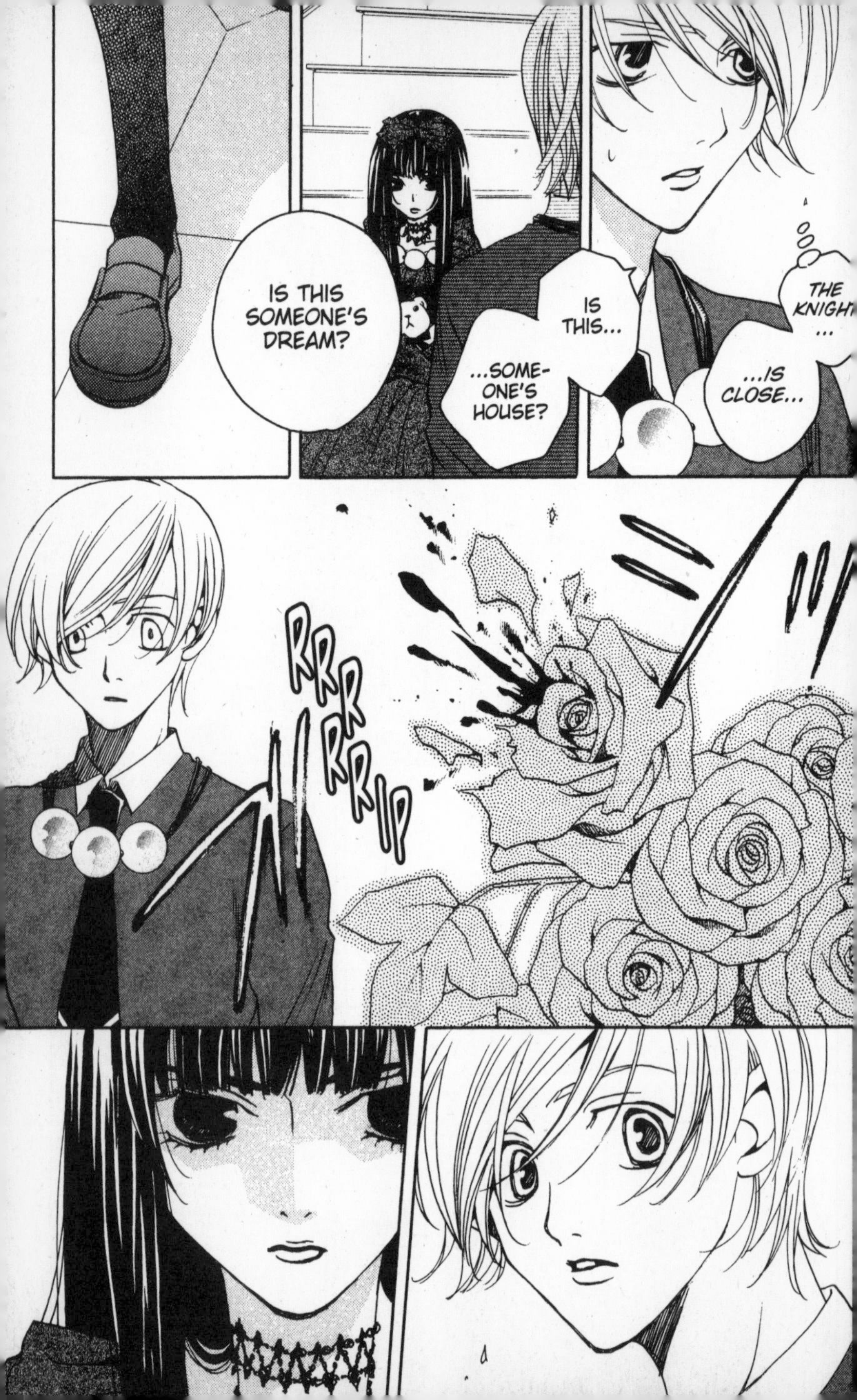
THE KNIGHT ...
...IS CLOSE...
IS THIS...
...SOME-ONE'S HOUSE?
IS THIS SOMEONE'S DREAM?
RRRRRRIP

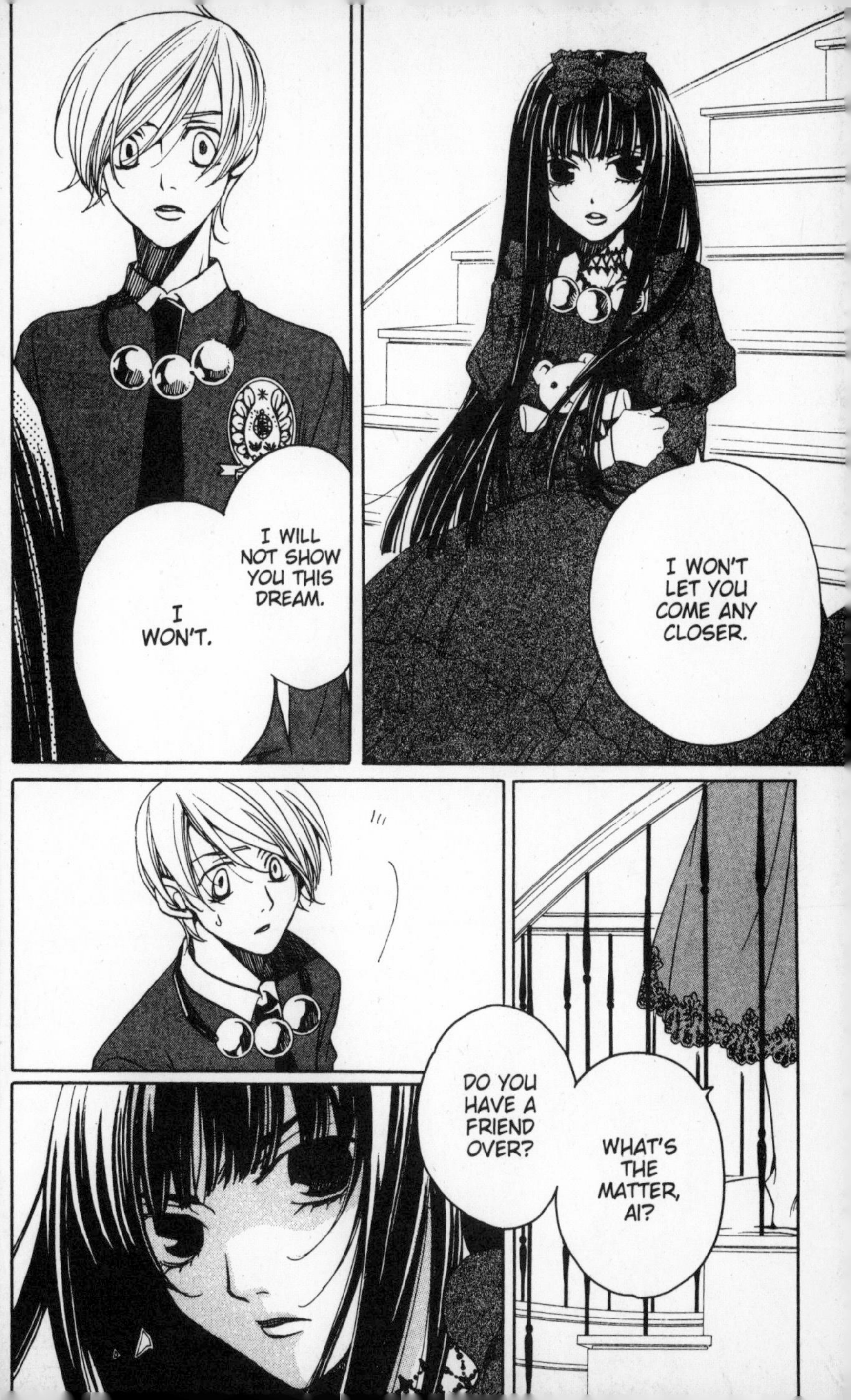
I WON'T LET YOU COME ANY CLOSER.
I WILL NOT SHOW YOU THIS DREAM.
I WON'T.
WHAT'S THE MATTER, AI?
DO YOU HAVE A FRIEND OVER?

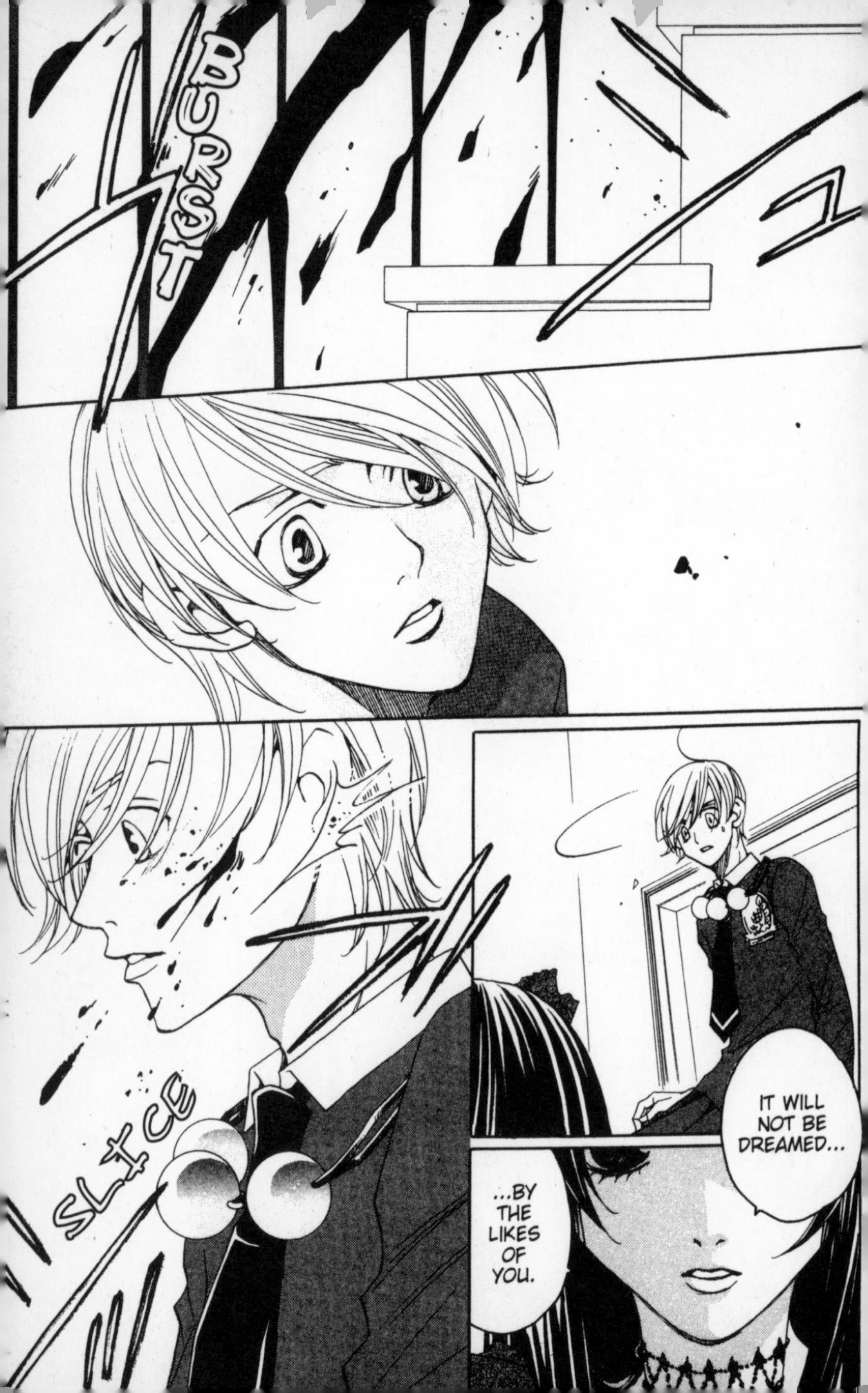
BURST
IT WILL NOT BE DREAMED...
...BY THE LIKES OF YOU.
SLICE

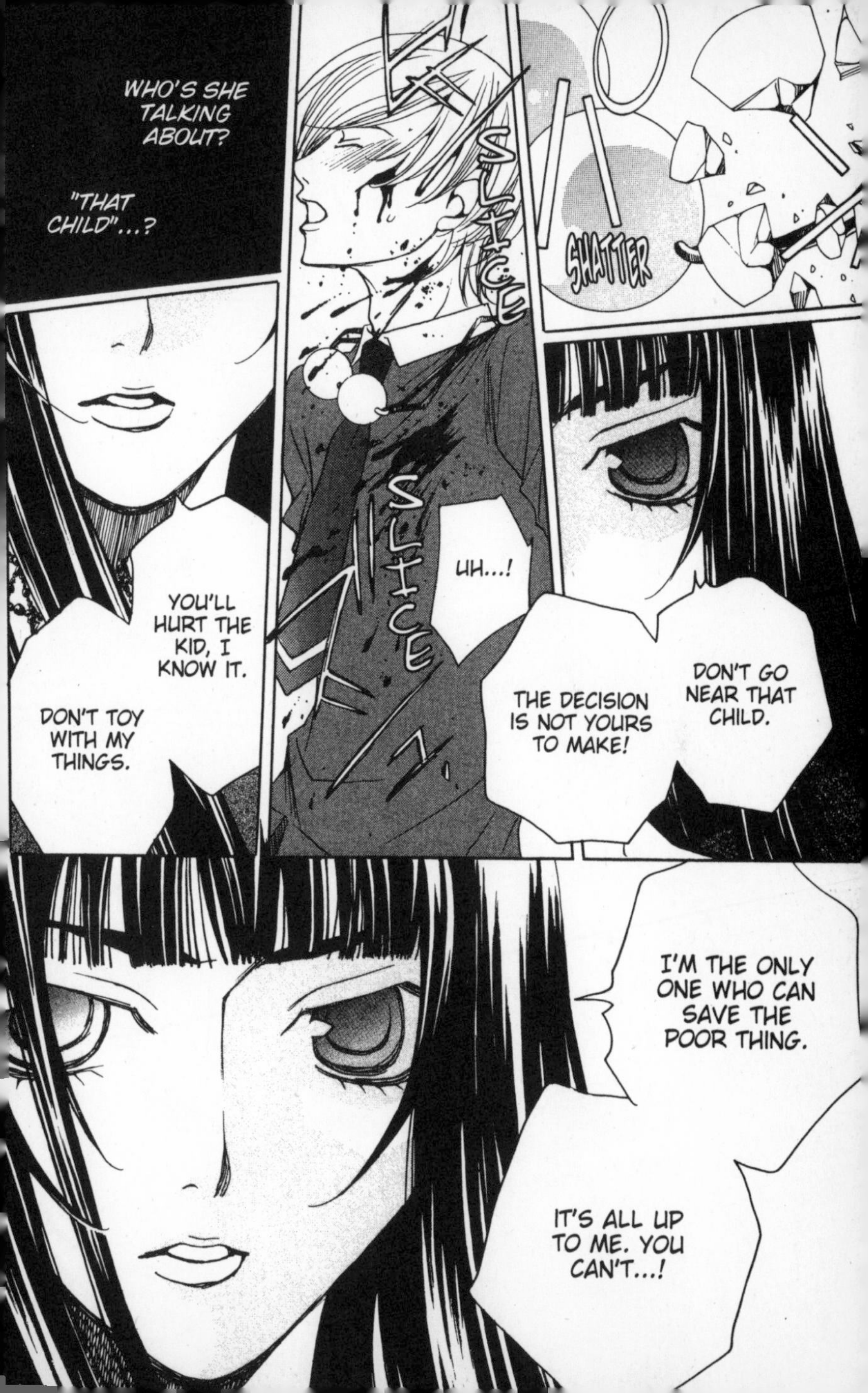
SHATTER
DON'T GO NEAR THAT CHILD.
THE DECISION IS NOT YOURS TO MAKE!
SLICE
SLICE
UH...!
WHO'S SHE TALKING ABOUT?
"THAT CHILD"...?
YOU'LL HURT THE KID, I KNOW IT.
DON'T TOY WITH MY THINGS.
I'M THE ONLY ONE WHO CAN SAVE THE POOR THING.
IT'S ALL UP TO ME. YOU CAN'T...!

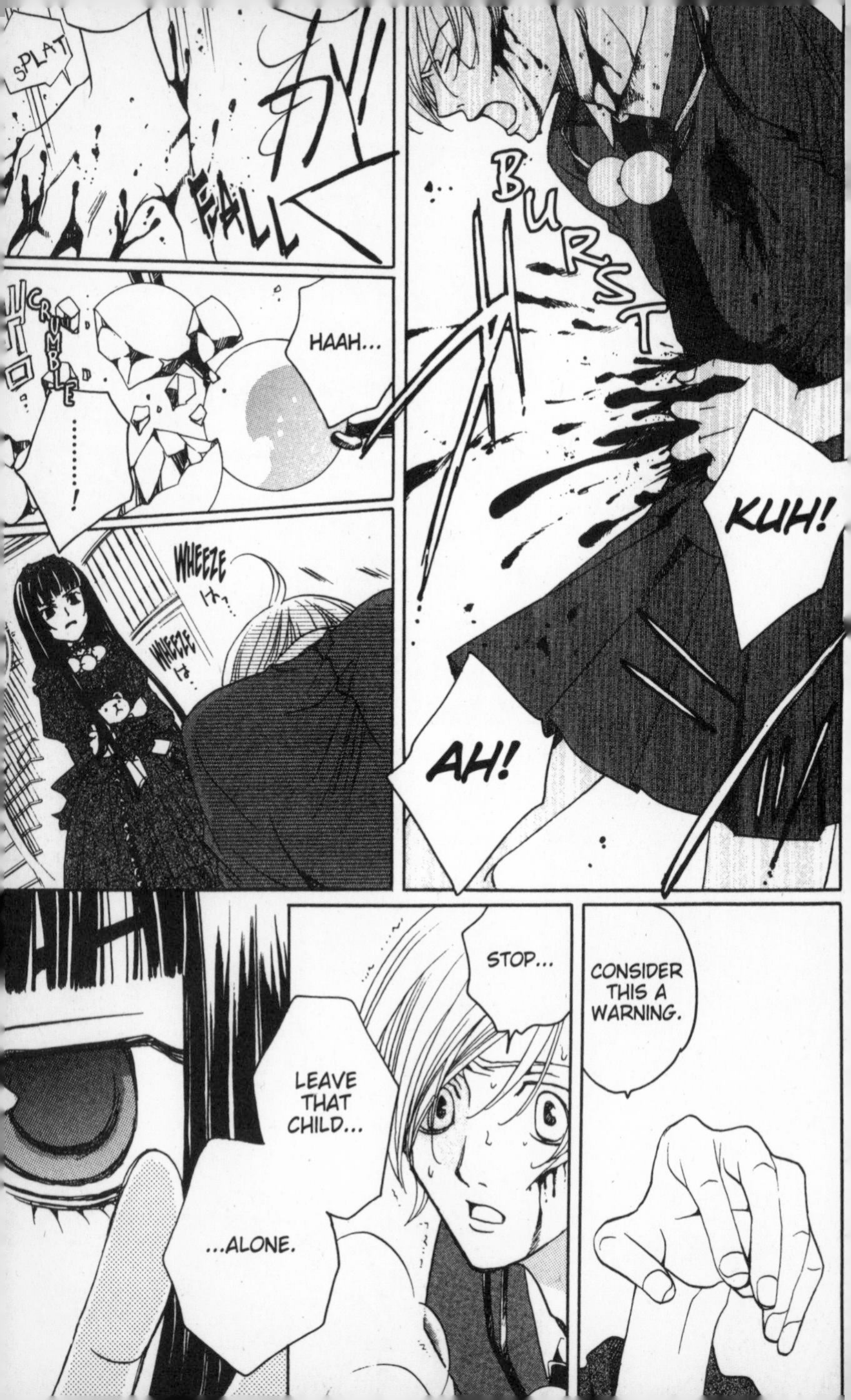
BURST
KUH!
AH!
SPLAT
FALL
HAAH...
CRUMBLE
......!
WHEEZE は...
WHEEZE は...
CONSIDER THIS A WARNING.
STOP...
LEAVE THAT CHILD...
...ALONE.

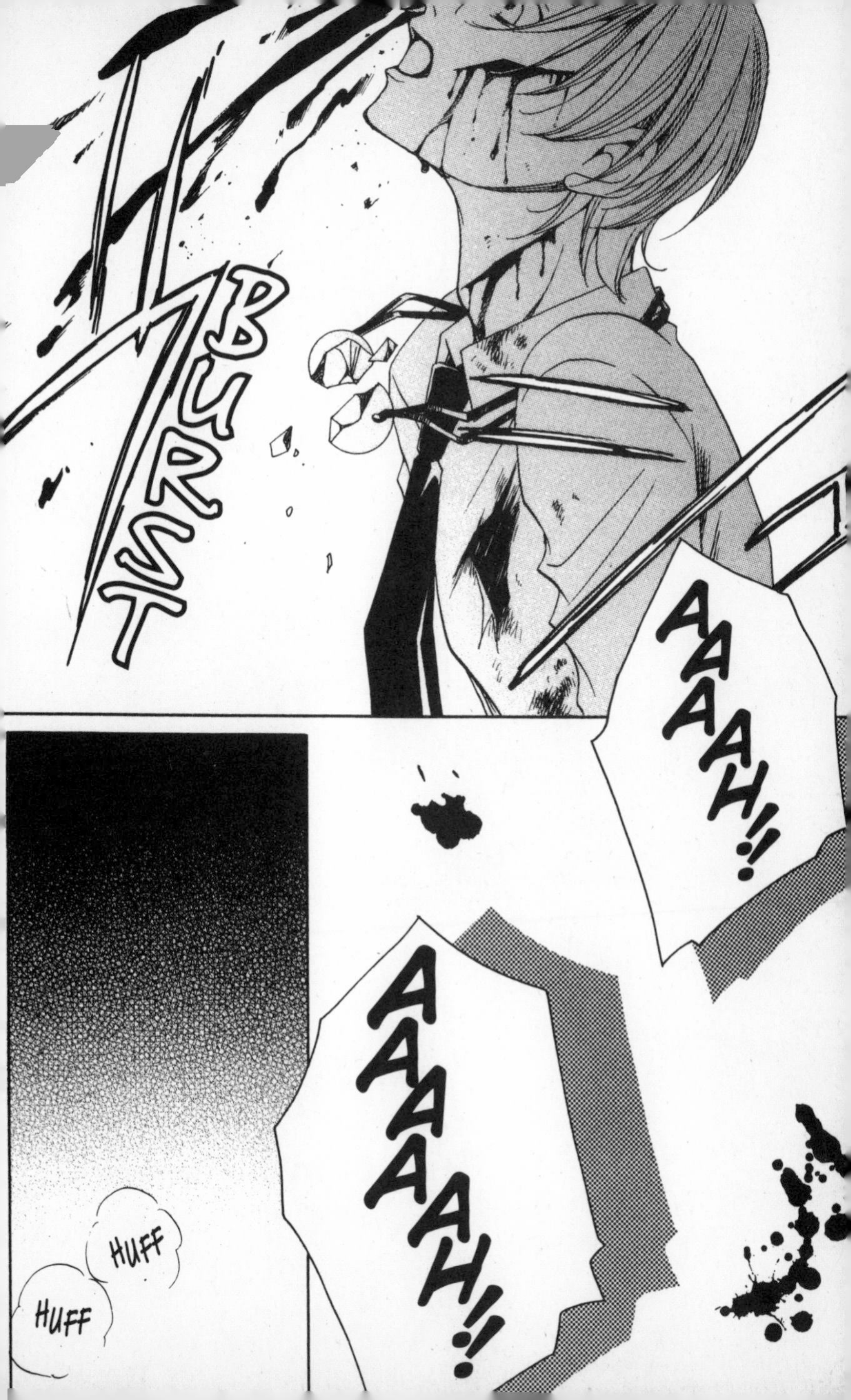
BURST
AAAAH!!
AAAAAH!!
HUFF
HUFF

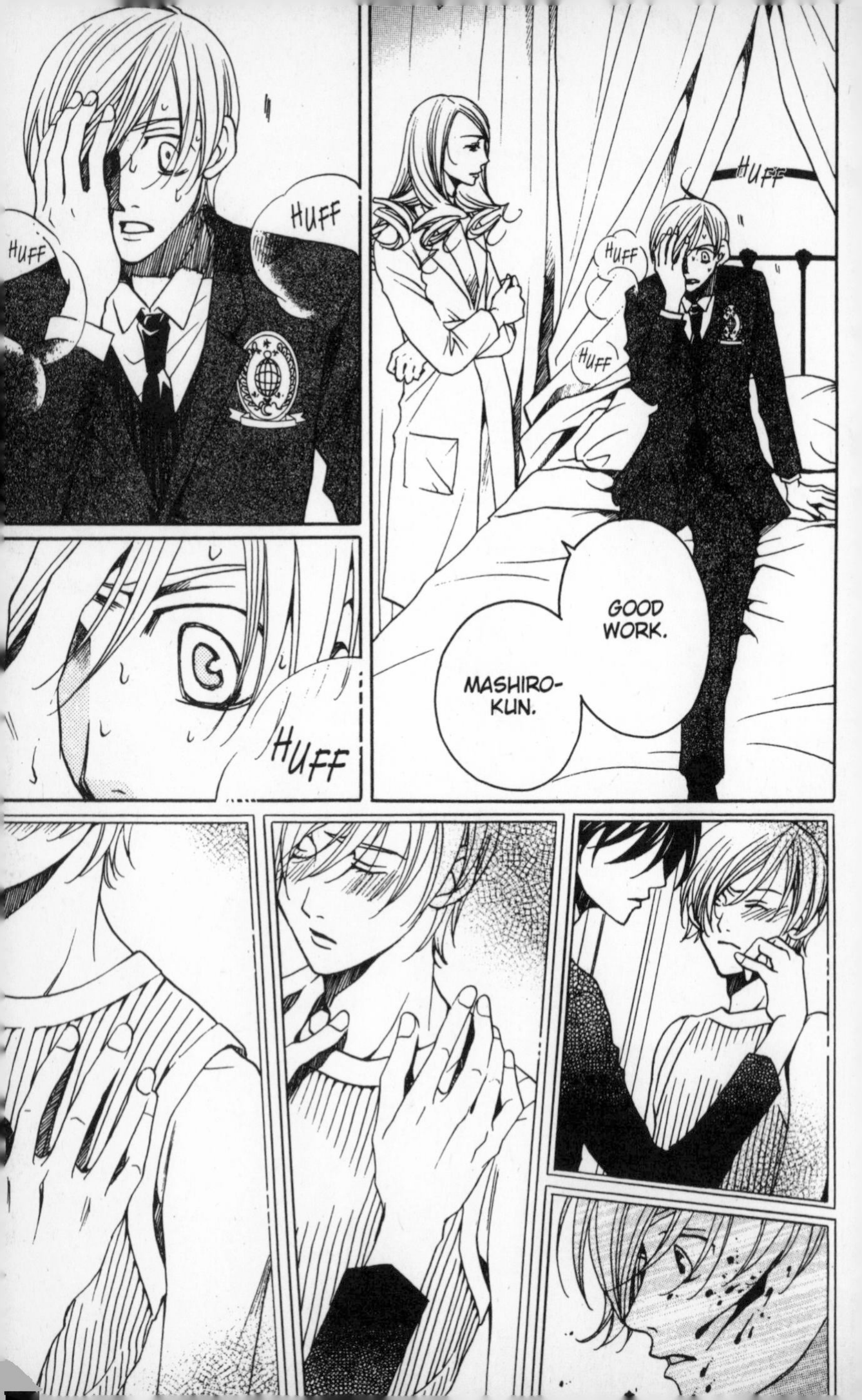
HUFF
HUFF
HUFF
GOOD WORK.
MASHIRO-KUN.
HUFF
HUFF
HUFF

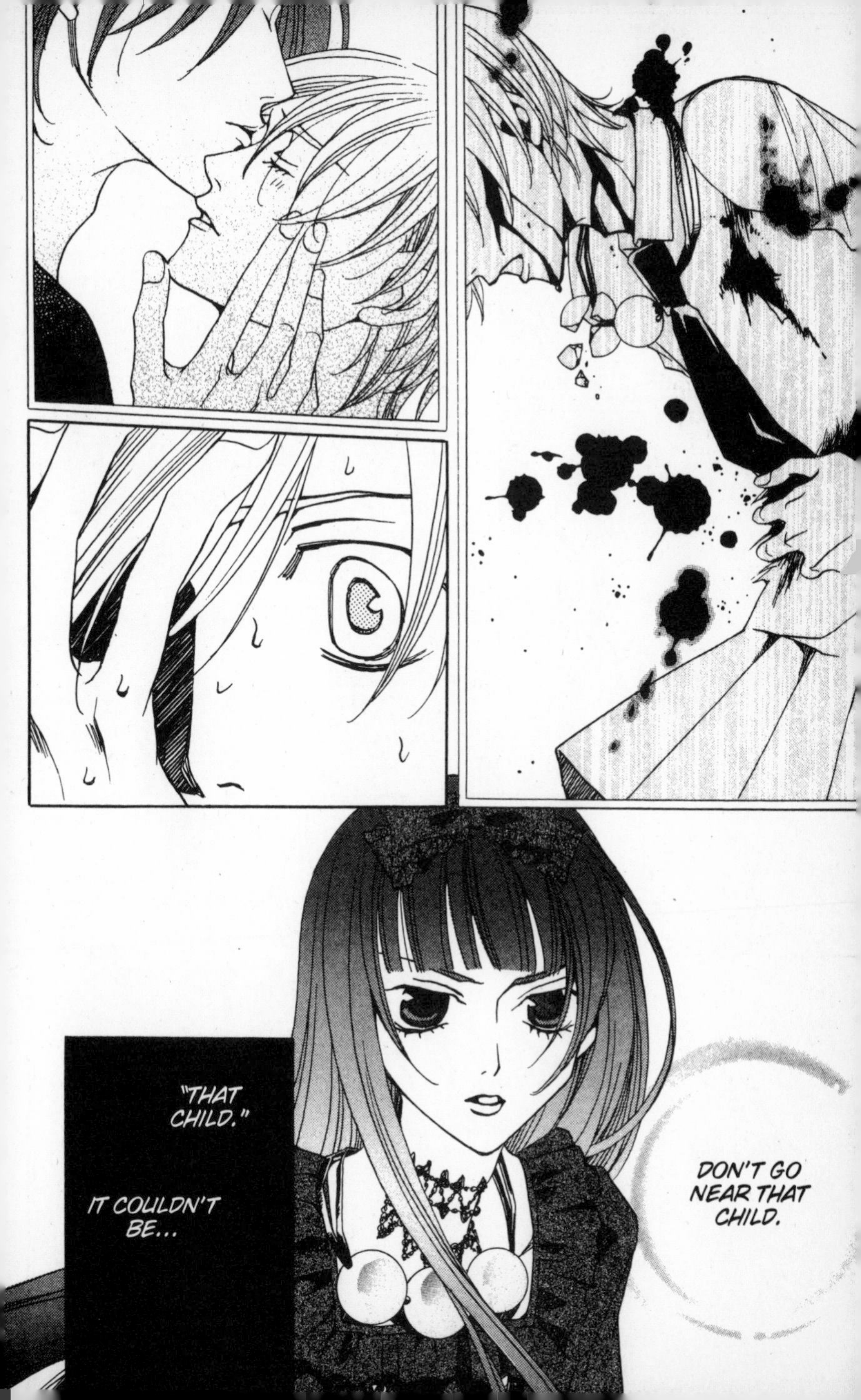
DON'T GO NEAR THAT CHILD.
"THAT CHILD."
IT COULDN'T BE...

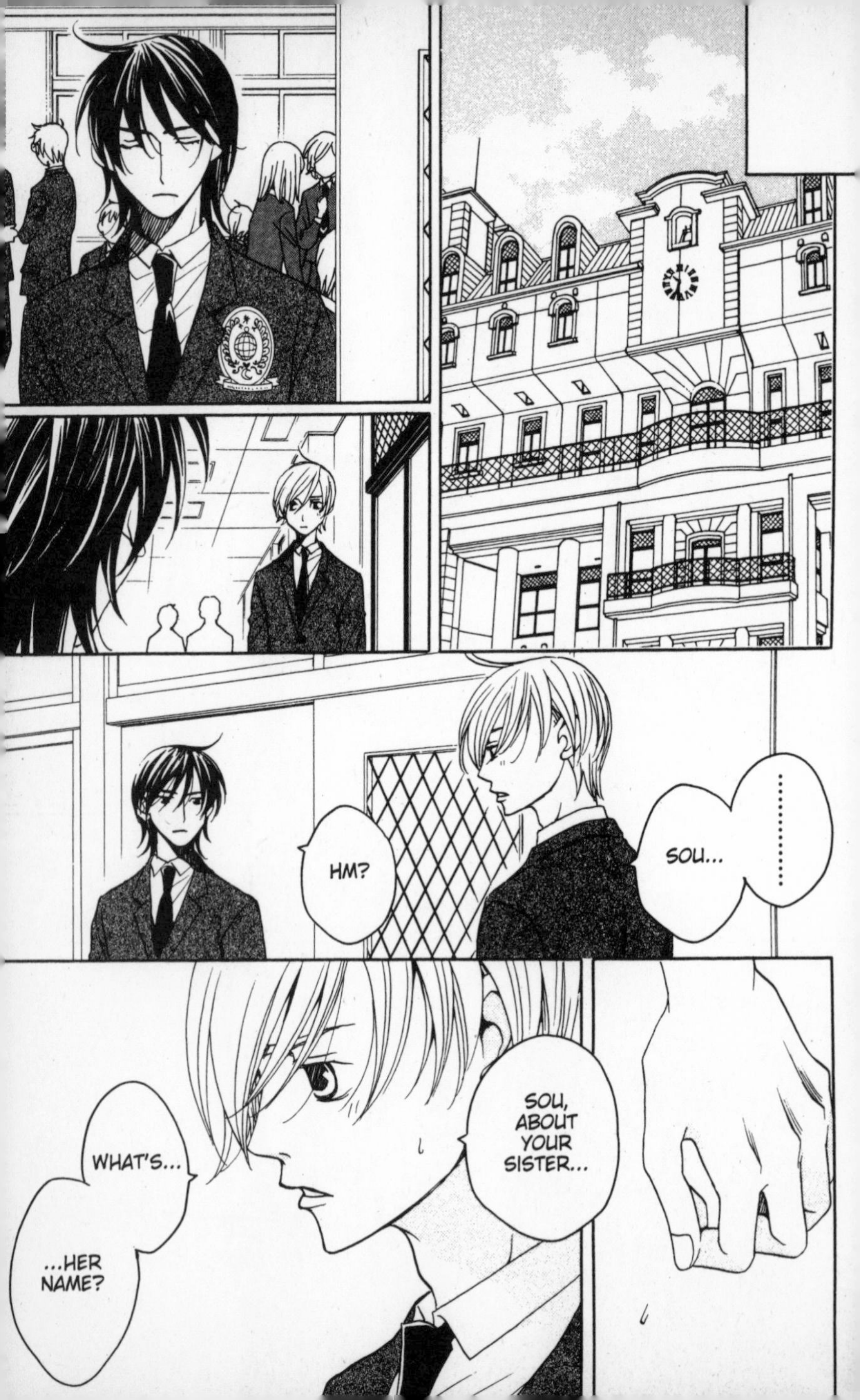
......
SOU...
HM?
SOU, ABOUT YOUR SISTER...
WHAT'S...
...HER NAME?

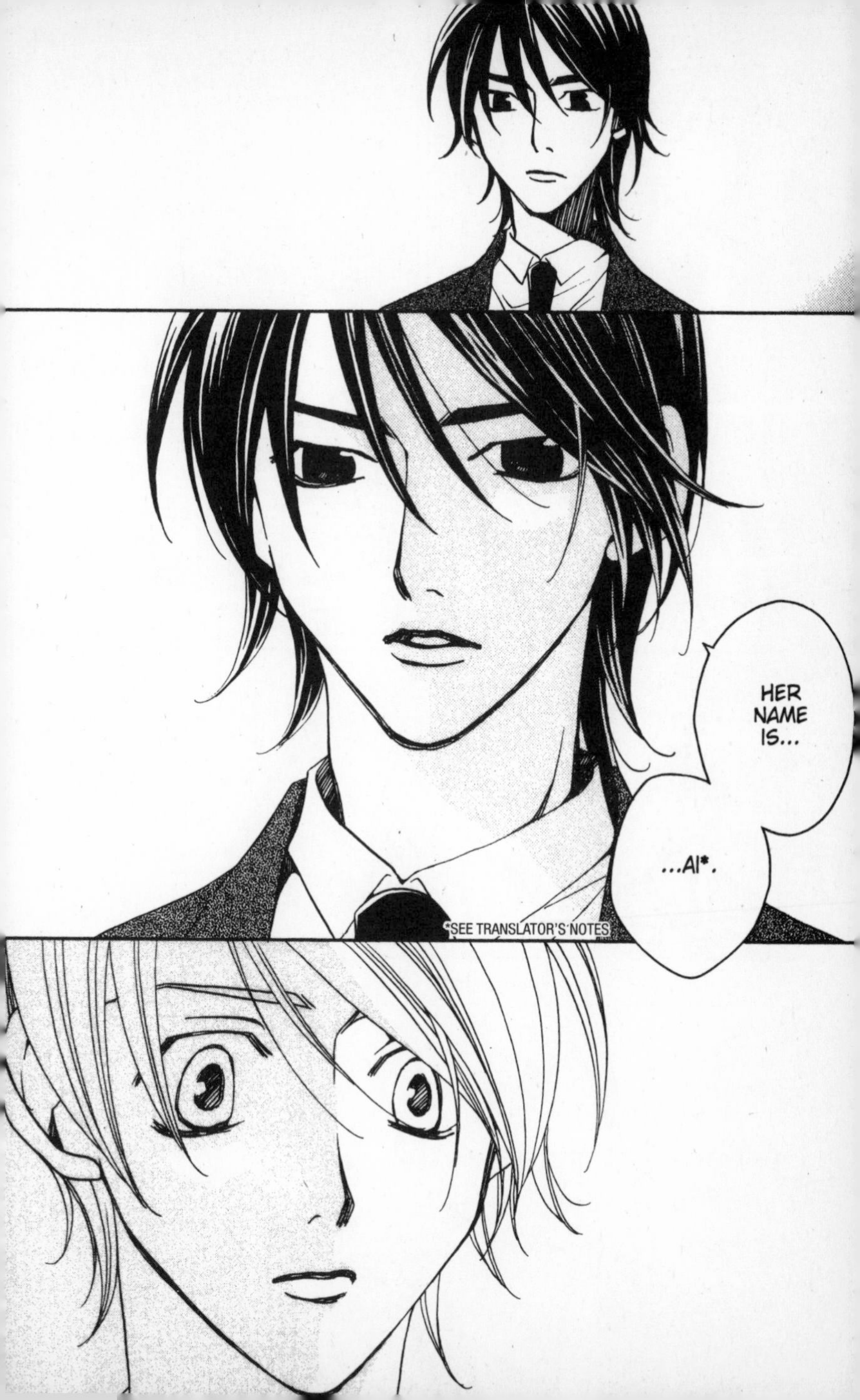
HER NAME IS...
...AI*.
*SEE TRANSLATOR'S NOTES

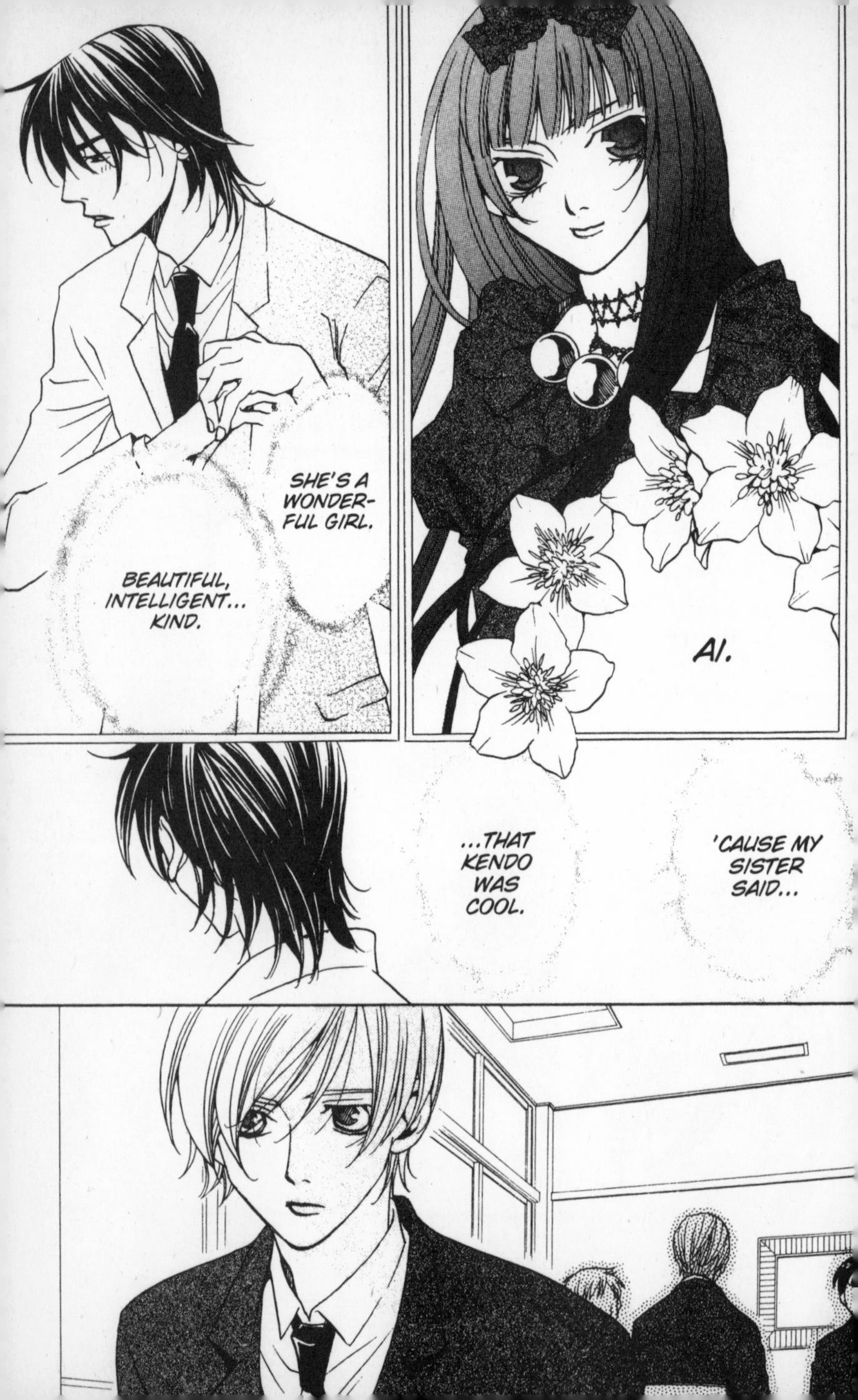
AI.
SHE'S A WONDERFUL GIRL.
BEAUTIFUL, INTELLIGENT... KIND.
'CAUSE MY SISTER SAID...
...THAT KENDO WAS COOL.

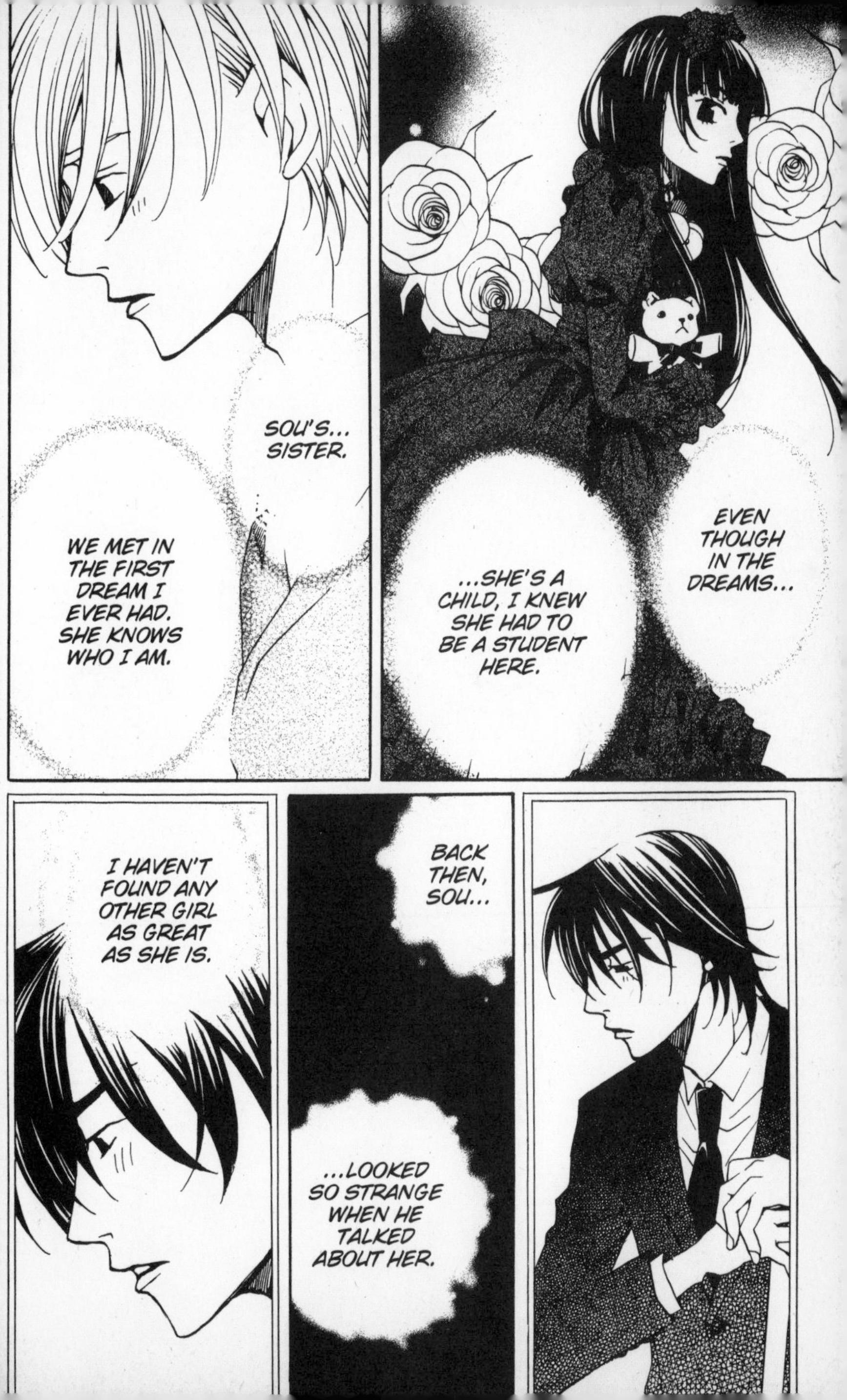
EVEN THOUGH IN THE DREAMS...
...SHE'S A CHILD, I KNEW SHE HAD TO BE A STUDENT HERE.
SOU'S... SISTER.
WE MET IN THE FIRST DREAM I EVER HAD. SHE KNOWS WHO I AM.
BACK THEN, SOU...
...LOOKED SO STRANGE WHEN HE TALKED ABOUT HER.
I HAVEN'T FOUND ANY OTHER GIRL AS GREAT AS SHE IS.

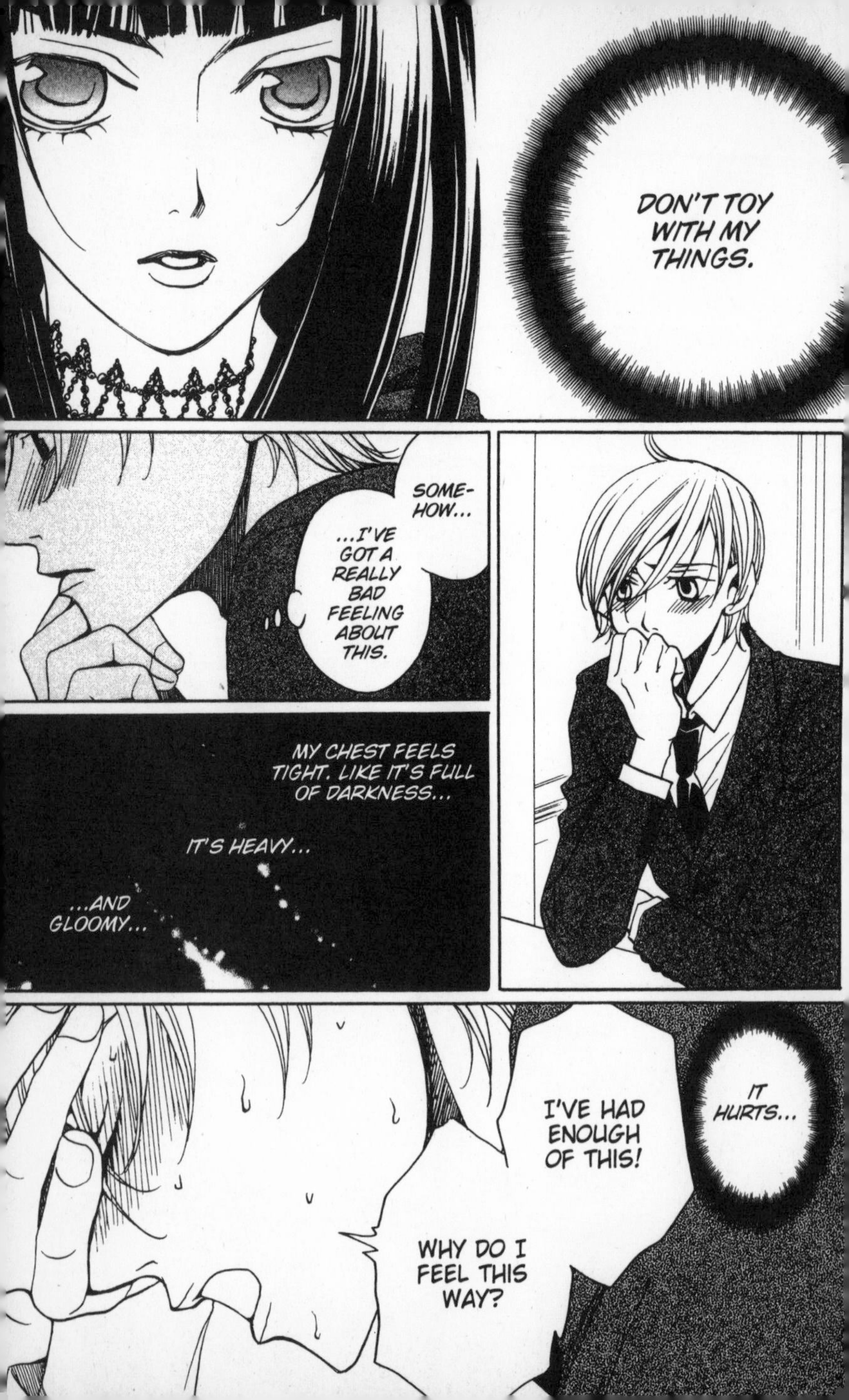
DON'T TOY WITH MY THINGS.
SOME-HOW...
...I'VE GOT A REALLY BAD FEELING ABOUT THIS.
MY CHEST FEELS TIGHT. LIKE IT'S FULL OF DARKNESS...
IT'S HEAVY...
...AND GLOOMY...
IT HURTS...
I'VE HAD ENOUGH OF THIS!
WHY DO I FEEL THIS WAY?

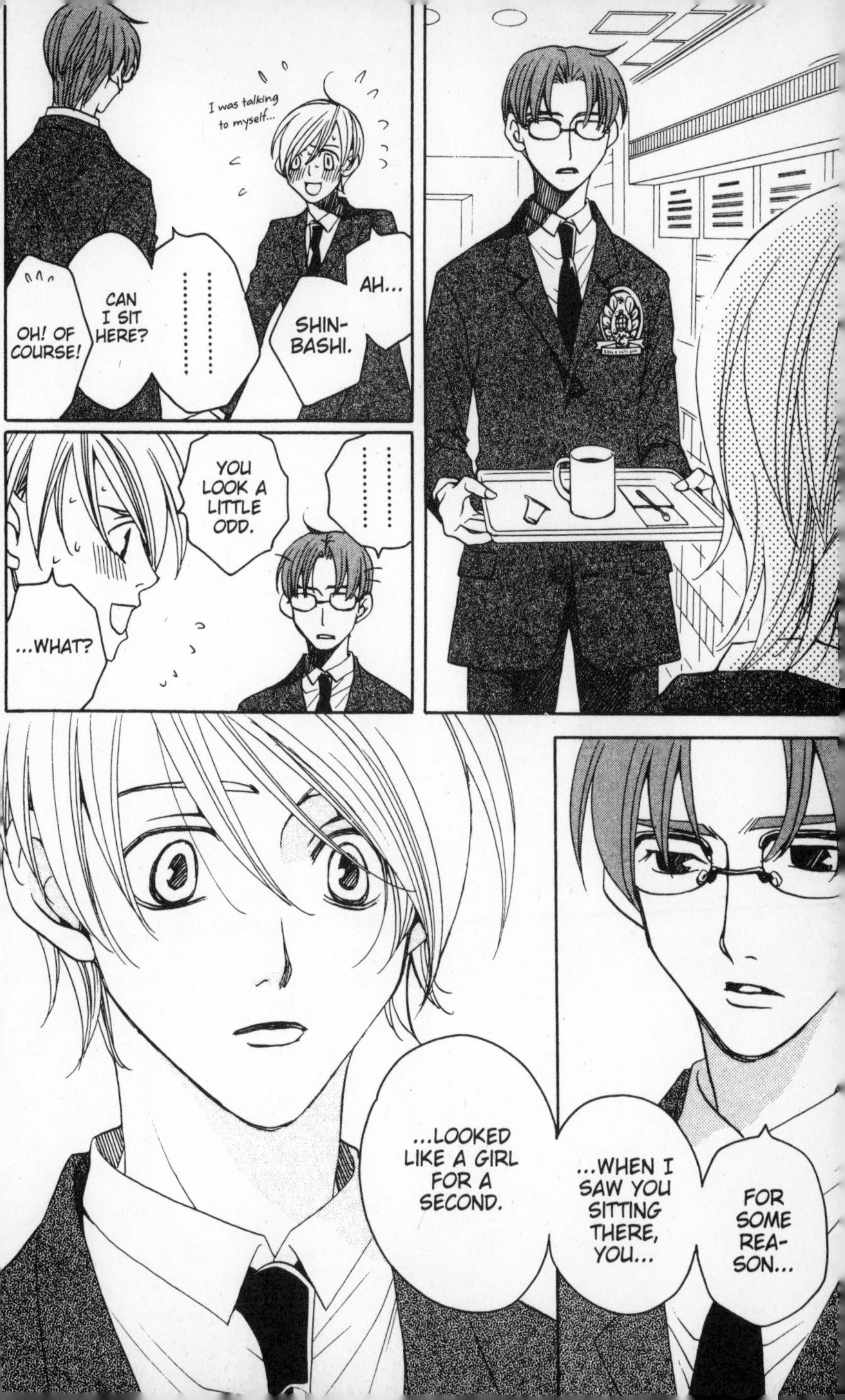
I was talking to myself...
AH... SHIN-BASHI.
......
CAN I SIT HERE?
OH! OF COURSE!
......
YOU LOOK A LITTLE ODD.
...WHAT?
FOR SOME REA-SON...
...WHEN I SAW YOU SITTING THERE, YOU...
...LOOKED LIKE A GIRL FOR A SECOND.

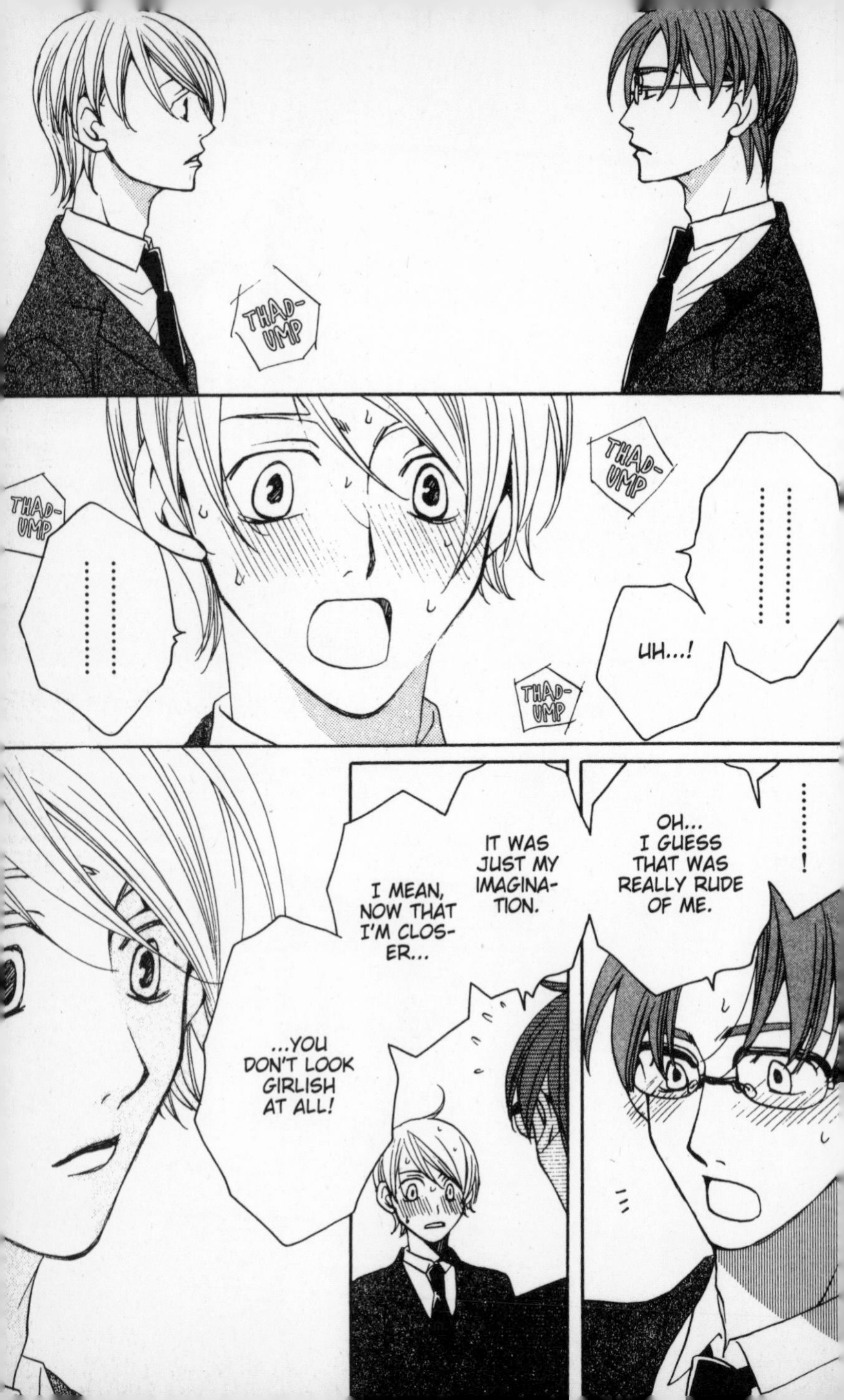
THAD-UMP
THAD-UMP
......
UH...!
THAD-UMP
......
THAD-UMP
......!
OH... I GUESS THAT WAS REALLY RUDE OF ME.
IT WAS JUST MY IMAGINATION.
I MEAN, NOW THAT I'M CLOS-ER...
...YOU DON'T LOOK GIRLISH AT ALL!

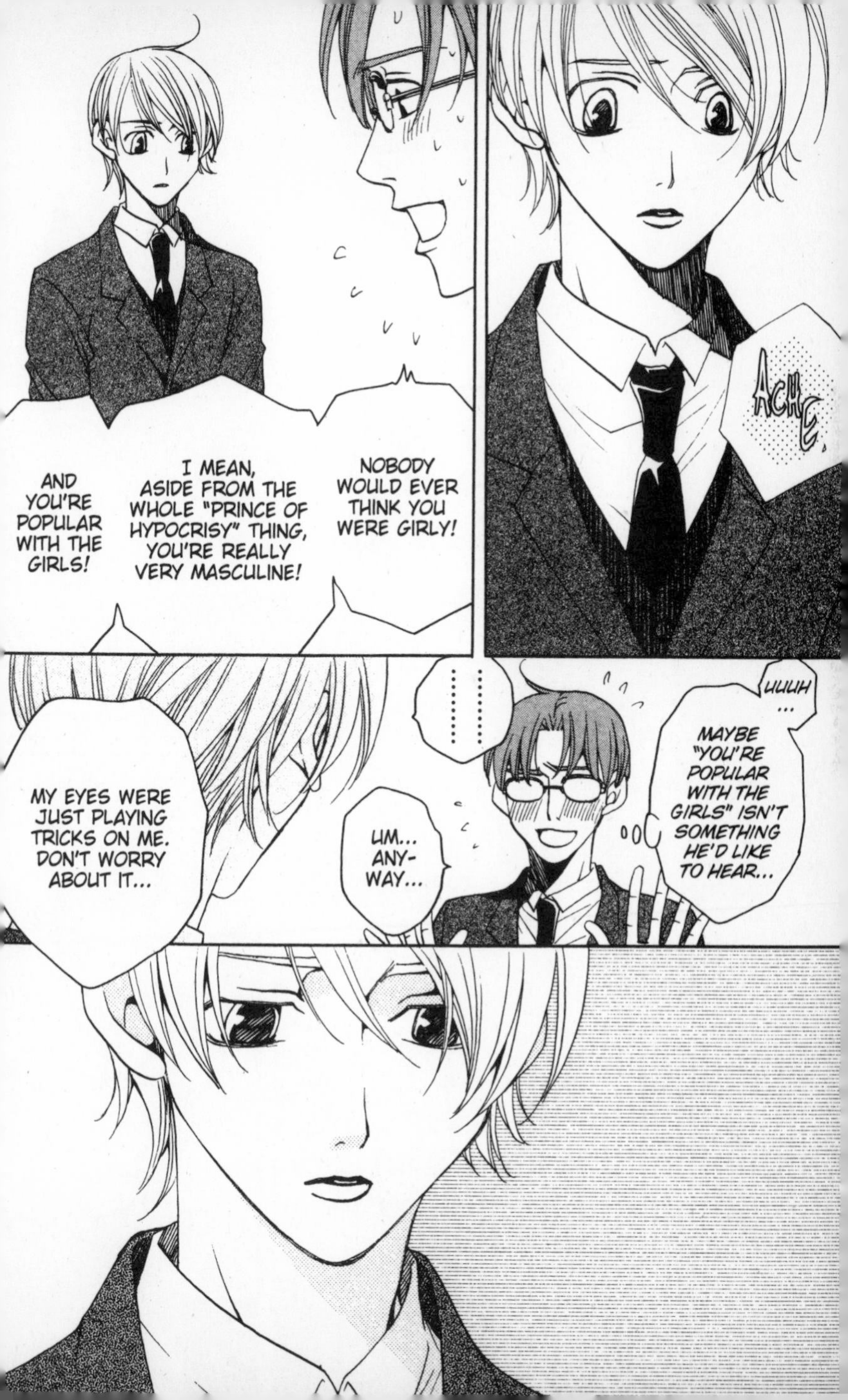
ACHE
NOBODY WOULD EVER THINK YOU WERE GIRLY!
I MEAN, ASIDE FROM THE WHOLE "PRINCE OF HYPOCRISY" THING, YOU'RE REALLY VERY MASCULINE!
AND YOU'RE POPULAR WITH THE GIRLS!
UUUH ...
......
MAYBE "YOU'RE POPULAR WITH THE GIRLS" ISN'T SOMETHING HE'D LIKE TO HEAR...
UM... ANYWAY...
MY EYES WERE JUST PLAYING TRICKS ON ME. DON'T WORRY ABOUT IT...

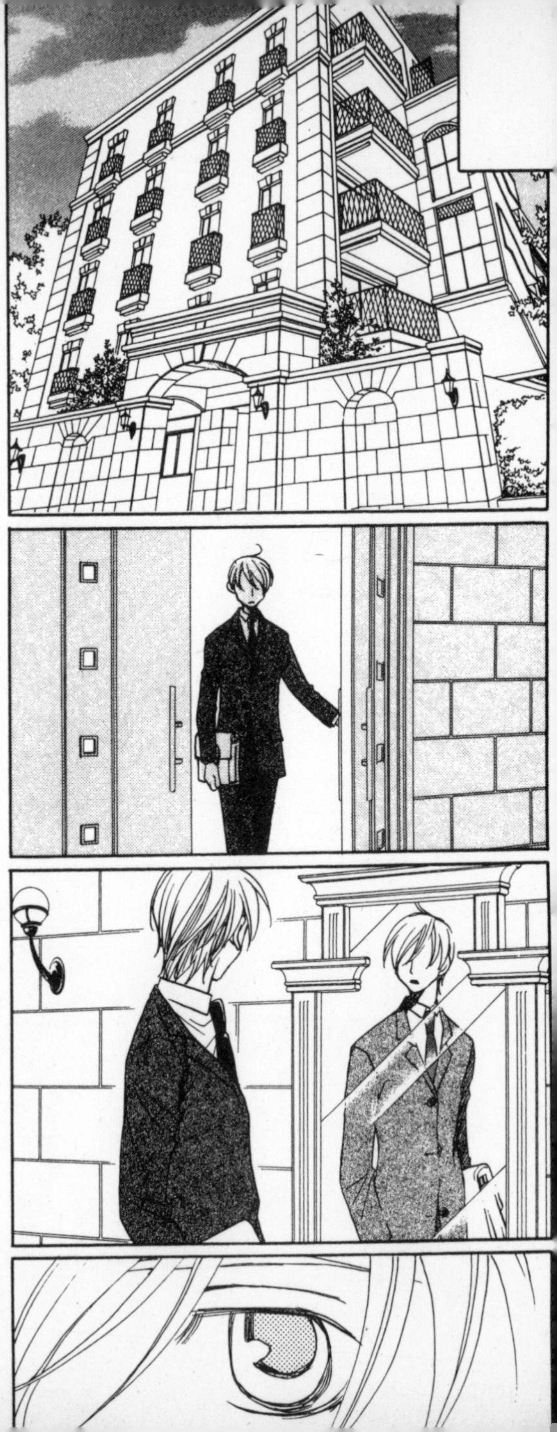

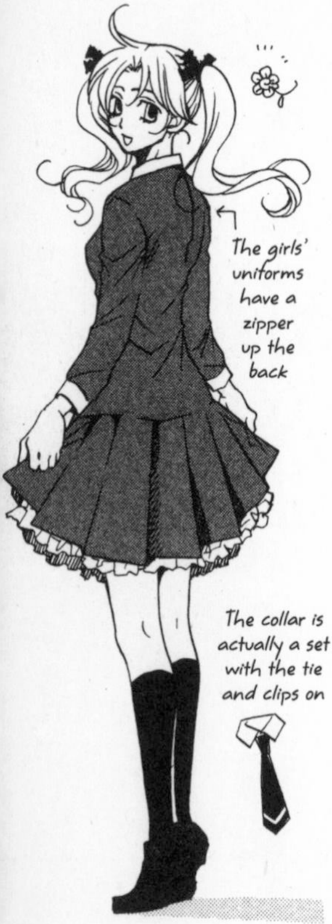
The girls' uniforms have a zipper up the back
The collar is actually a set with the tie and clips on

Only Kureha wears a petticoat under her uniform. It's very girlish!

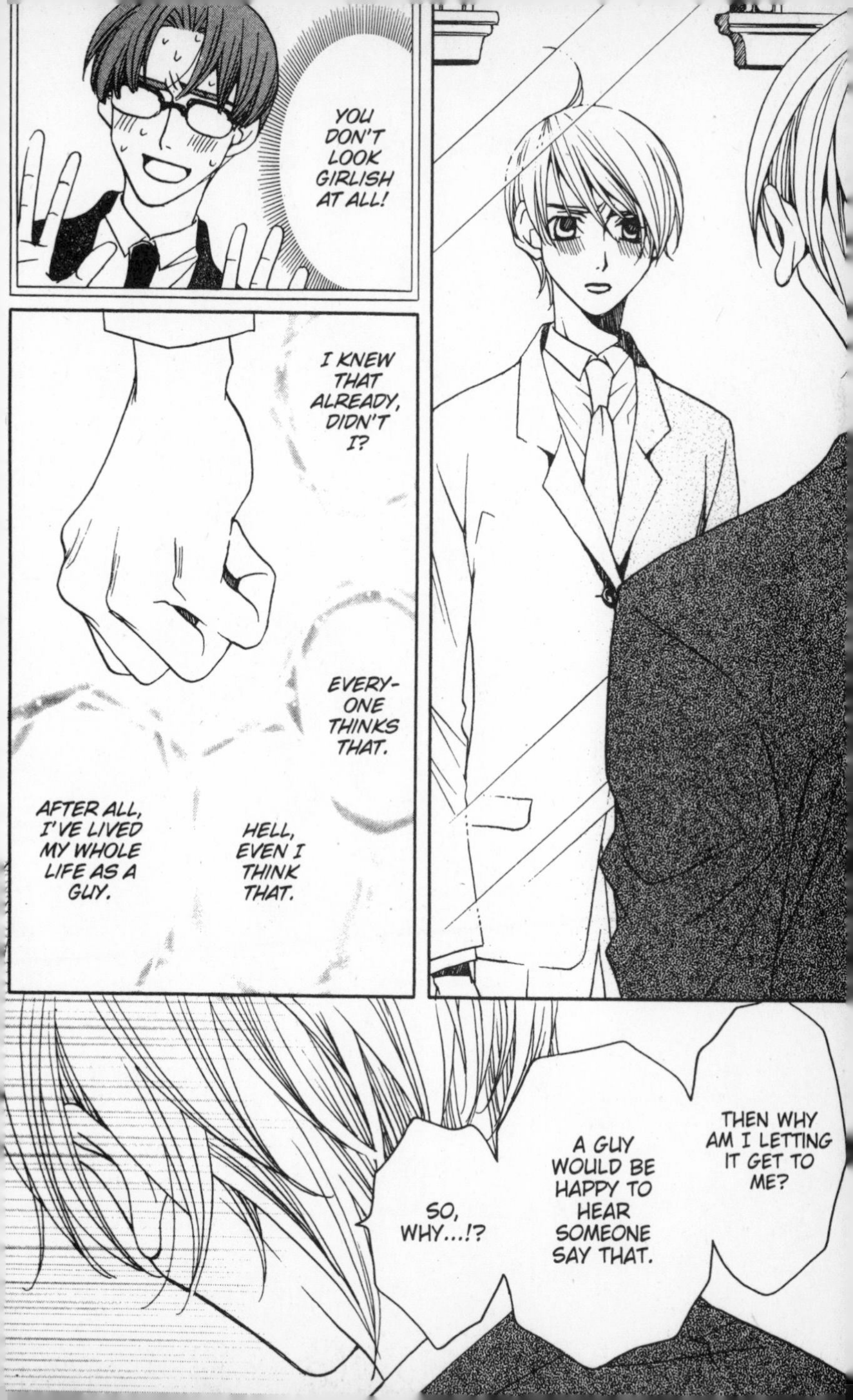
YOU DON'T LOOK GIRLISH AT ALL!
I KNEW THAT ALREADY, DIDN'T I?
EVERY-ONE THINKS THAT.
HELL, EVEN I THINK THAT.
AFTER ALL, I'VE LIVED MY WHOLE LIFE AS A GUY.
THEN WHY AM I LETTING IT GET TO ME?
A GUY WOULD BE HAPPY TO HEAR SOMEONE SAY THAT.
SO, WHY...!?

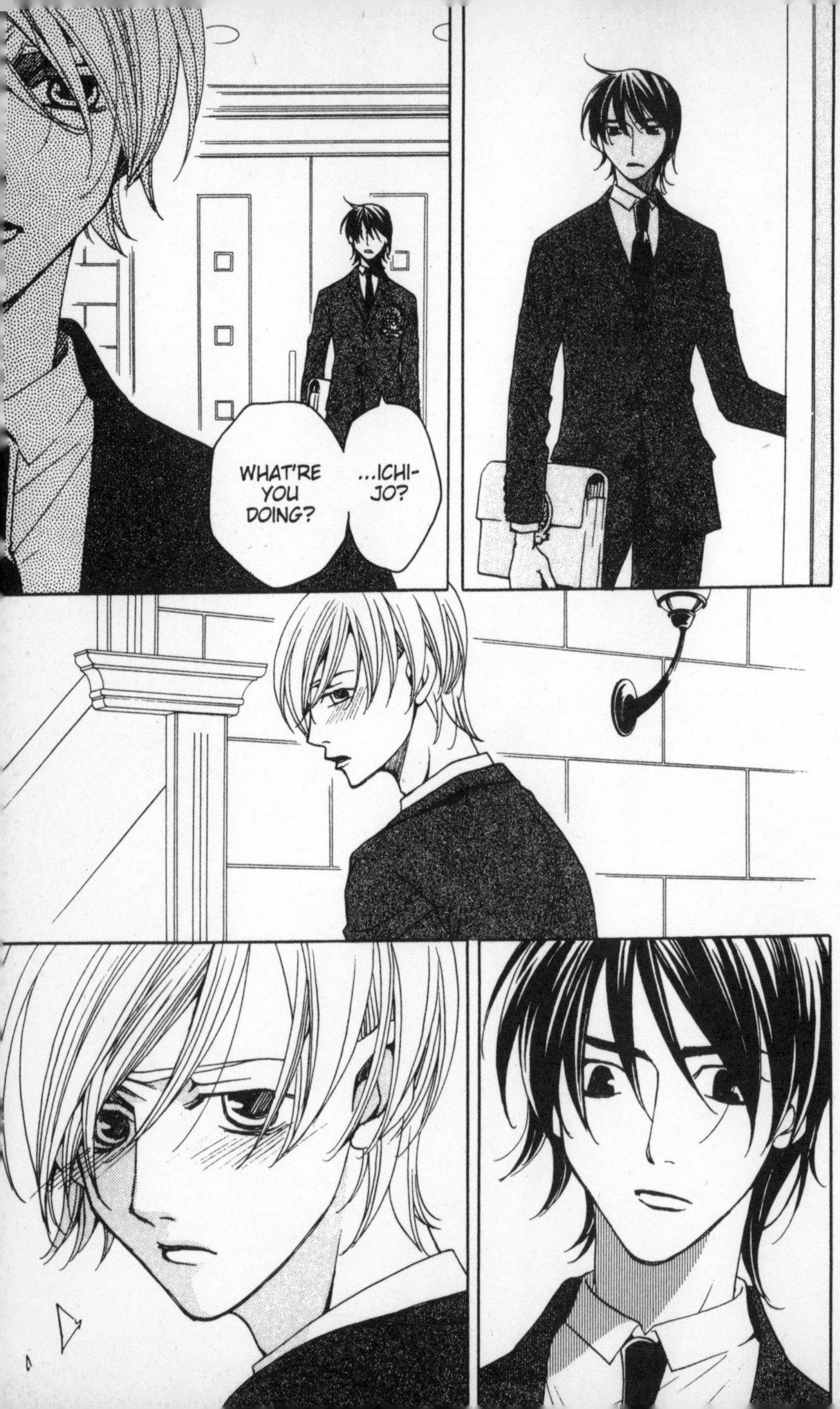
...ICHI-JO?
WHAT'RE YOU DOING?

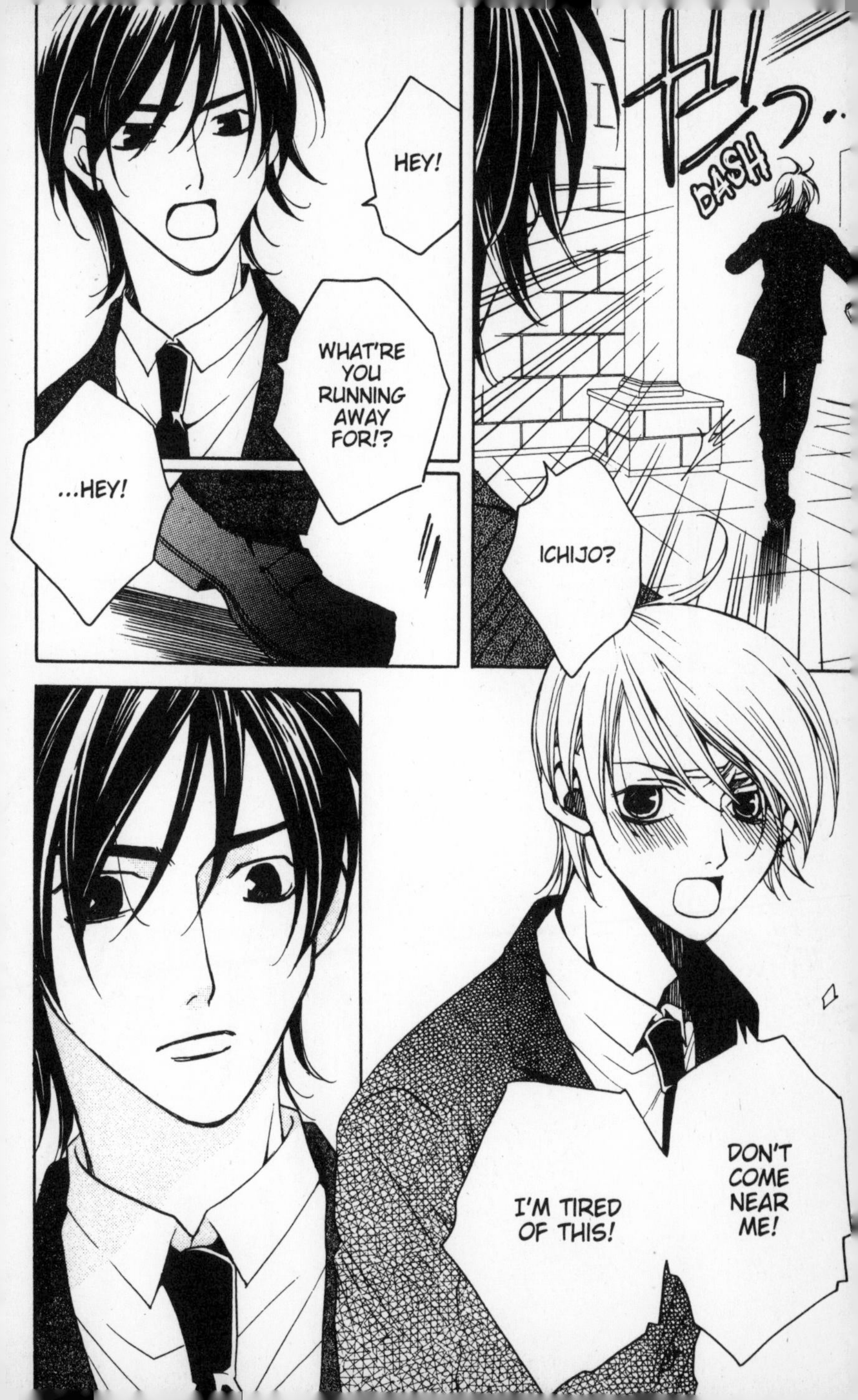
DASH
ICHIJO?
HEY!
WHAT'RE YOU RUNNING AWAY FOR!?
...HEY!
DON'T COME NEAR ME!
I'M TIRED OF THIS!

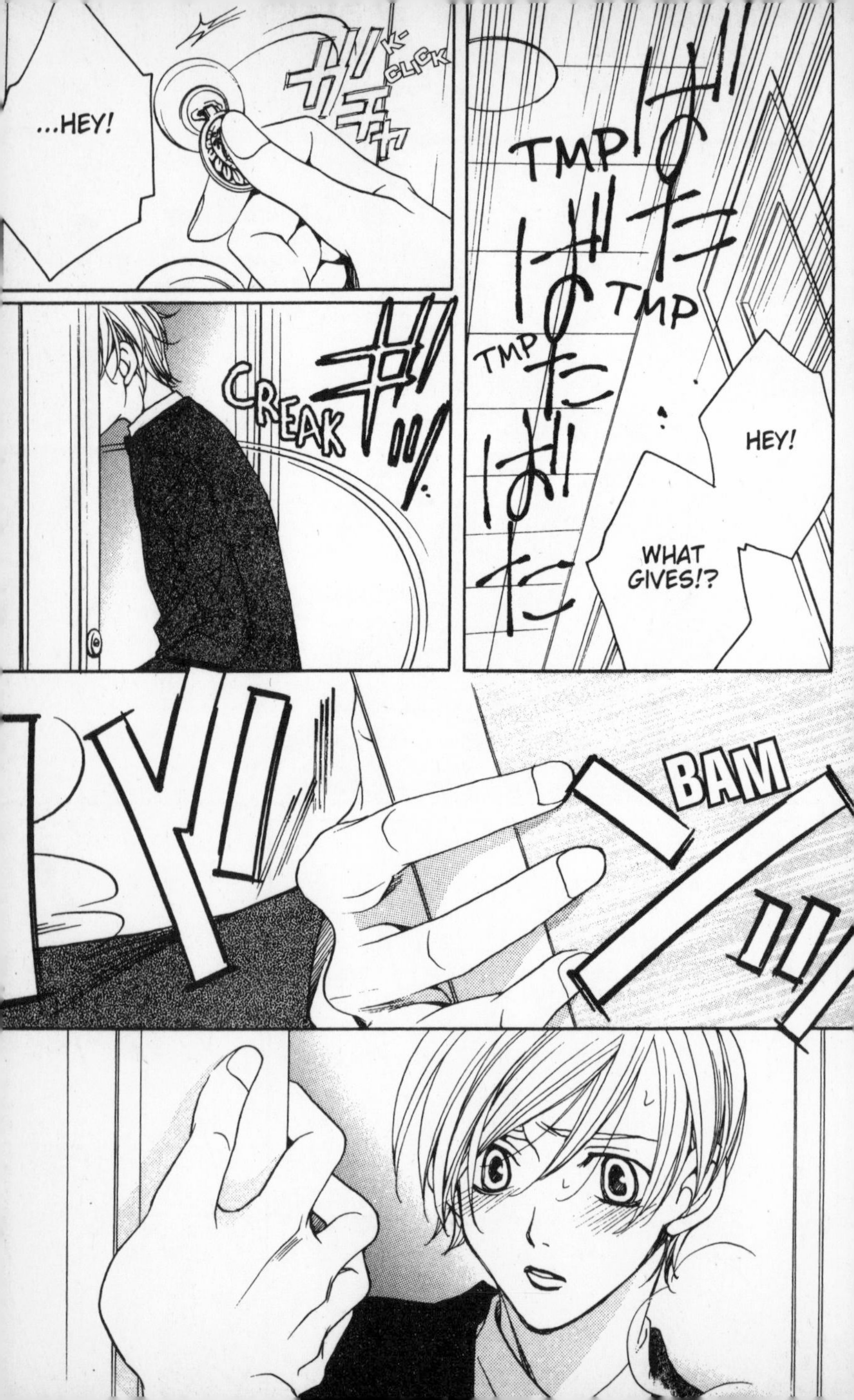
TMP
TMP
TMP
HEY!
WHAT GIVES!?
K-CLICK
...HEY!
CREAK
BAM

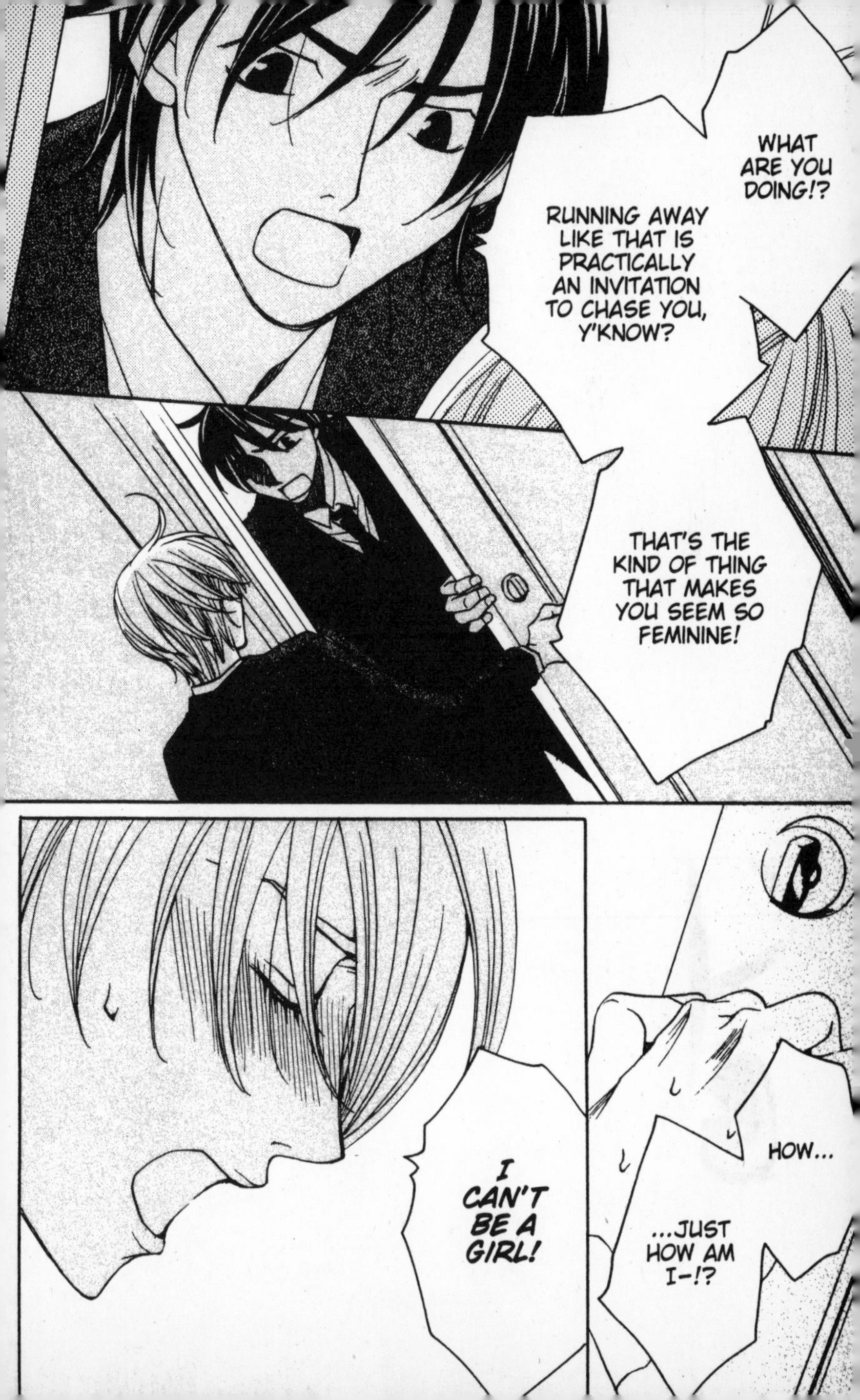
WHAT ARE YOU DOING!?
RUNNING AWAY LIKE THAT IS PRACTICALLY AN INVITATION TO CHASE YOU, Y'KNOW?
THAT'S THE KIND OF THING THAT MAKES YOU SEEM SO FEMININE!
HOW...
...JUST HOW AM I-!?
I CAN'T BE A GIRL!

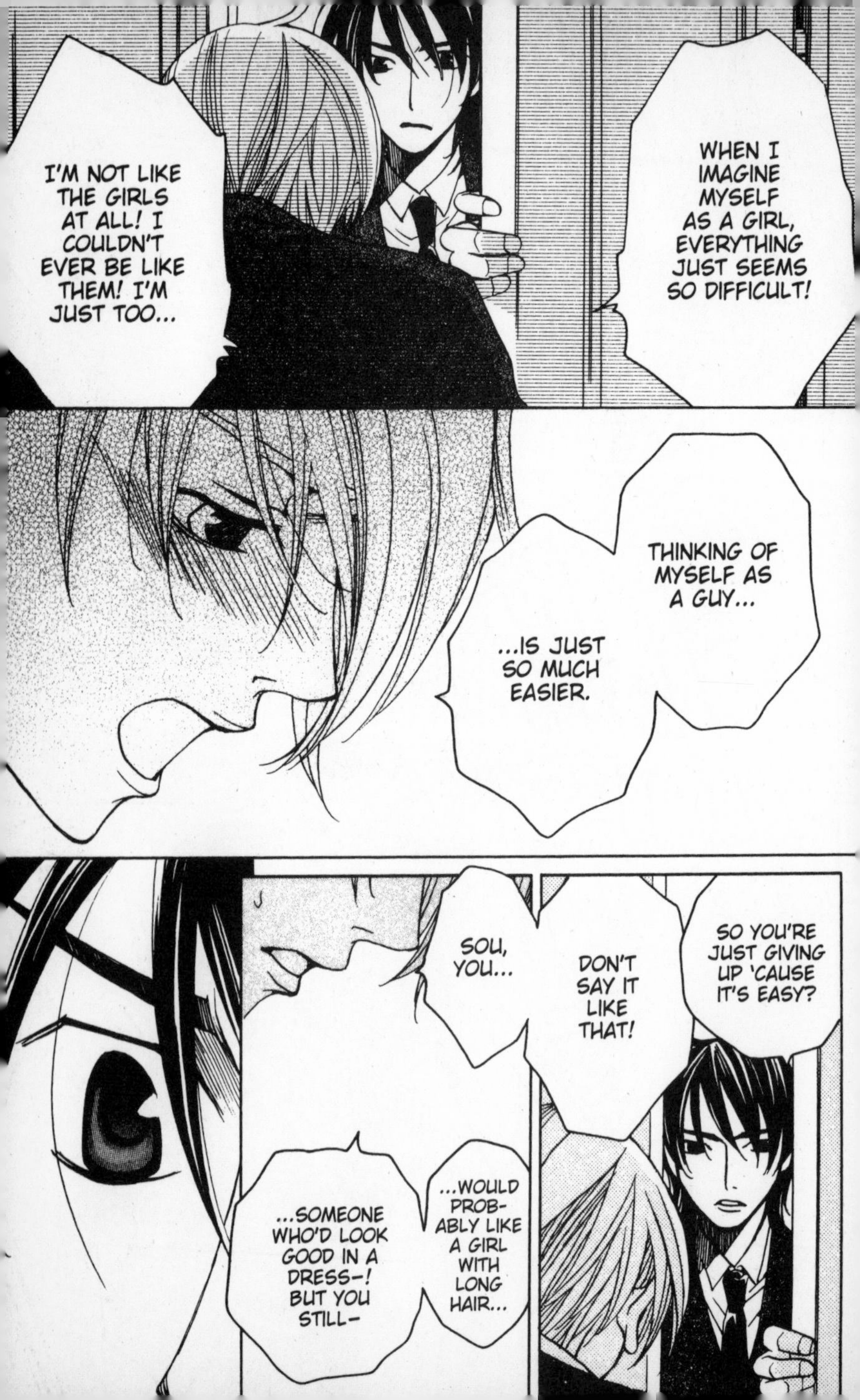
WHEN I IMAGINE MYSELF AS A GIRL, EVERYTHING JUST SEEMS SO DIFFICULT!
I'M NOT LIKE THE GIRLS AT ALL! I COULDN'T EVER BE LIKE THEM! I'M JUST TOO...
THINKING OF MYSELF AS A GUY...
...IS JUST SO MUCH EASIER.
SO YOU'RE JUST GIVING UP 'CAUSE IT'S EASY?
DON'T SAY IT LIKE THAT!
SOU, YOU...
...WOULD PROB-ABLY LIKE A GIRL WITH LONG HAIR...
...SOMEONE WHO'D LOOK GOOD IN A DRESS-! BUT YOU STILL-

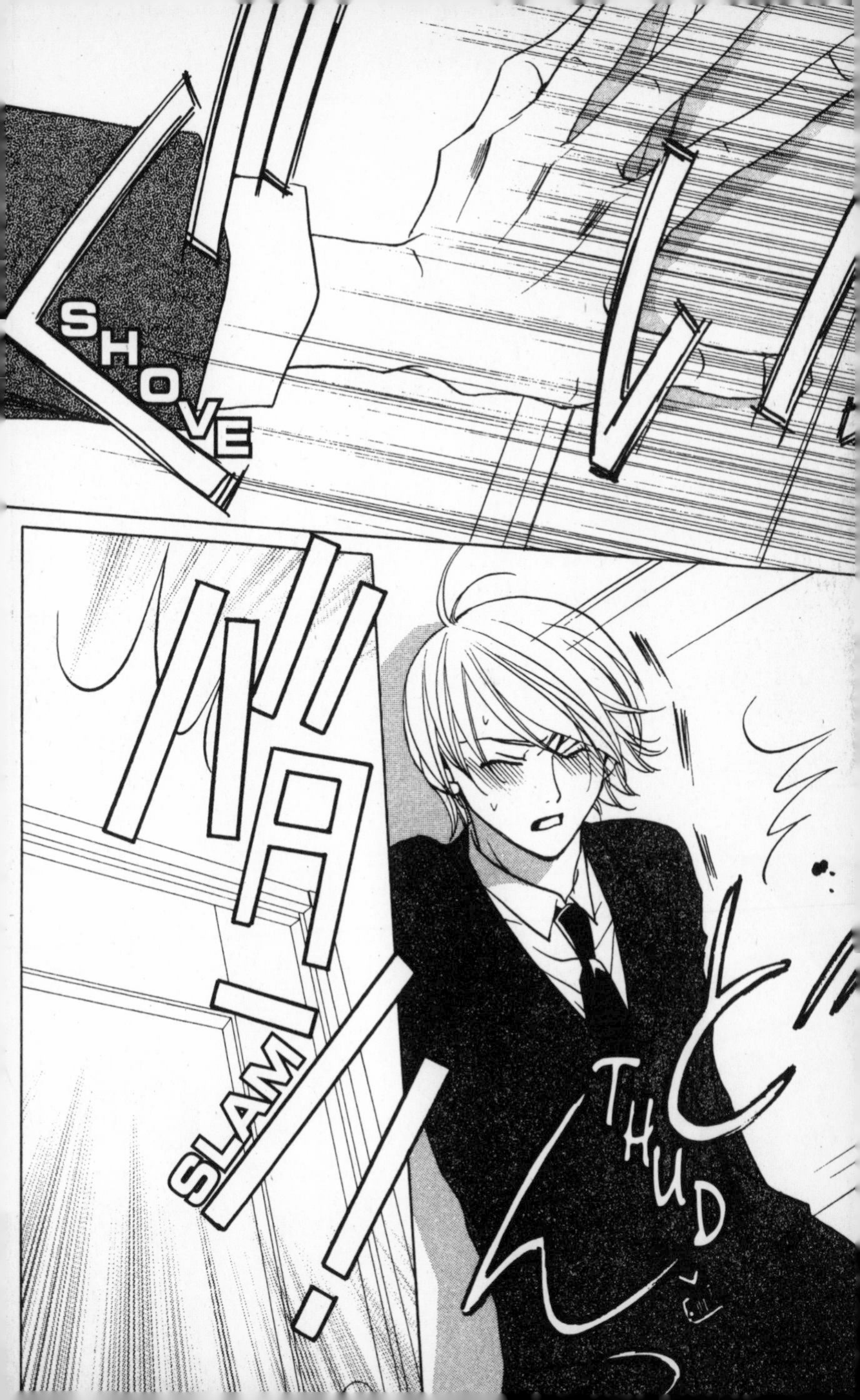
SHOVE
THUD
SLAM

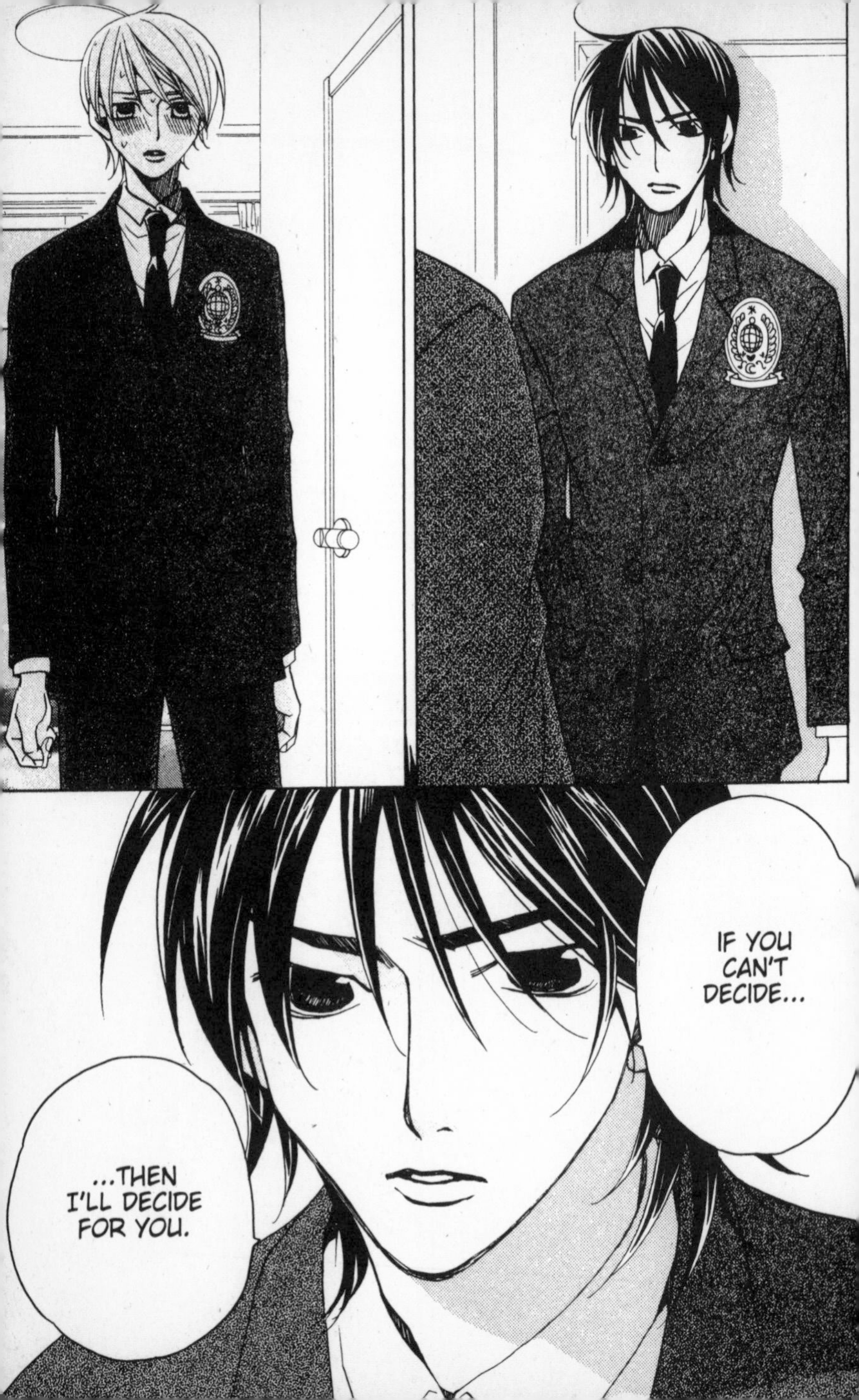
IF YOU CAN'T DECIDE...
...THEN I'LL DECIDE FOR YOU.

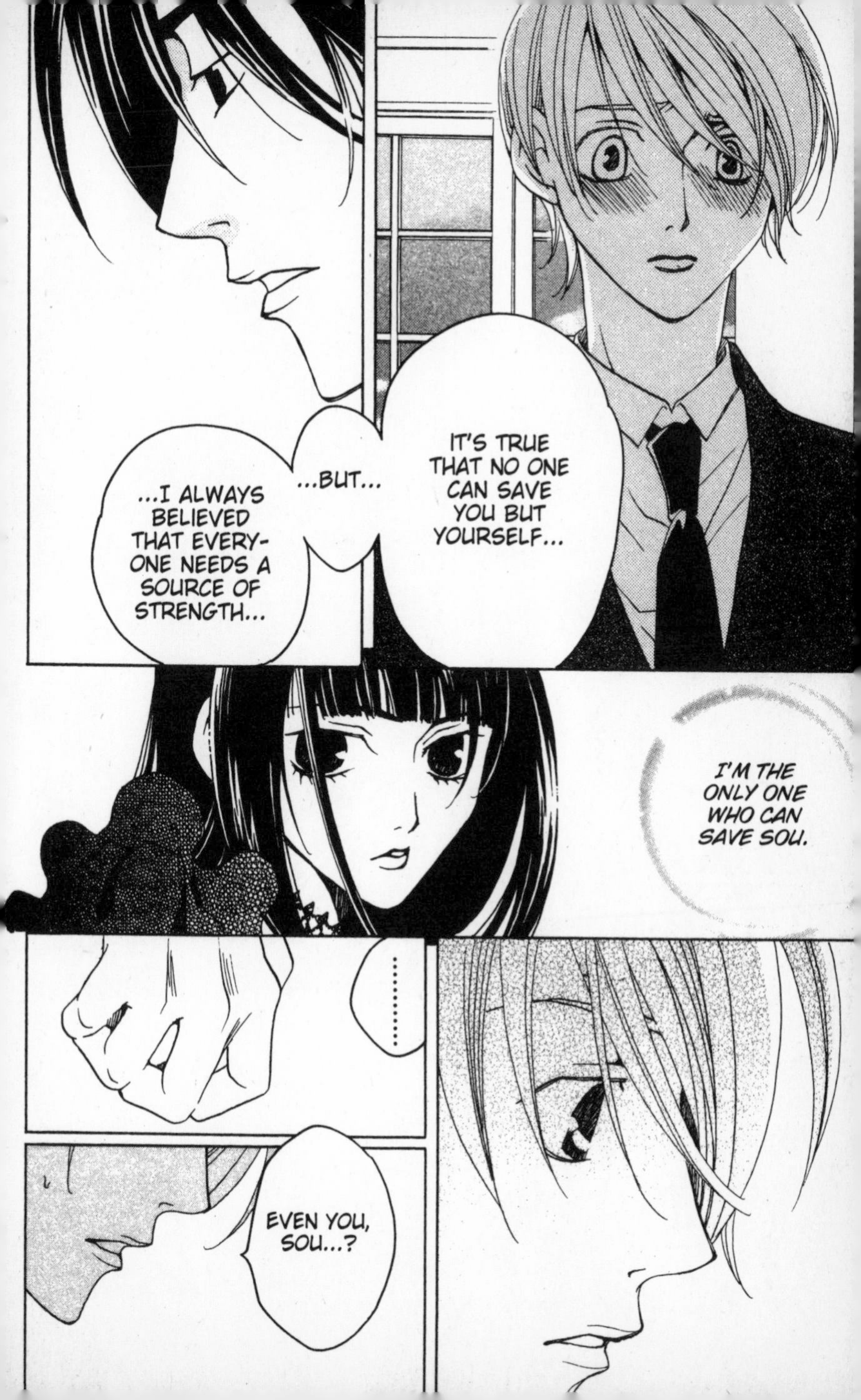
IT'S TRUE THAT NO ONE CAN SAVE YOU BUT YOURSELF...
...BUT...
...I ALWAYS BELIEVED THAT EVERY-ONE NEEDS A SOURCE OF STRENGTH...
I'M THE ONLY ONE WHO CAN SAVE SOU.
......
EVEN YOU, SOU...?

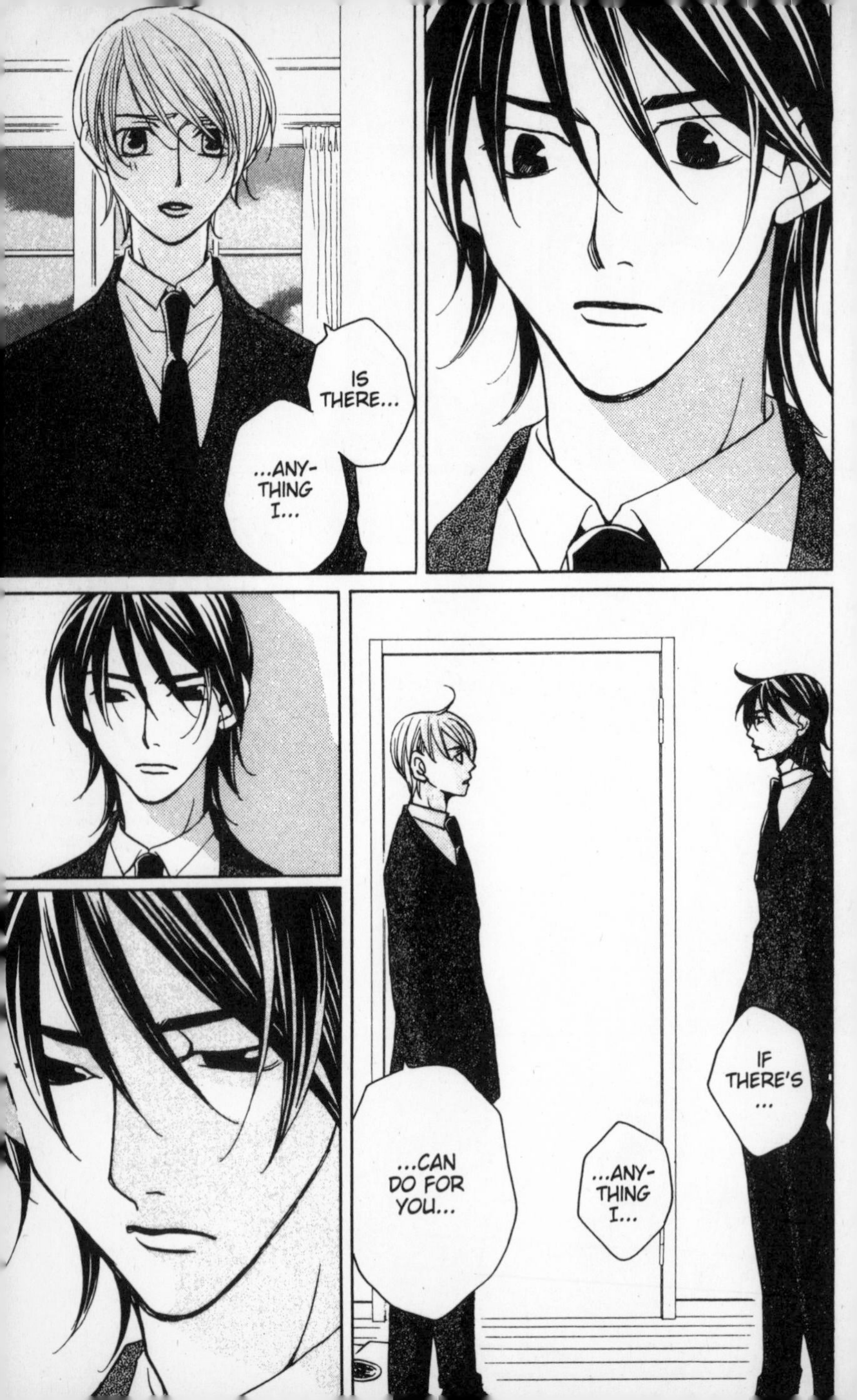
IS THERE...
...ANY-THING I...
IF THERE'S ...
...ANY-THING I...
...CAN DO FOR YOU...

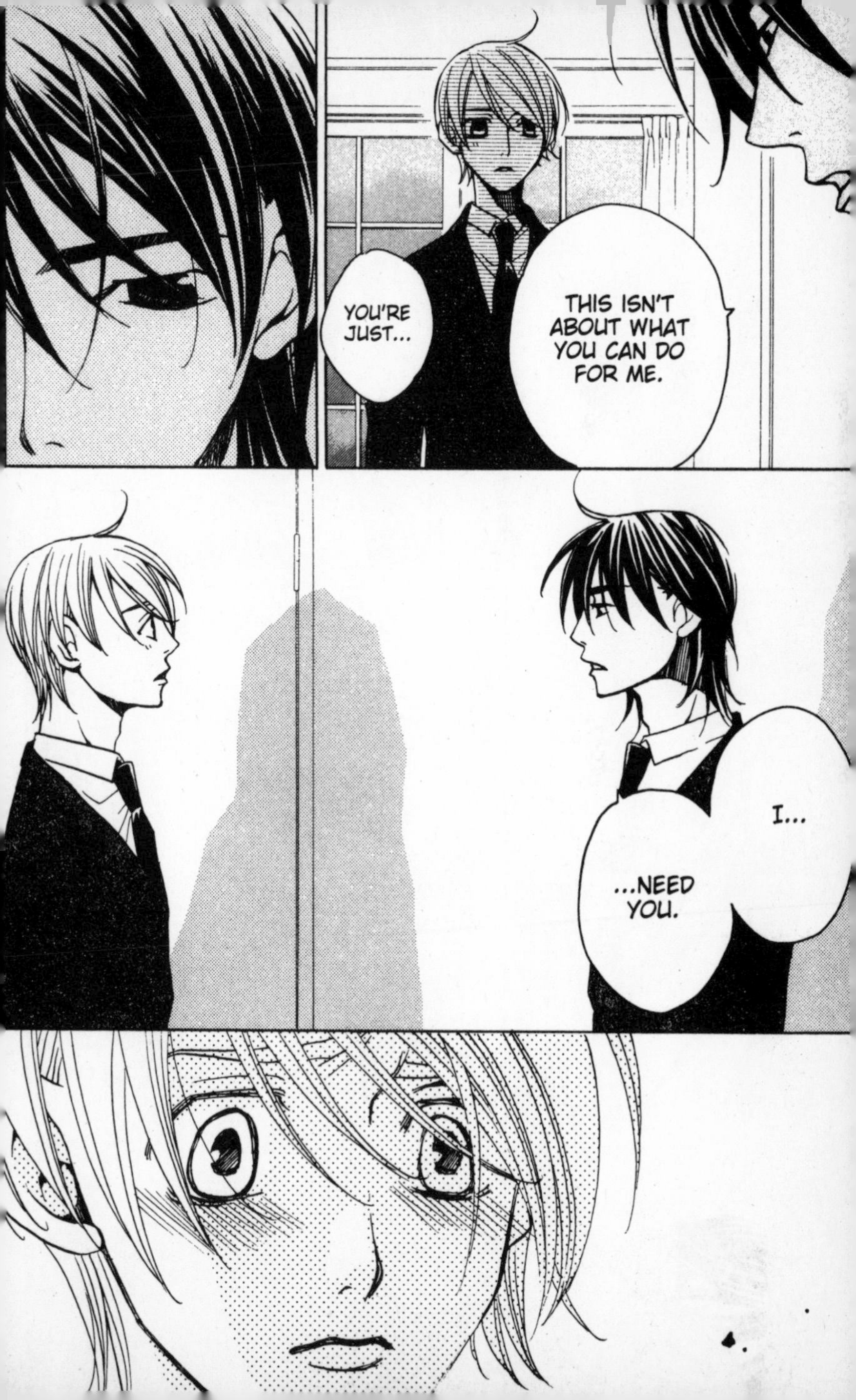
THIS ISN'T ABOUT WHAT YOU CAN DO FOR ME.
YOU'RE JUST...
I...
...NEED YOU.

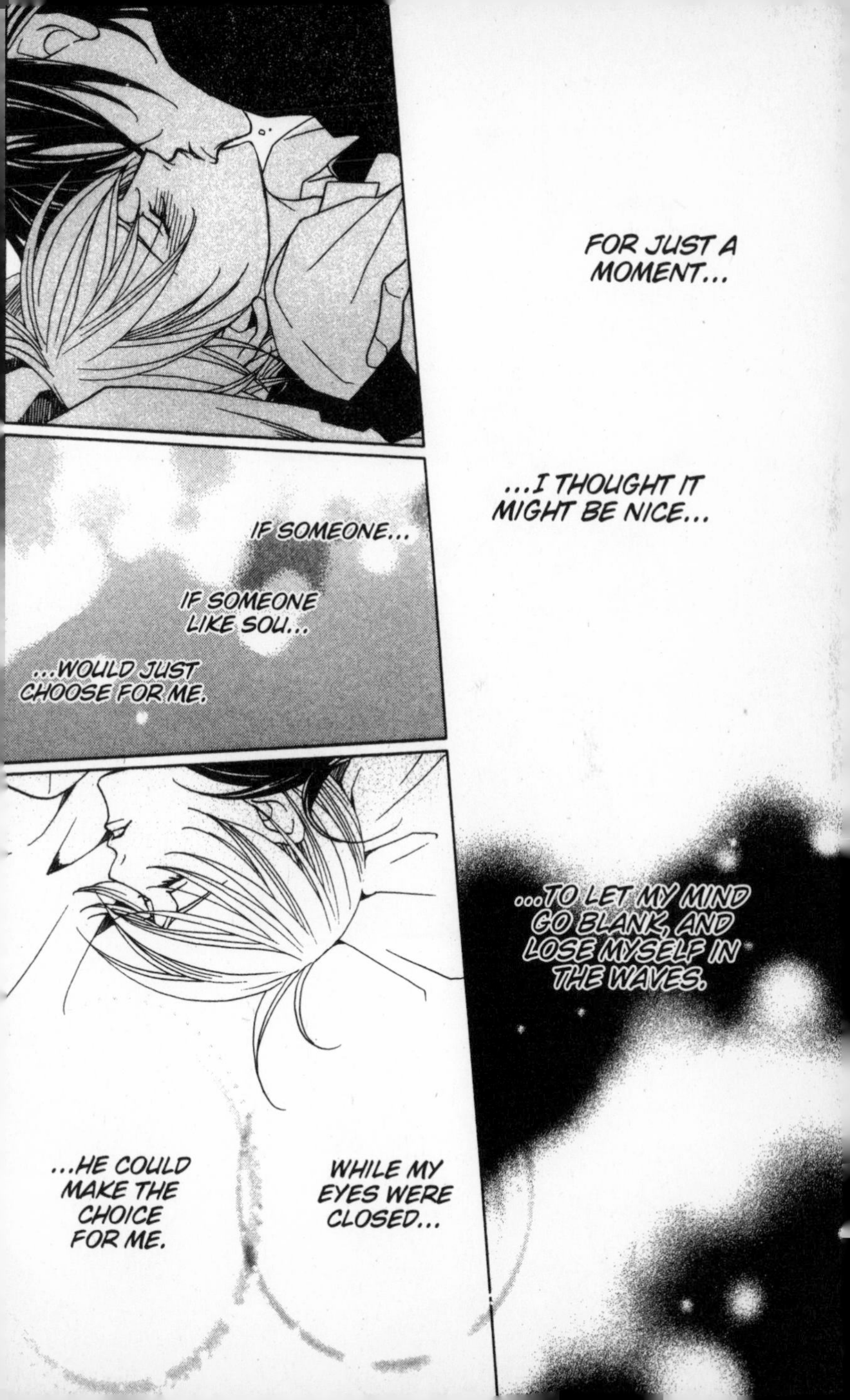
FOR JUST A MOMENT...
...I THOUGHT IT MIGHT BE NICE...
...TO LET MY MIND GO BLANK, AND LOSE MYSELF IN THE WAVES.
IF SOMEONE...
IF SOMEONE LIKE SOU...
...WOULD JUST CHOOSE FOR ME.
WHILE MY EYES WERE CLOSED...
...HE COULD MAKE THE CHOICE FOR ME.

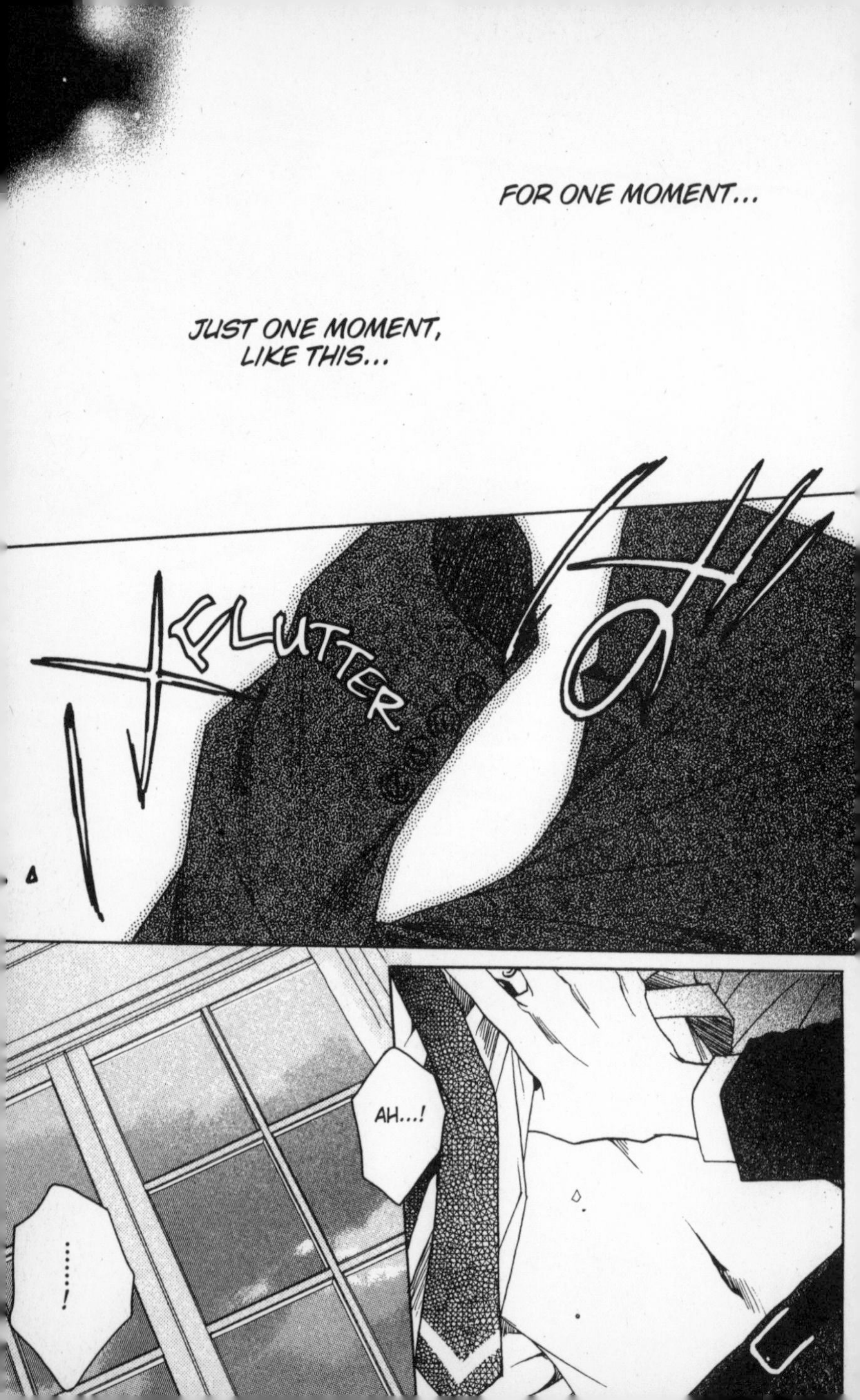
FOR ONE MOMENT...
JUST ONE MOMENT, LIKE THIS...
FLUTTER
AH...!
......!

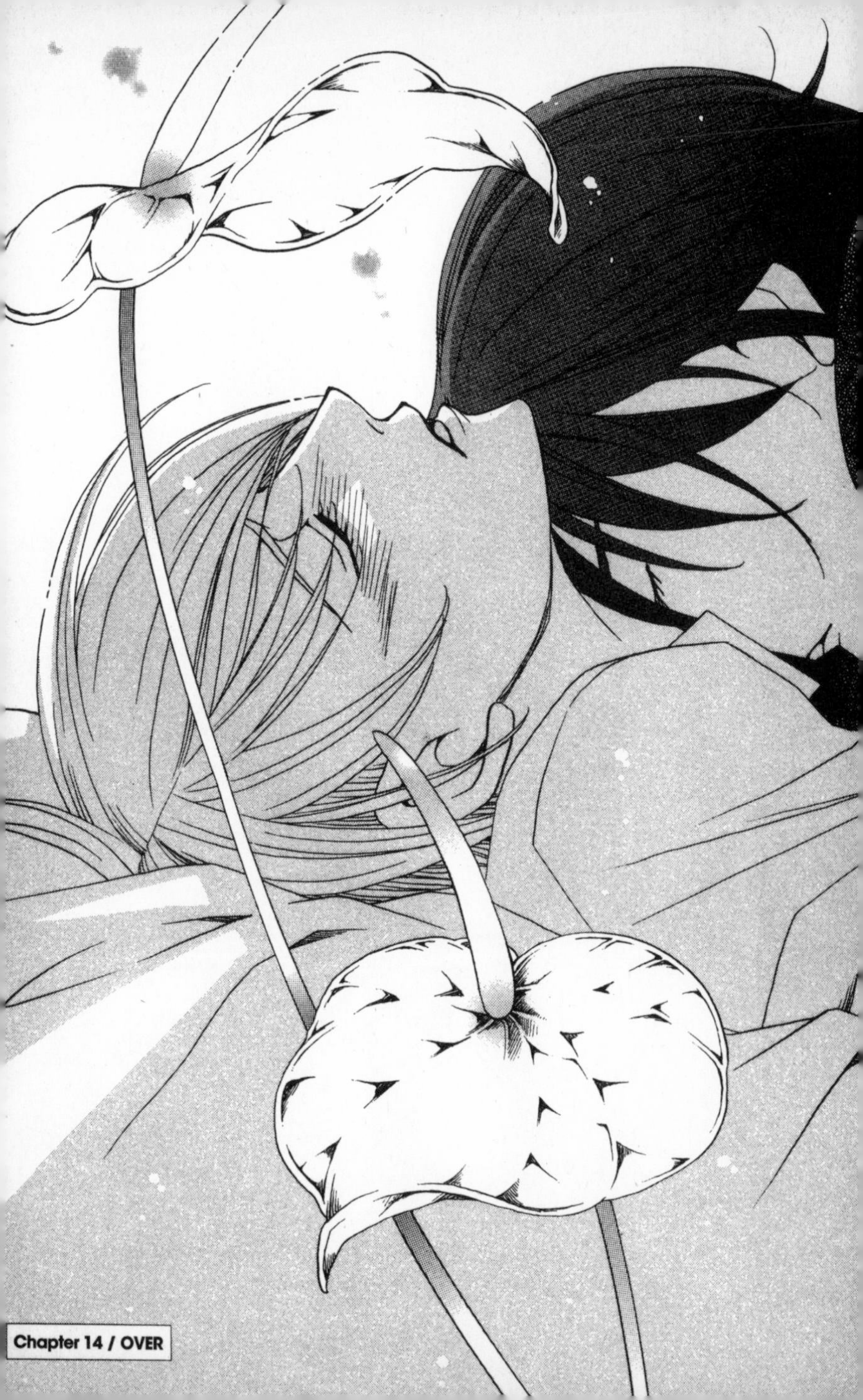
Chapter 14 / OVER

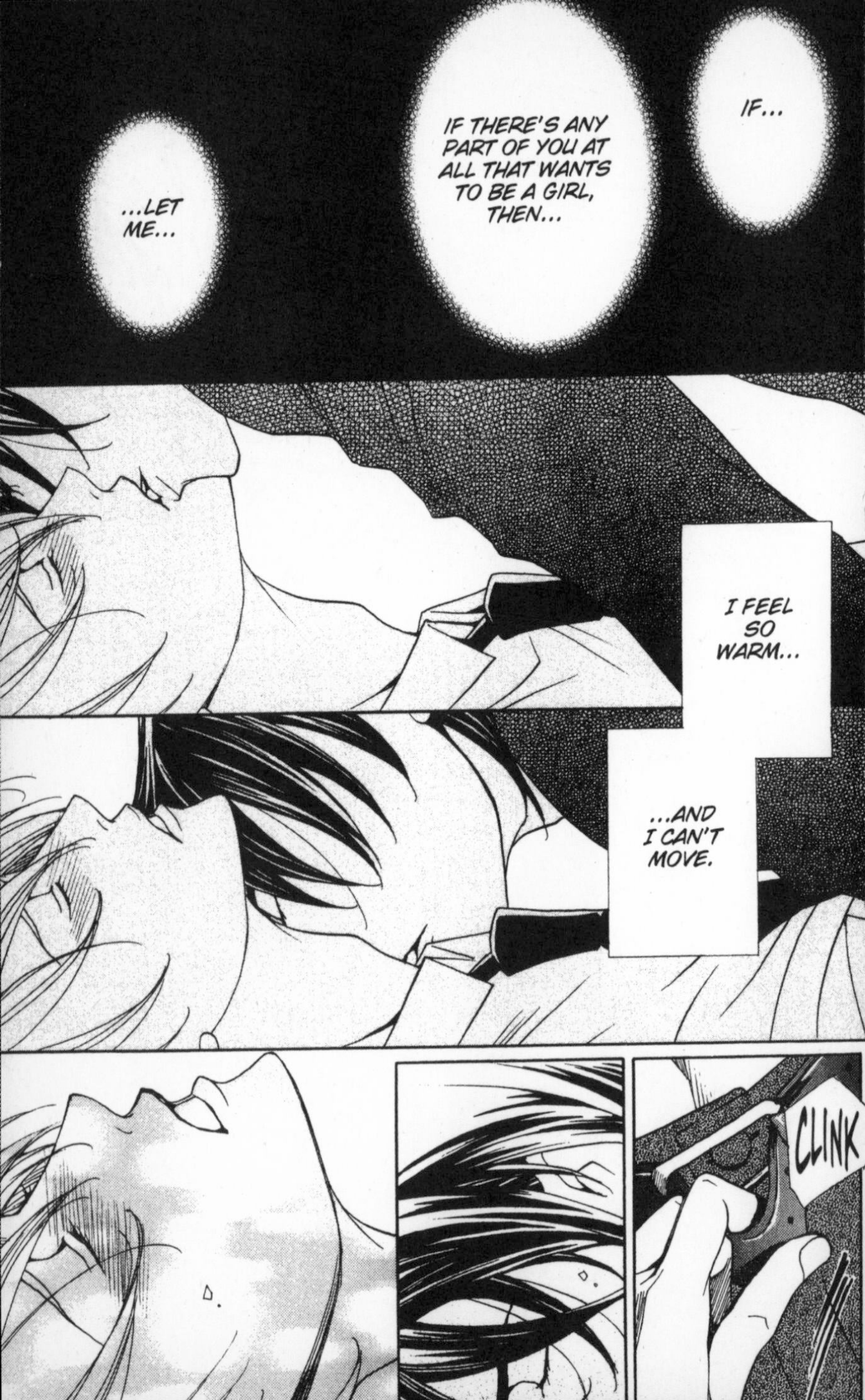
IF...
IF THERE'S ANY PART OF YOU AT ALL THAT WANTS TO BE A GIRL, THEN...
...LET ME...
I FEEL SO WARM...
...AND I CAN'T MOVE.
CLINK

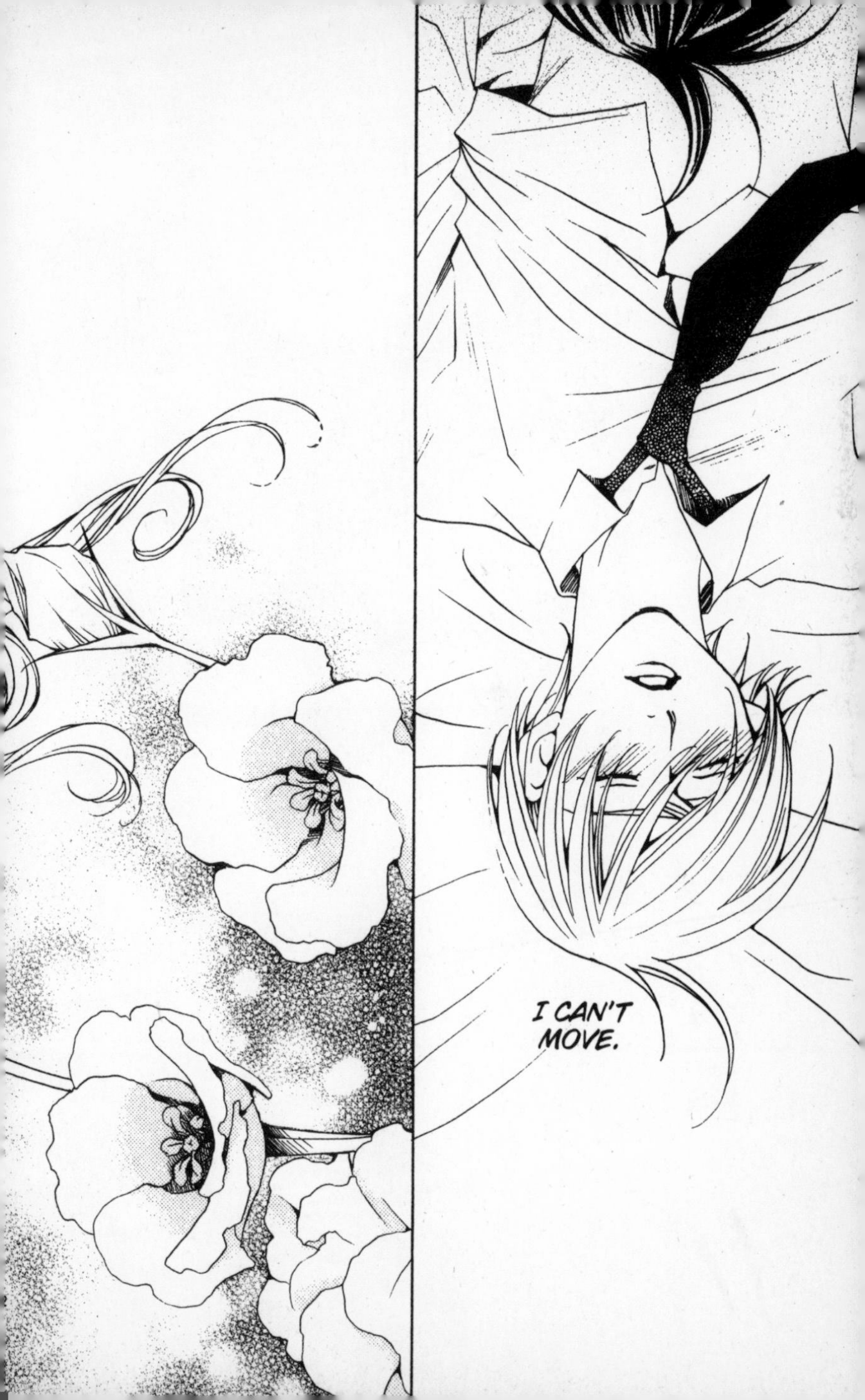
I CAN'T MOVE.

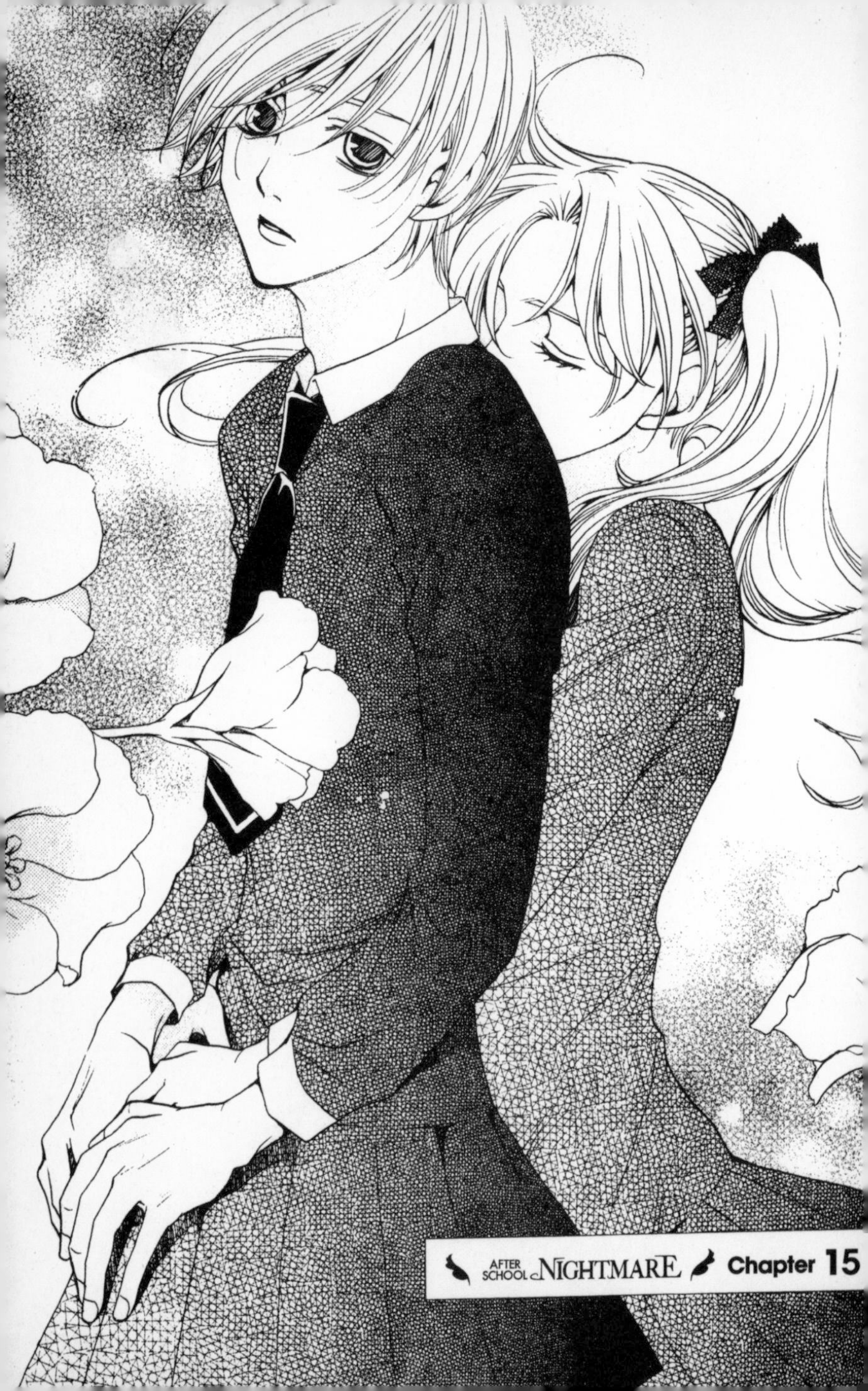
AFTER SCHOOL NIGHTMARE Chapter 15

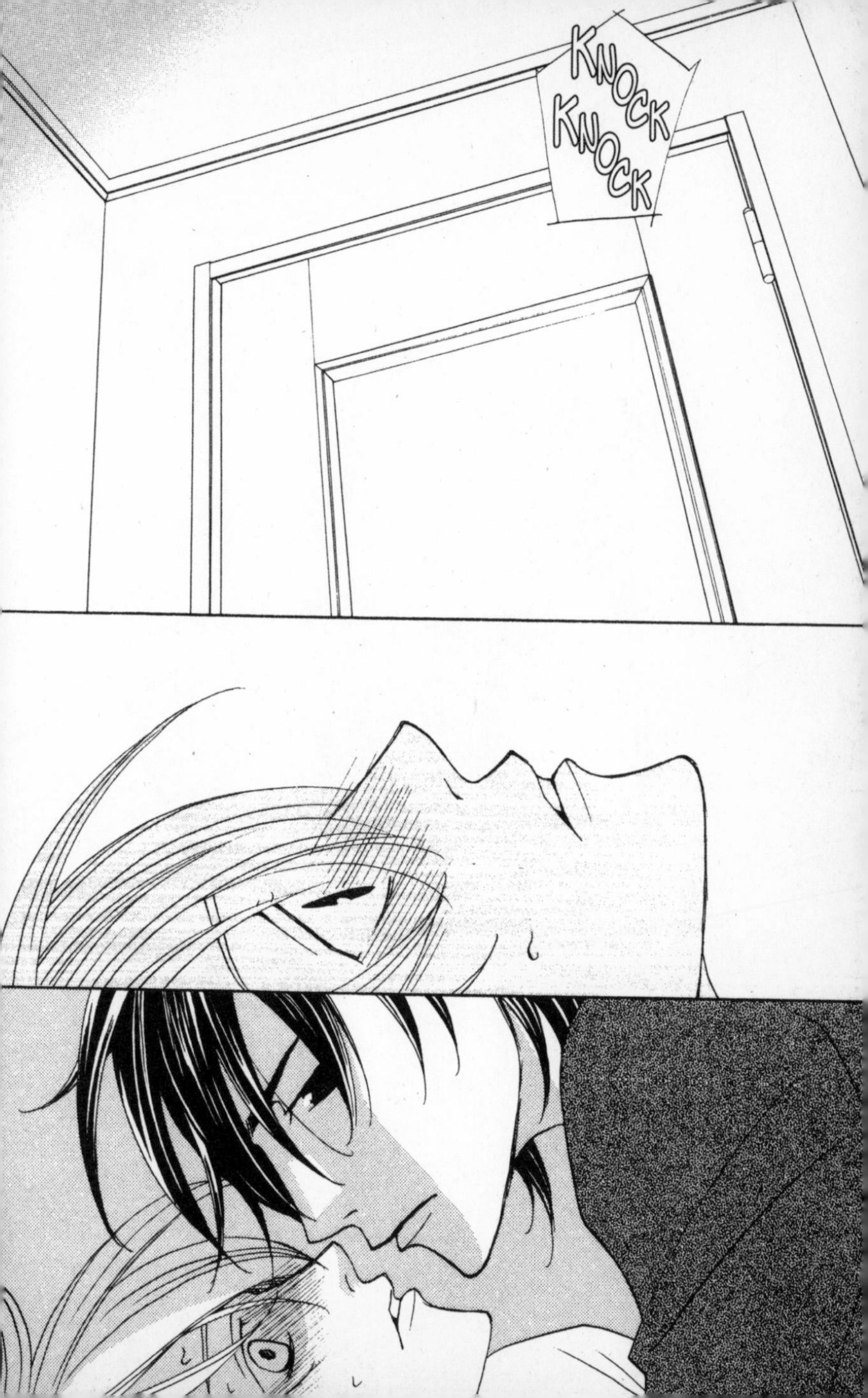
KNOCK KNOCK

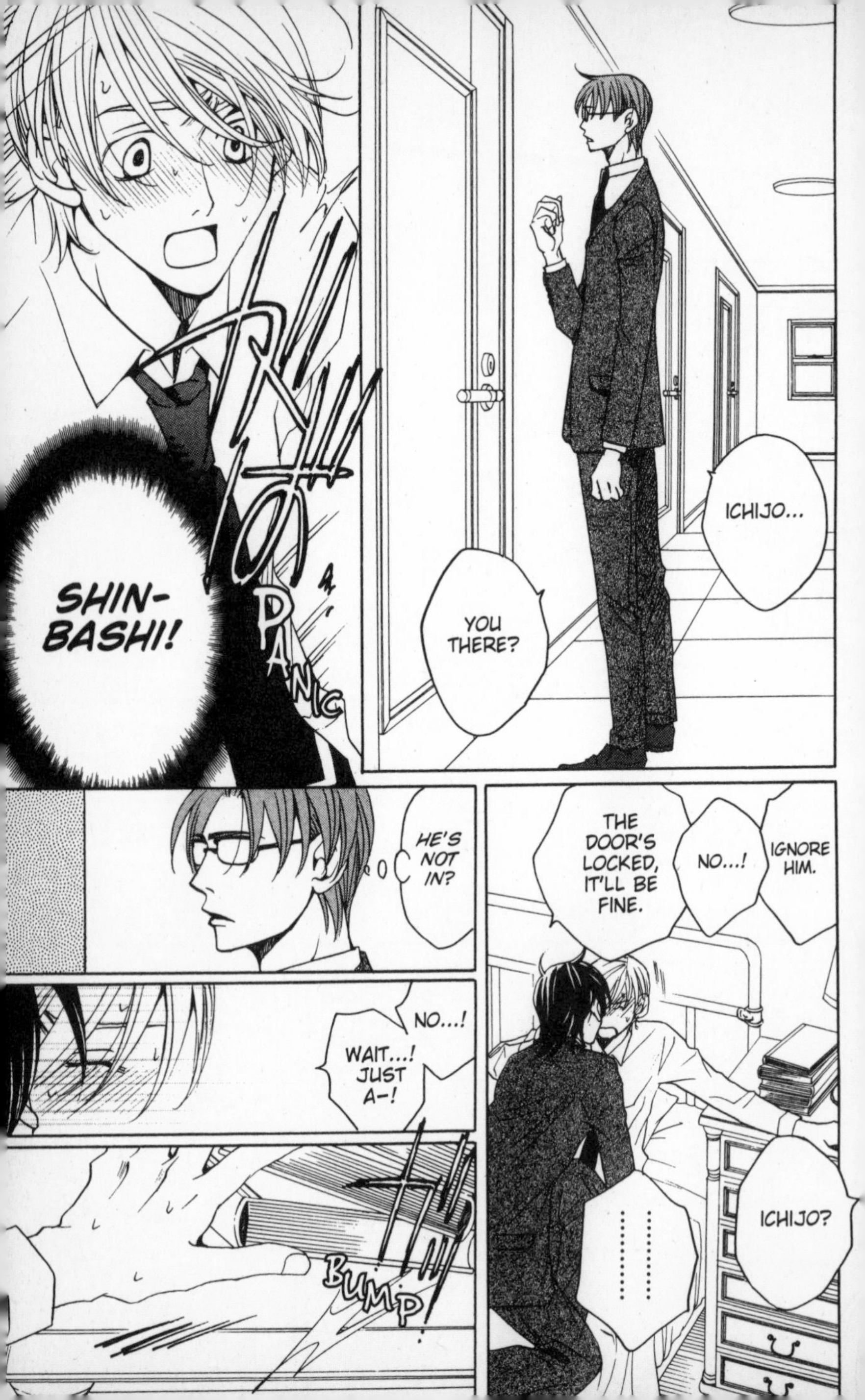

ICHIJO...
YOU THERE?
PANIC
SHIN-BASHI!
IGNORE HIM.
NO...!
THE DOOR'S LOCKED, IT'LL BE FINE.
ICHIJO?
......
HE'S NOT IN?
NO...!
WAIT...! JUST A-!
BUMP

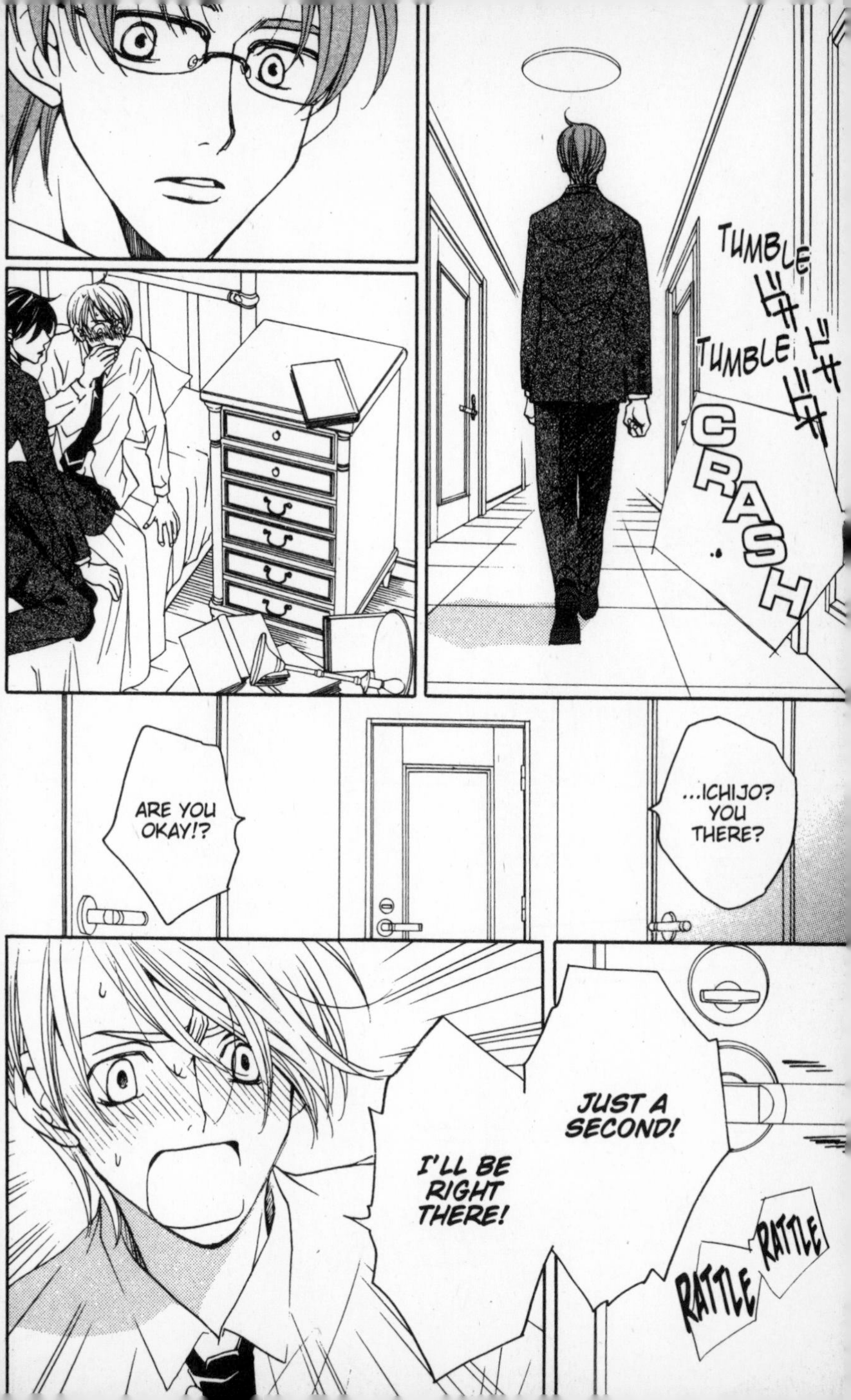
TUMBLE
TUMBLE
CRASH
...ICHIJO? YOU THERE?
ARE YOU OKAY!?
RATTLE RATTLE
JUST A SECOND!
I'LL BE RIGHT THERE!

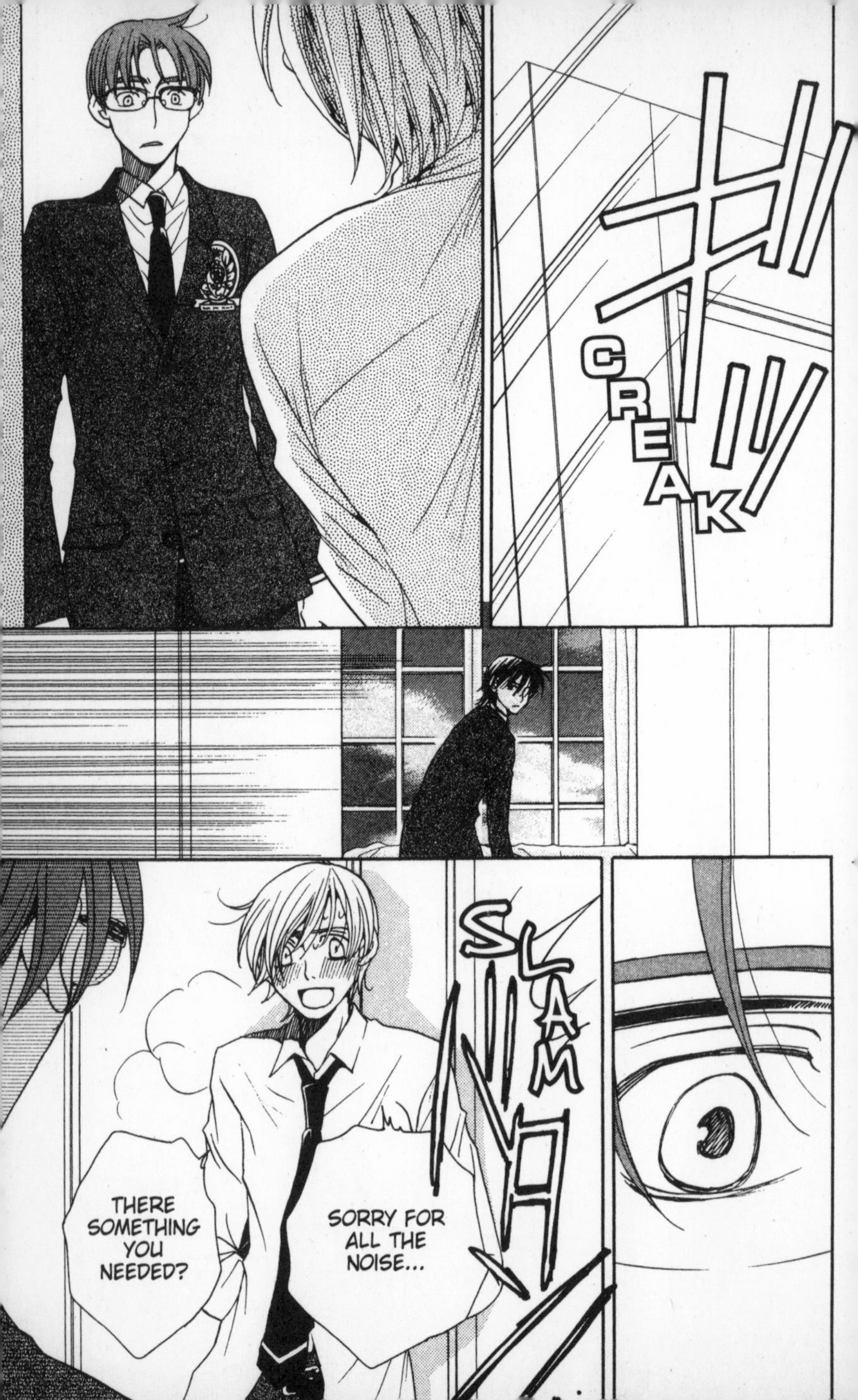

CREAK
SLAM
SORRY FOR ALL THE NOISE...
THERE SOMETHING YOU NEEDED?

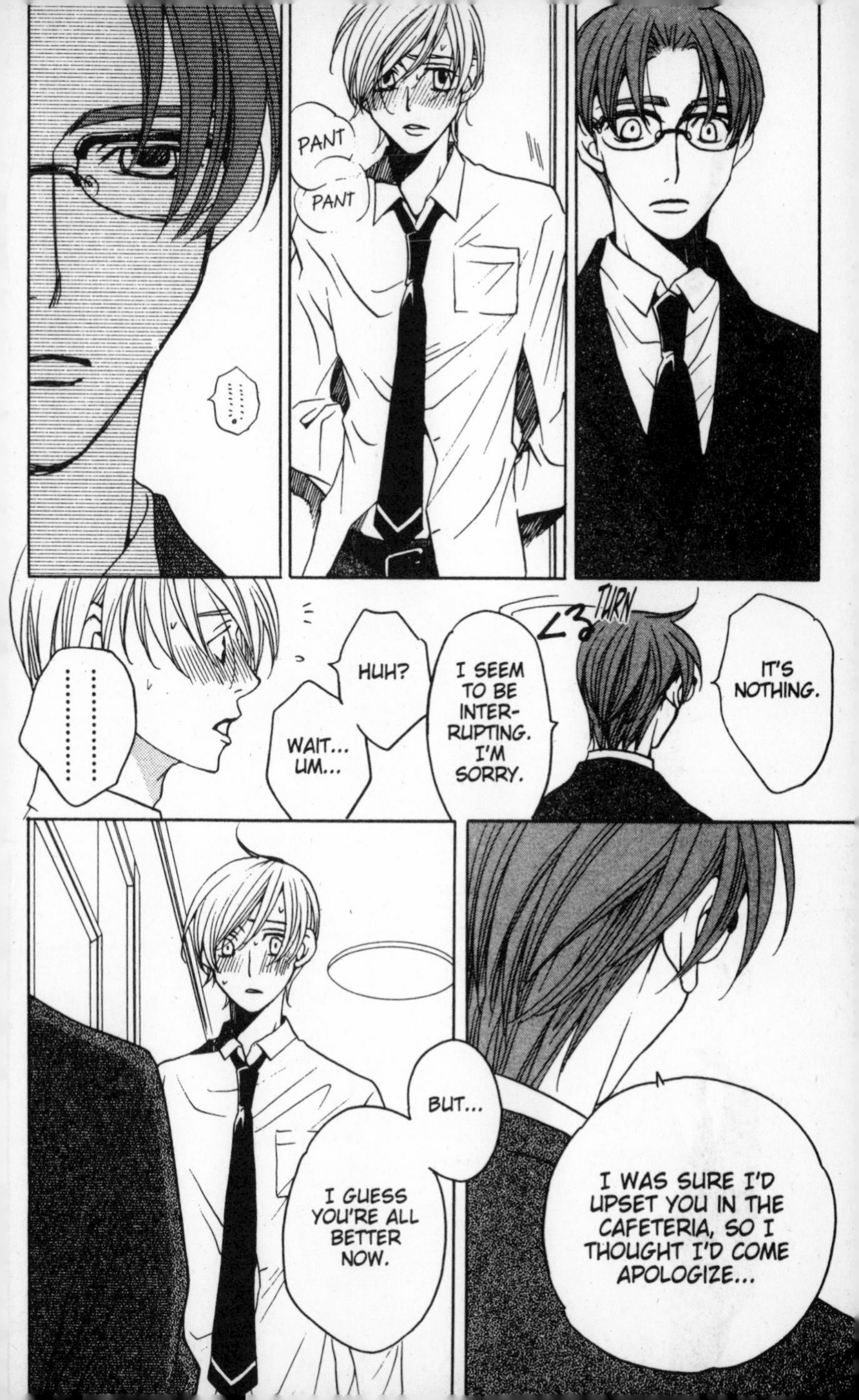
PANT
PANT
......
IT'S NOTHING.
TURN
I SEEM TO BE INTER-RUPTING. I'M SORRY.
HUH?
WAIT... UM...
......
I WAS SURE I'D UPSET YOU IN THE CAFETERIA, SO I THOUGHT I'D COME APOLOGIZE...
BUT...
I GUESS YOU'RE ALL BETTER NOW.

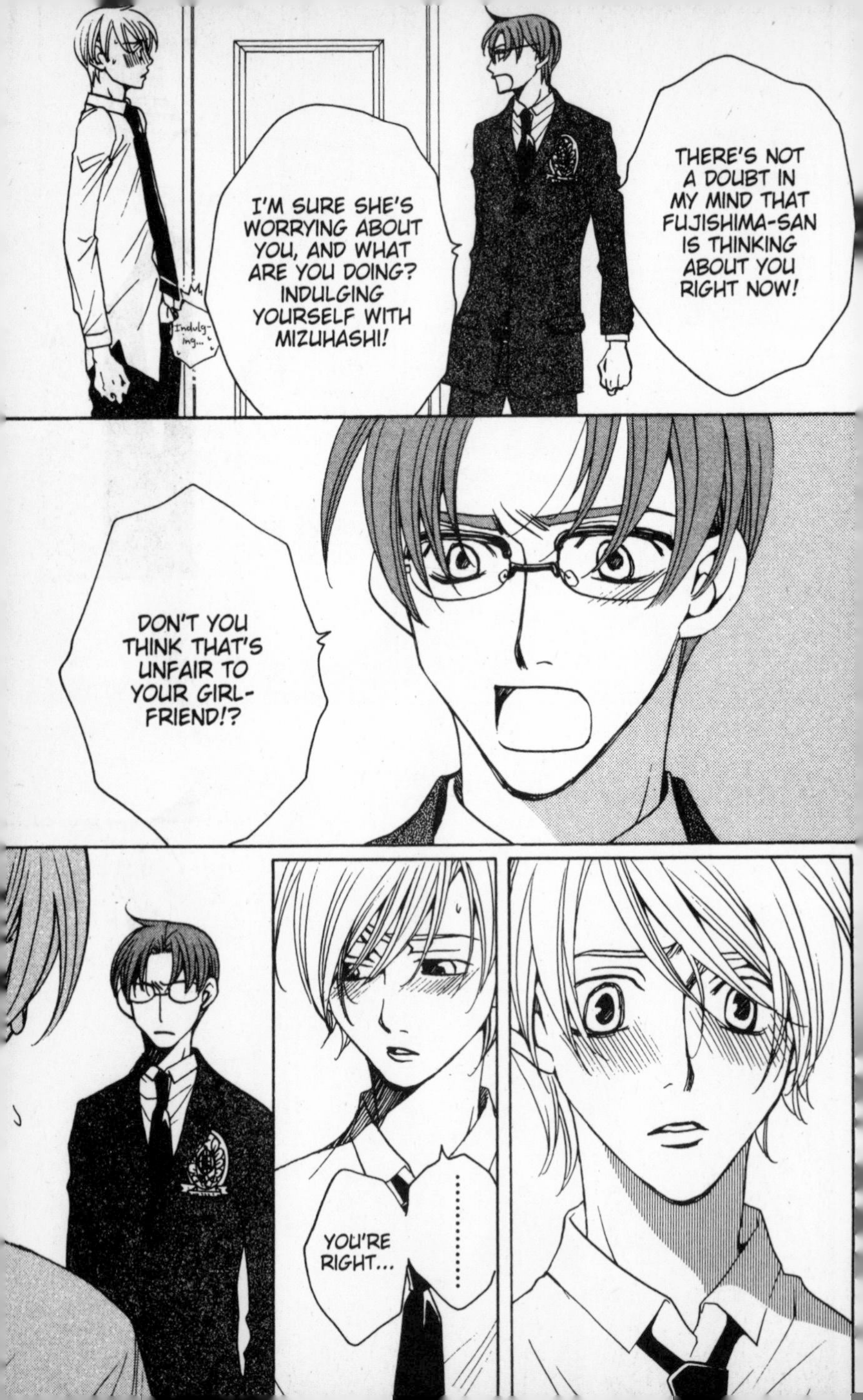
THERE'S NOT A DOUBT IN MY MIND THAT FUJISHIMA-SAN IS THINKING ABOUT YOU RIGHT NOW!
I'M SURE SHE'S WORRYING ABOUT YOU, AND WHAT ARE YOU DOING? INDULGING YOURSELF WITH MIZUHASHI!
Indulg-ing...
DON'T YOU THINK THAT'S UNFAIR TO YOUR GIRL-FRIEND!?
......
YOU'RE RIGHT...

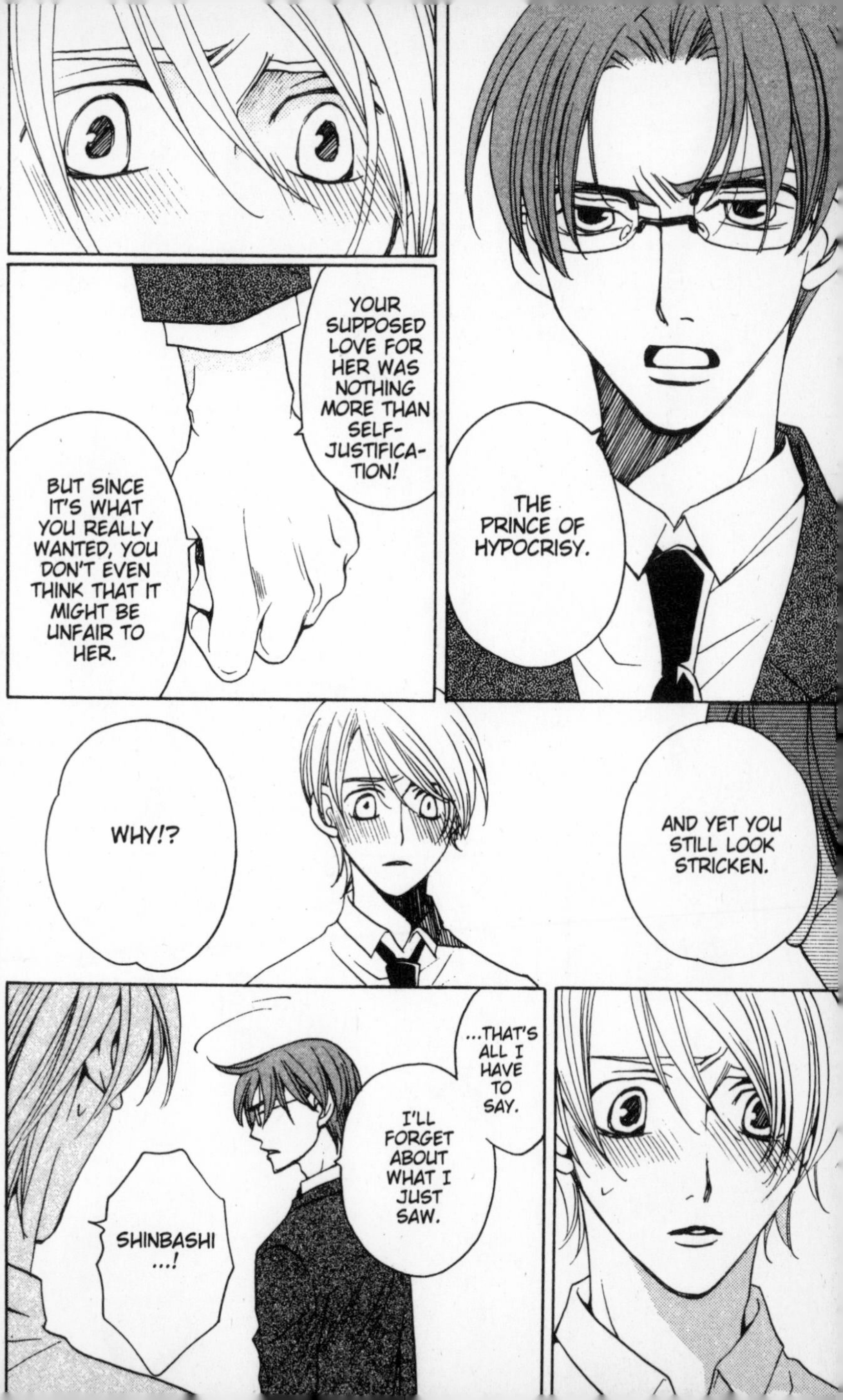
THE PRINCE OF HYPOCRISY.
YOUR SUPPOSED LOVE FOR HER WAS NOTHING MORE THAN SELF-JUSTIFICATION!
BUT SINCE IT'S WHAT YOU REALLY WANTED, YOU DON'T EVEN THINK THAT IT MIGHT BE UNFAIR TO HER.
AND YET YOU STILL LOOK STRICKEN.
WHY!?
...THAT'S ALL I HAVE TO SAY.
I'LL FORGET ABOUT WHAT I JUST SAW.
SHINBASHI ...!

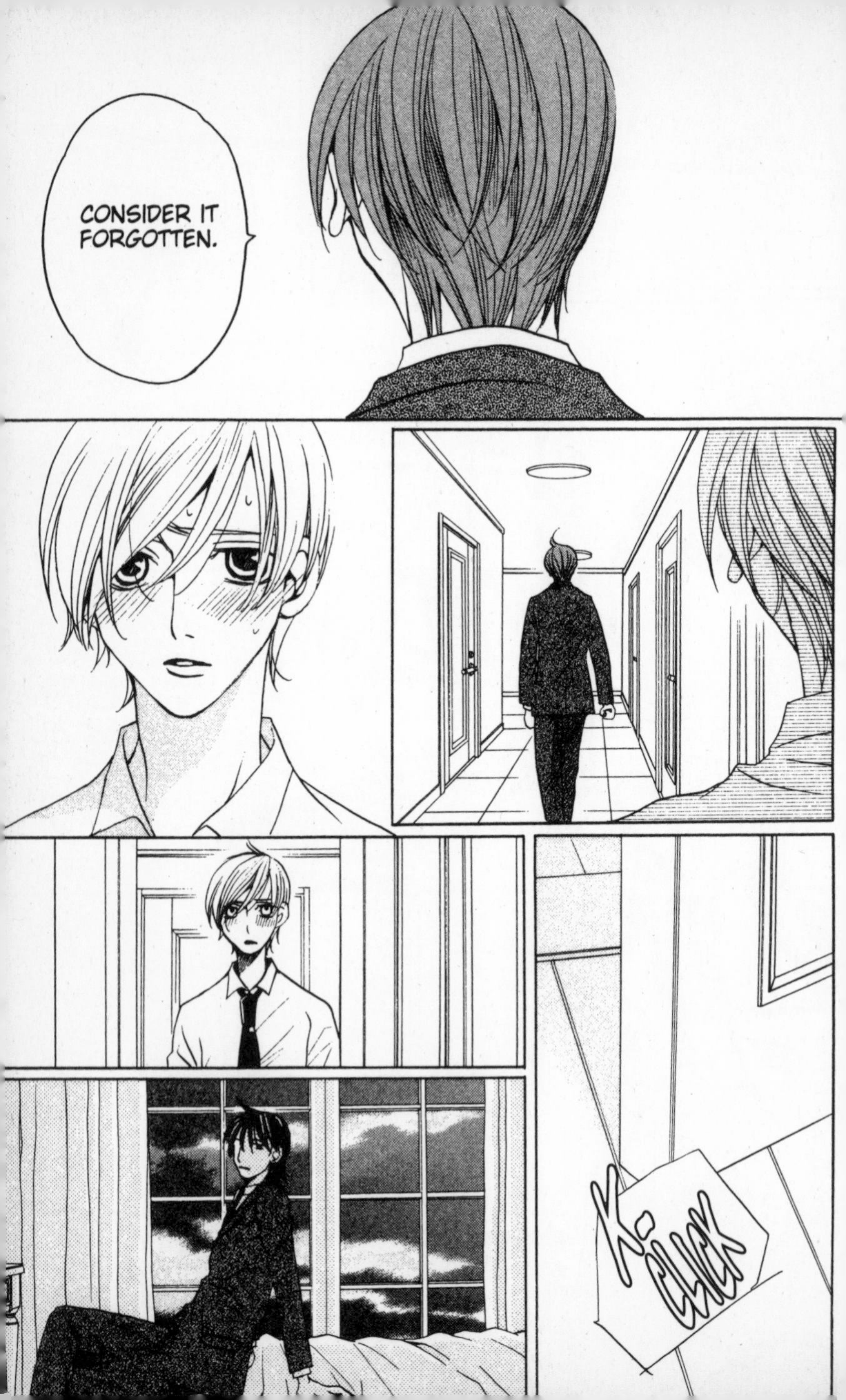
CONSIDER IT FORGOTTEN.
K-CLICK

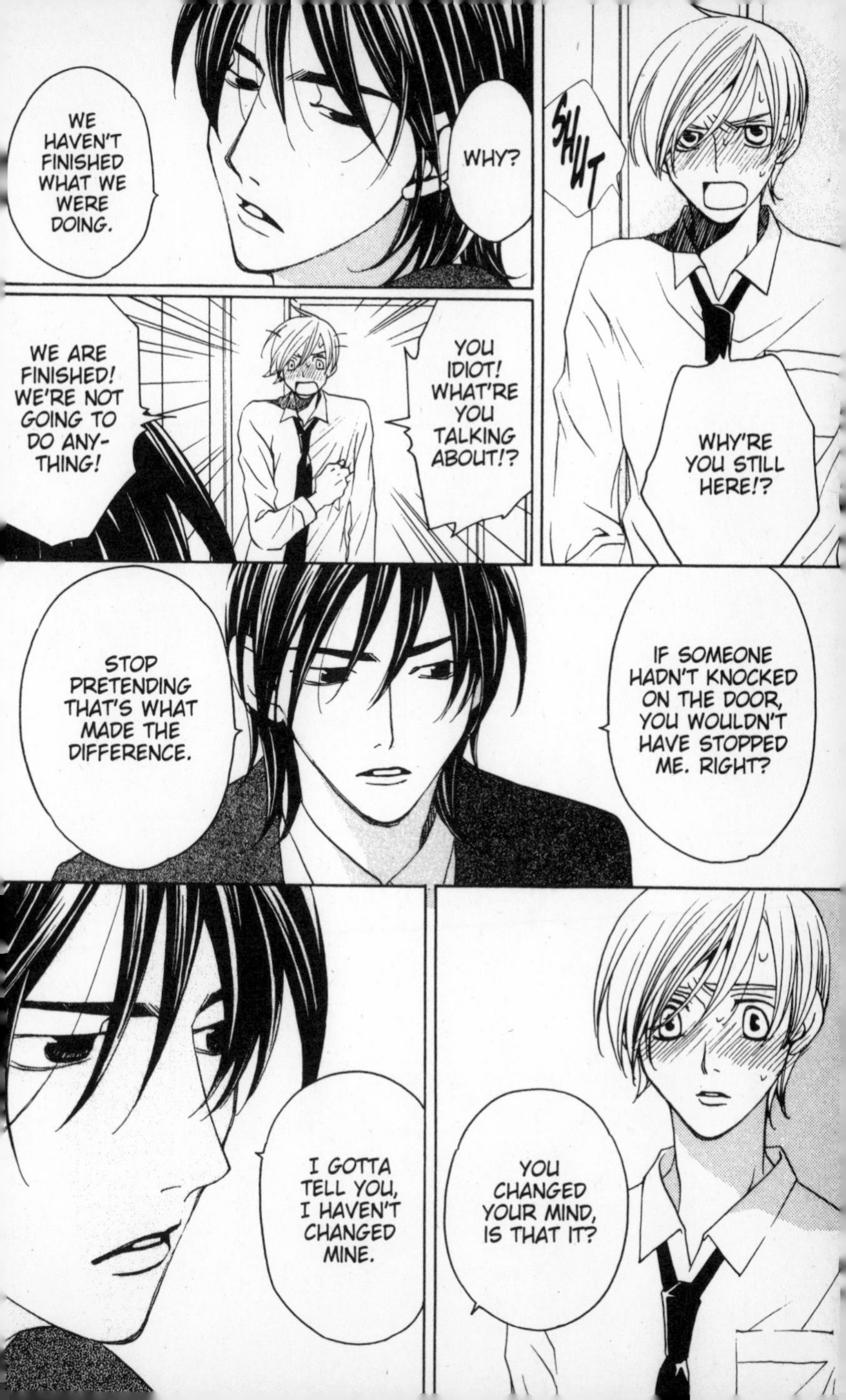
SHUT
WHY'RE YOU STILL HERE!?
WHY?
WE HAVEN'T FINISHED WHAT WE WERE DOING.
YOU IDIOT! WHAT'RE YOU TALKING ABOUT!?
WE ARE FINISHED! WE'RE NOT GOING TO DO ANY-THING!
IF SOMEONE HADN'T KNOCKED ON THE DOOR, YOU WOULDN'T HAVE STOPPED ME. RIGHT?
STOP PRETENDING THAT'S WHAT MADE THE DIFFERENCE.
YOU CHANGED YOUR MIND, IS THAT IT?
I GOTTA TELL YOU, I HAVEN'T CHANGED MINE.

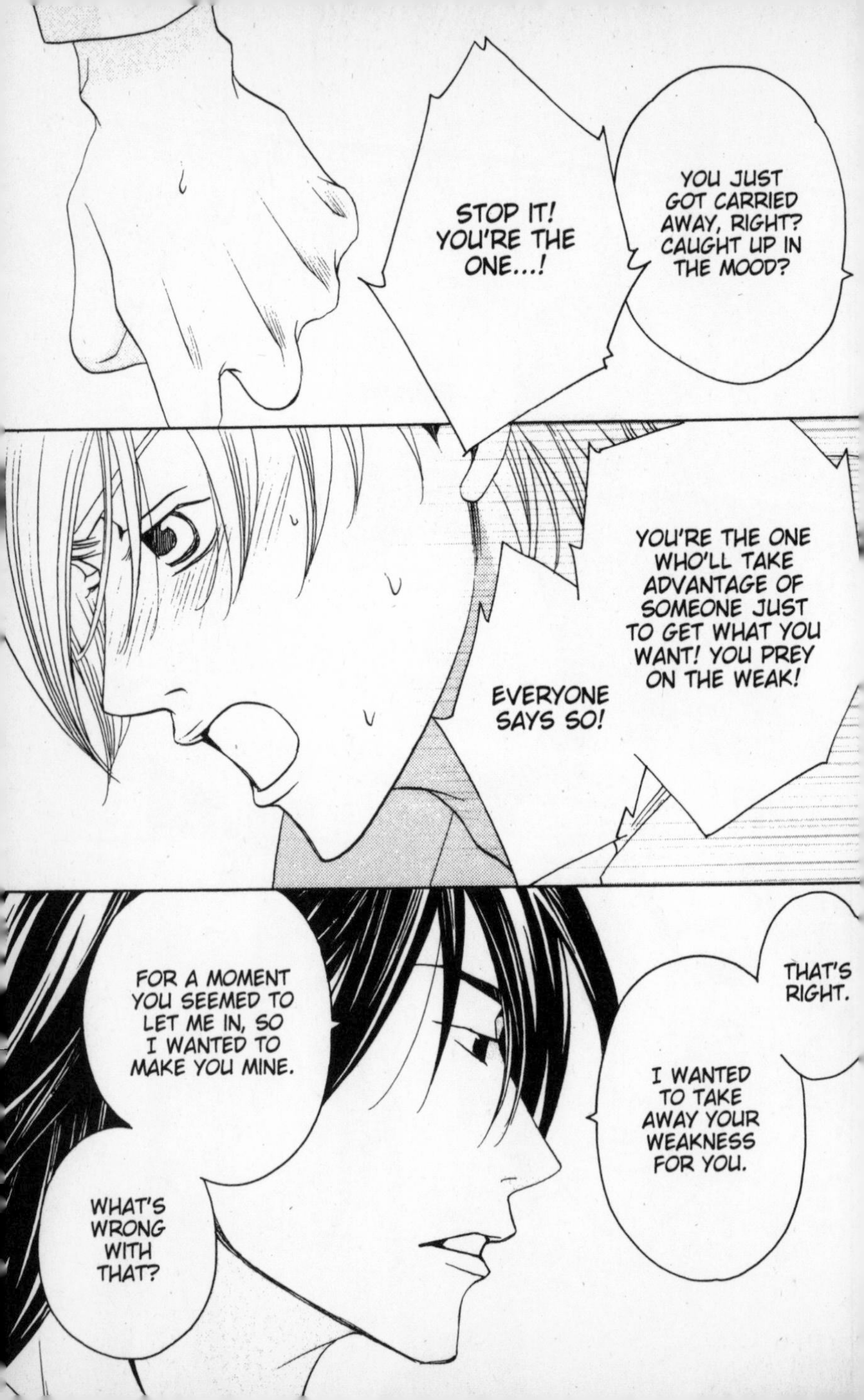
YOU JUST GOT CARRIED AWAY, RIGHT? CAUGHT UP IN THE MOOD?
STOP IT! YOU'RE THE ONE...!
YOU'RE THE ONE WHO'LL TAKE ADVANTAGE OF SOMEONE JUST TO GET WHAT YOU WANT! YOU PREY ON THE WEAK!
EVERYONE SAYS SO!
THAT'S RIGHT.
I WANTED TO TAKE AWAY YOUR WEAKNESS FOR YOU.
FOR A MOMENT YOU SEEMED TO LET ME IN, SO I WANTED TO MAKE YOU MINE.
WHAT'S WRONG WITH THAT?

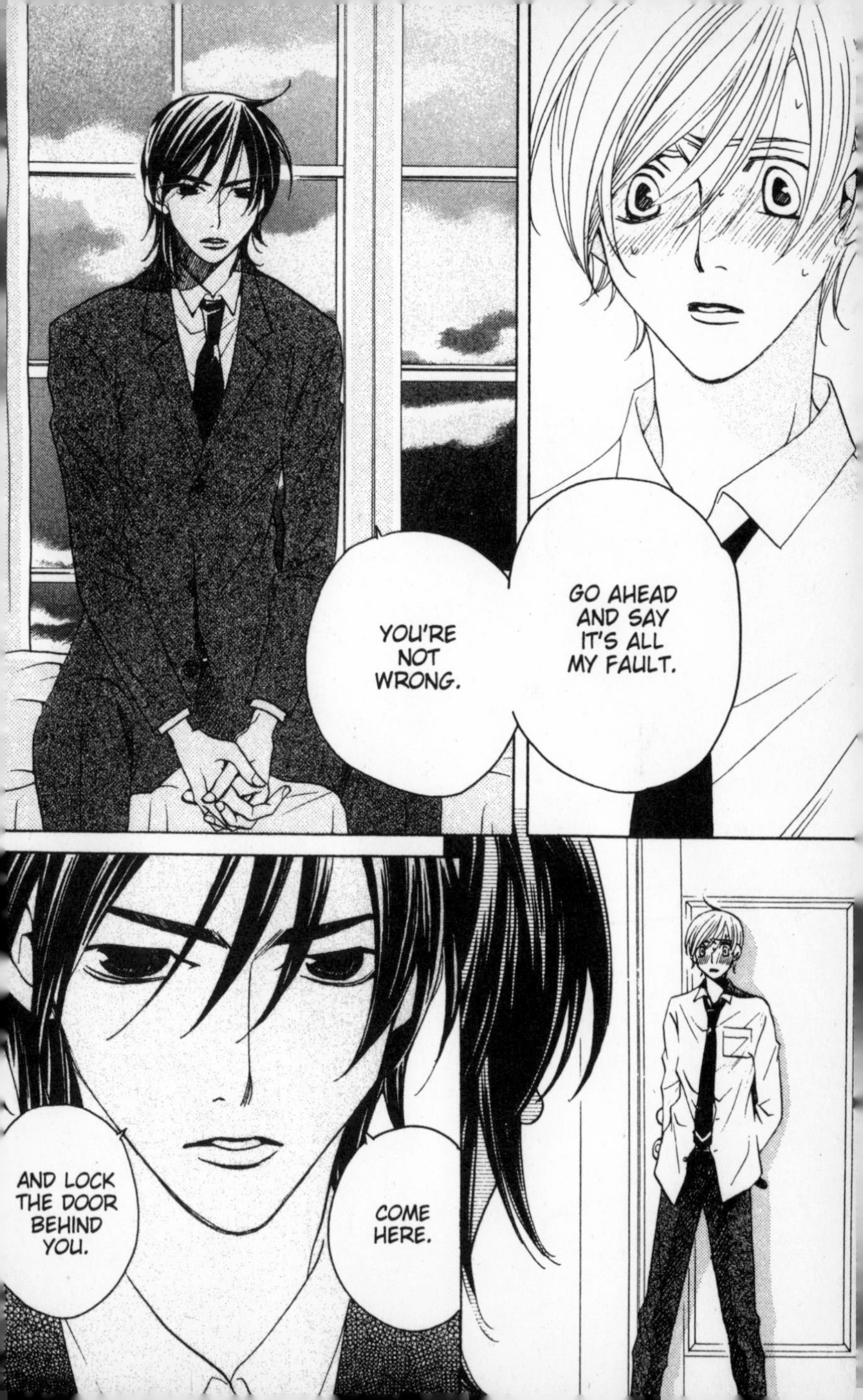
GO AHEAD AND SAY IT'S ALL MY FAULT.
YOU'RE NOT WRONG.
COME HERE.
AND LOCK THE DOOR BEHIND YOU.

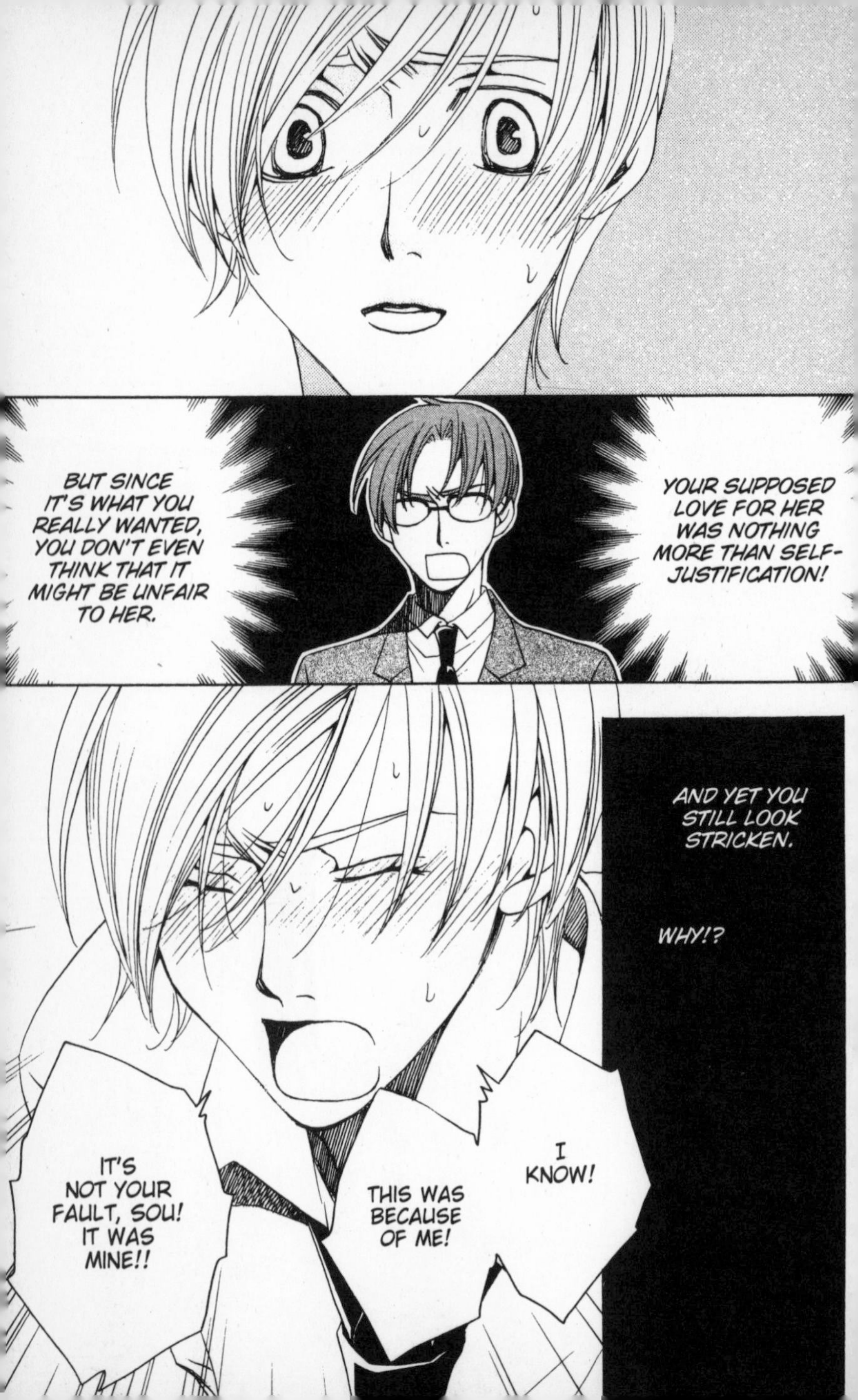
YOUR SUPPOSED LOVE FOR HER WAS NOTHING MORE THAN SELF-JUSTIFICATION!
BUT SINCE IT'S WHAT YOU REALLY WANTED, YOU DON'T EVEN THINK THAT IT MIGHT BE UNFAIR TO HER.
AND YET YOU STILL LOOK STRICKEN.
WHY!?
I KNOW!
THIS WAS BECAUSE OF ME!
IT'S NOT YOUR FAULT, SOU! IT WAS MINE!!

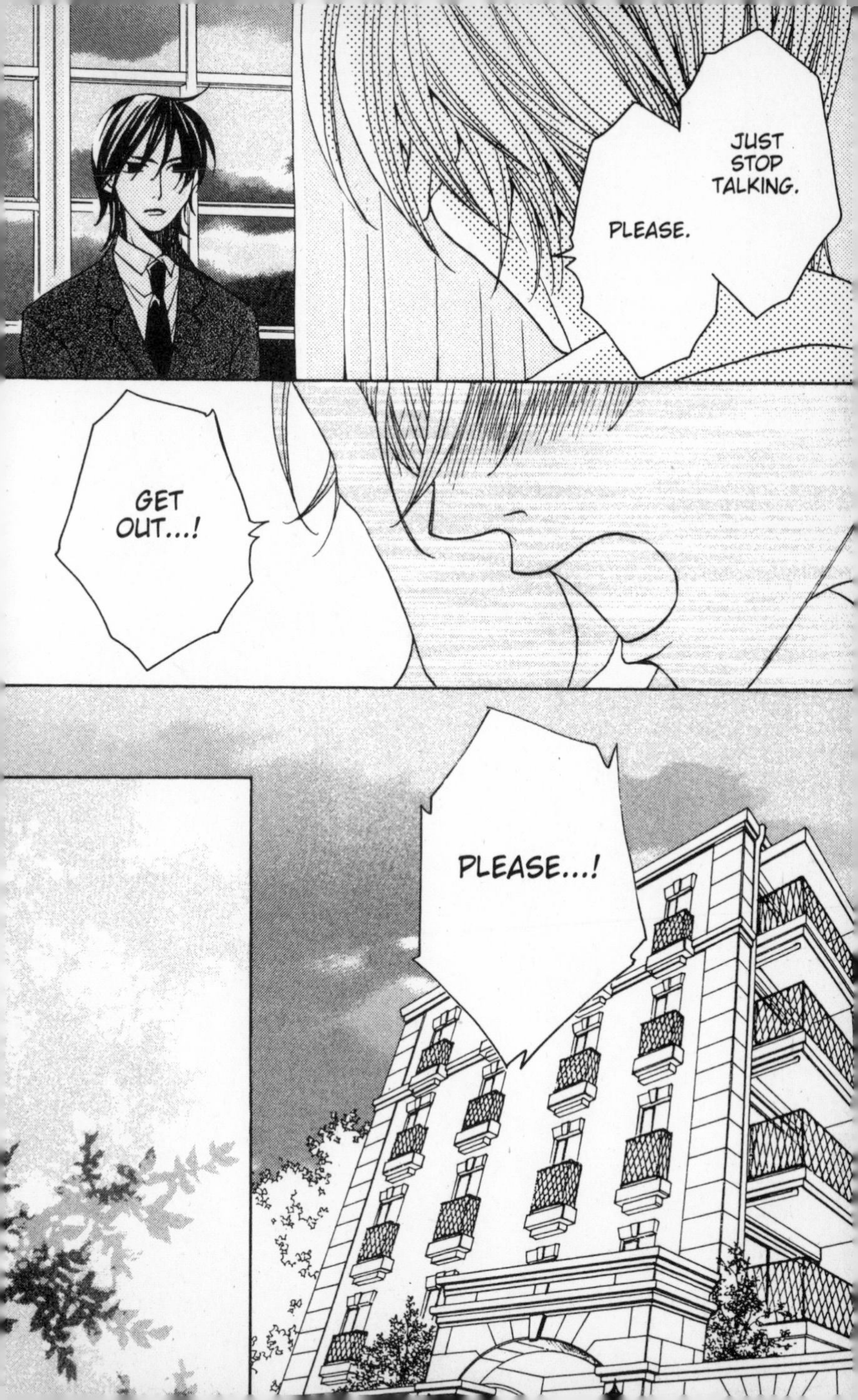
JUST STOP TALKING.
PLEASE.
GET OUT...!
PLEASE...!

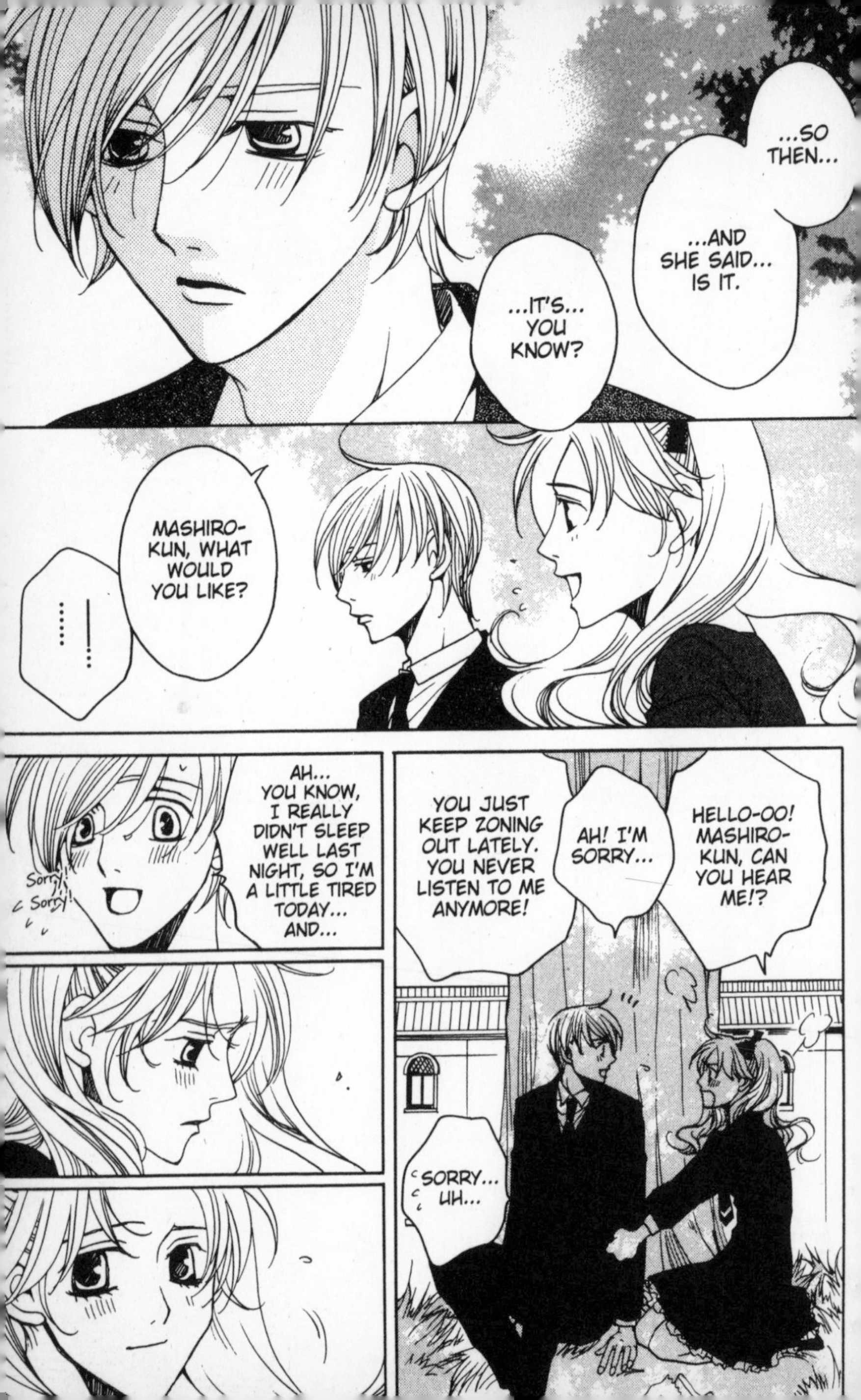
...SO THEN...
...AND SHE SAID... IS IT.
...IT'S... YOU KNOW?
MASHIRO-KUN, WHAT WOULD YOU LIKE?
......!
HELLO-OO! MASHIRO-KUN, CAN YOU HEAR ME!?
AH! I'M SORRY...
YOU JUST KEEP ZONING OUT LATELY. YOU NEVER LISTEN TO ME ANYMORE!
SORRY... UH...
AH... YOU KNOW, I REALLY DIDN'T SLEEP WELL LAST NIGHT, SO I'M A LITTLE TIRED TODAY... AND...
Sorry! Sorry!

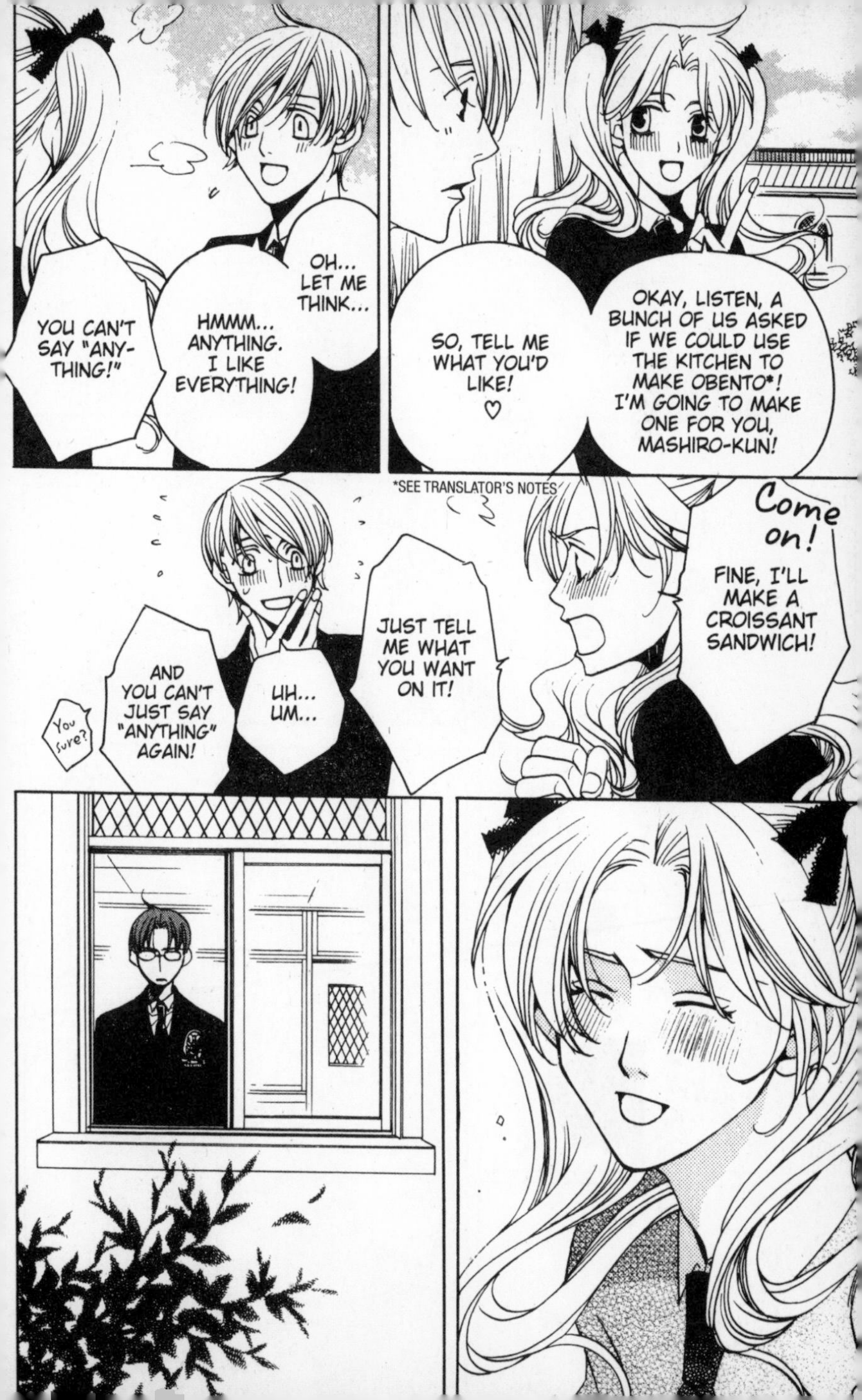
OKAY, LISTEN, A BUNCH OF US ASKED IF WE COULD USE THE KITCHEN TO MAKE OBENTO*! I'M GOING TO MAKE ONE FOR YOU, MASHIRO-KUN!
SO, TELL ME WHAT YOU'D LIKE! ♡
OH... LET ME THINK...
HMMM... ANYTHING. I LIKE EVERYTHING!
YOU CAN'T SAY "ANY-THING!"
*SEE TRANSLATOR'S NOTES
Come on!
FINE, I'LL MAKE A CROISSANT SANDWICH!
JUST TELL ME WHAT YOU WANT ON IT!
UH... UM...
AND YOU CAN'T JUST SAY "ANYTHING" AGAIN!
You sure?

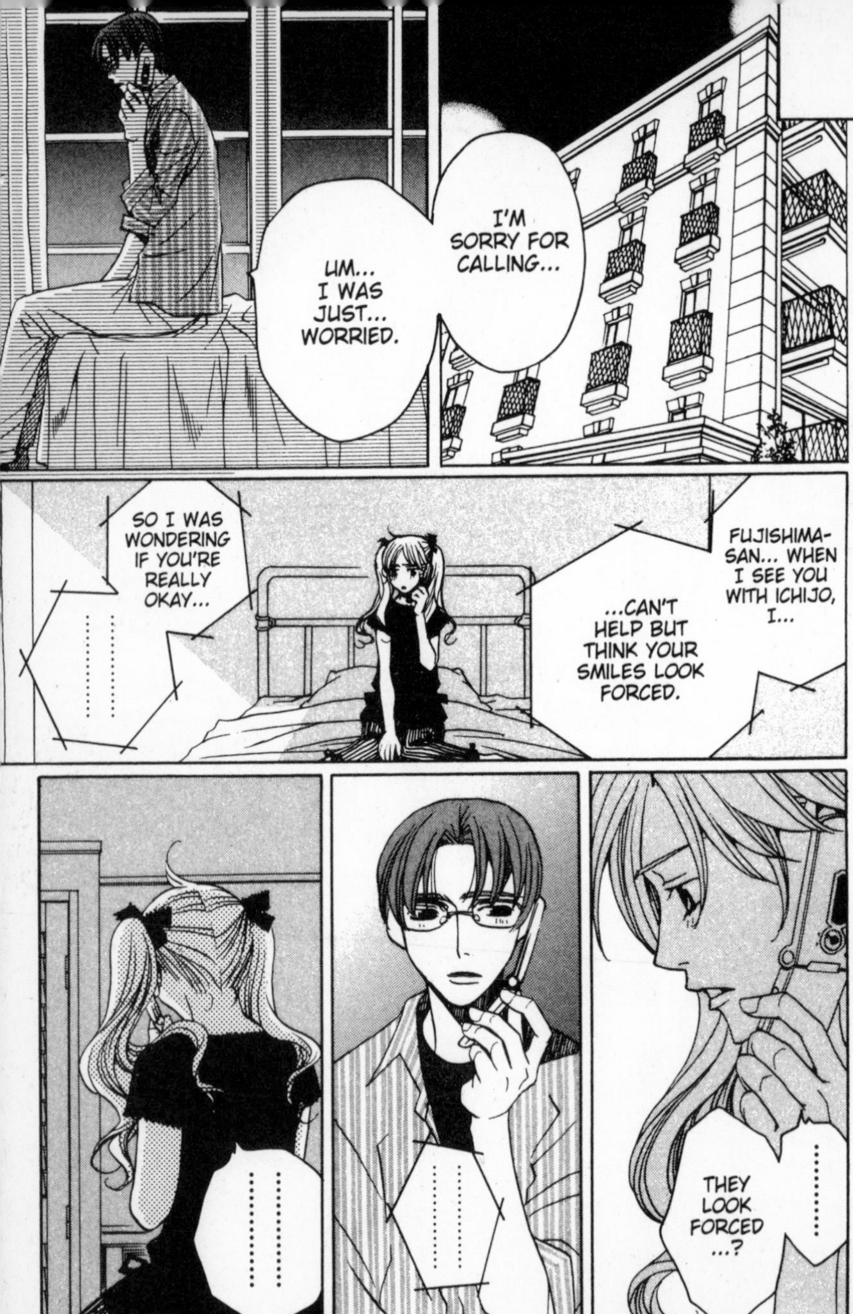
I'M SORRY FOR CALLING...
UM... I WAS JUST... WORRIED.
FUJISHIMA-SAN... WHEN I SEE YOU WITH ICHIJO, I...
...CAN'T HELP BUT THINK YOUR SMILES LOOK FORCED.
SO I WAS WONDERING IF YOU'RE REALLY OKAY...
......
......
THEY LOOK FORCED ...?
......
......

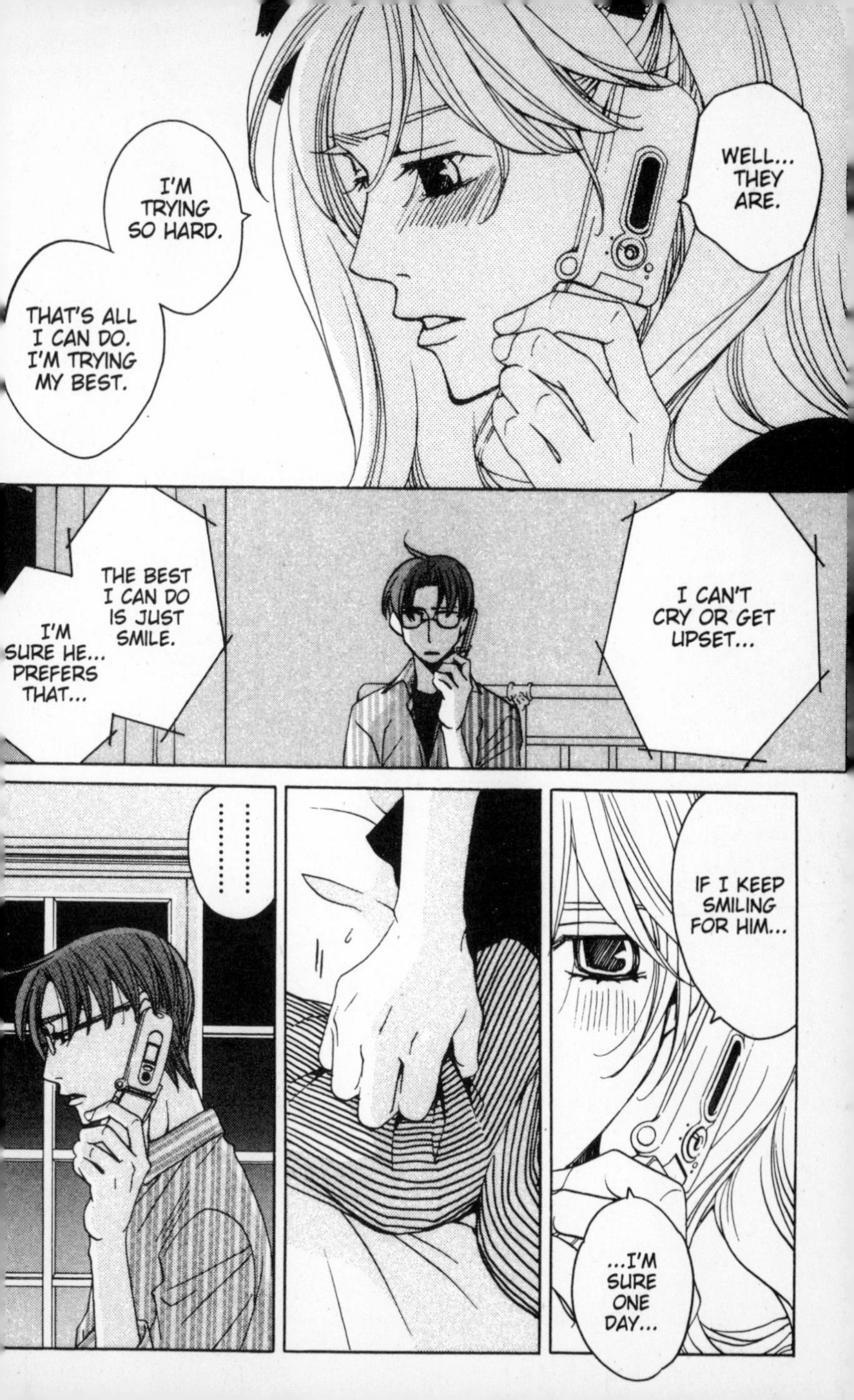
WELL... THEY ARE.
I'M TRYING SO HARD.
THAT'S ALL I CAN DO. I'M TRYING MY BEST.
I CAN'T CRY OR GET UPSET...
THE BEST I CAN DO IS JUST SMILE.
I'M SURE HE... PREFERS THAT...
IF I KEEP SMILING FOR HIM...
...I'M SURE ONE DAY...
......

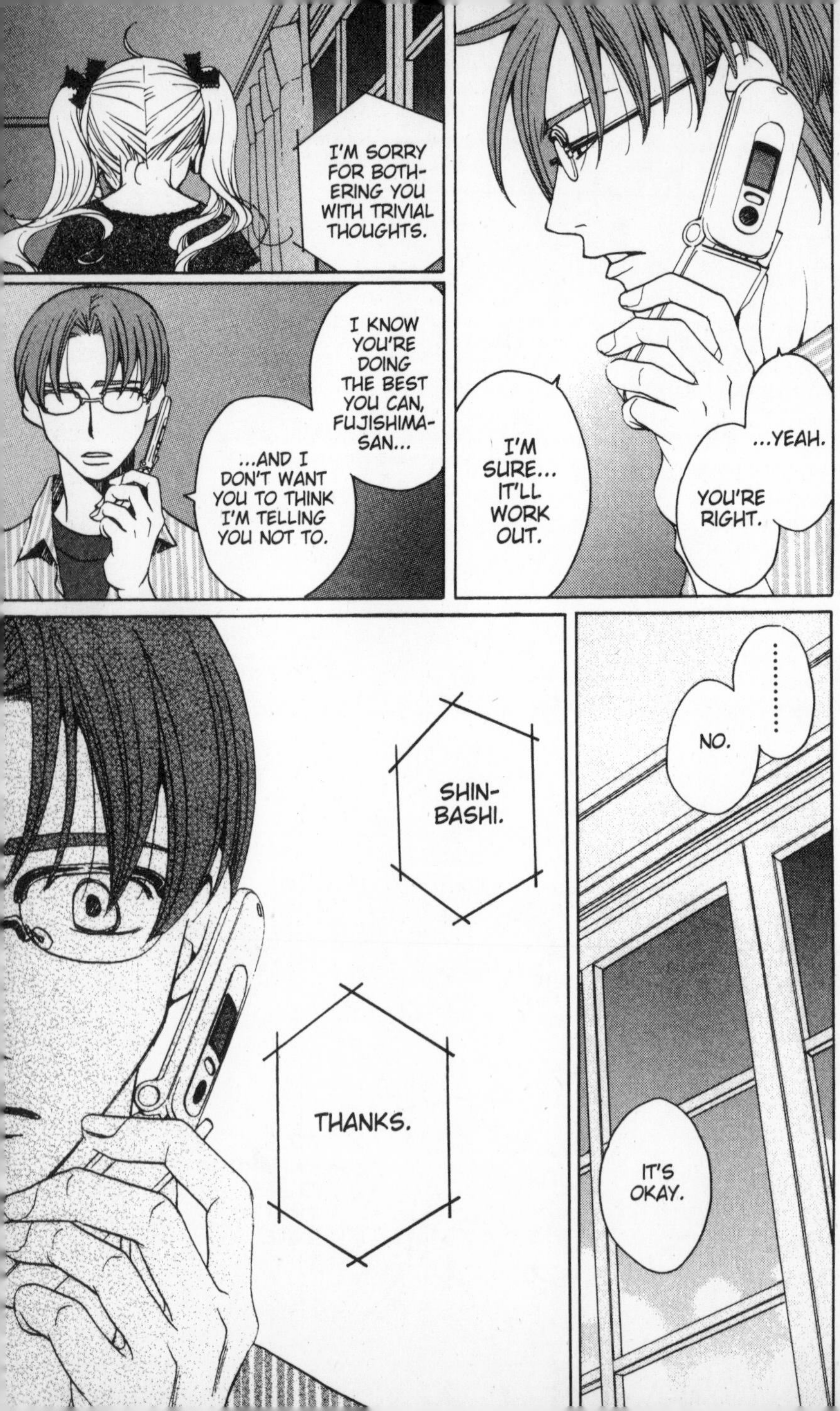
...YEAH.
YOU'RE RIGHT.
I'M SURE... IT'LL WORK OUT.
I'M SORRY FOR BOTH-ERING YOU WITH TRIVIAL THOUGHTS.
I KNOW YOU'RE DOING THE BEST YOU CAN, FUJISHIMA-SAN...
...AND I DON'T WANT YOU TO THINK I'M TELLING YOU NOT TO.
......
NO.
IT'S OKAY.
SHIN-BASHI.
THANKS.

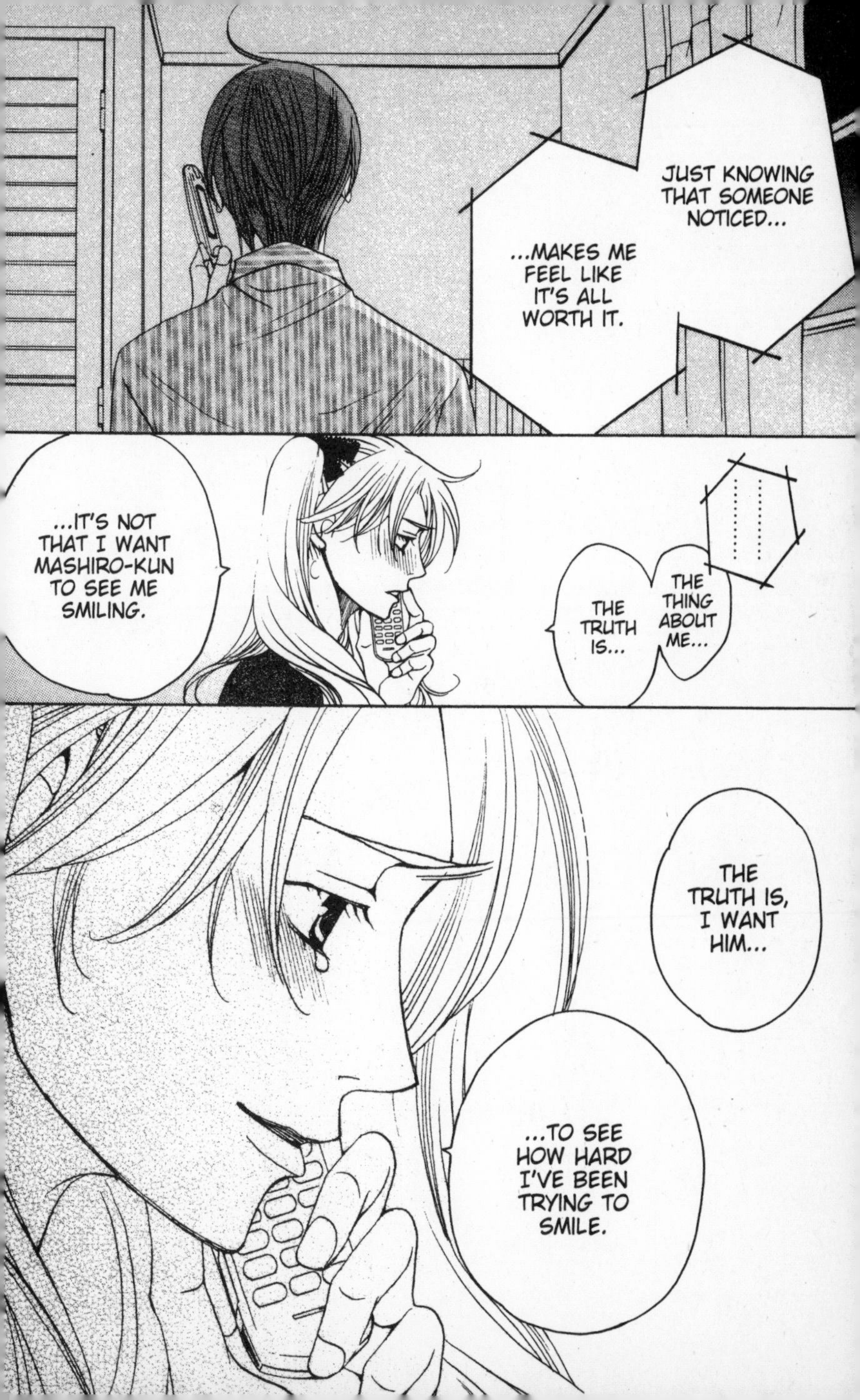

JUST KNOWING THAT SOMEONE NOTICED...
...MAKES ME FEEL LIKE IT'S ALL WORTH IT.
THE THING ABOUT ME...
THE TRUTH IS...
...IT'S NOT THAT I WANT MASHIRO-KUN TO SEE ME SMILING.
THE TRUTH IS, I WANT HIM...
...TO SEE HOW HARD I'VE BEEN TRYING TO SMILE.

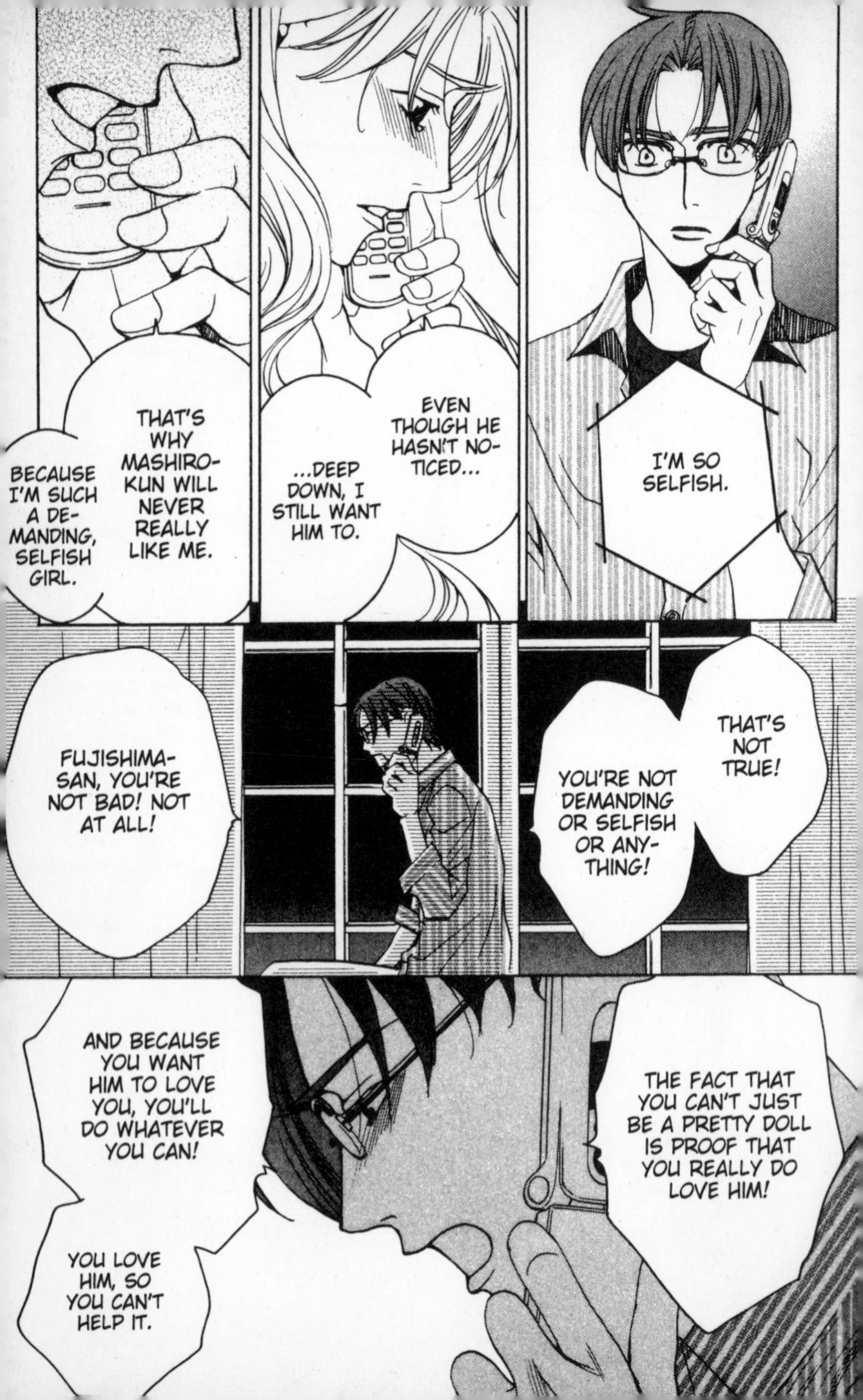

I'M SO SELFISH.
EVEN THOUGH HE HASN'T NOTICED...
...DEEP DOWN, I STILL WANT HIM TO.
THAT'S WHY MASHIRO-KUN WILL NEVER REALLY LIKE ME.
BECAUSE I'M SUCH A DEMANDING, SELFISH GIRL.
THAT'S NOT TRUE!
YOU'RE NOT DEMANDING OR SELFISH OR ANYTHING!
FUJISHIMA-SAN, YOU'RE NOT BAD! NOT AT ALL!
THE FACT THAT YOU CAN'T JUST BE A PRETTY DOLL IS PROOF THAT YOU REALLY DO LOVE HIM!
AND BECAUSE YOU WANT HIM TO LOVE YOU, YOU'LL DO WHATEVER YOU CAN!
YOU LOVE HIM, SO YOU CAN'T HELP IT.

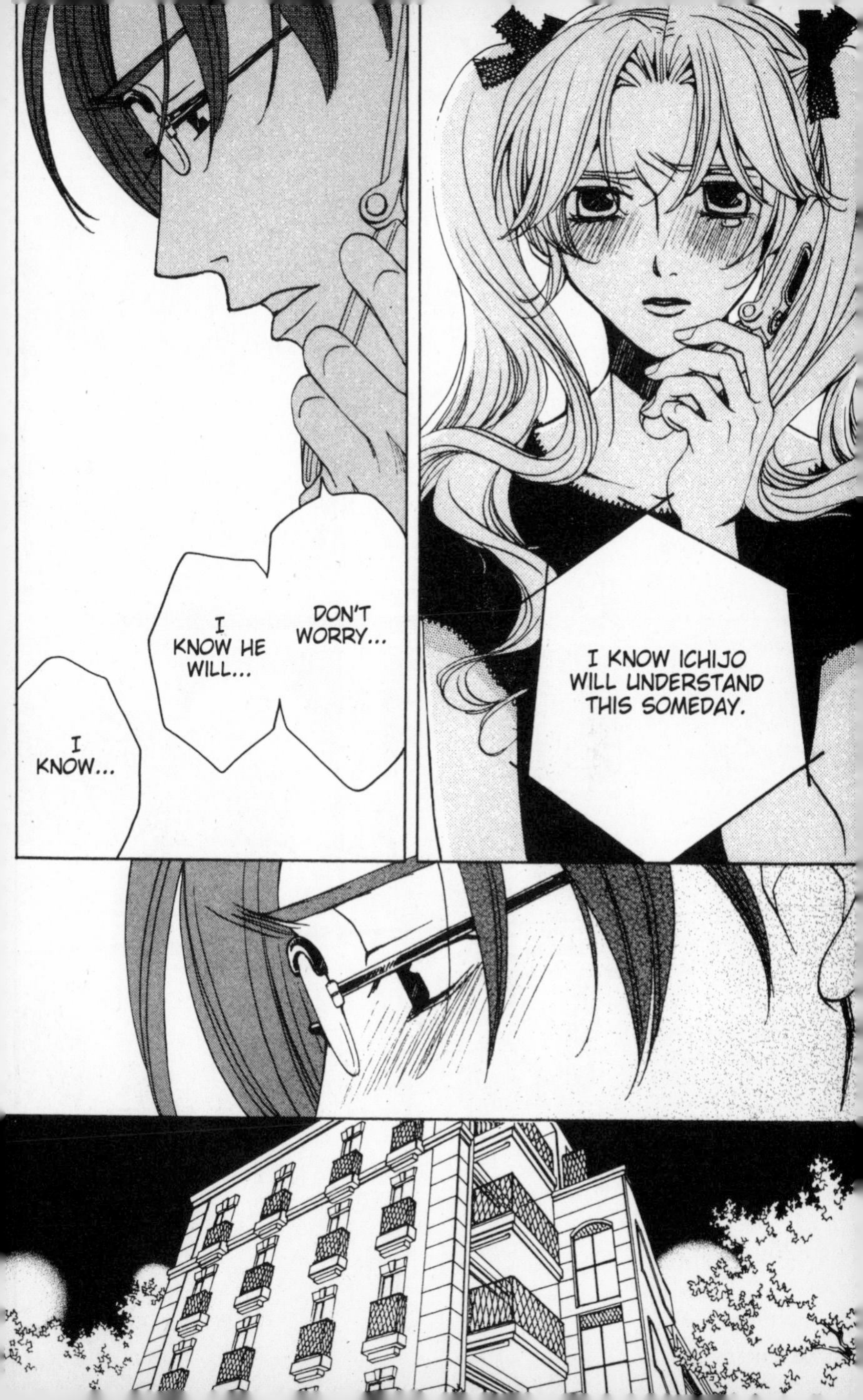
I KNOW ICHIJO WILL UNDERSTAND THIS SOMEDAY.
DON'T WORRY...
I KNOW HE WILL...
I KNOW...

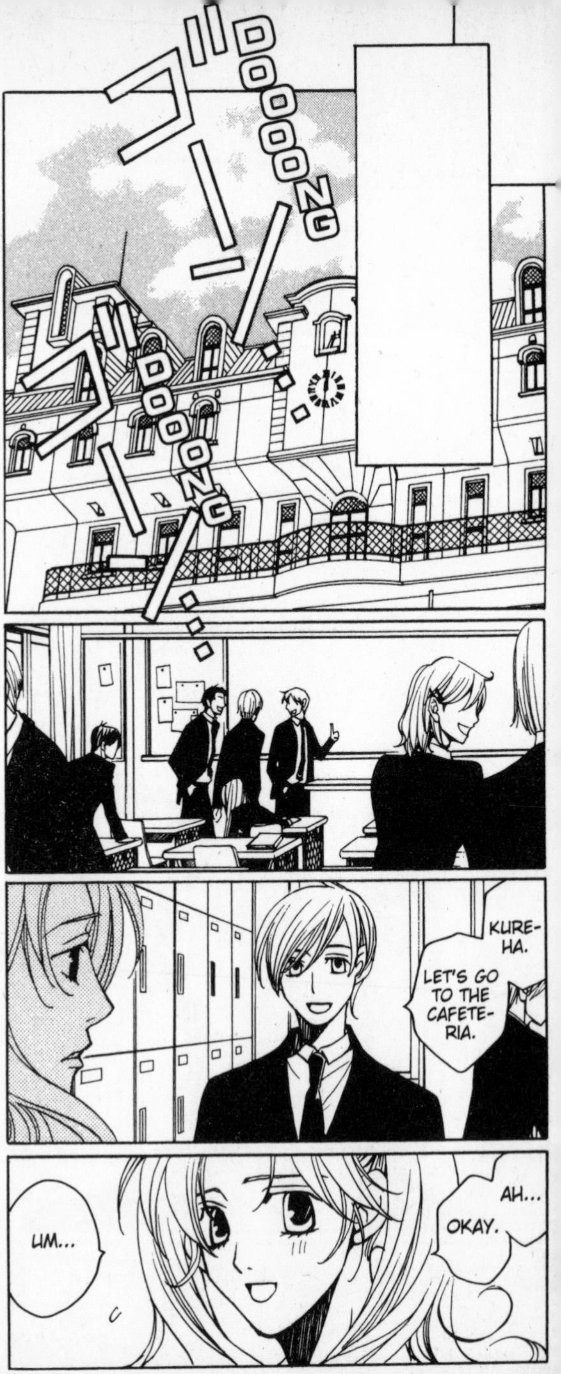
DOOOOONG
DOOONG
KURE-HA.
LET'S GO TO THE CAFETE-RIA.
AH... OKAY.
UM...

This is the earlier design of the bead cord. The middle bead was supported by metal fixtures modeled after cherry blossoms, because of the "graduation" theme...*

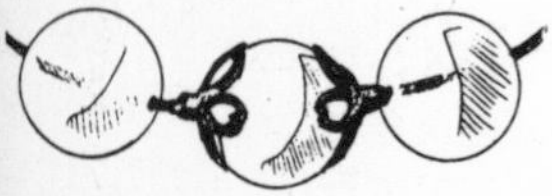

For some reason, that felt too Japanese, so I scrapped the idea... but the real reason was because I started thinking "this is gonna be a pain to have to draw in every panel..."

*SEE TRANSLATOR'S NOTES

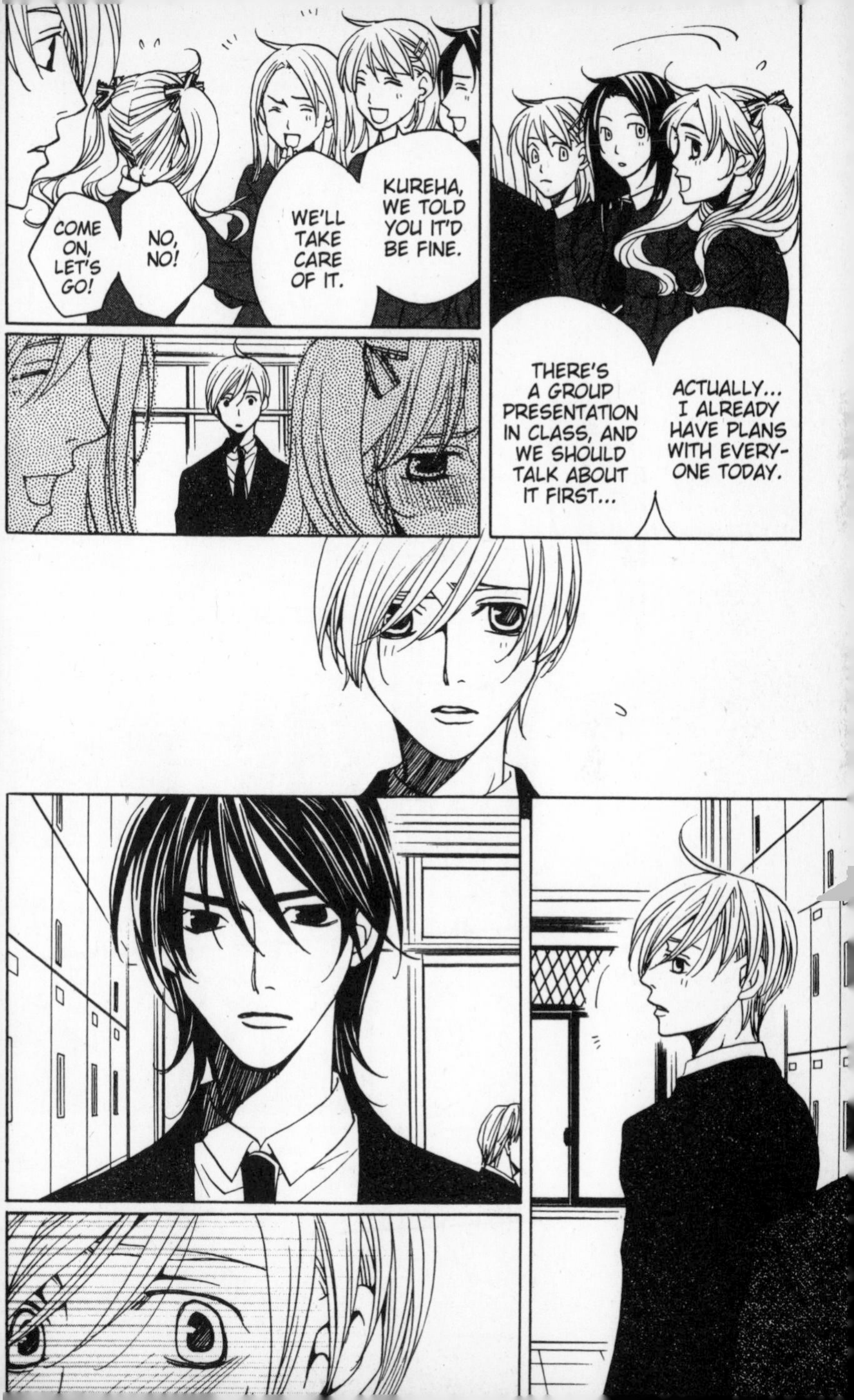

ACTUALLY... I ALREADY HAVE PLANS WITH EVERY-ONE TODAY.
THERE'S A GROUP PRESENTATION IN CLASS, AND WE SHOULD TALK ABOUT IT FIRST...
KUREHA, WE TOLD YOU IT'D BE FINE.
WE'LL TAKE CARE OF IT.
NO, NO!
COME ON, LET'S GO!

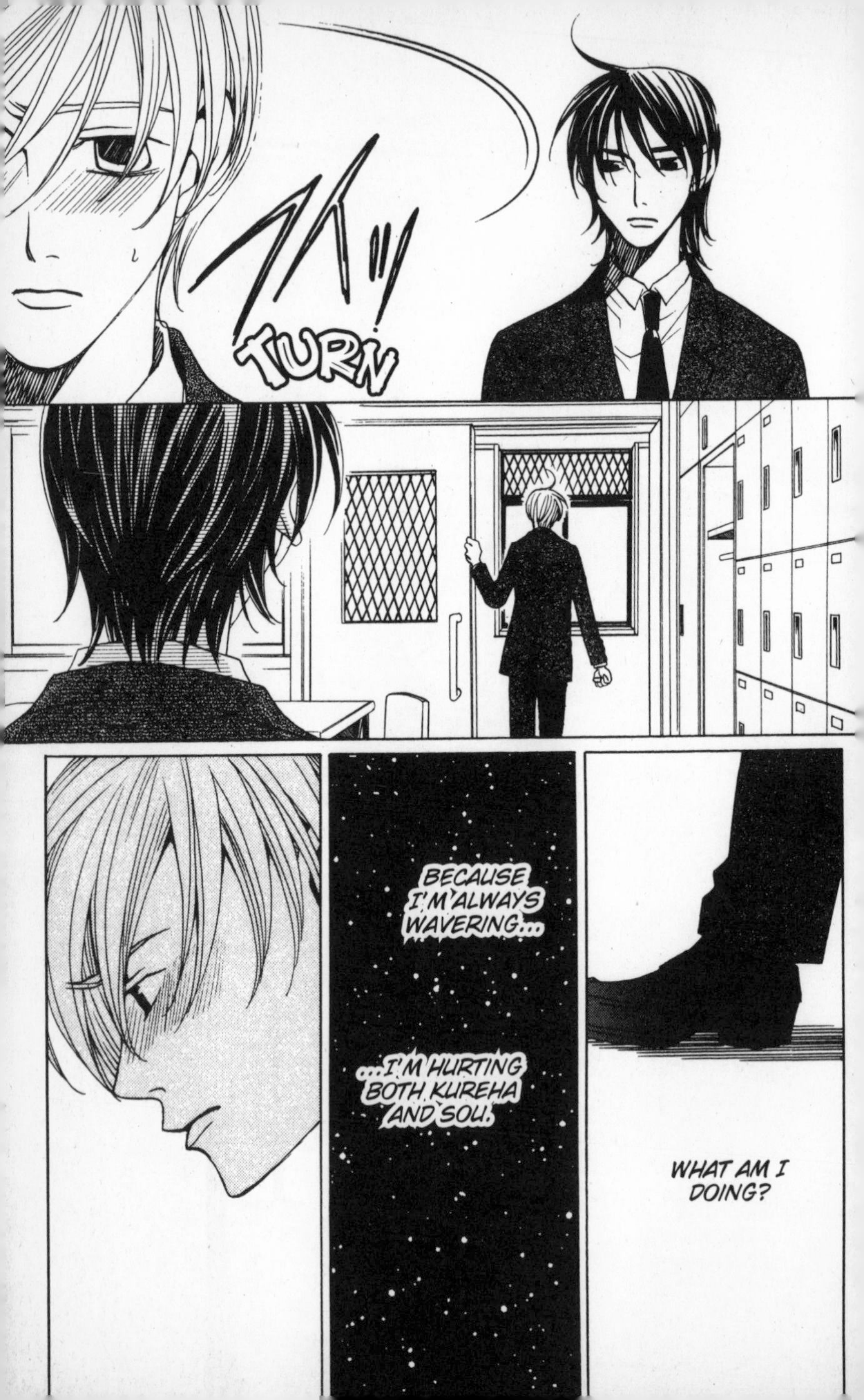
TURN
WHAT AM I DOING?
BECAUSE I'M ALWAYS WAVERING...
...I'M HURTING BOTH KUREHA AND SOU.

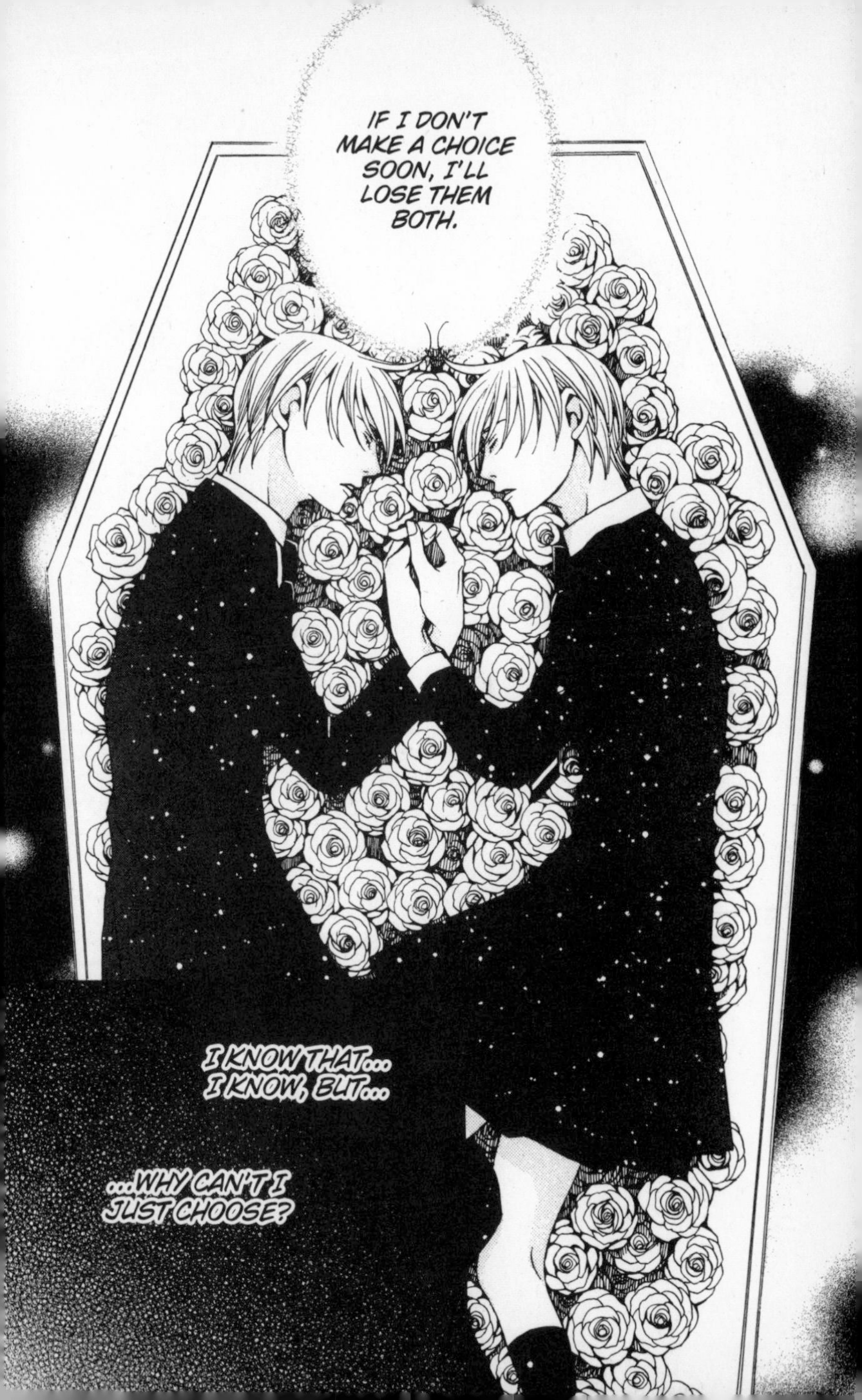
IF I DON'T MAKE A CHOICE SOON, I'LL LOSE THEM BOTH.
I KNOW THAT... I KNOW, BUT...
...WHY CAN'T I JUST CHOOSE?

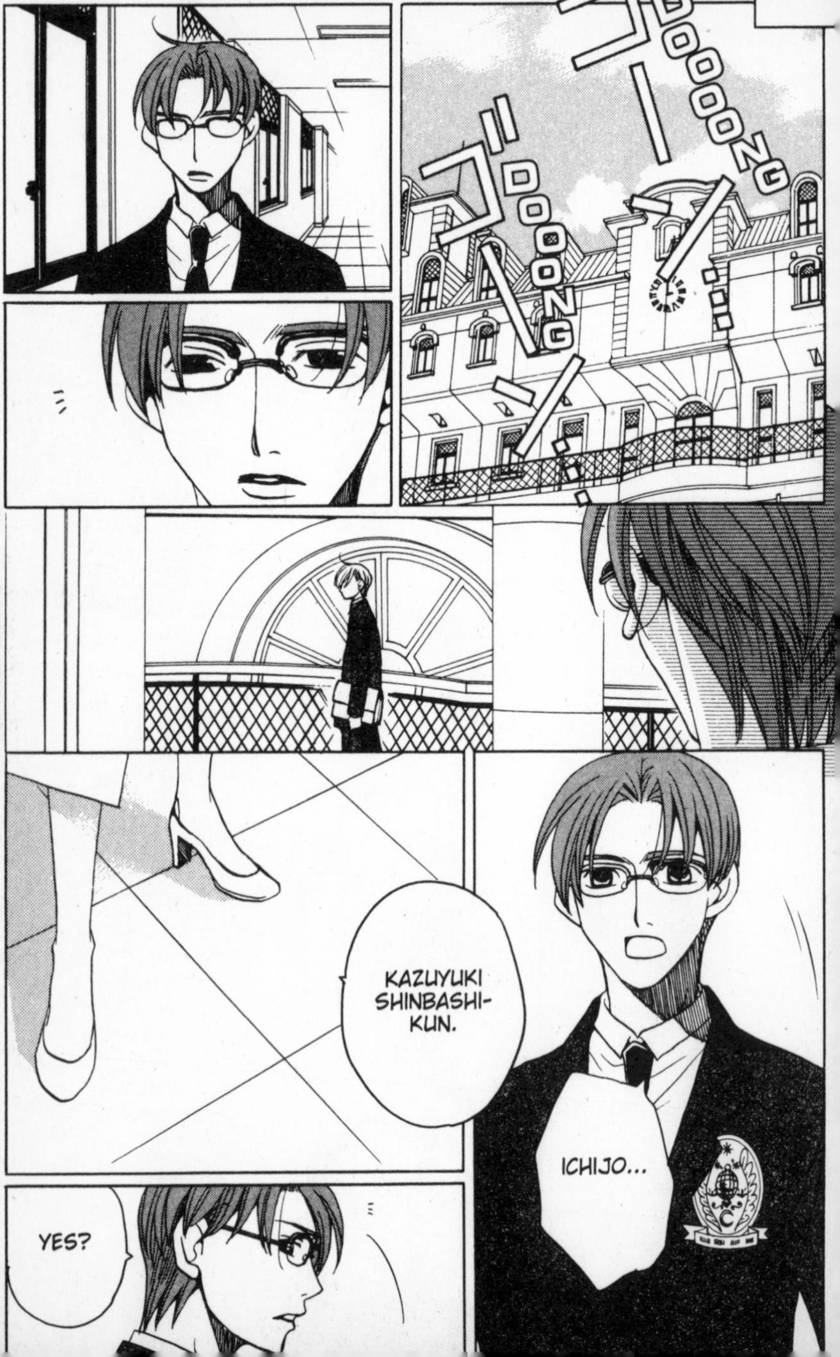
DOOOONG
DOOONG
ICHIJO...
KAZUYUKI SHINBASHI-KUN.
YES?

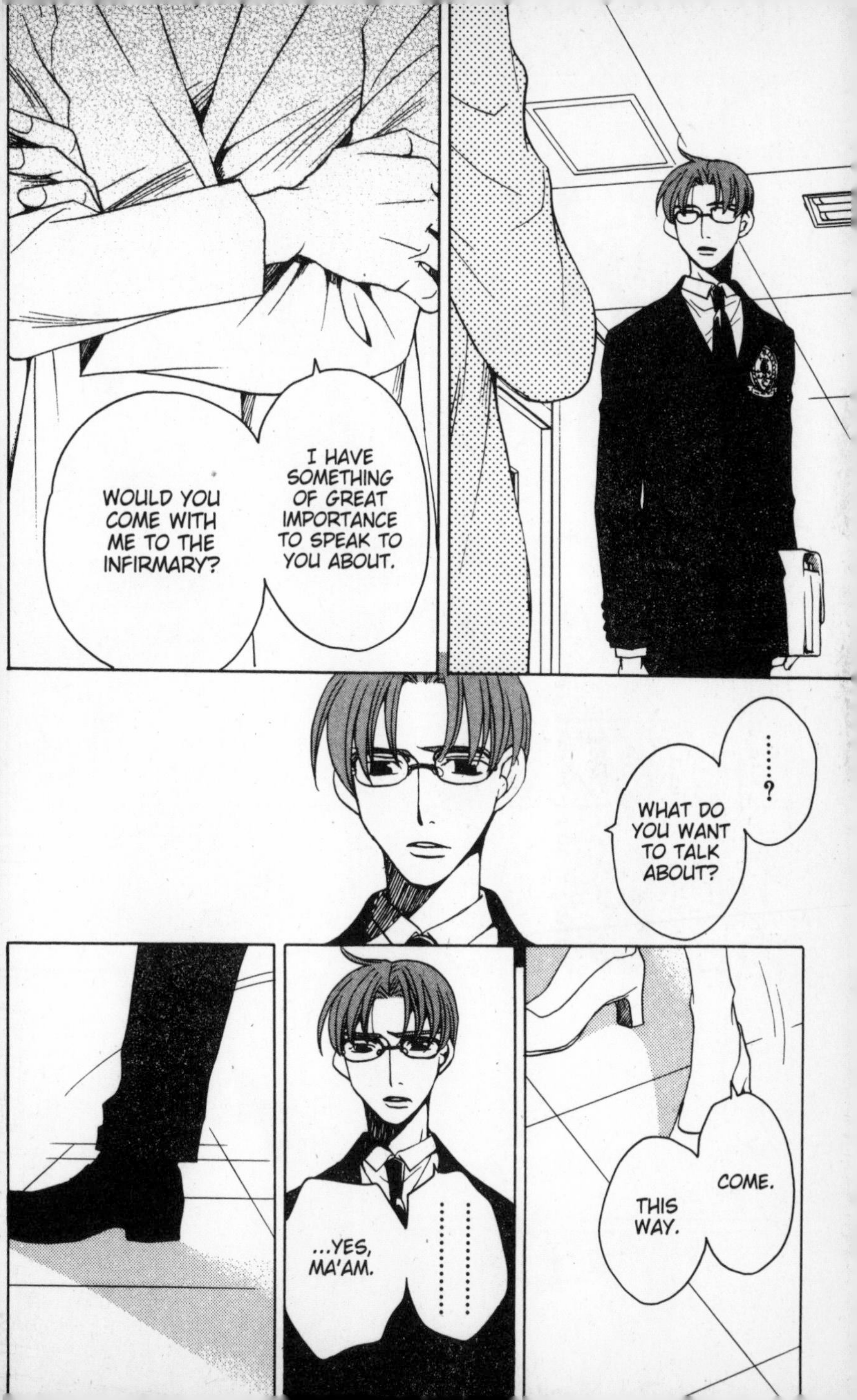
I HAVE SOMETHING OF GREAT IMPORTANCE TO SPEAK TO YOU ABOUT.
WOULD YOU COME WITH ME TO THE INFIRMARY?
......?
WHAT DO YOU WANT TO TALK ABOUT?
COME.
THIS WAY.
......
...YES, MA'AM.

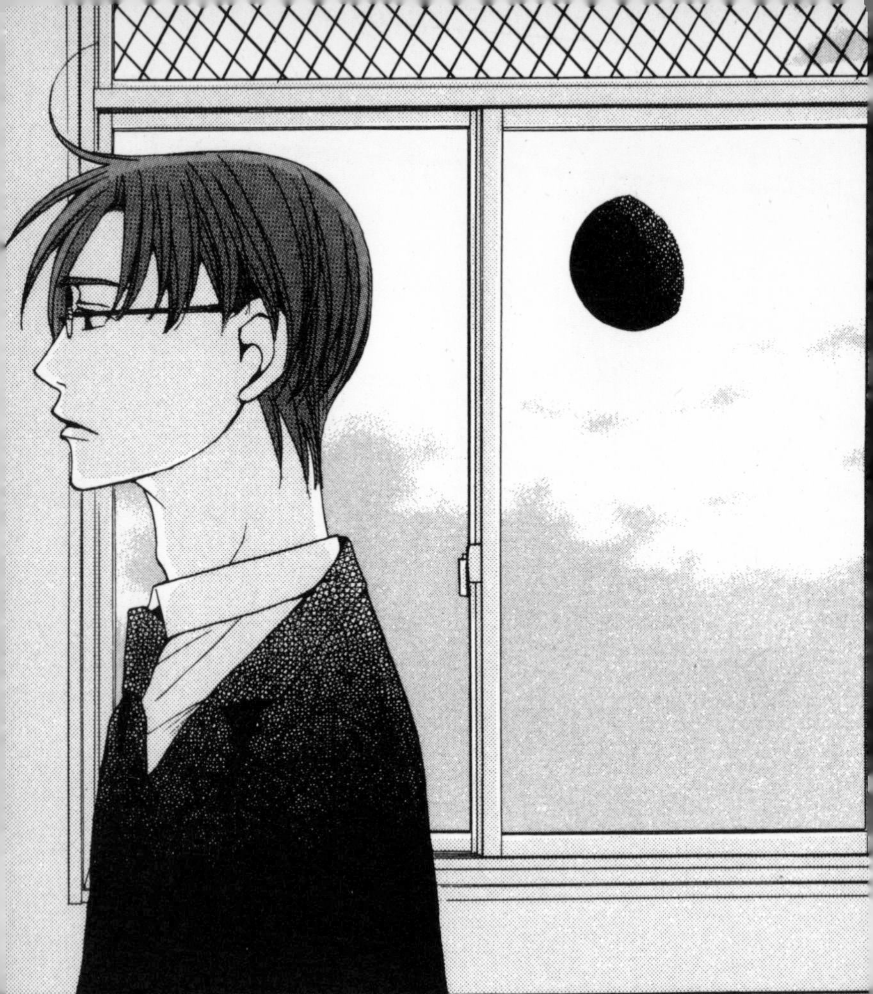
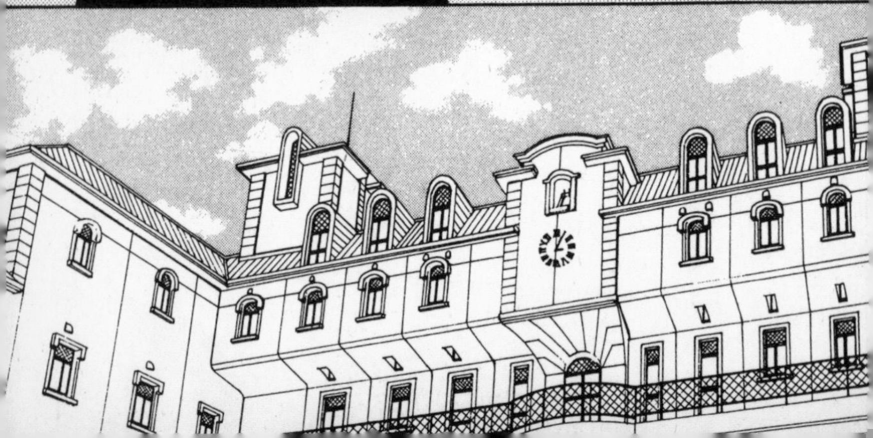

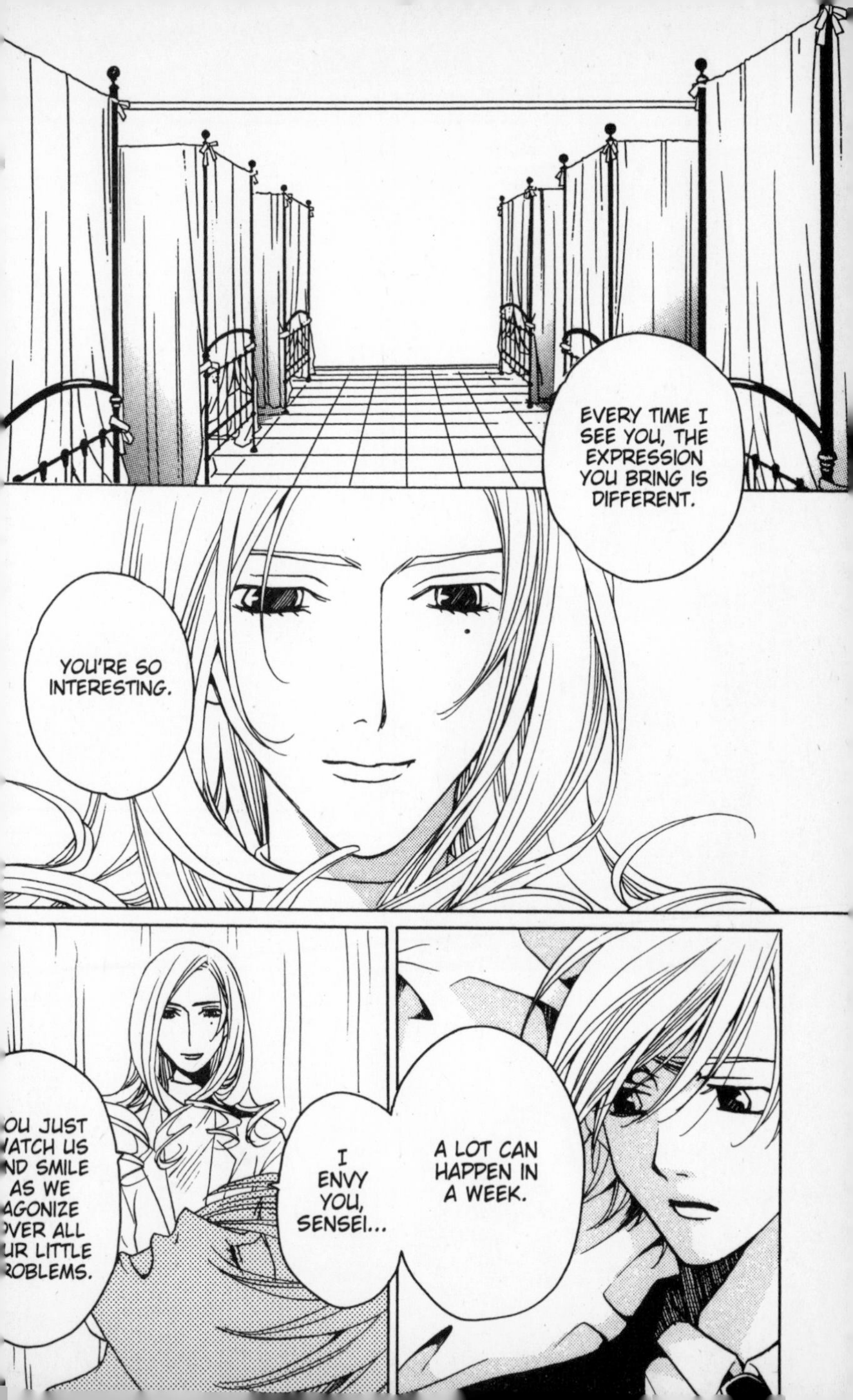
EVERY TIME I SEE YOU, THE EXPRESSION YOU BRING IS DIFFERENT.
YOU'RE SO INTERESTING.
A LOT CAN HAPPEN IN A WEEK.
I ENVY YOU, SENSEI...
OU JUST ATCH US ND SMILE AS WE AGONIZE VER ALL UR LITTLE ROBLEMS.

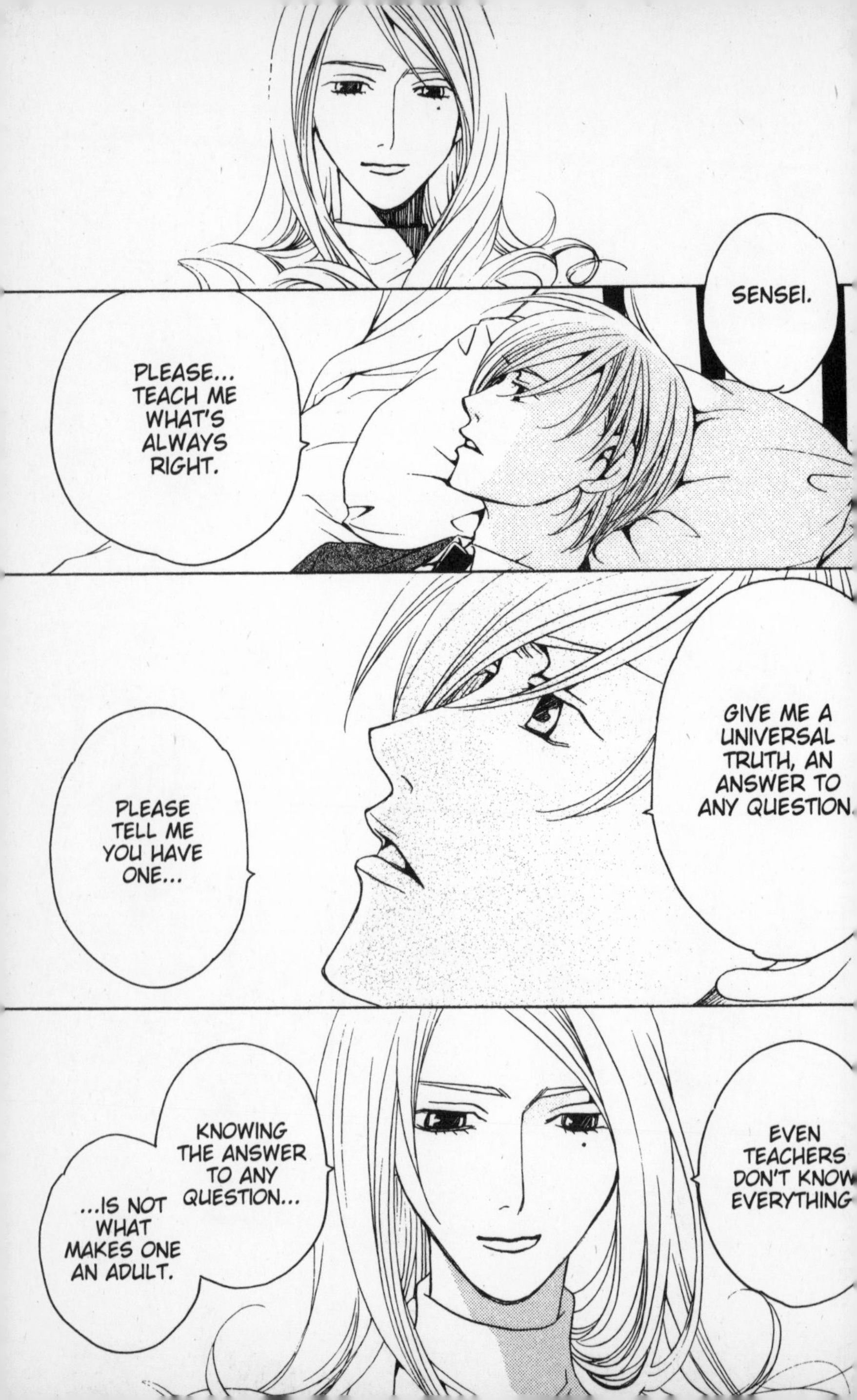
SENSEI.
PLEASE... TEACH ME WHAT'S ALWAYS RIGHT.
GIVE ME A UNIVERSAL TRUTH, AN ANSWER TO ANY QUESTION.
PLEASE TELL ME YOU HAVE ONE...
EVEN TEACHERS DON'T KNOW EVERYTHING
KNOWING THE ANSWER TO ANY QUESTION...
...IS NOT WHAT MAKES ONE AN ADULT.

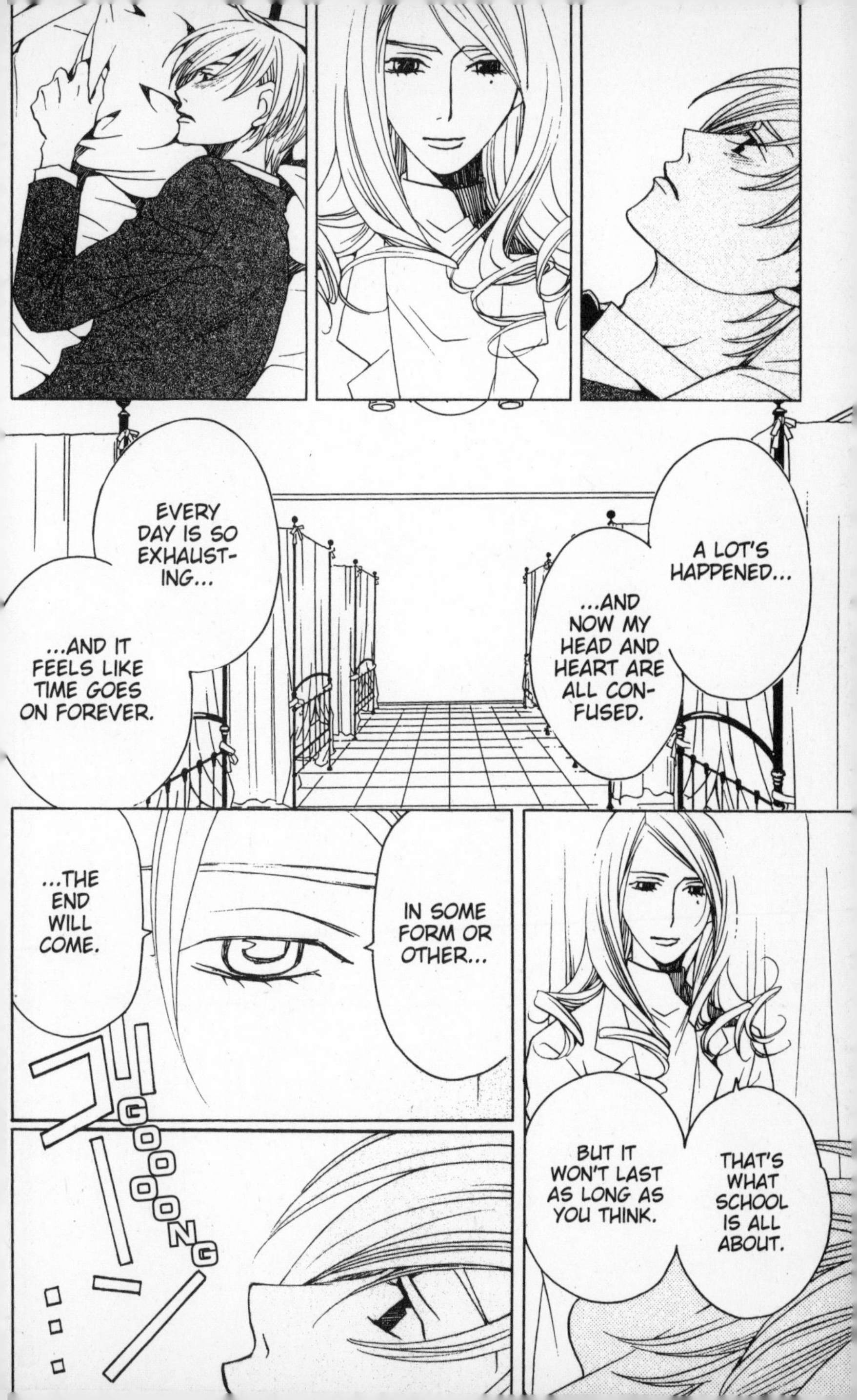
A LOT'S HAPPENED...
...AND NOW MY HEAD AND HEART ARE ALL CON-FUSED.
EVERY DAY IS SO EXHAUST-ING...
...AND IT FEELS LIKE TIME GOES ON FOREVER.
THAT'S WHAT SCHOOL IS ALL ABOUT.
BUT IT WON'T LAST AS LONG AS YOU THINK.
IN SOME FORM OR OTHER...
...THE END WILL COME.
GOOOONG

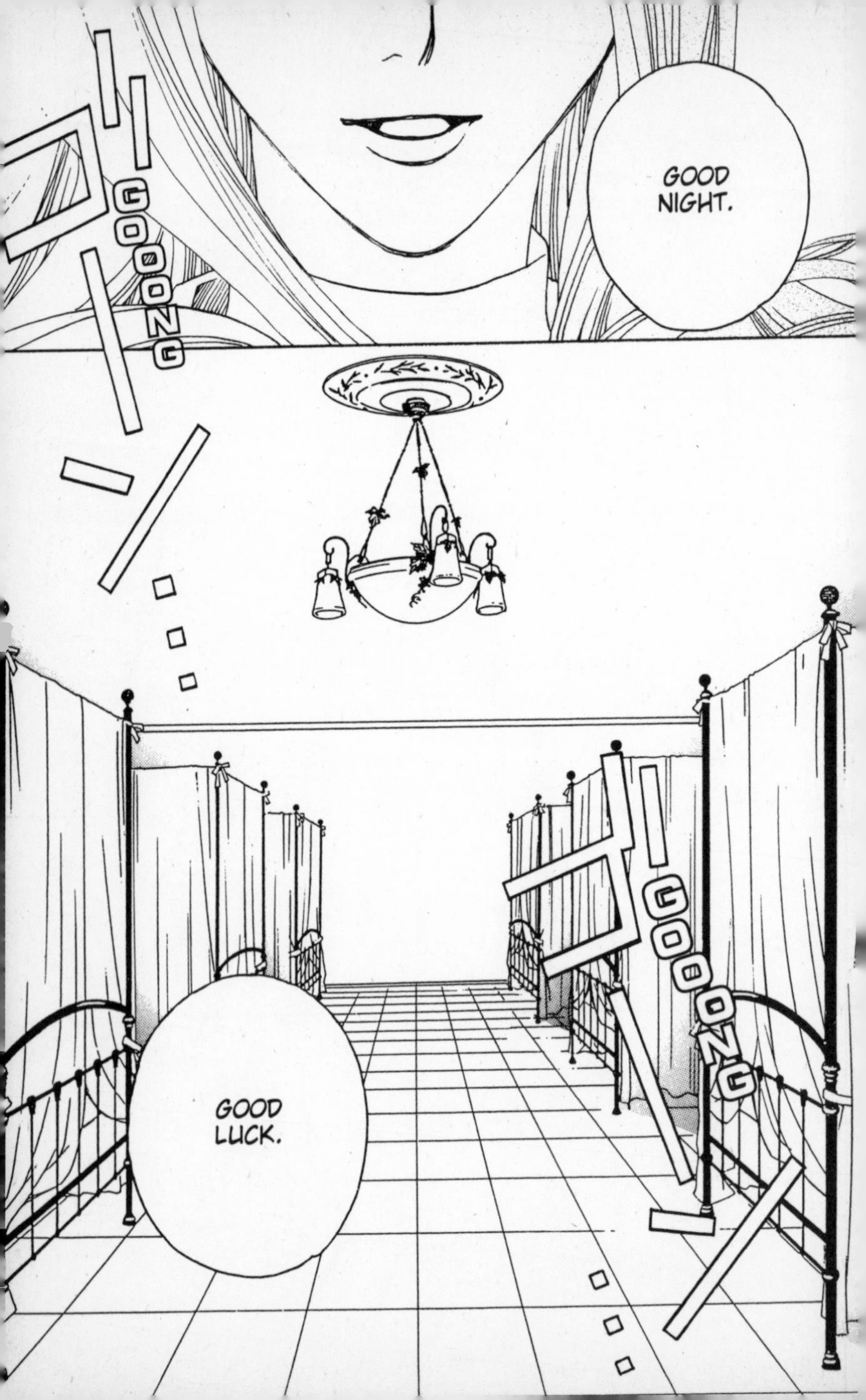
GOOD NIGHT.
GOOONG
GOOD LUCK.
GOOONG

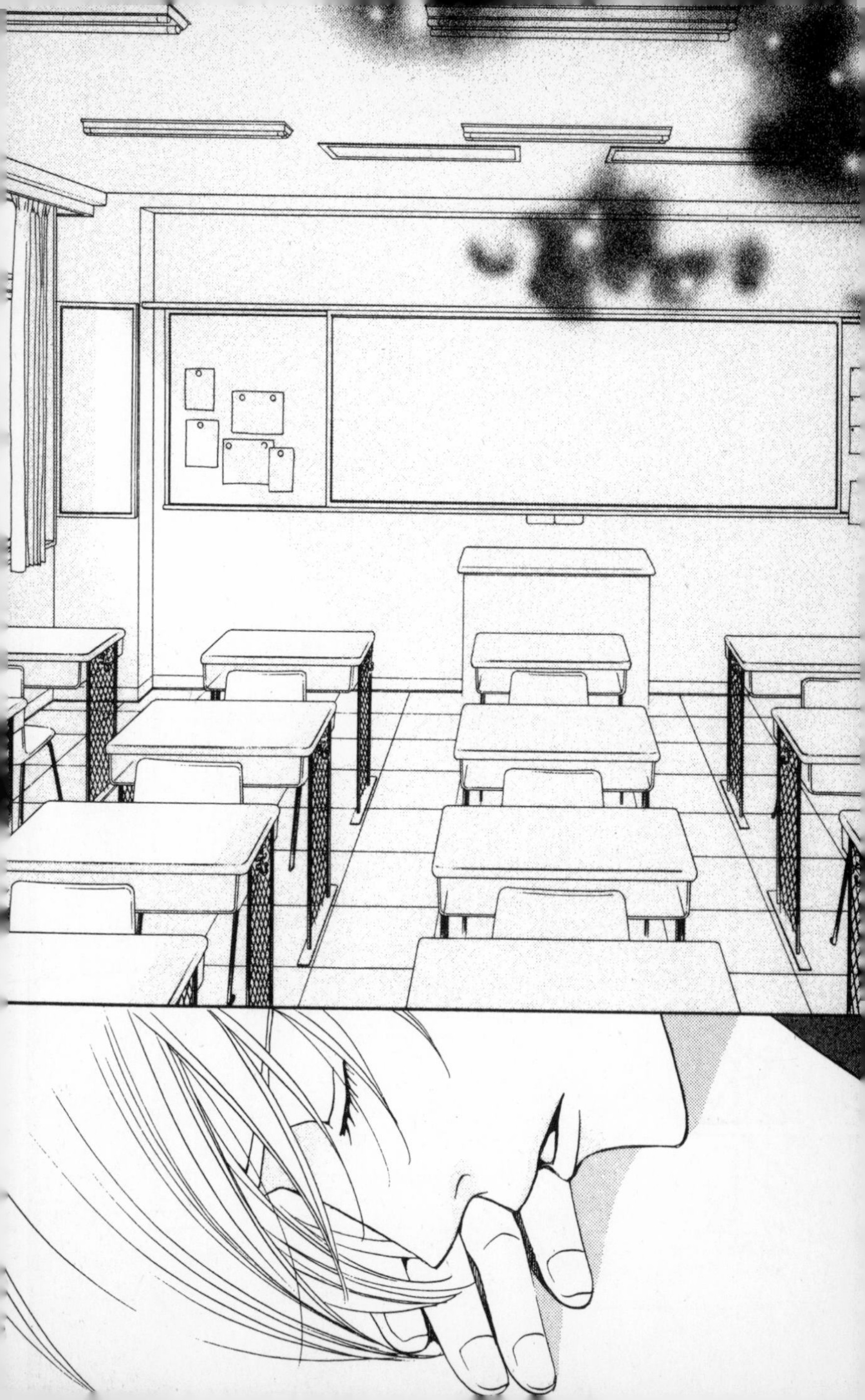

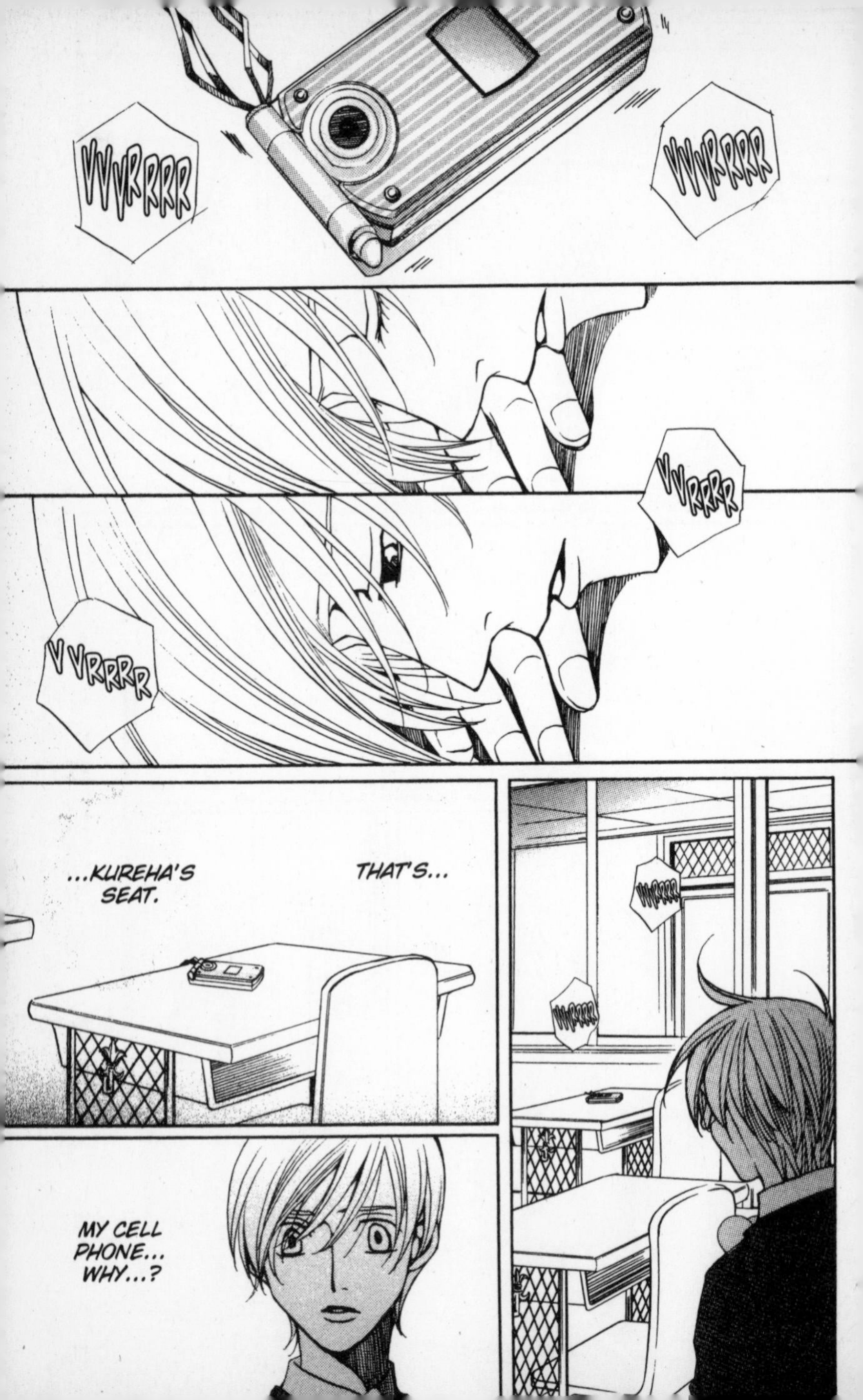
VVVRRRR
VVVRRRR
VVRRRR
VVRRRR
VVVRRRR
VVVRRRR
THAT'S...
...KUREHA'S SEAT.
MY CELL PHONE... WHY...?

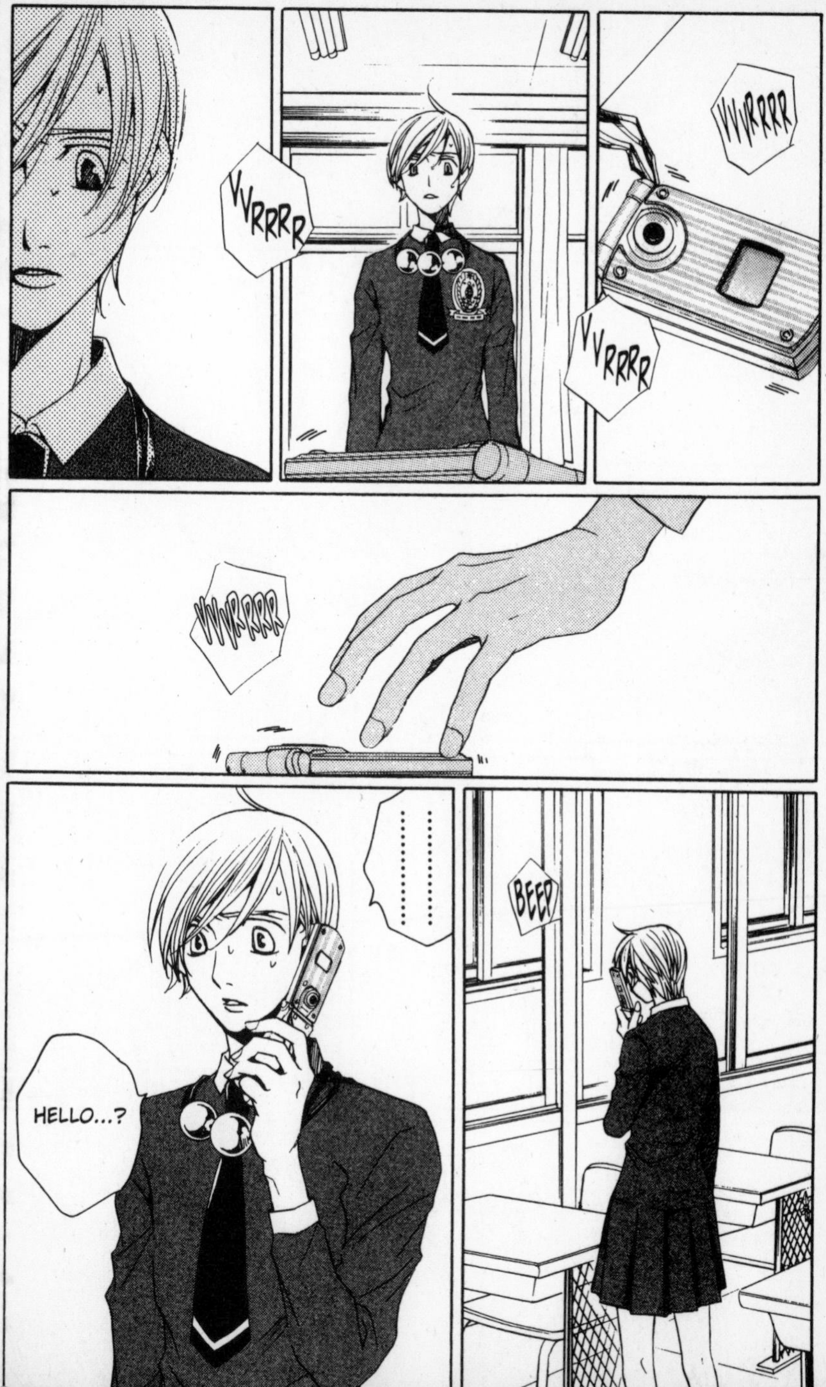

VVVRRRR
VVRRRR
VVRRRR
VVVRRRR
BEEP
......
HELLO...?

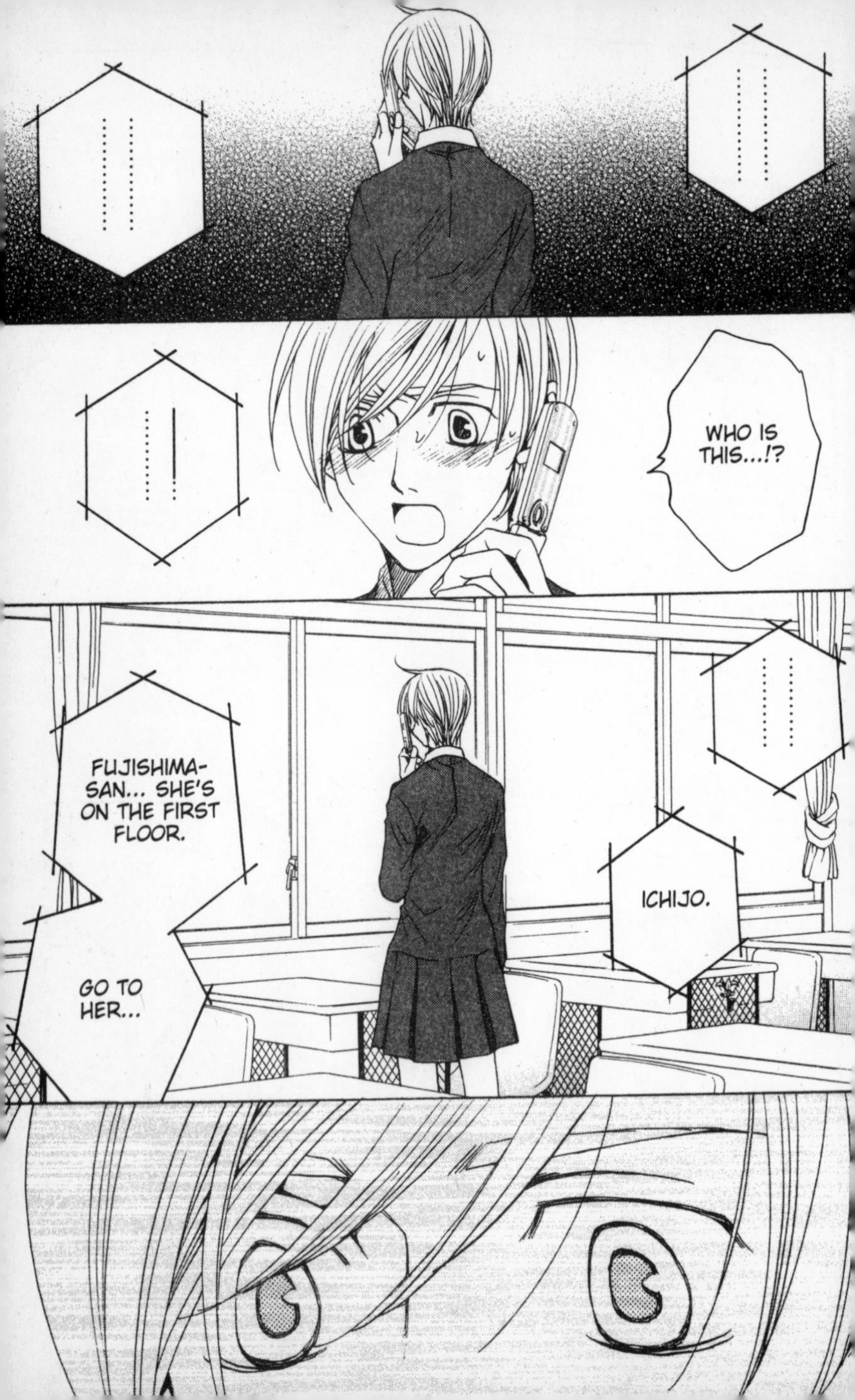
......
......
WHO IS THIS...!?
......!
......
ICHIJO.
FUJISHIMA-SAN... SHE'S ON THE FIRST FLOOR.
GO TO HER...

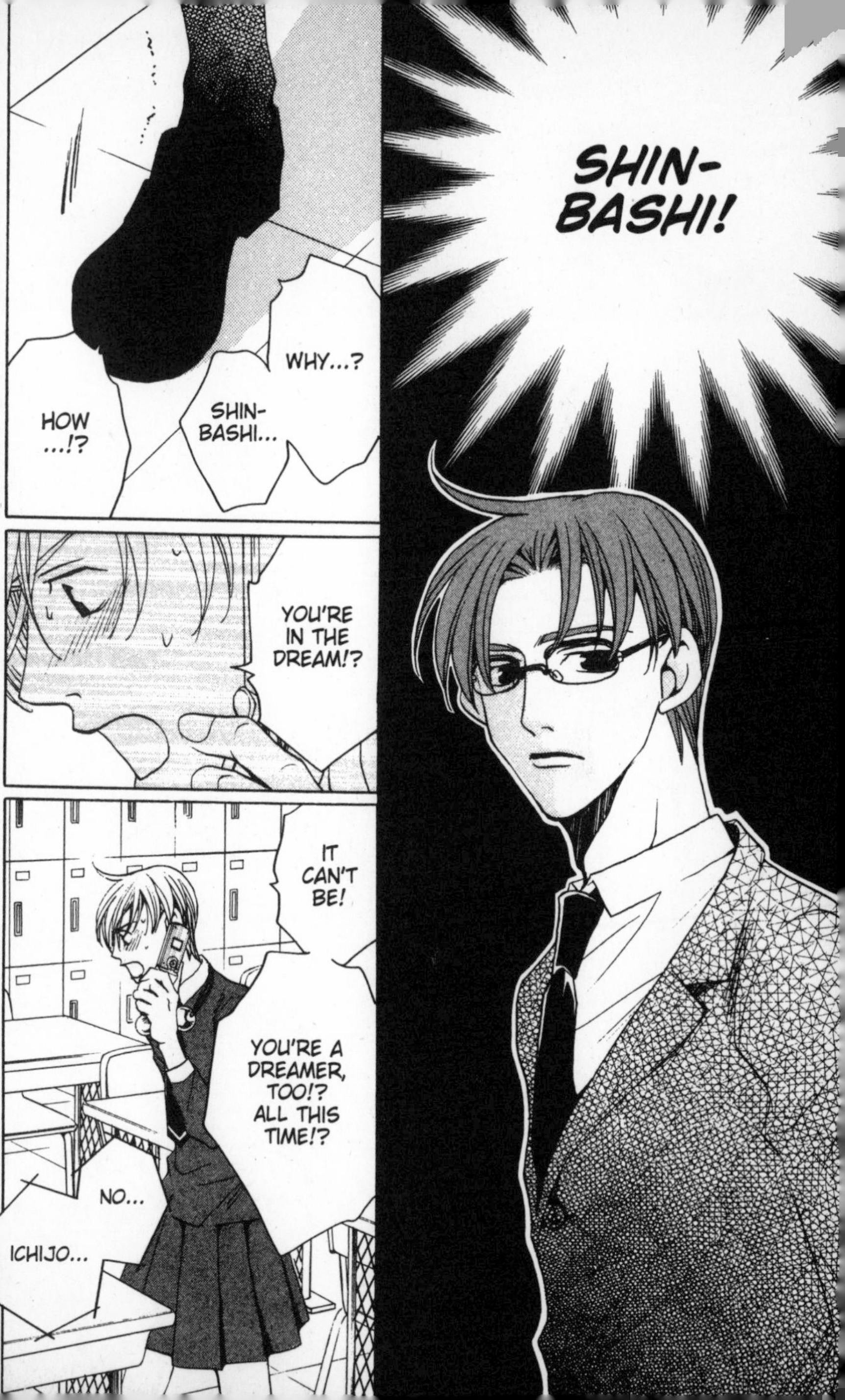
SHIN-BASHI!
WHY...?
SHIN-BASHI...
HOW ...!?
YOU'RE IN THE DREAM!?
IT CAN'T BE!
YOU'RE A DREAMER, TOO!? ALL THIS TIME!?
NO...
ICHIJO...

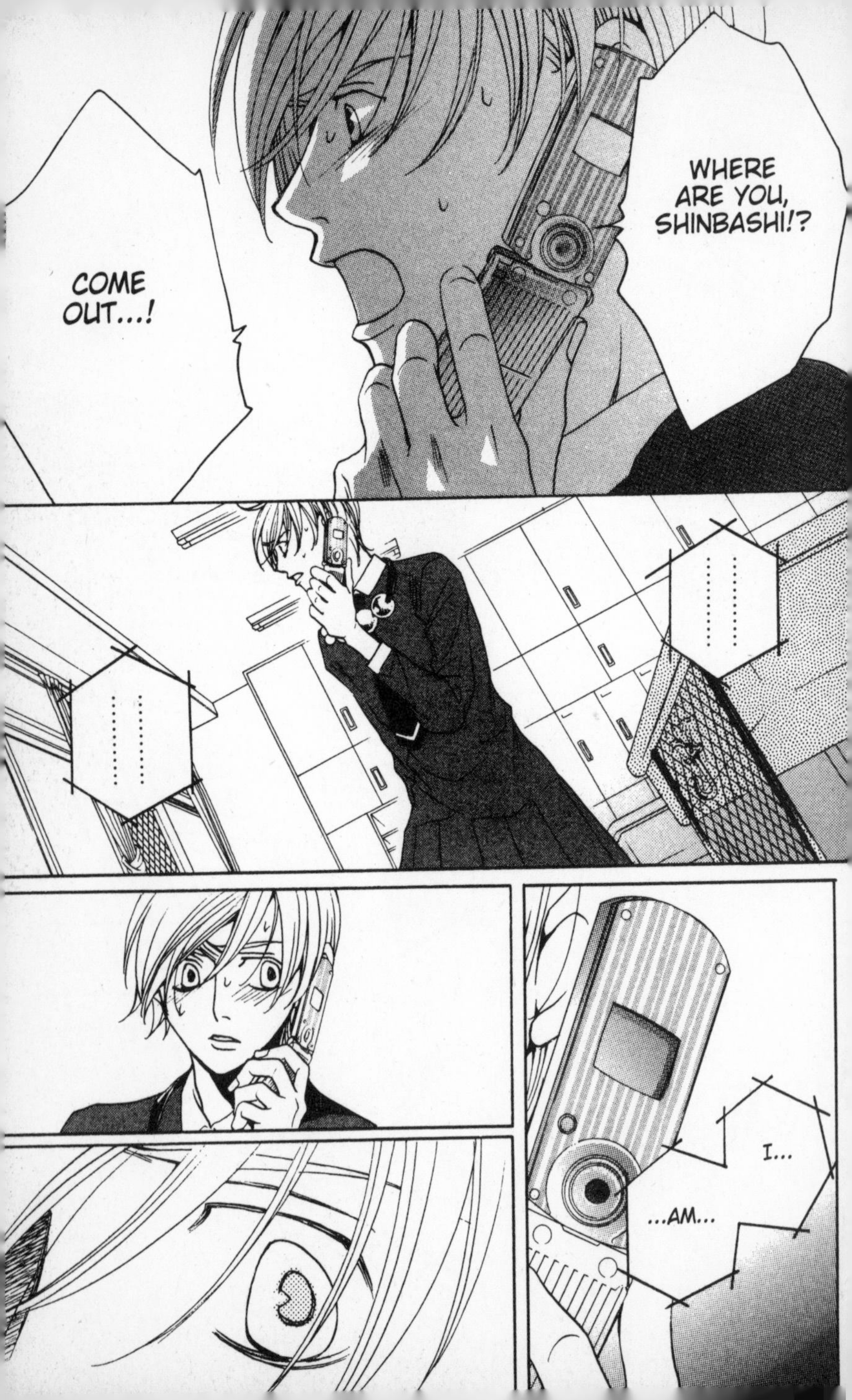
WHERE ARE YOU, SHINBASHI!?
COME OUT...!
I...
...AM...

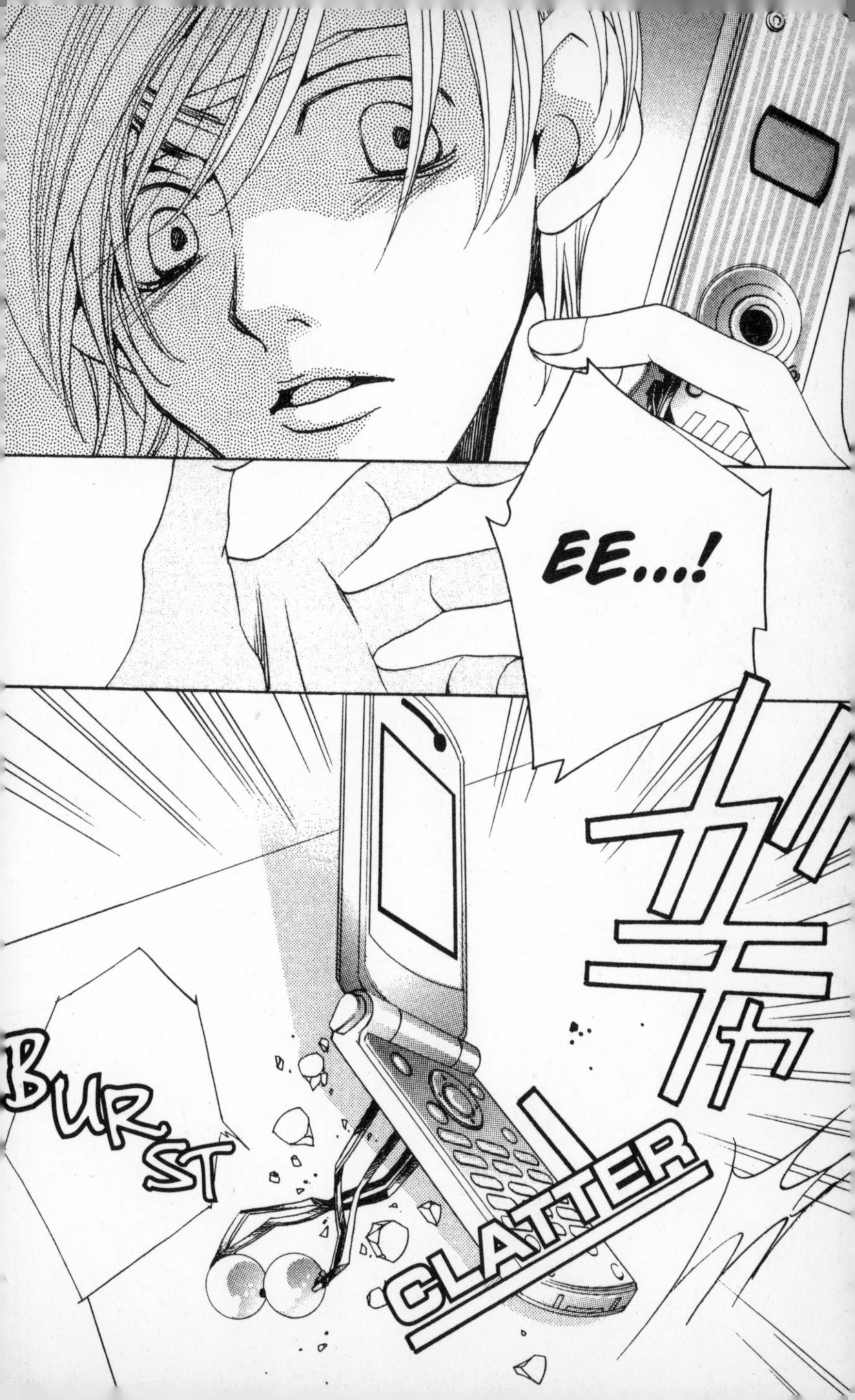
EE...!
BURST
CLATTER

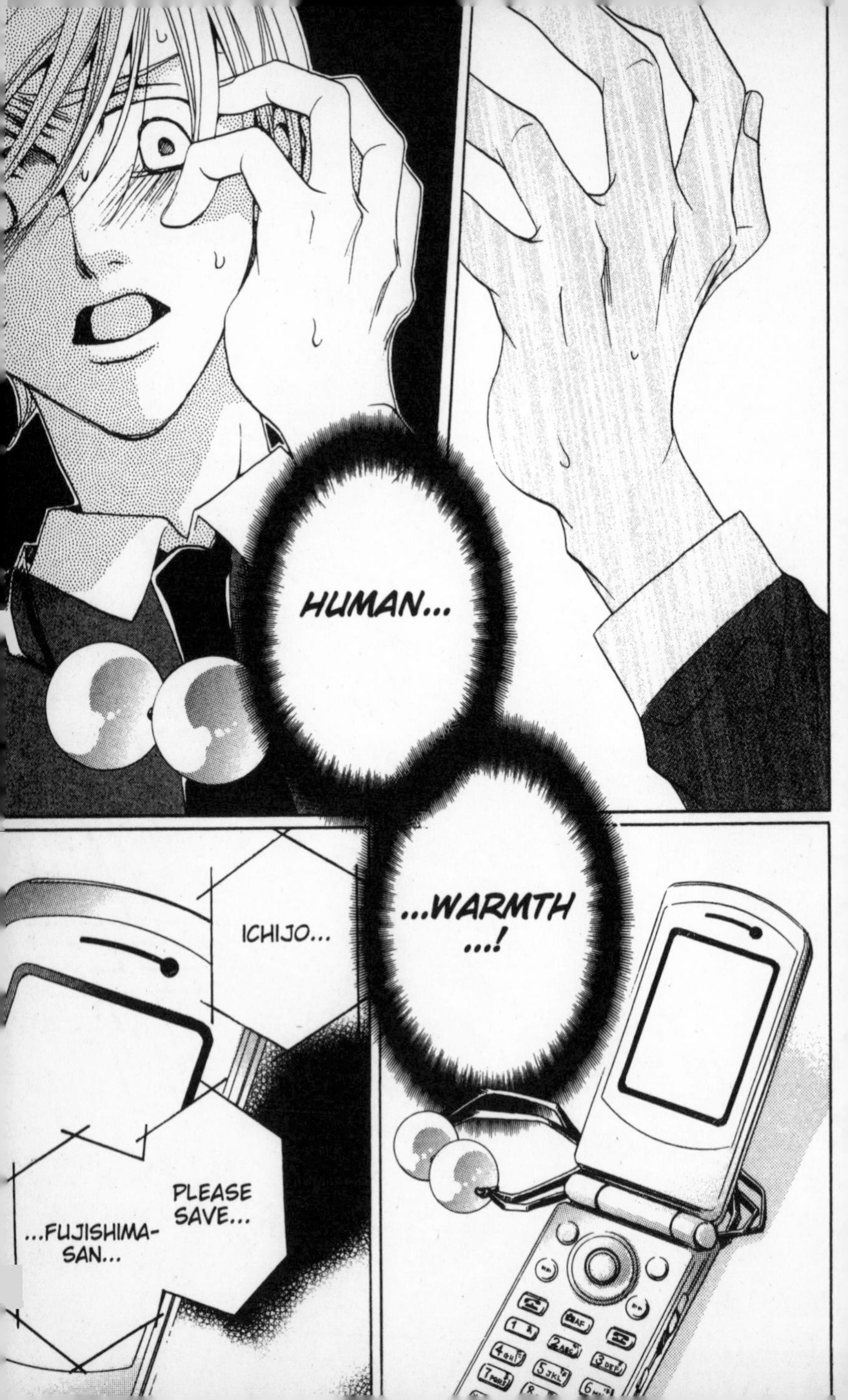
HUMAN...
...WARMTH ...!
ICHIJO...
PLEASE SAVE...
...FUJISHIMA-SAN...

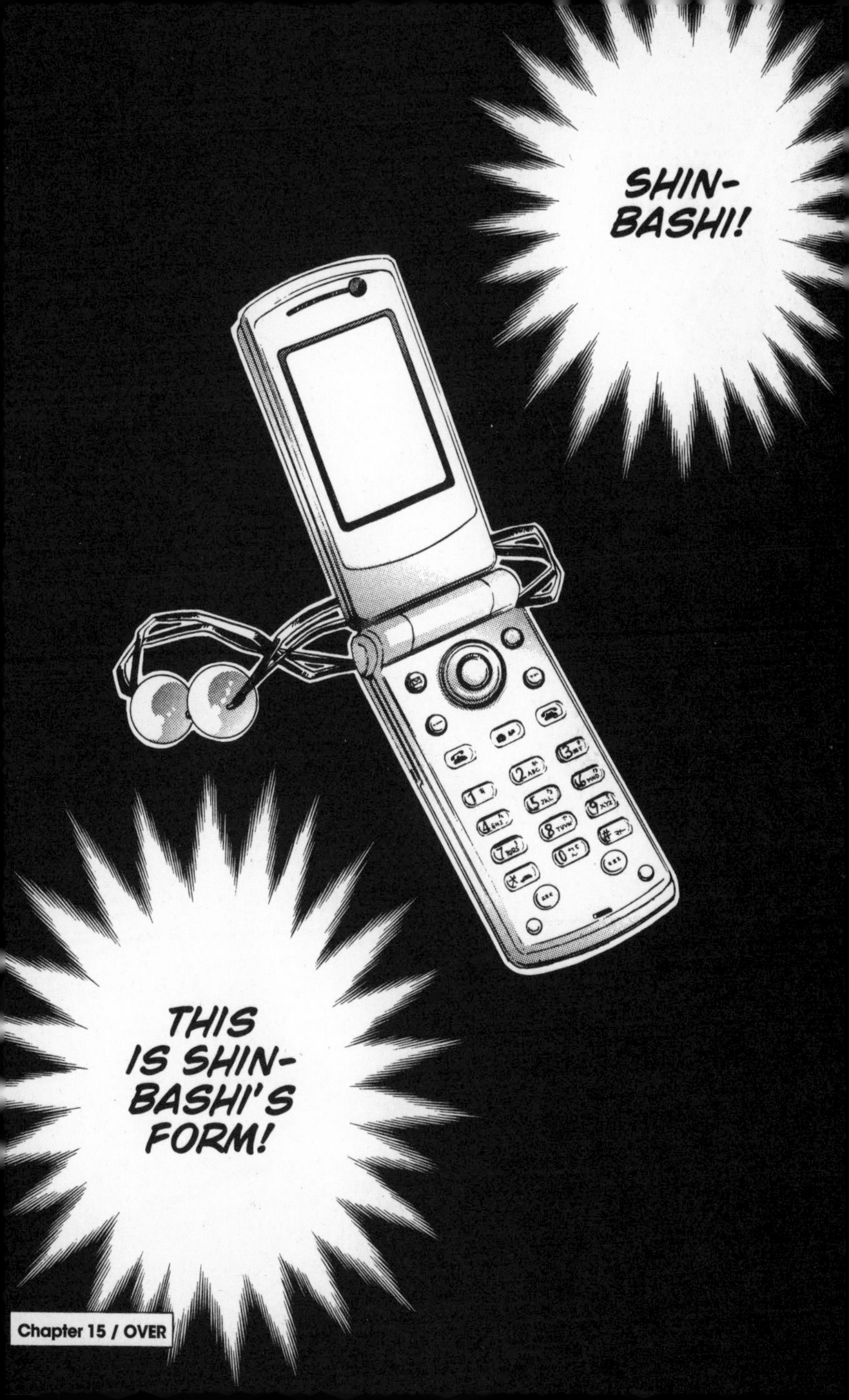
SHIN-BASHI!
THIS IS SHIN-BASHI'S FORM!

Chapter 15 / OVER

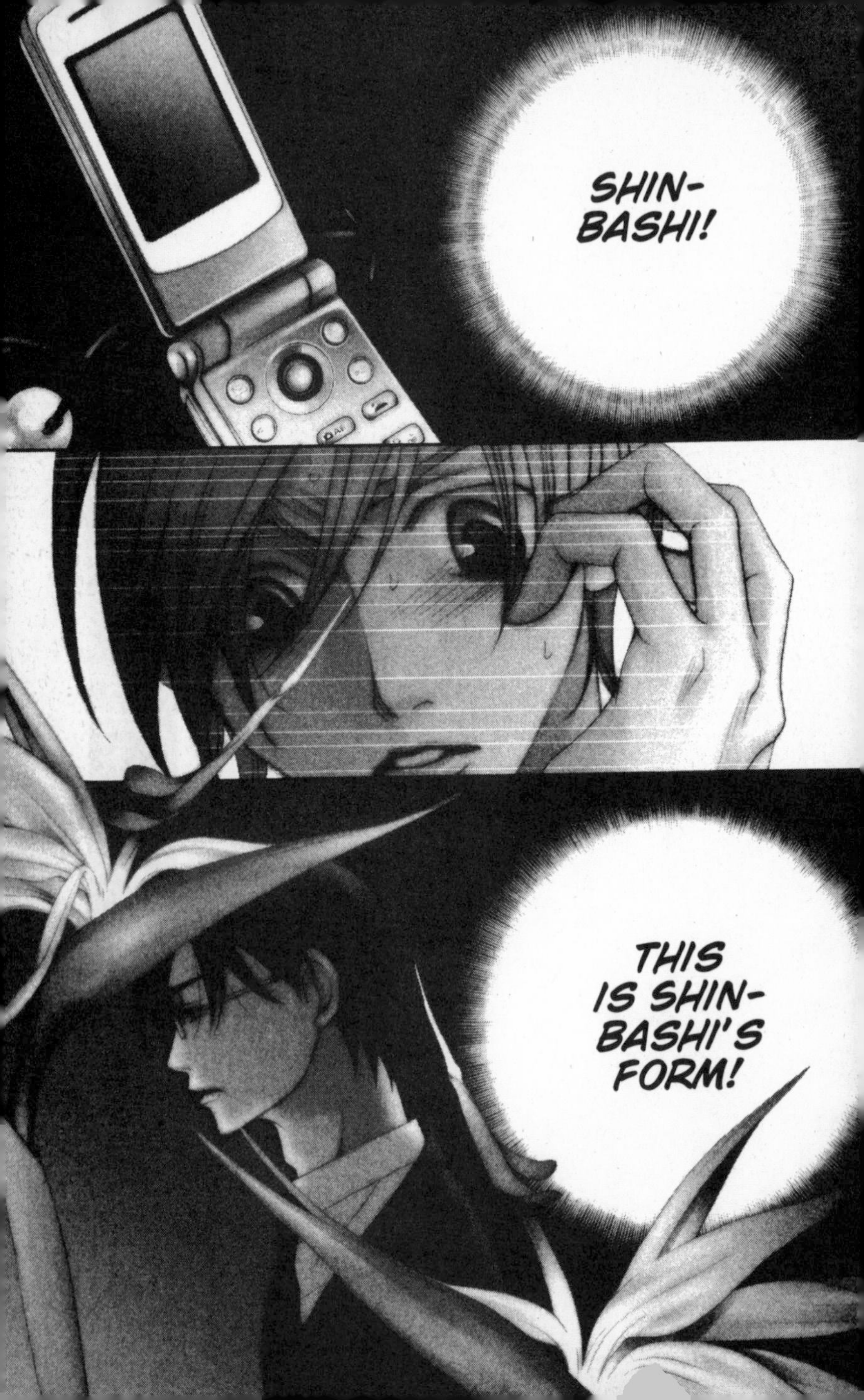
SHIN-
BASHI!
THIS
IS SHIN-
BASHI'S
FORM!

AFTER SCHOOL NIGHTMARE Chapter 16

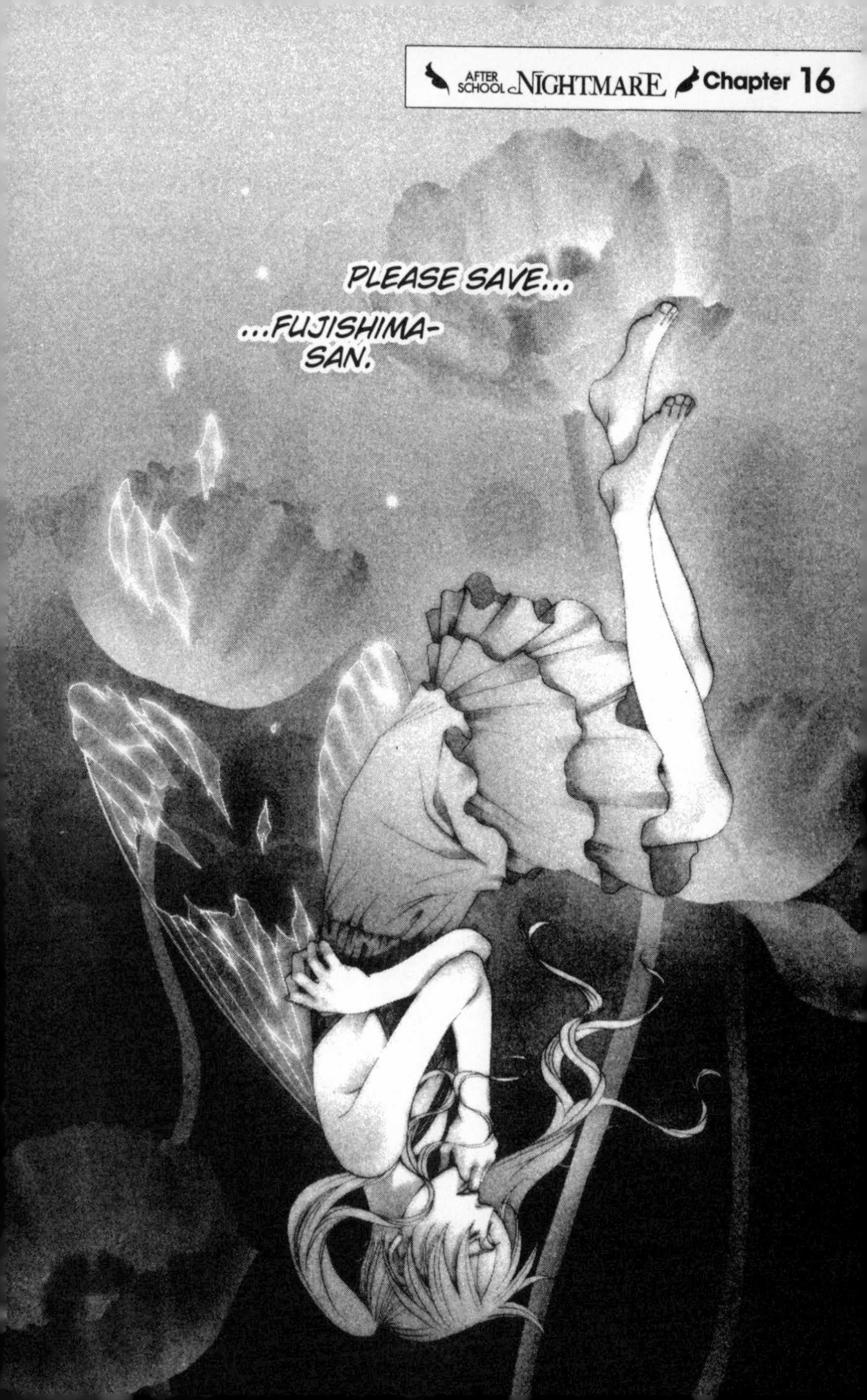
PLEASE SAVE...
...FUJISHIMA-SAN.

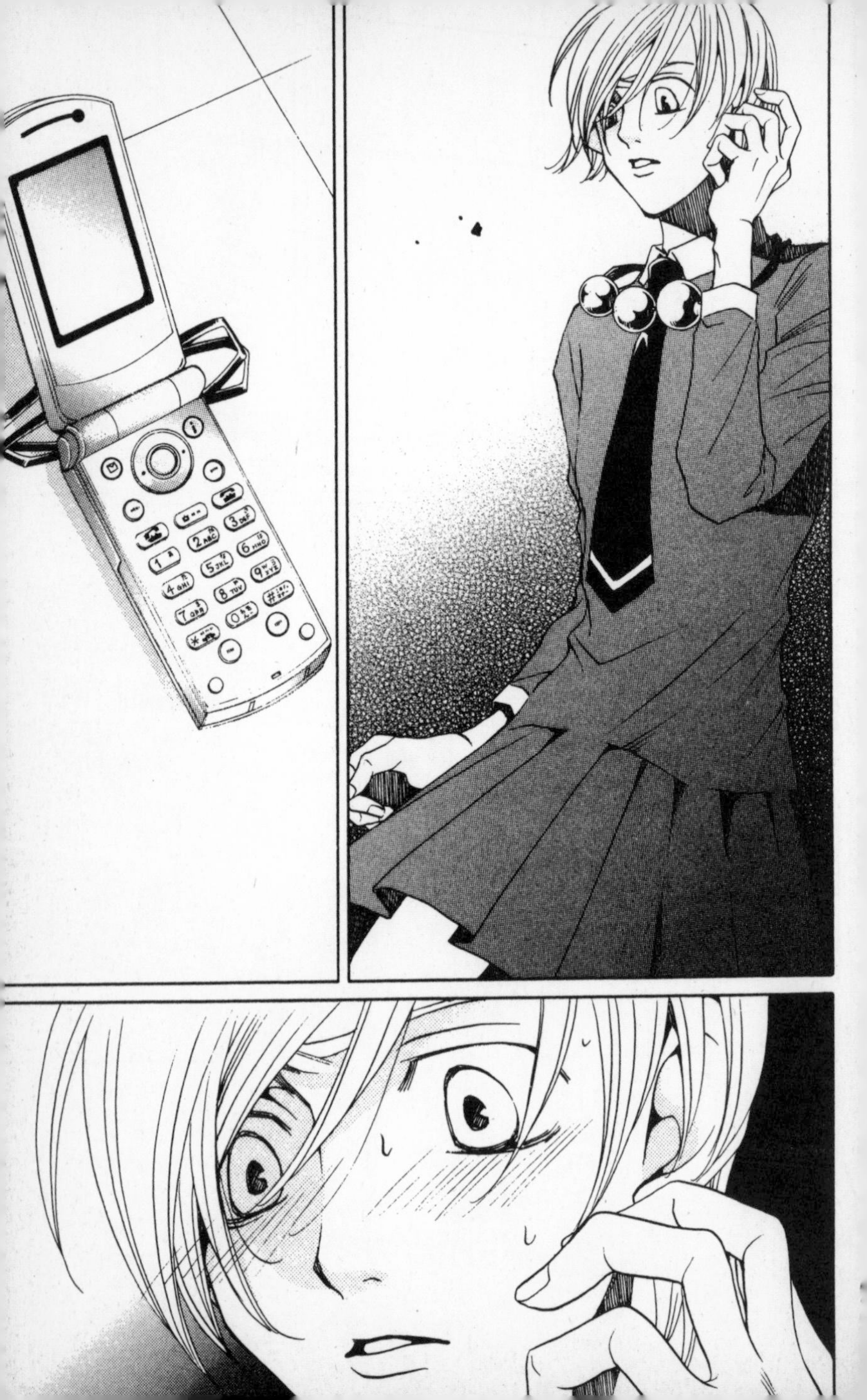

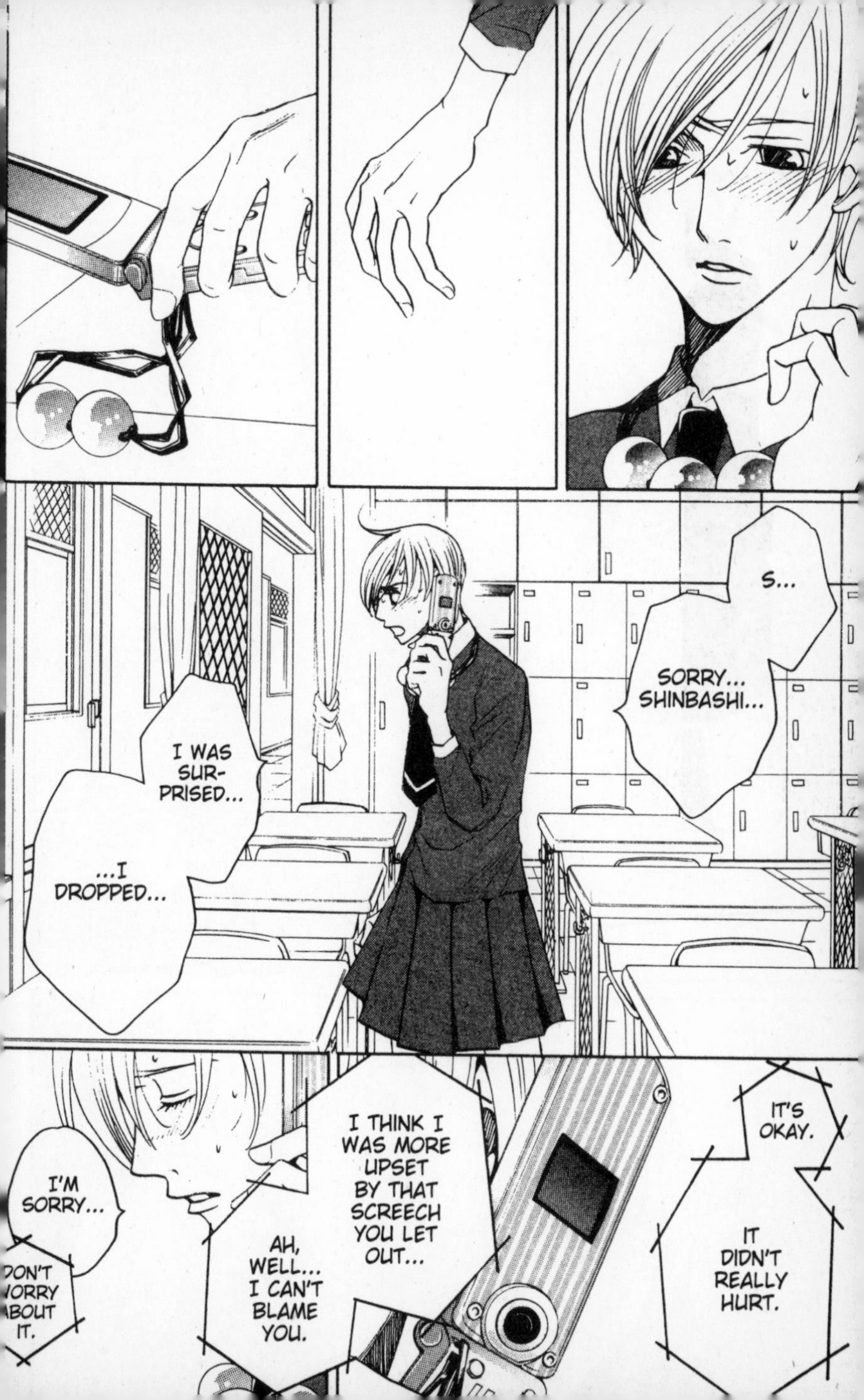
S...
SORRY... SHINBASHI...
I WAS SUR-PRISED...
...I DROPPED...
IT'S OKAY.
IT DIDN'T REALLY HURT.
I THINK I WAS MORE UPSET BY THAT SCREECH YOU LET OUT...
AH, WELL... I CAN'T BLAME YOU.
I'M SORRY...
DON'T WORRY ABOUT IT.

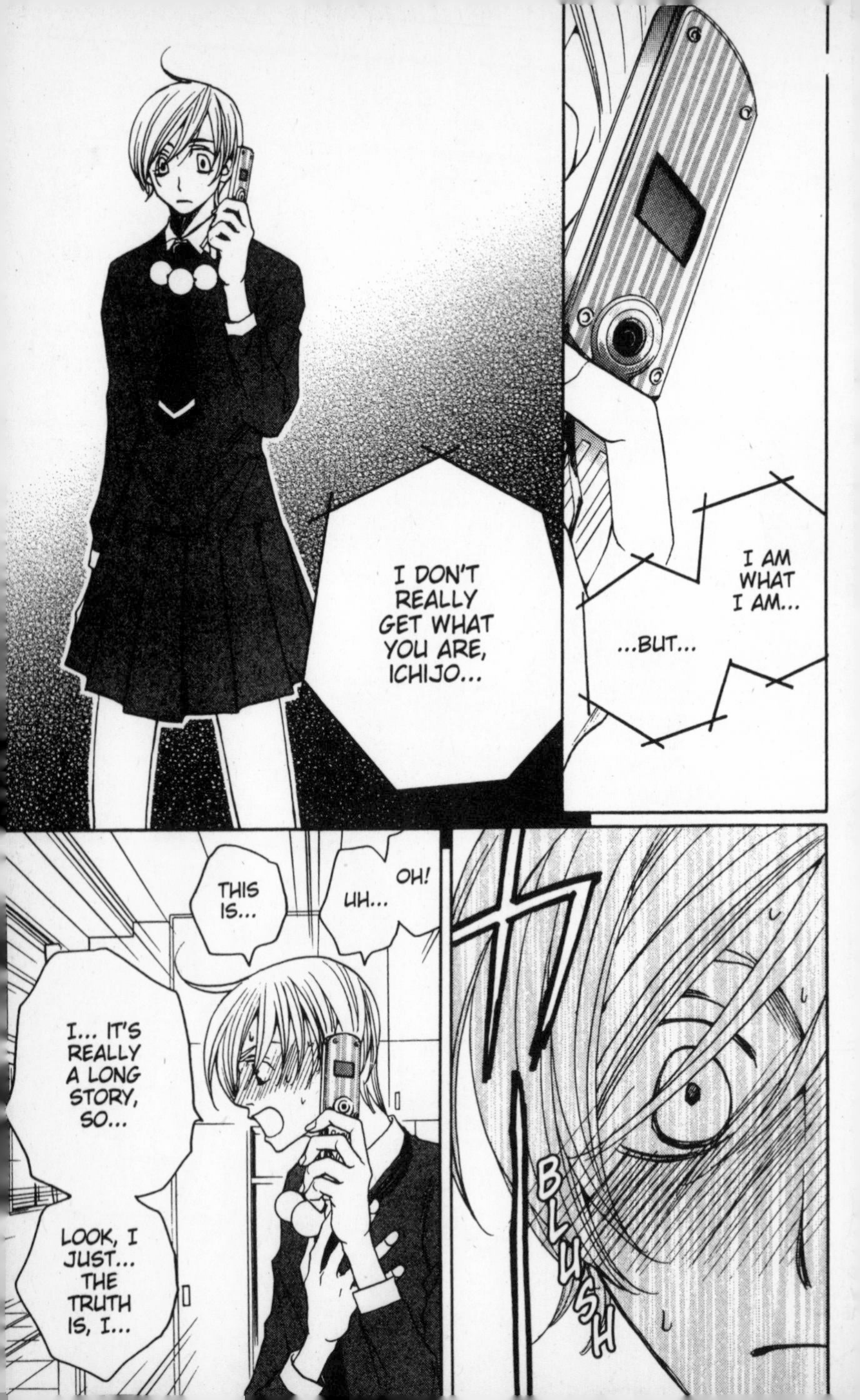
I AM WHAT I AM...
...BUT...
I DON'T REALLY GET WHAT YOU ARE, ICHIJO...
BLUSH
OH!
UH...
THIS IS...
I... IT'S REALLY A LONG STORY, SO...
LOOK, I JUST... THE TRUTH IS, I...

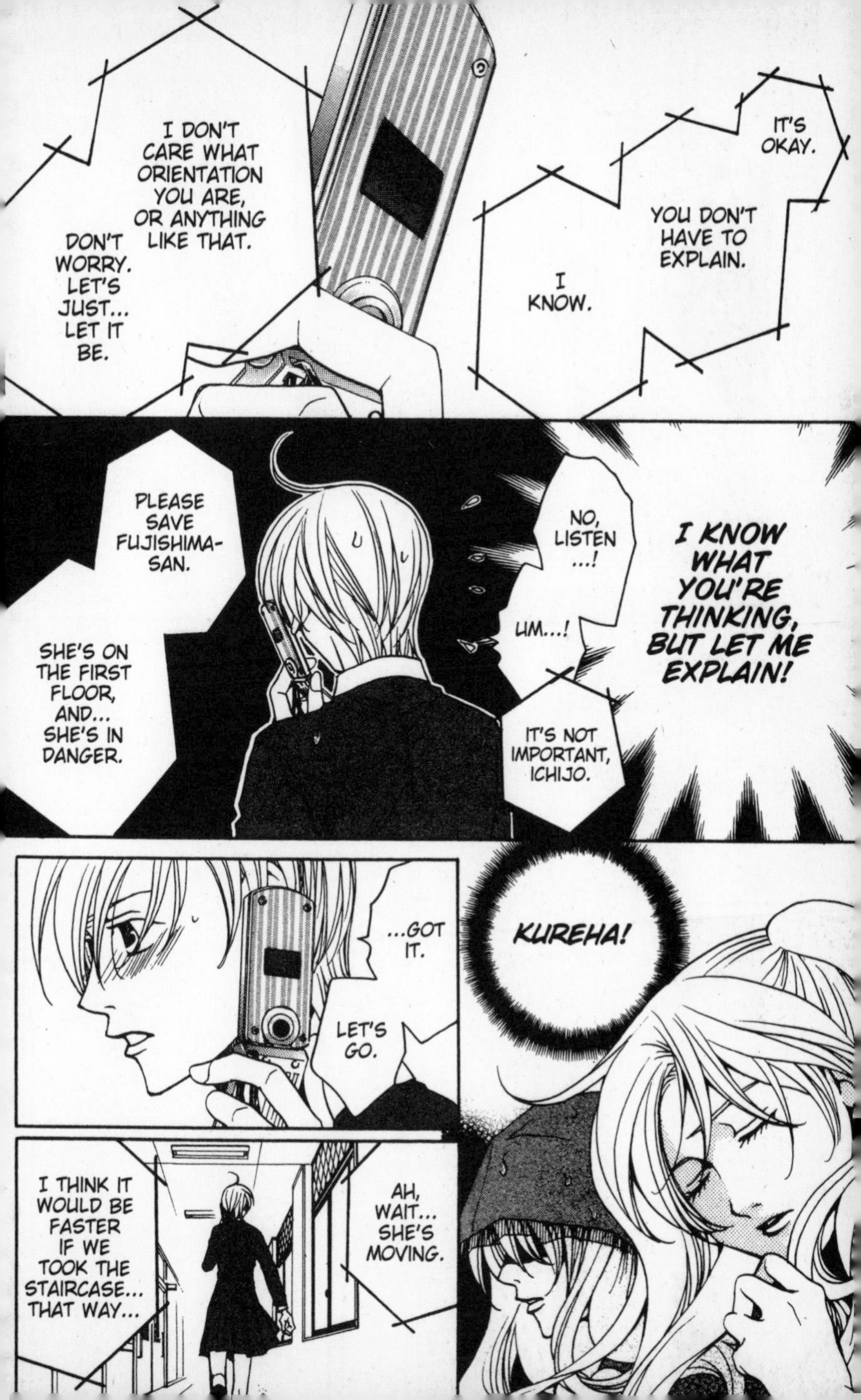
IT'S OKAY.
YOU DON'T HAVE TO EXPLAIN.
I KNOW.
I DON'T CARE WHAT ORIENTATION YOU ARE, OR ANYTHING LIKE THAT.
DON'T WORRY. LET'S JUST... LET IT BE.
I KNOW WHAT YOU'RE THINKING, BUT LET ME EXPLAIN!
NO, LISTEN ...!
UM...!
IT'S NOT IMPORTANT, ICHIJO.
PLEASE SAVE FUJISHIMA-SAN.
SHE'S ON THE FIRST FLOOR, AND... SHE'S IN DANGER.
KUREHA!
...GOT IT.
LET'S GO.
AH, WAIT... SHE'S MOVING.
I THINK IT WOULD BE FASTER IF WE TOOK THE STAIRCASE... THAT WAY...

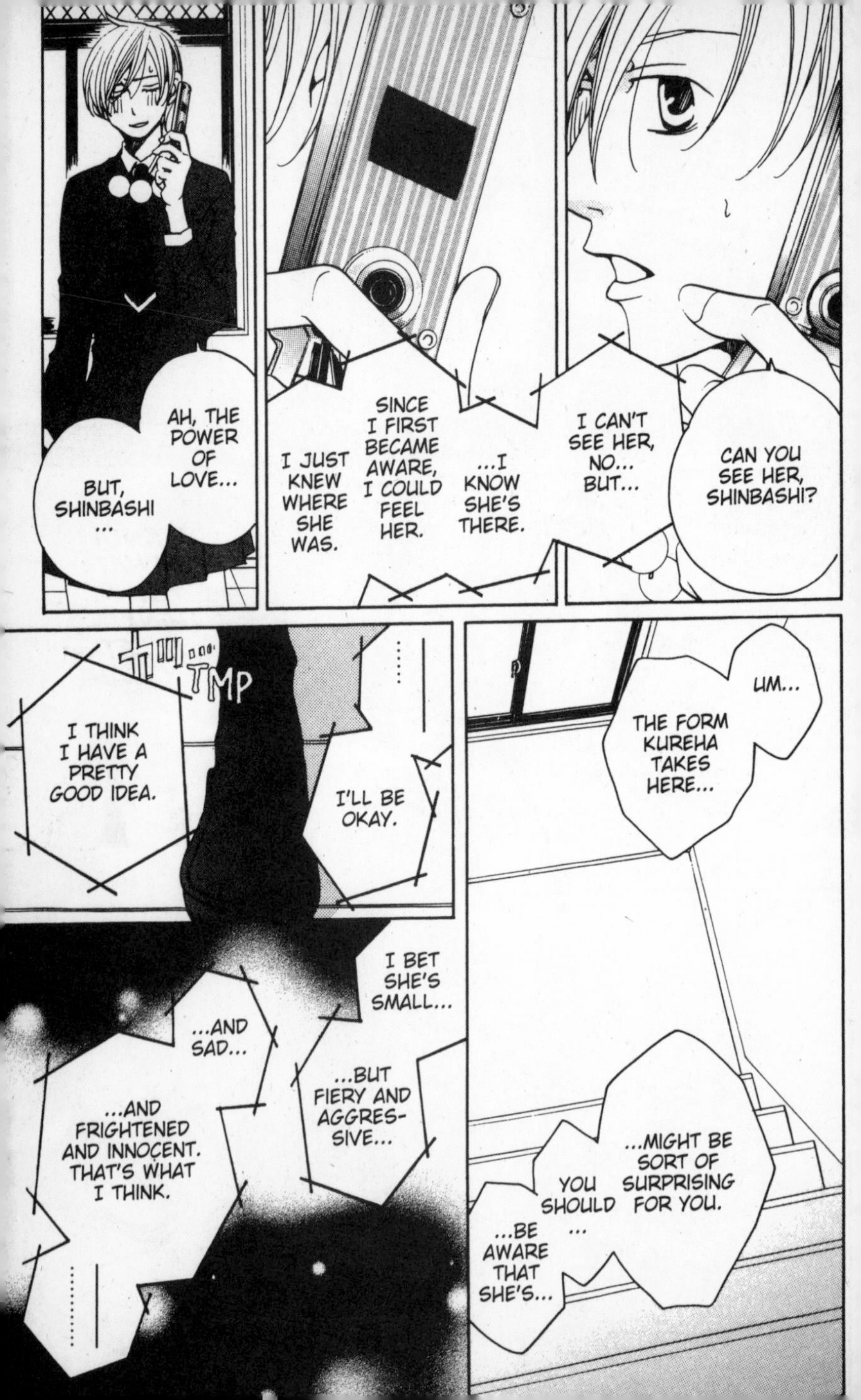
CAN YOU SEE HER, SHINBASHI?
I CAN'T SEE HER, NO... BUT...
...I KNOW SHE'S THERE.
SINCE I FIRST BECAME AWARE, I COULD FEEL HER.
I JUST KNEW WHERE SHE WAS.
AH, THE POWER OF LOVE...
BUT, SHINBASHI...
UM...
THE FORM KUREHA TAKES HERE...
...MIGHT BE SORT OF SURPRISING FOR YOU.
YOU SHOULD...
...BE AWARE THAT SHE'S...
......
I'LL BE OKAY.
TMP
I THINK I HAVE A PRETTY GOOD IDEA.
I BET SHE'S SMALL...
...AND SAD...
...BUT FIERY AND AGGRES-SIVE...
...AND FRIGHTENED AND INNOCENT. THAT'S WHAT I THINK.
......

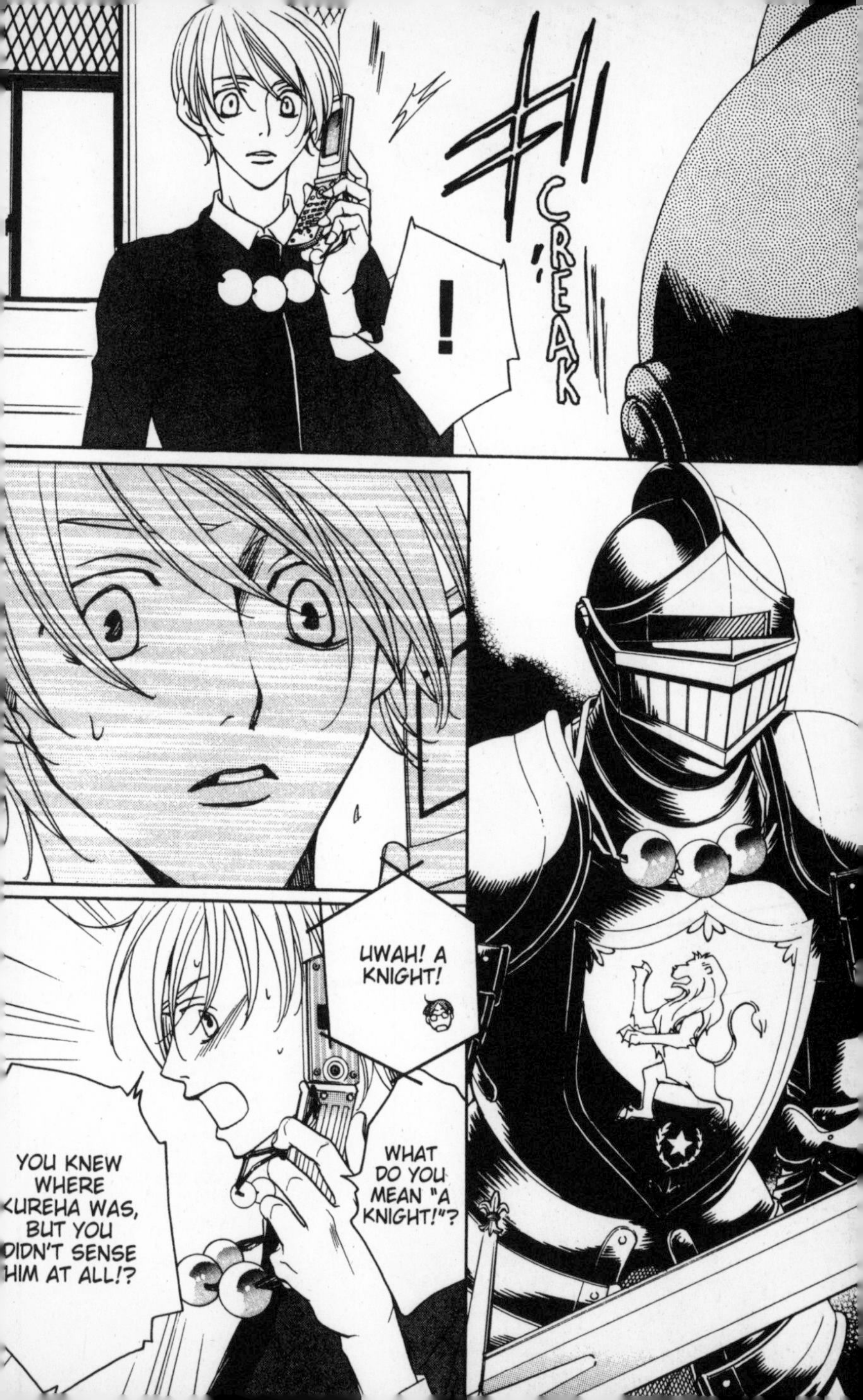
CREAK
!
UWAH! A KNIGHT!
WHAT DO YOU MEAN "A KNIGHT!"?
YOU KNEW WHERE KUREHA WAS, BUT YOU DIDN'T SENSE HIM AT ALL!?

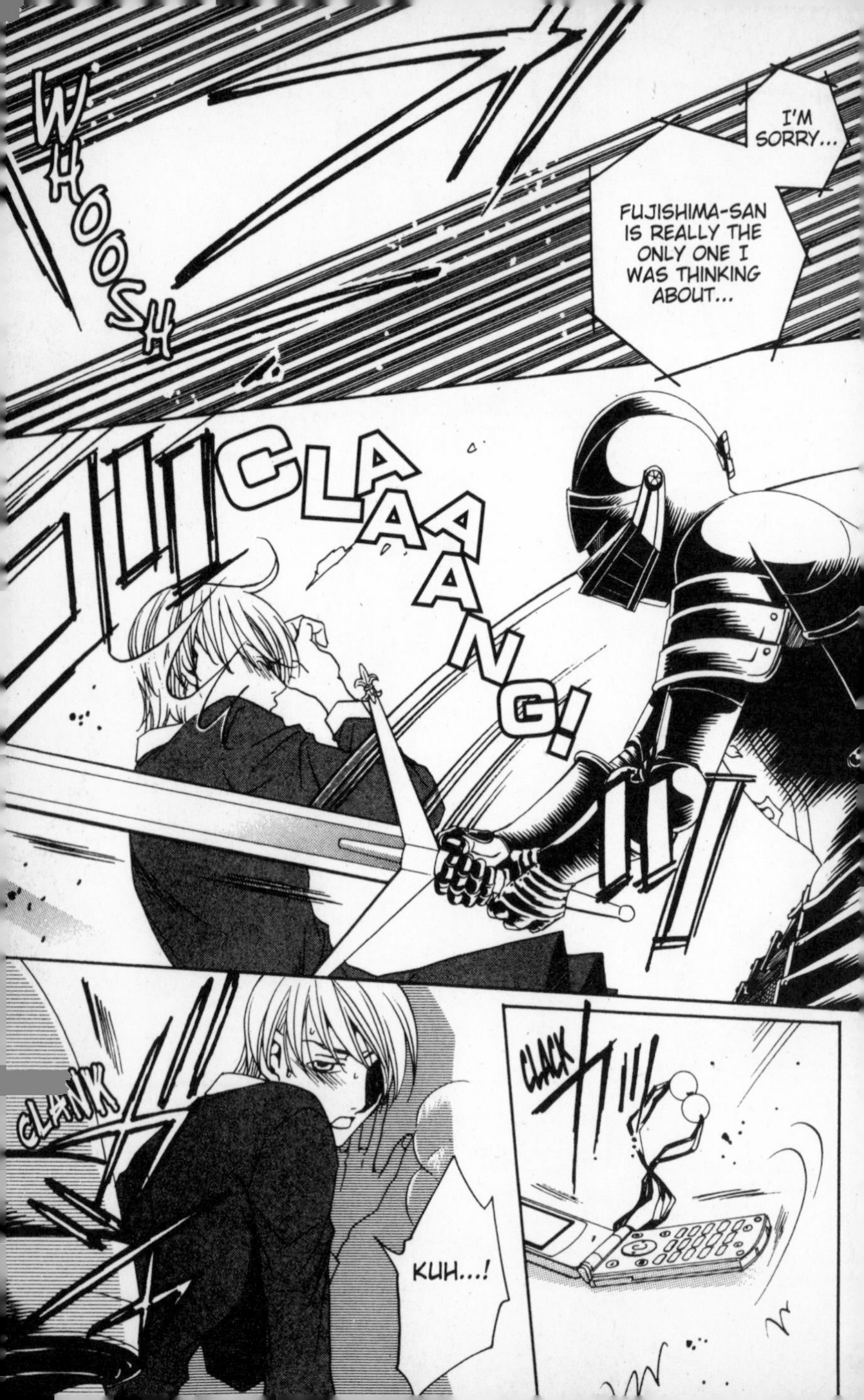
I'M SORRY...
FUJISHIMA-SAN IS REALLY THE ONLY ONE I WAS THINKING ABOUT...
WHOOSH
CLAAAANG!
CLACK
KUH...!
CLANK

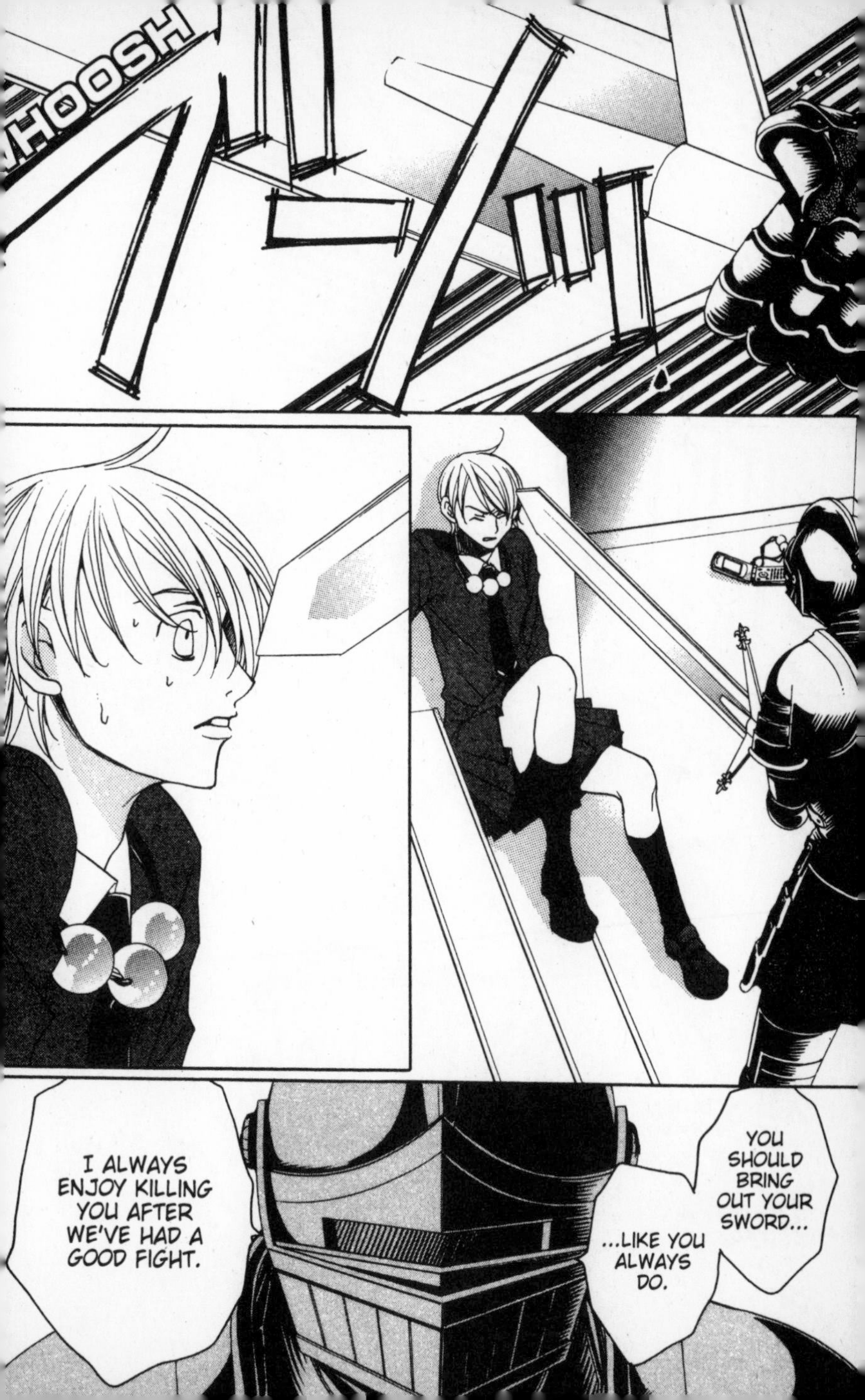
HOOSH
YOU SHOULD BRING OUT YOUR SWORD...
...LIKE YOU ALWAYS DO.
I ALWAYS ENJOY KILLING YOU AFTER WE'VE HAD A GOOD FIGHT.

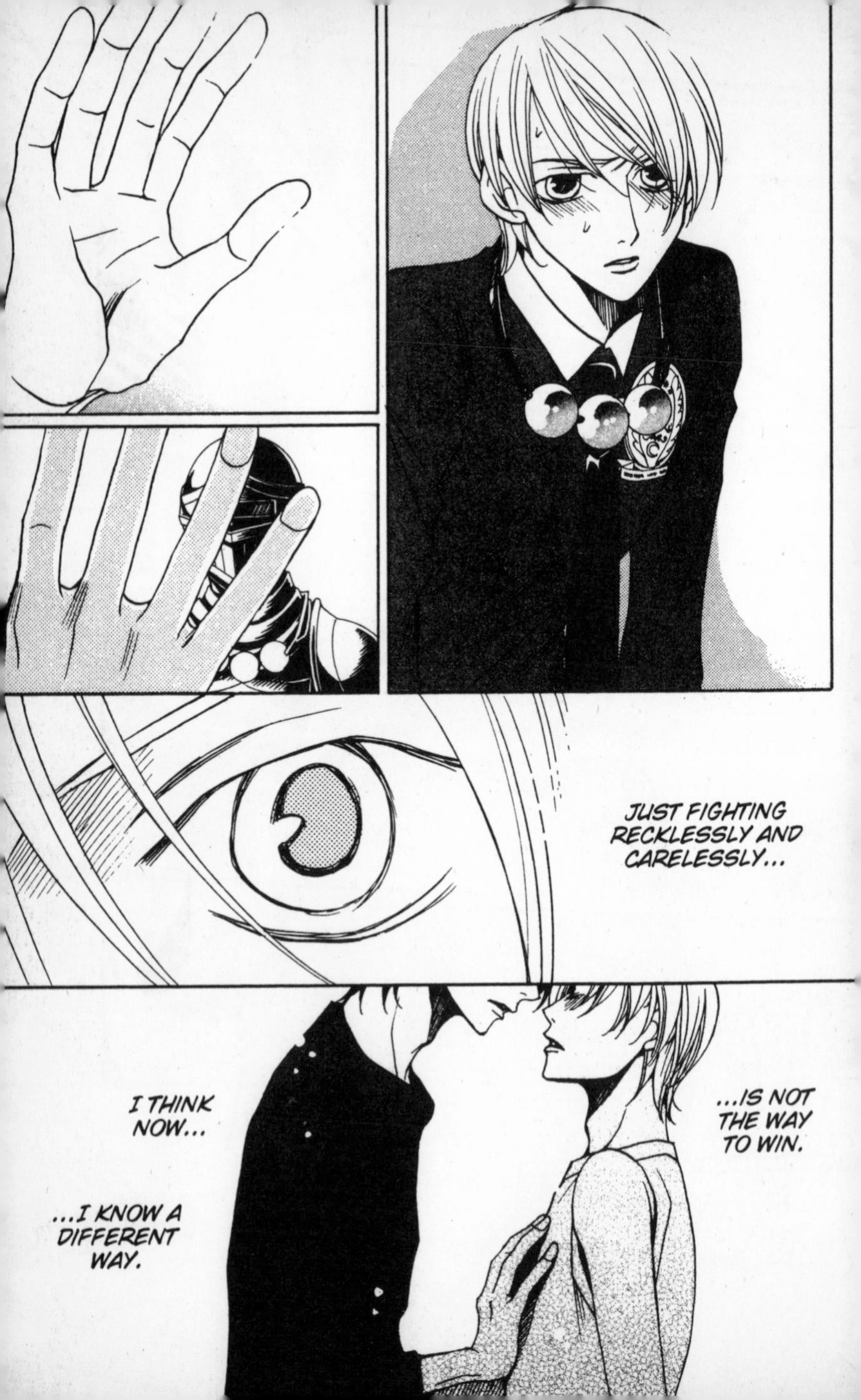
JUST FIGHTING RECKLESSLY AND CARELESSLY...
...IS NOT THE WAY TO WIN.
I THINK NOW...
...I KNOW A DIFFERENT WAY.

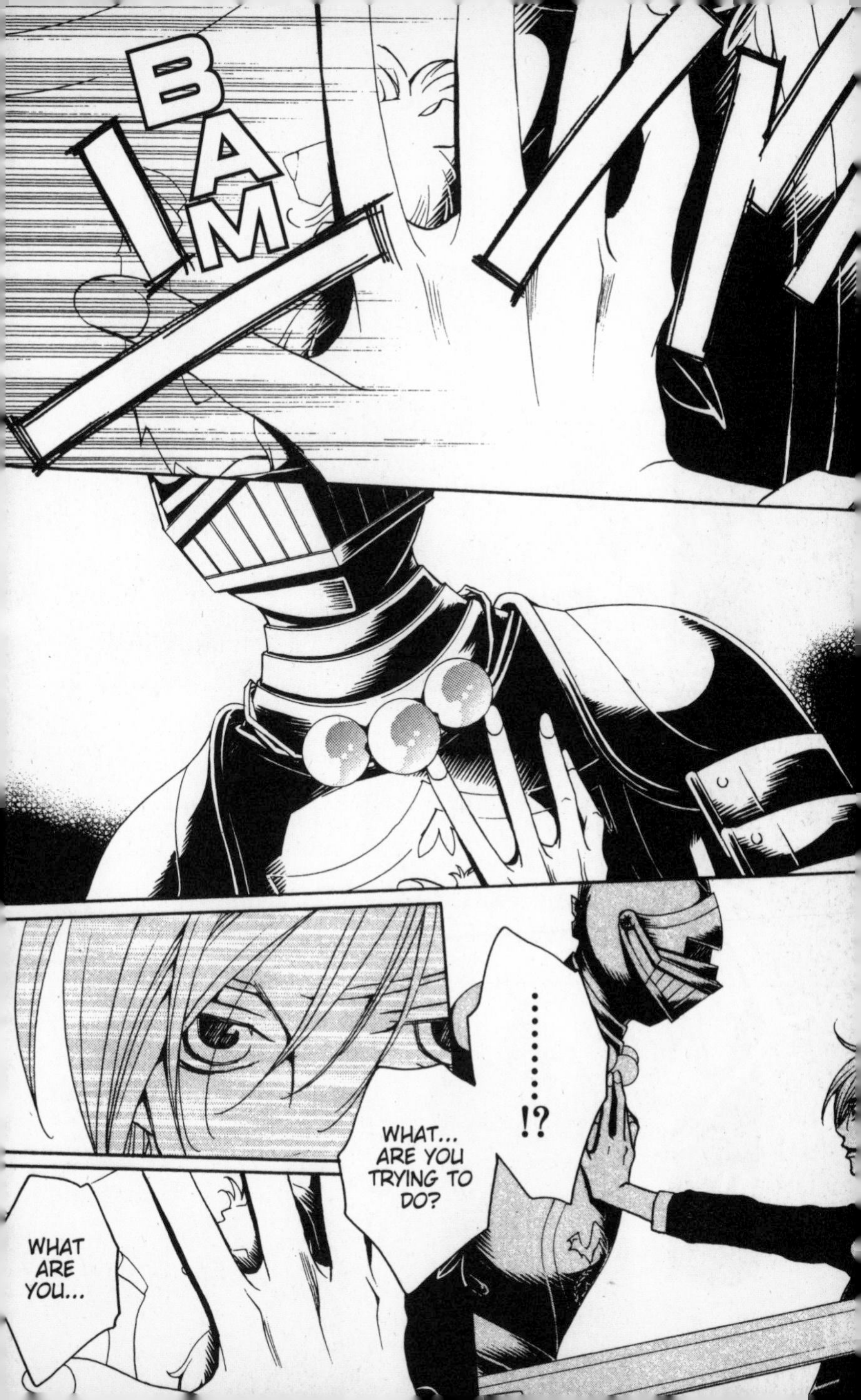
BAM
......!?
WHAT... ARE YOU TRYING TO DO?
WHAT ARE YOU...

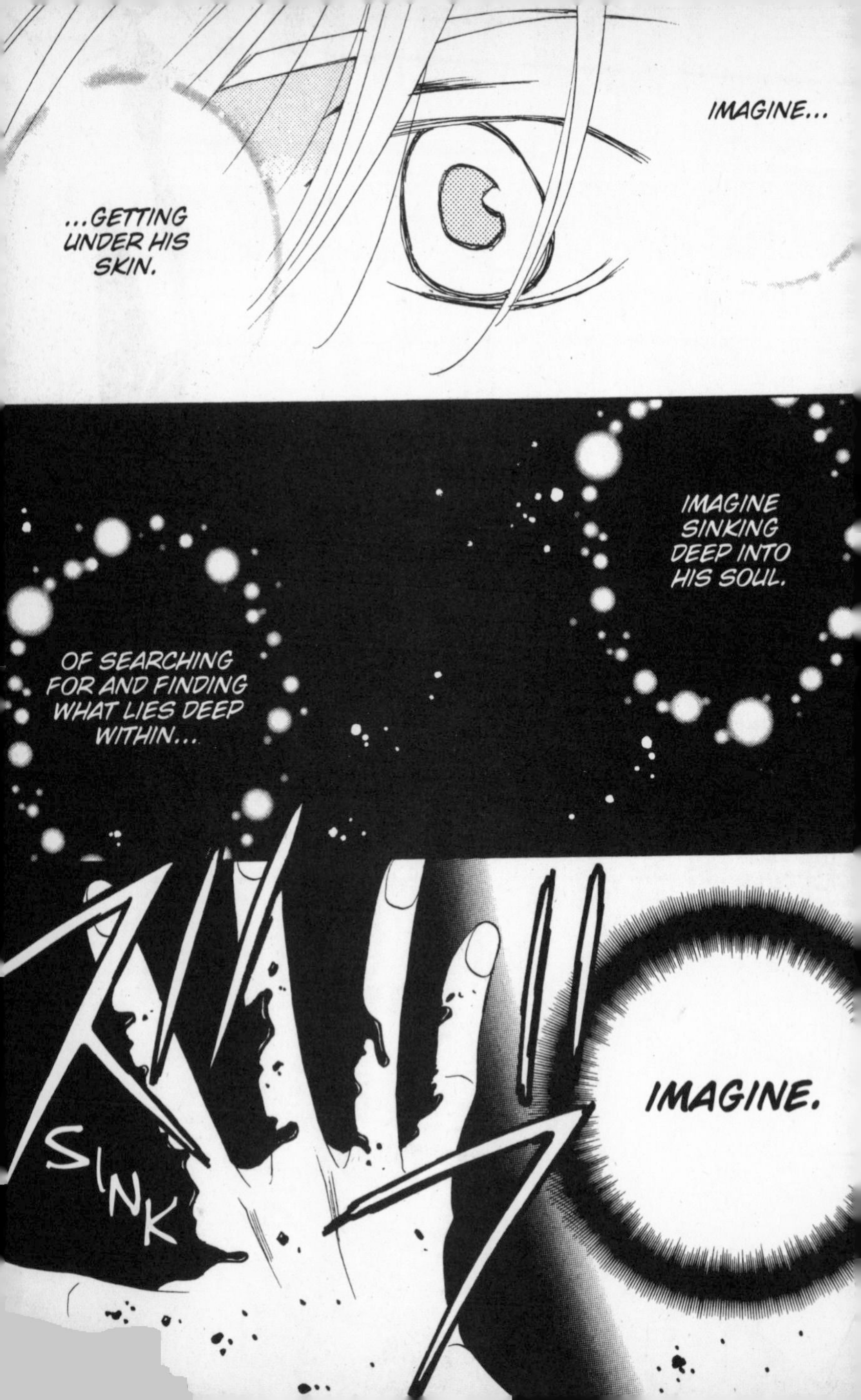
IMAGINE...
...GETTING UNDER HIS SKIN.
IMAGINE SINKING DEEP INTO HIS SOUL.
OF SEARCHING FOR AND FINDING WHAT LIES DEEP WITHIN...
IMAGINE.
SINK

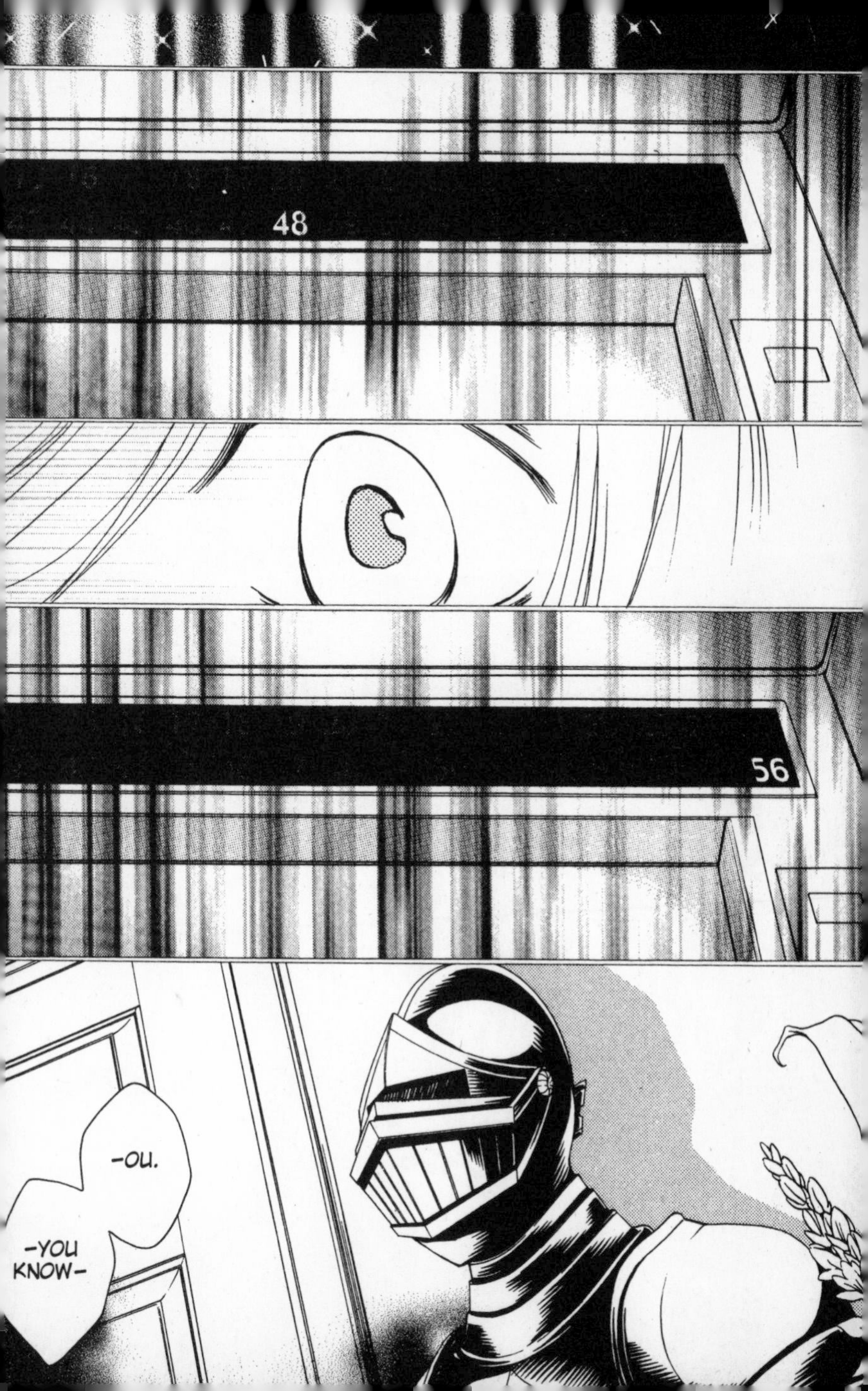
48
56
-OU.
-YOU KNOW-

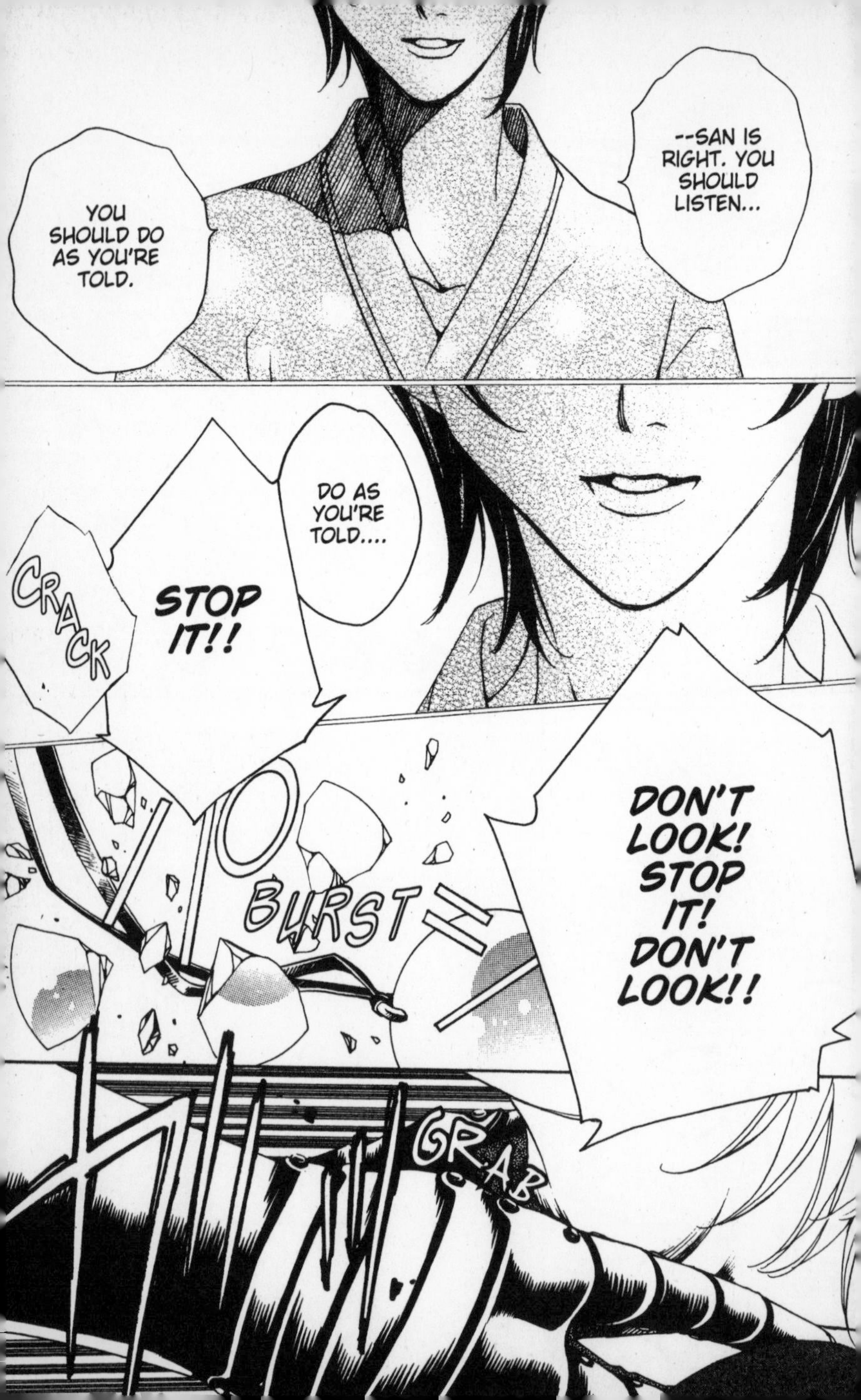
--SAN IS RIGHT. YOU SHOULD LISTEN...
YOU SHOULD DO AS YOU'RE TOLD.
DO AS YOU'RE TOLD....
STOP IT!!
CRACK
DON'T LOOK! STOP IT! DON'T LOOK!!
BURST
GRAB

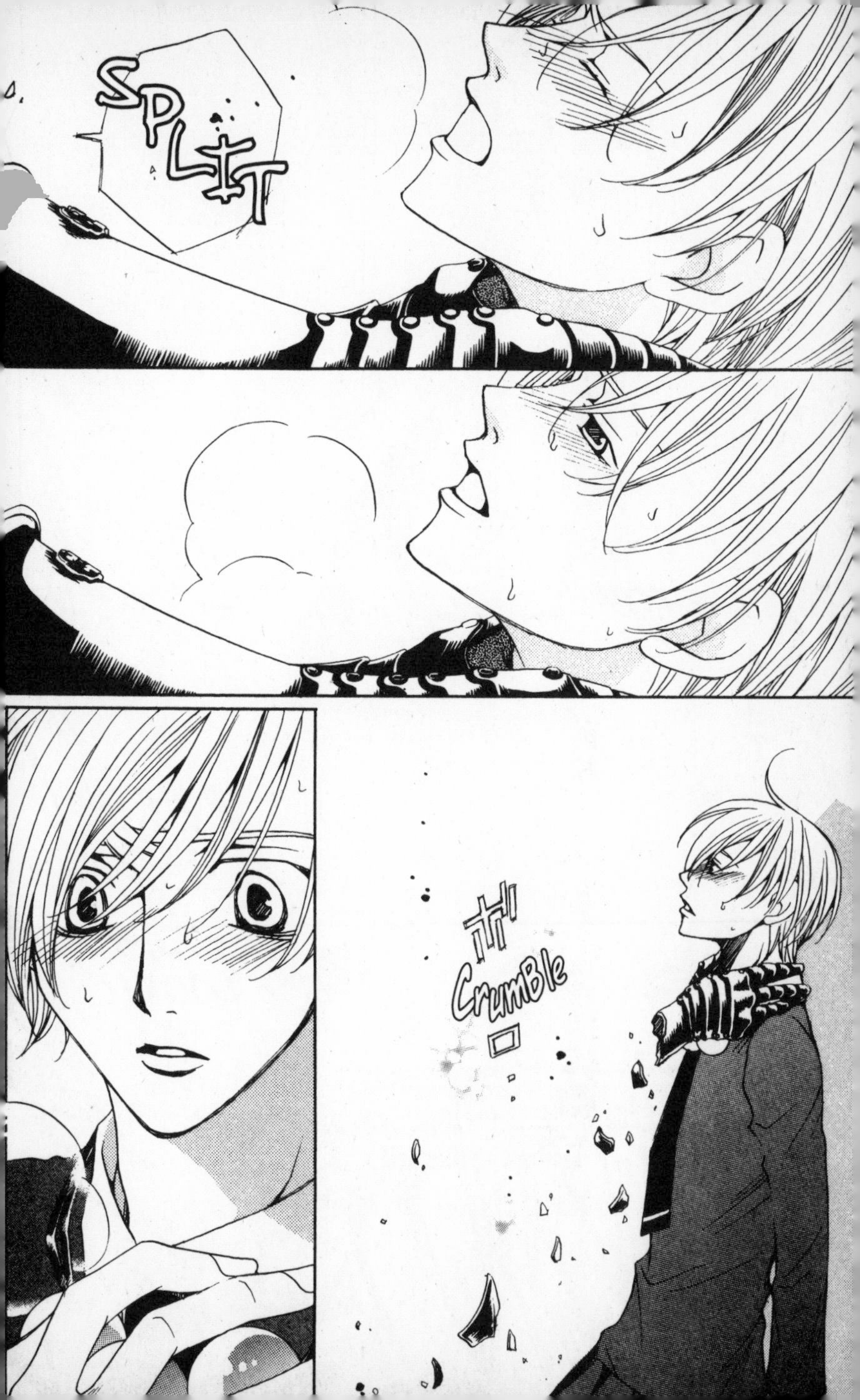
SPLIT
CrumBle

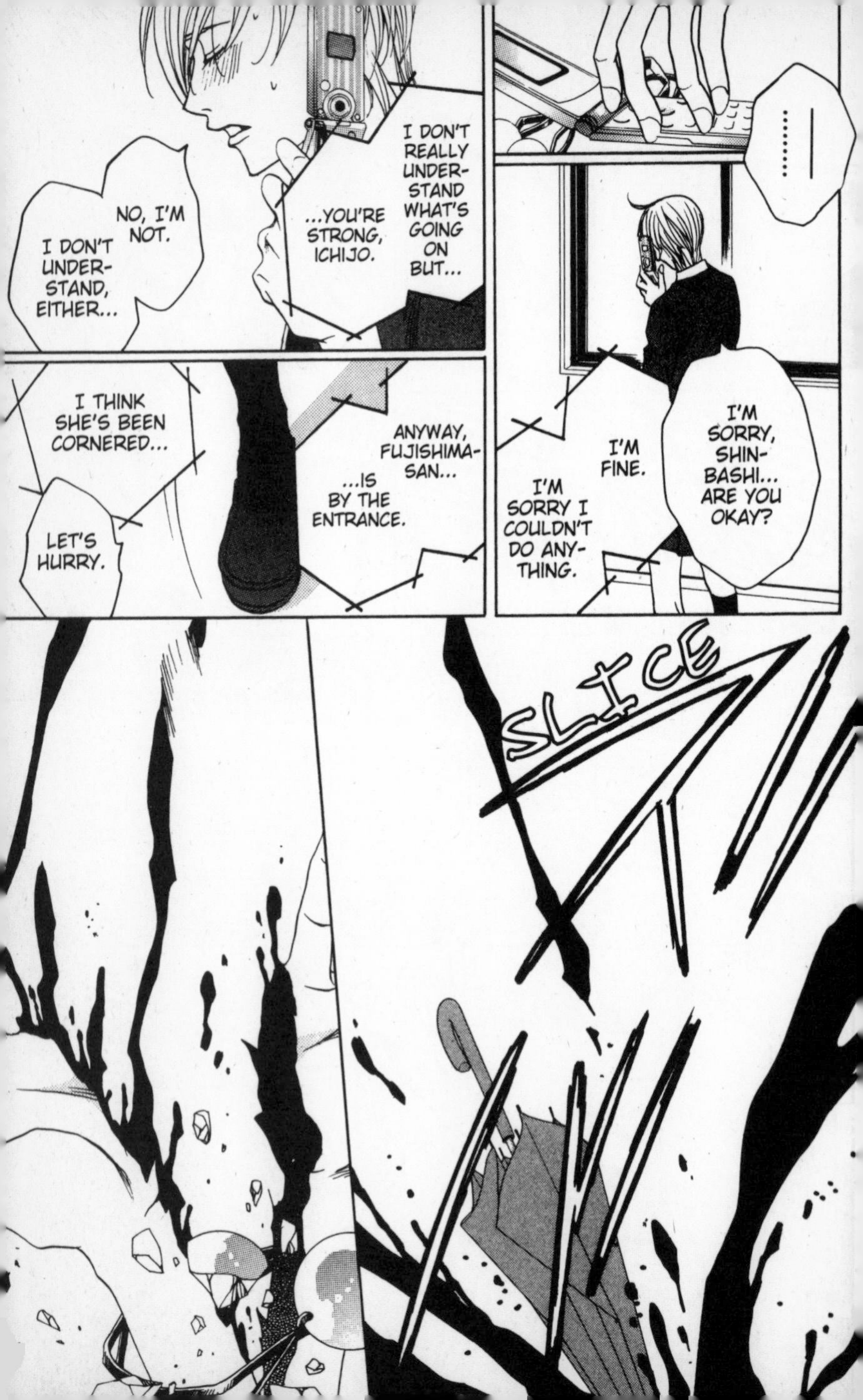
......!
I DON'T REALLY UNDERSTAND WHAT'S GOING ON BUT...
...YOU'RE STRONG, ICHIJO.
NO, I'M NOT.
I DON'T UNDERSTAND, EITHER...
I'M SORRY, SHINBASHI... ARE YOU OKAY?
I'M FINE.
I'M SORRY I COULDN'T DO ANYTHING.
ANYWAY, FUJISHIMA-SAN...
...IS BY THE ENTRANCE.
I THINK SHE'S BEEN CORNERED...
LET'S HURRY.
SLICE

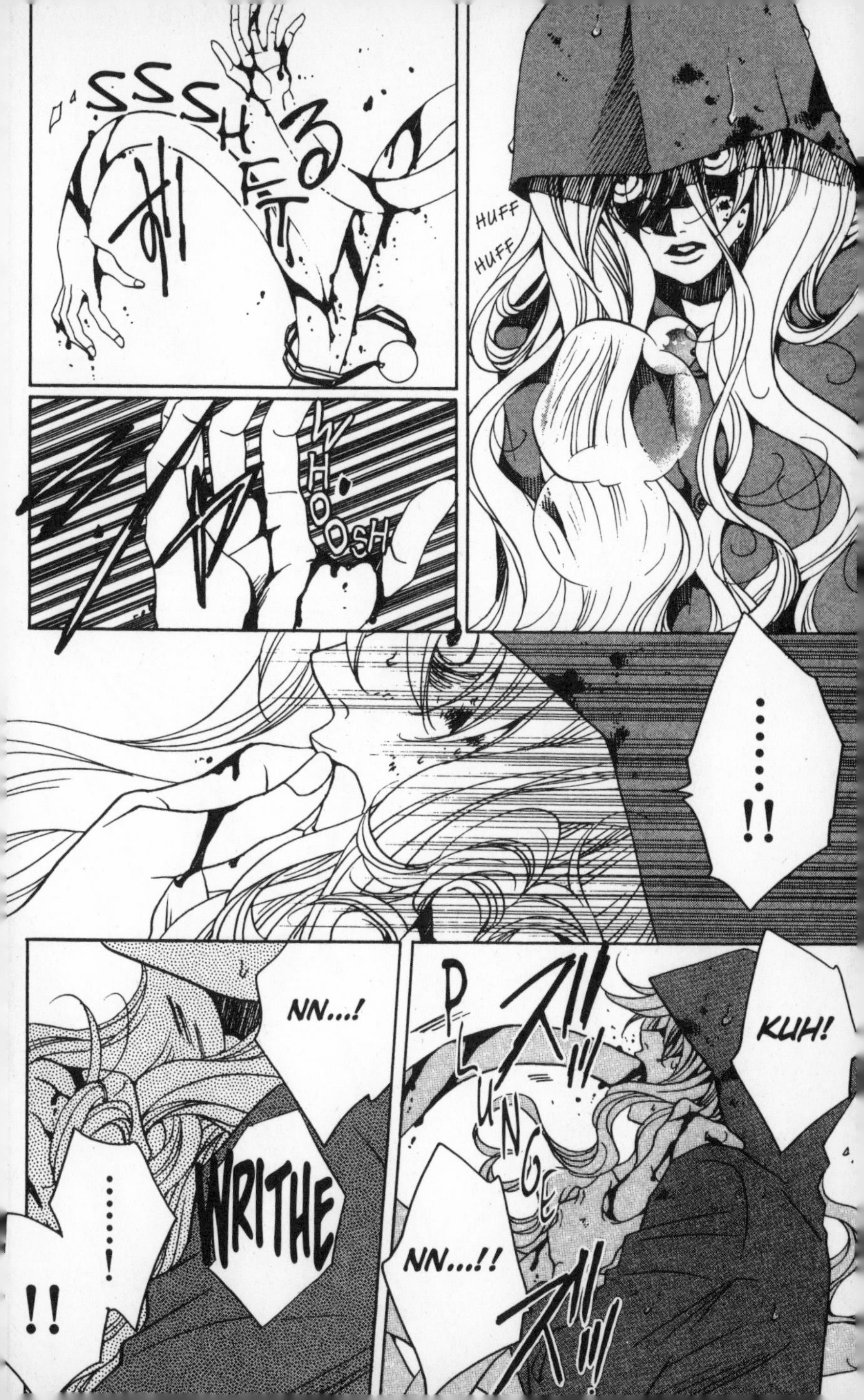
HUFF
HUFF
SSSHFT
WHOOSH
......!!
KUH!
PLUNGE
NN...!!
NN...!
WRITHE
......!
!!

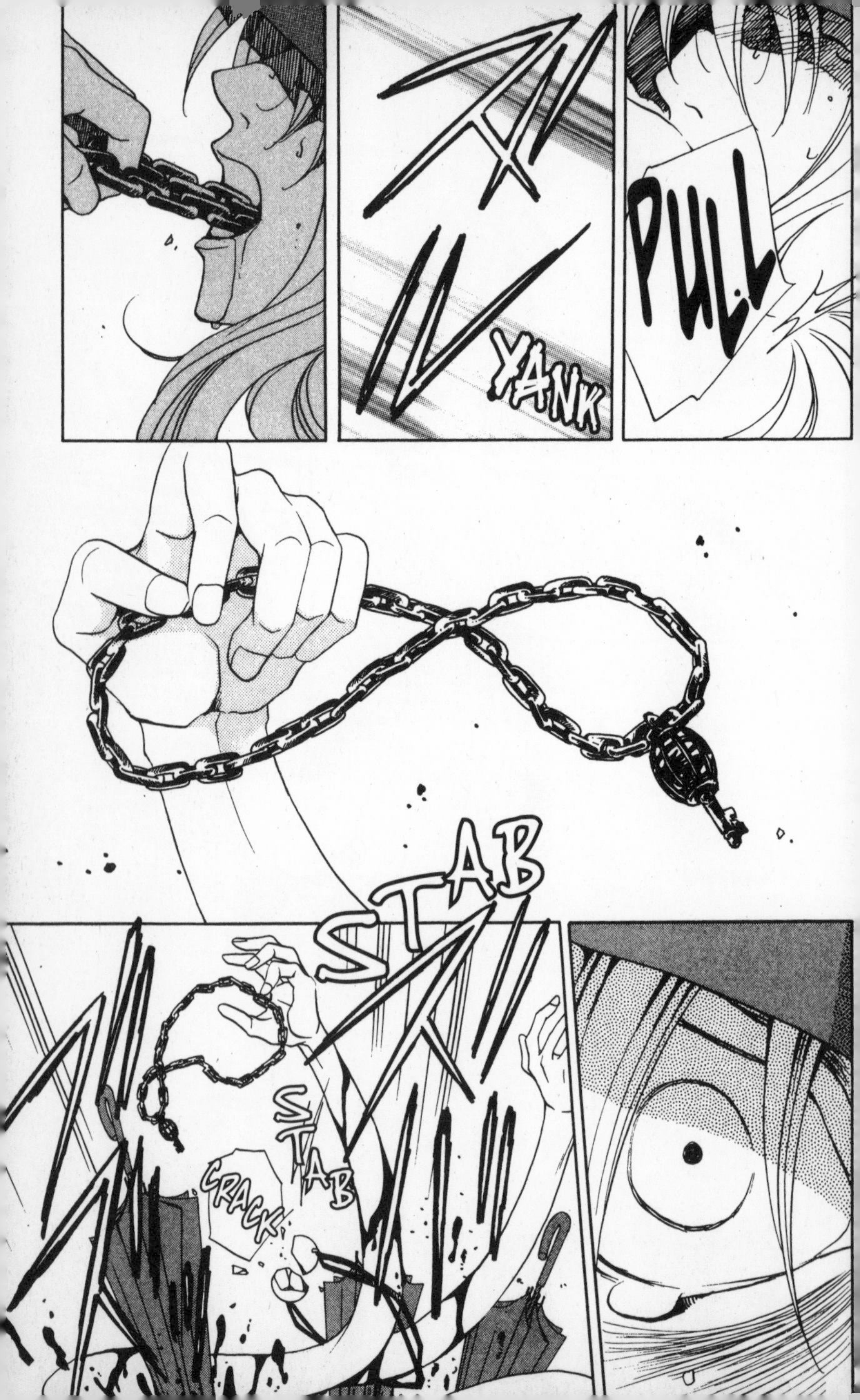
PULL
YANK
STAB
CRACK
STAB

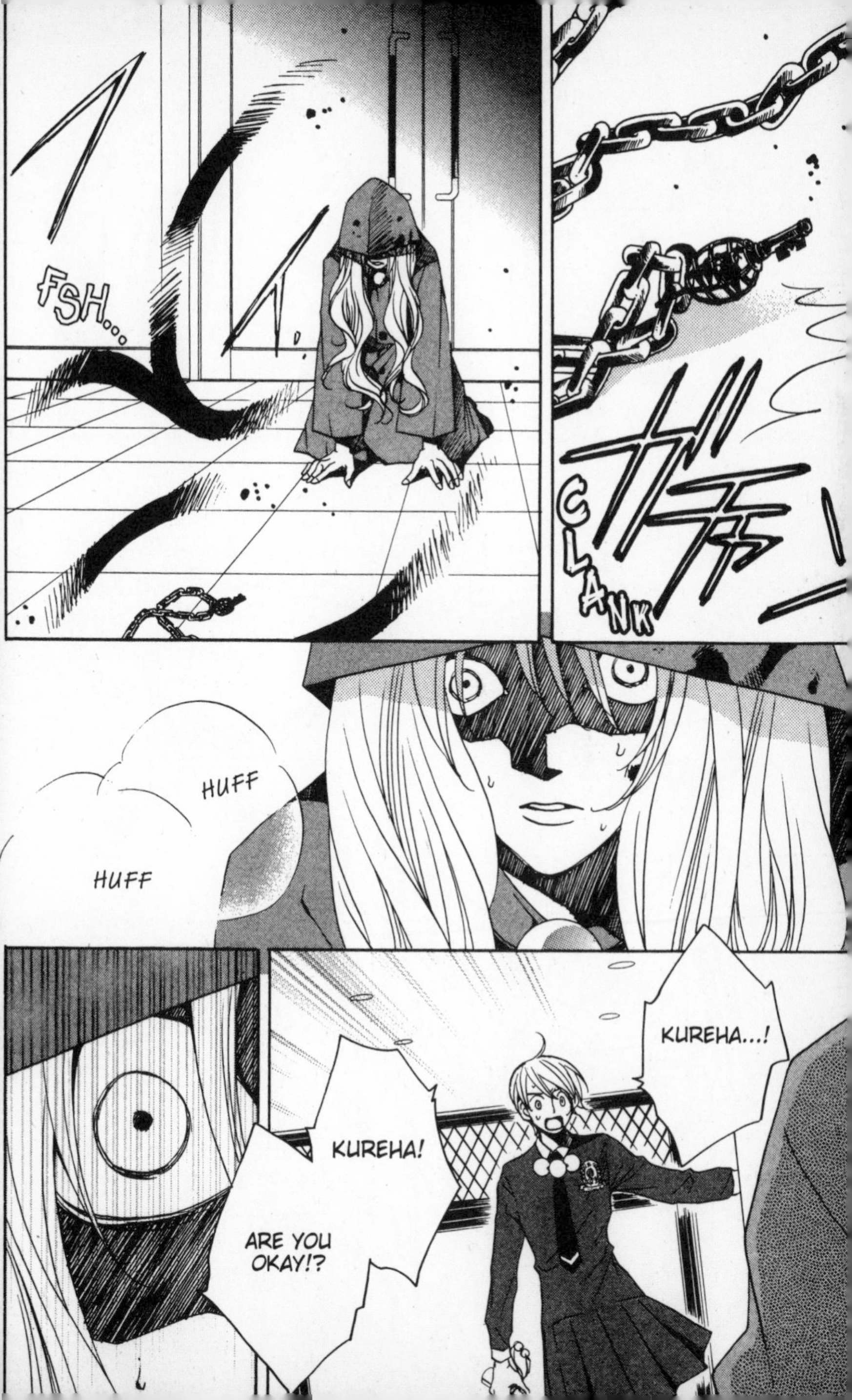
CLANK
FSH...
HUFF
HUFF
KUREHA...!
KUREHA!
ARE YOU OKAY!?

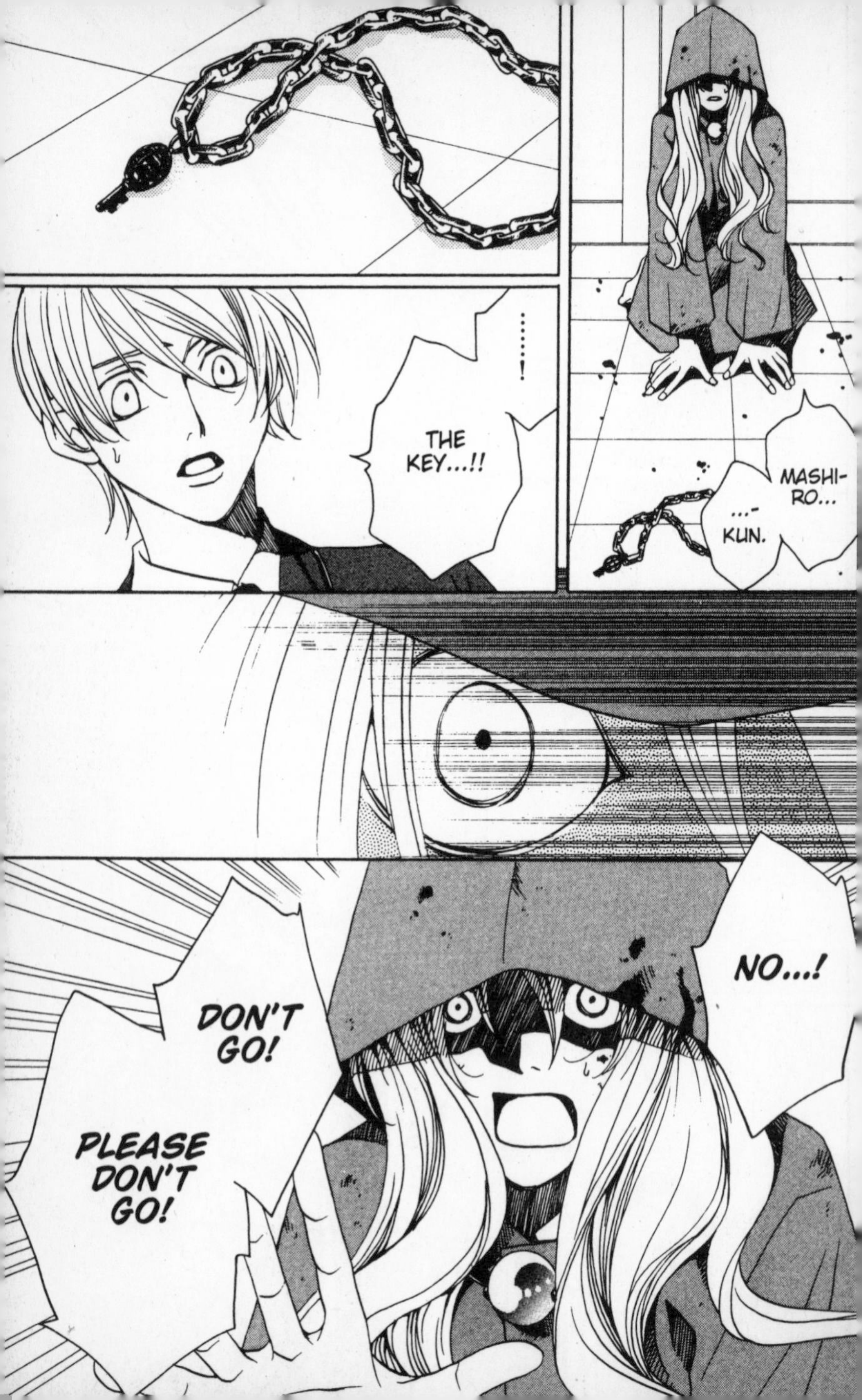
MASHIRO...
...-KUN.
......!
THE KEY...!!
NO...!
DON'T GO!
PLEASE DON'T GO!

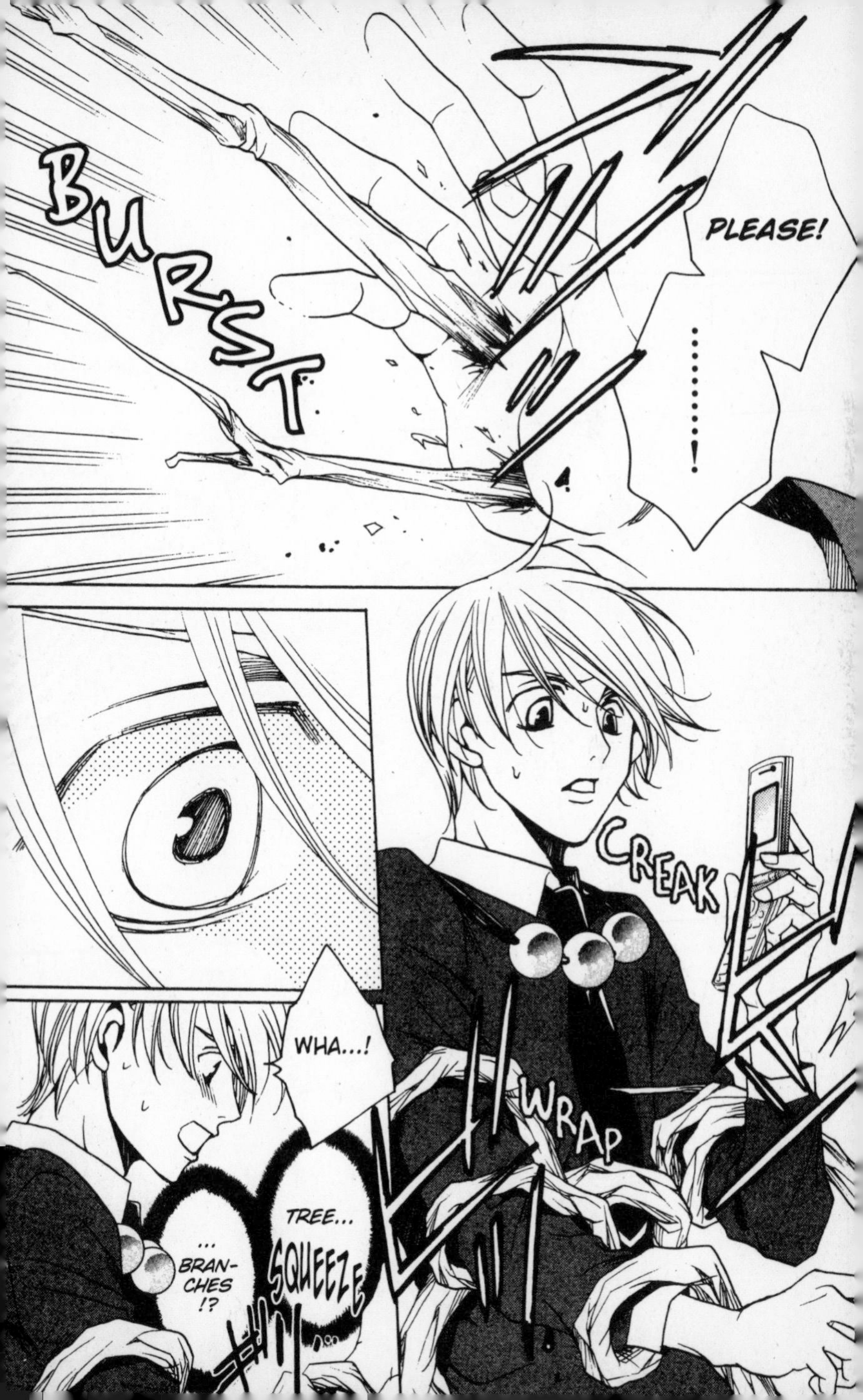
PLEASE!
......!
BURST
CREAK
WHA...!
WRAP
TREE...
... BRANCHES !?
SQUEEZE

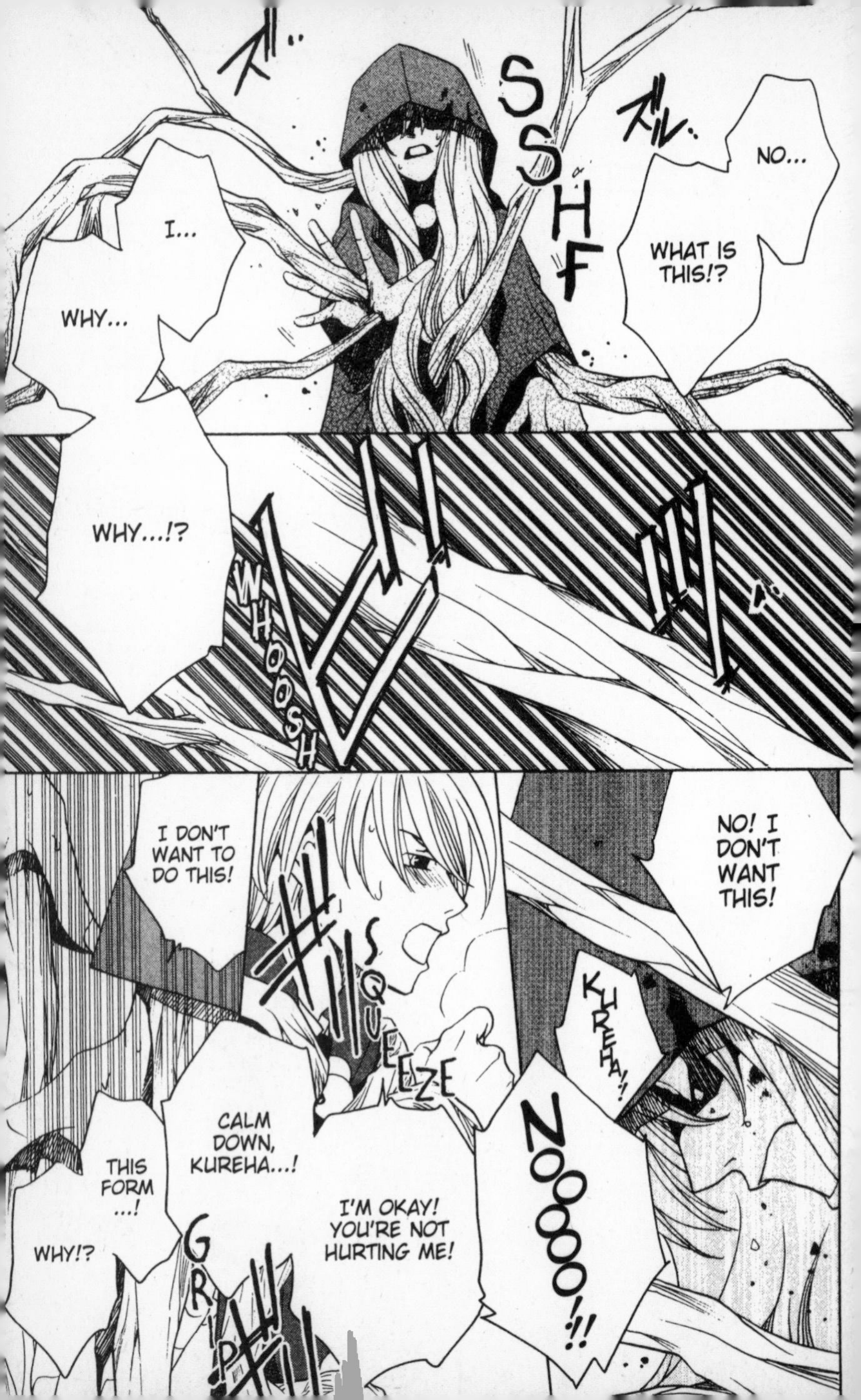
NO...
WHAT IS THIS!?
SSHF
I...
WHY...
WHY...!?
WHOOSH
NO! I DON'T WANT THIS!
KUREHA!!
NOOOOO!!!
I DON'T WANT TO DO THIS!
SQUEEZE
CALM DOWN, KUREHA...!
I'M OKAY! YOU'RE NOT HURTING ME!
GRIP
THIS FORM ...!
WHY!?

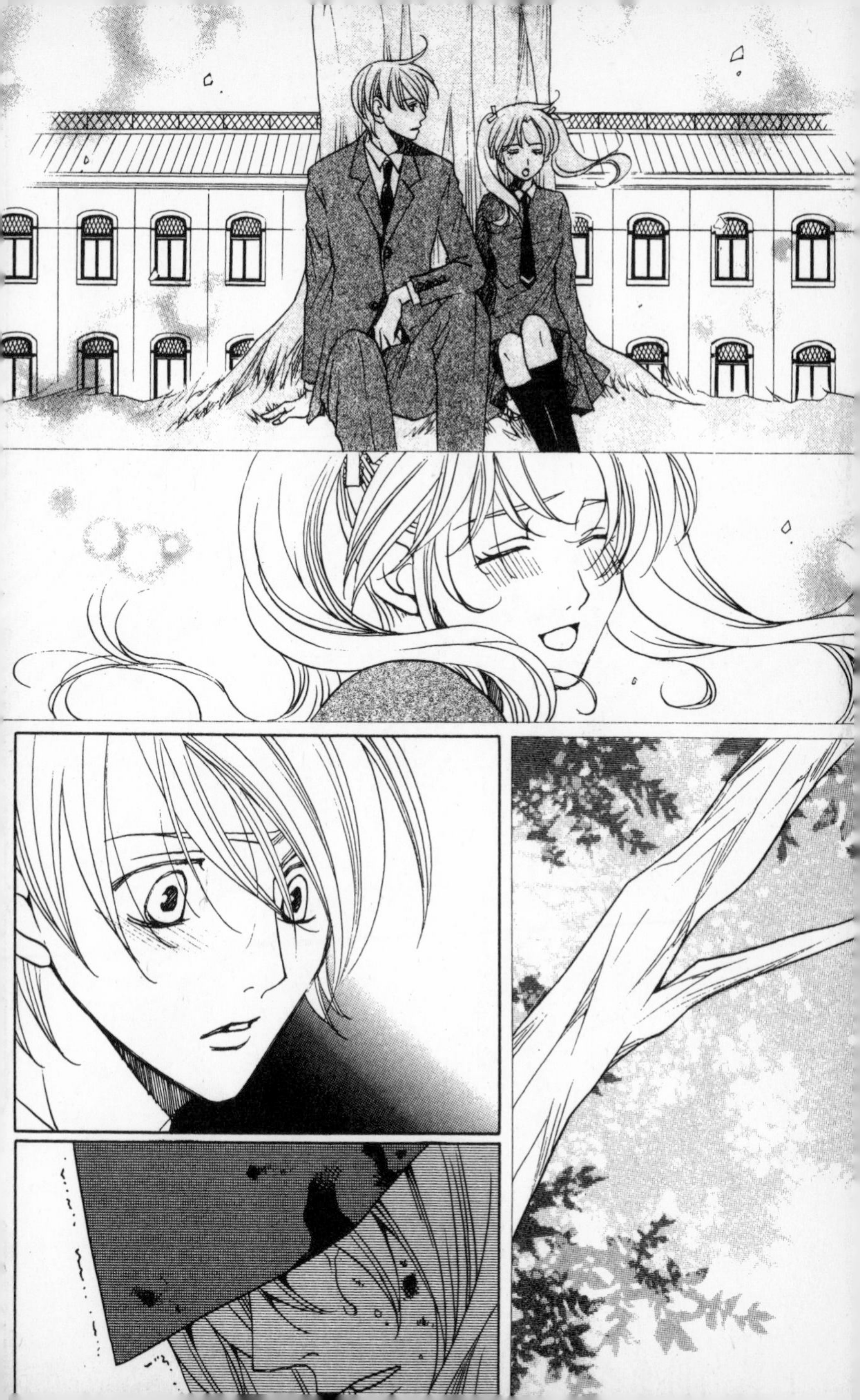

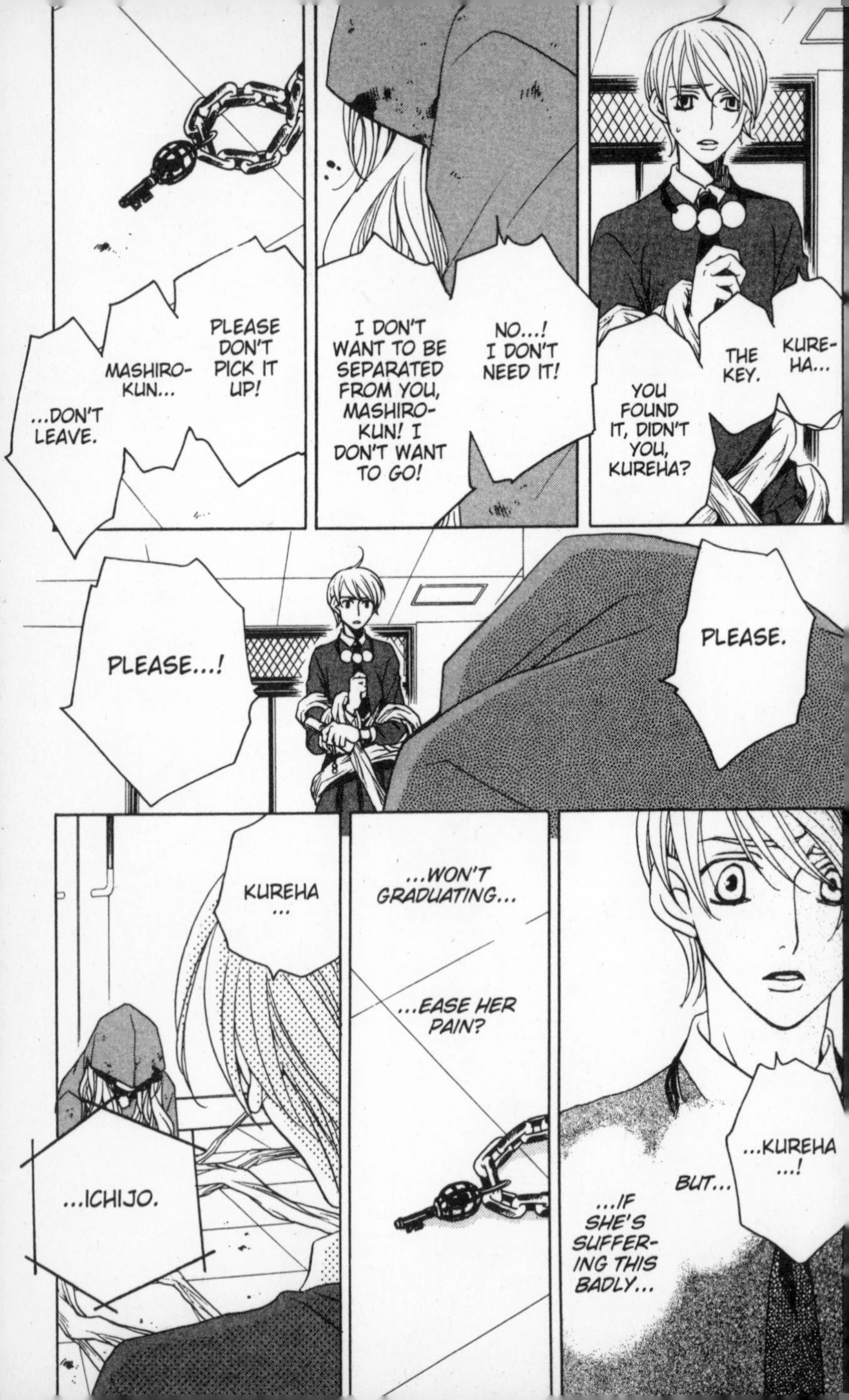
KURE-HA...
THE KEY.
YOU FOUND IT, DIDN'T YOU, KUREHA?
NO...! I DON'T NEED IT!
I DON'T WANT TO BE SEPARATED FROM YOU, MASHIRO-KUN! I DON'T WANT TO GO!
PLEASE DON'T PICK IT UP!
MASHIRO-KUN...
...DON'T LEAVE.
PLEASE.
PLEASE...!
...KUREHA ...!
BUT...
...IF SHE'S SUFFERING THIS BADLY...
...WON'T GRADUATING...
...EASE HER PAIN?
KUREHA ...
...ICHIJO.

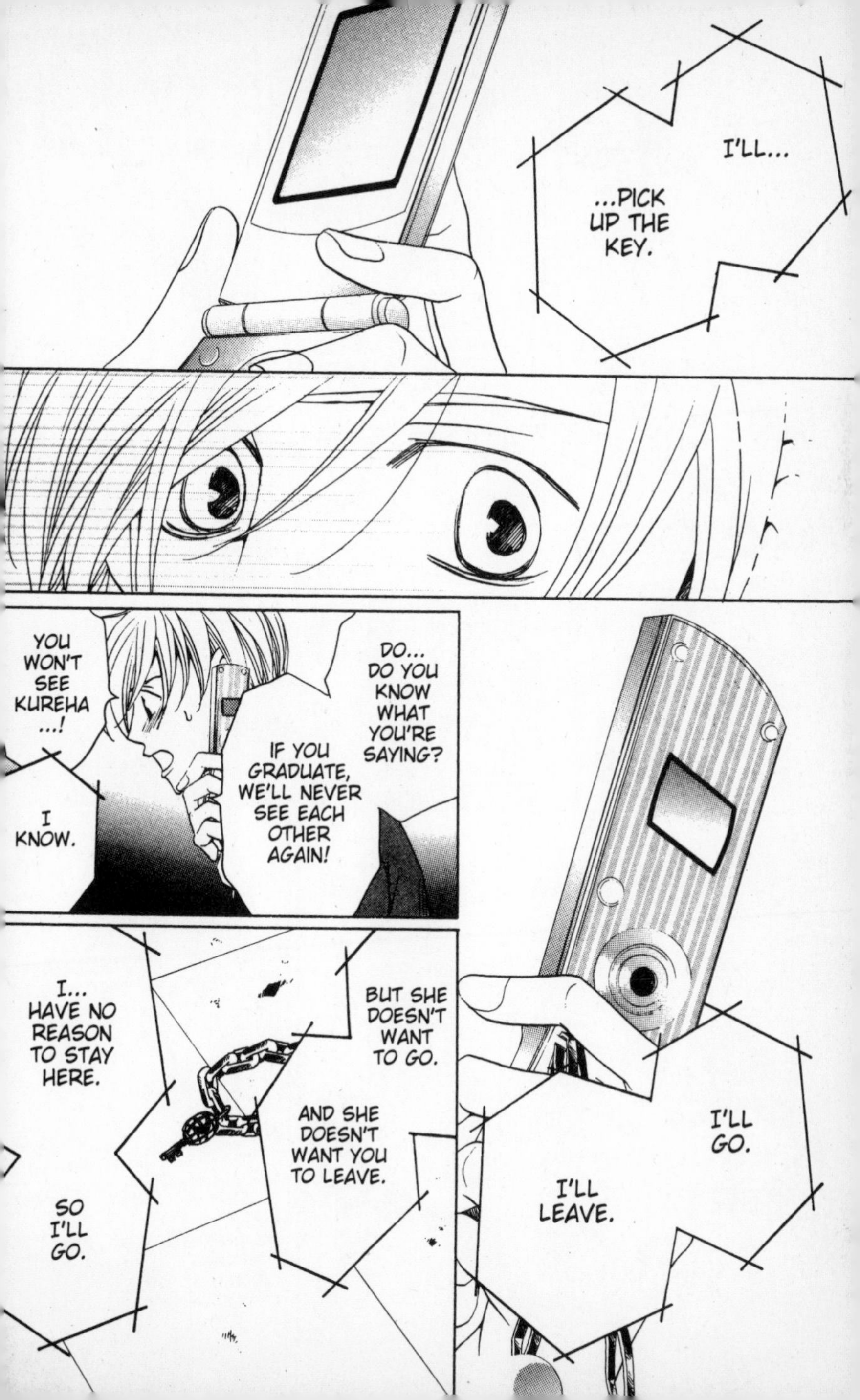

I'LL...
...PICK UP THE KEY.
I'LL GO.
I'LL LEAVE.
DO... DO YOU KNOW WHAT YOU'RE SAYING?
IF YOU GRADUATE, WE'LL NEVER SEE EACH OTHER AGAIN!
YOU WON'T SEE KUREHA...!
I KNOW.
BUT SHE DOESN'T WANT TO GO.
AND SHE DOESN'T WANT YOU TO LEAVE.
I... HAVE NO REASON TO STAY HERE.
SO I'LL GO.

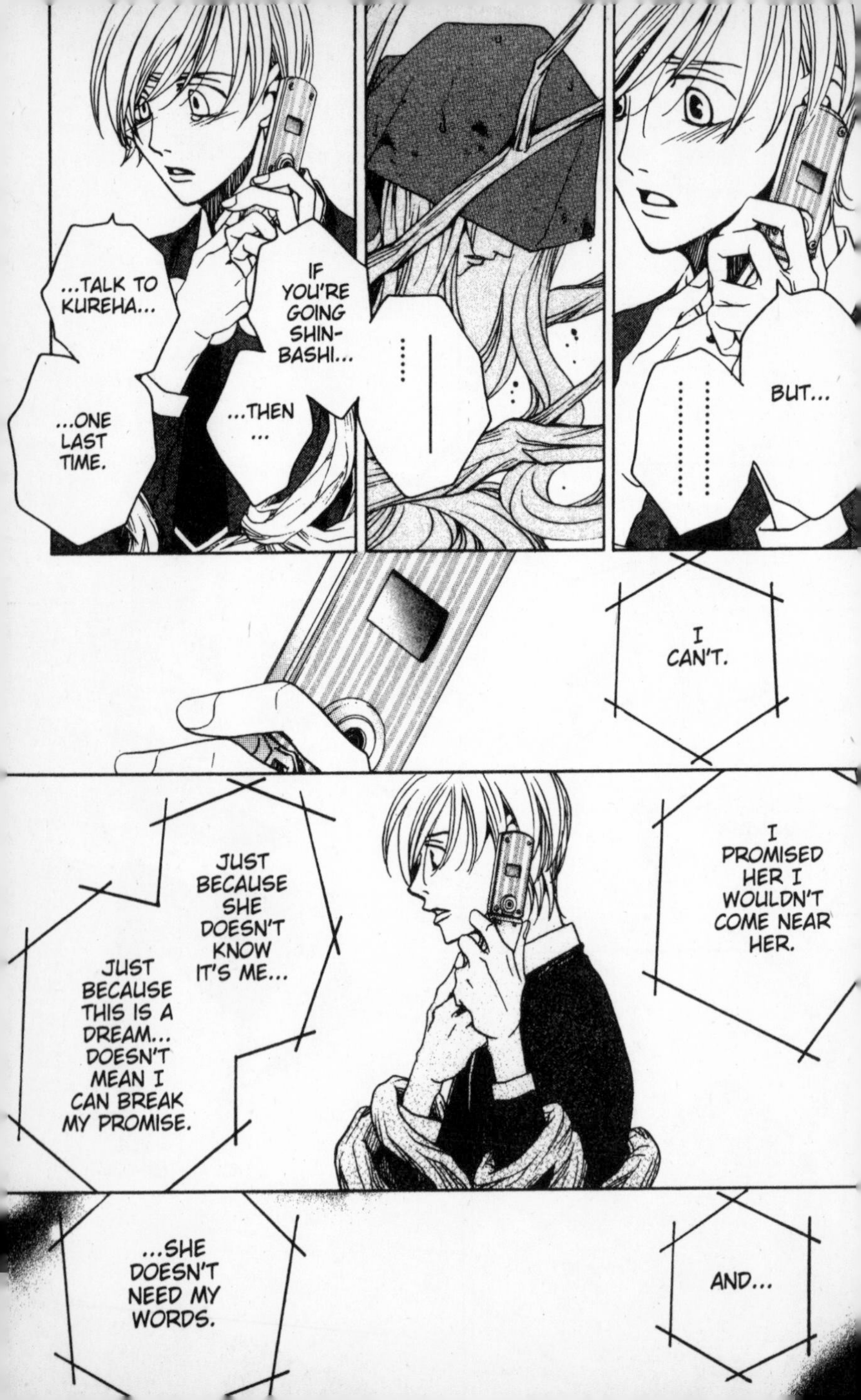
BUT...
… …
……
IF YOU'RE GOING SHIN-BASHI...
...THEN ...
...TALK TO KUREHA...
...ONE LAST TIME.
I CAN'T.
I PROMISED HER I WOULDN'T COME NEAR HER.
JUST BECAUSE SHE DOESN'T KNOW IT'S ME...
JUST BECAUSE THIS IS A DREAM... DOESN'T MEAN I CAN BREAK MY PROMISE.
AND...
...SHE DOESN'T NEED MY WORDS.

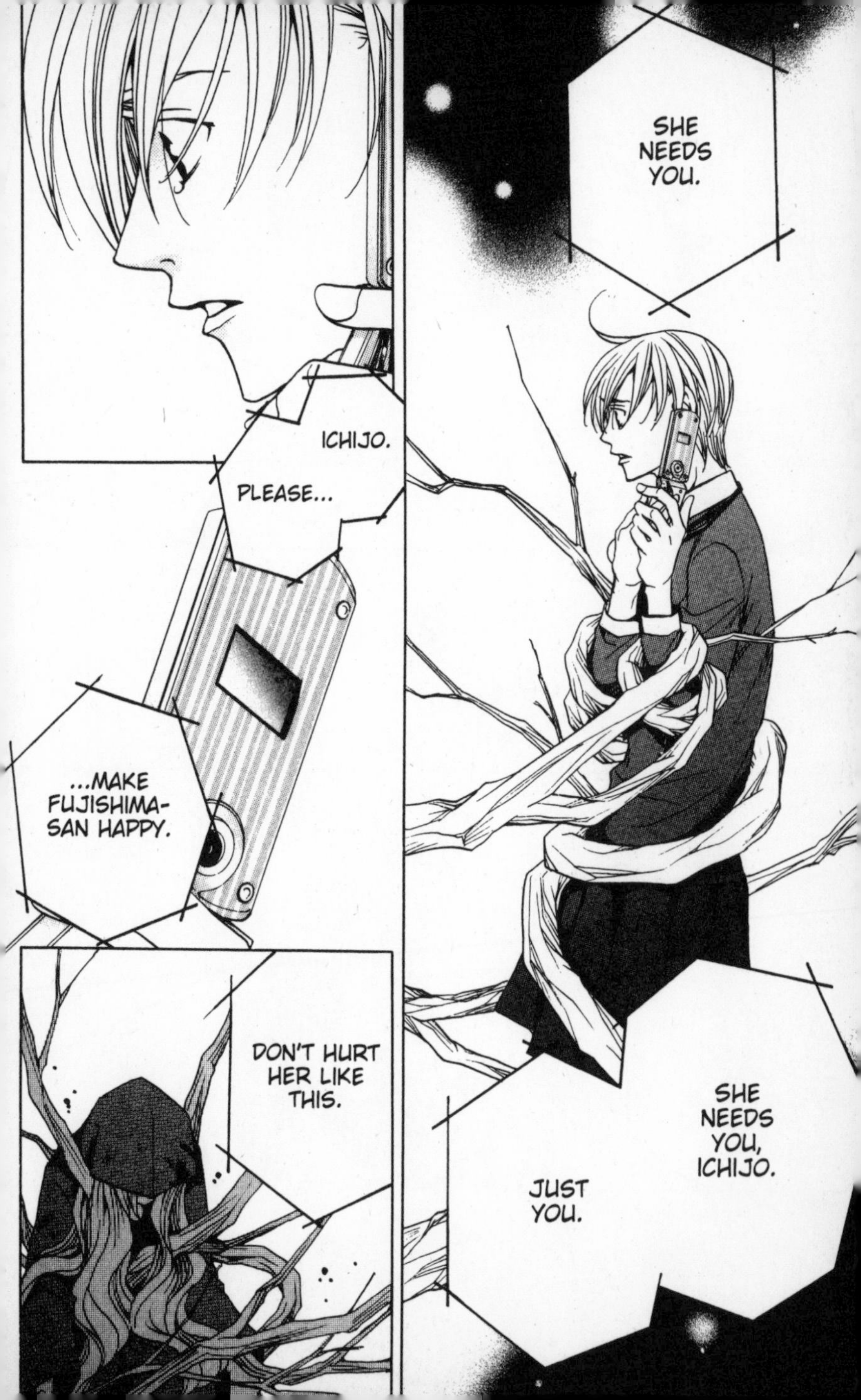
SHE NEEDS YOU.
SHE NEEDS YOU, ICHIJO.
JUST YOU.
ICHIJO.
PLEASE...
...MAKE FUJISHIMA-SAN HAPPY.
DON'T HURT HER LIKE THIS.

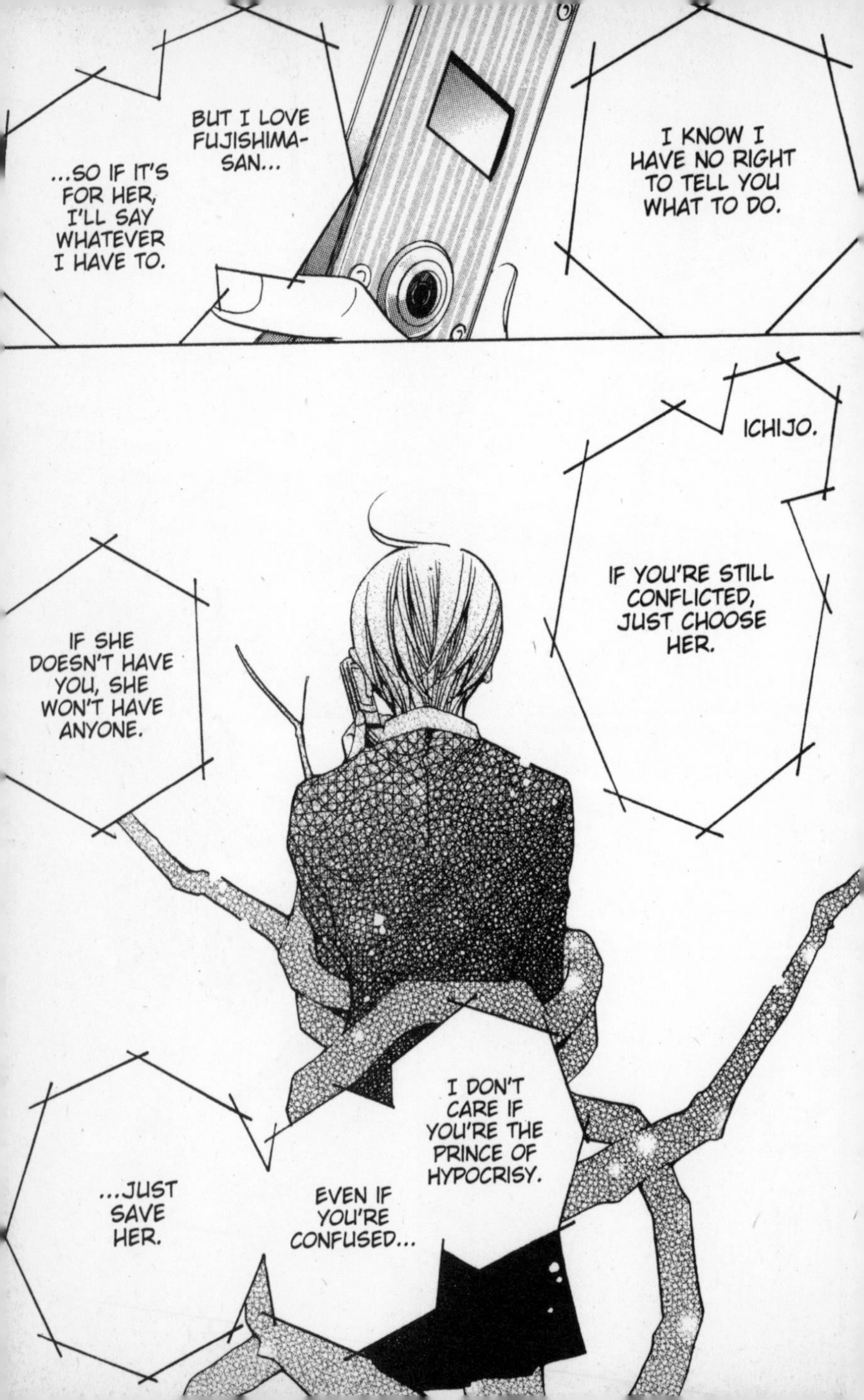
I KNOW I HAVE NO RIGHT TO TELL YOU WHAT TO DO.
BUT I LOVE FUJISHIMA-SAN...
...SO IF IT'S FOR HER, I'LL SAY WHATEVER I HAVE TO.
ICHIJO.
IF YOU'RE STILL CONFLICTED, JUST CHOOSE HER.
IF SHE DOESN'T HAVE YOU, SHE WON'T HAVE ANYONE.
I DON'T CARE IF YOU'RE THE PRINCE OF HYPOCRISY.
EVEN IF YOU'RE CONFUSED...
...JUST SAVE HER.

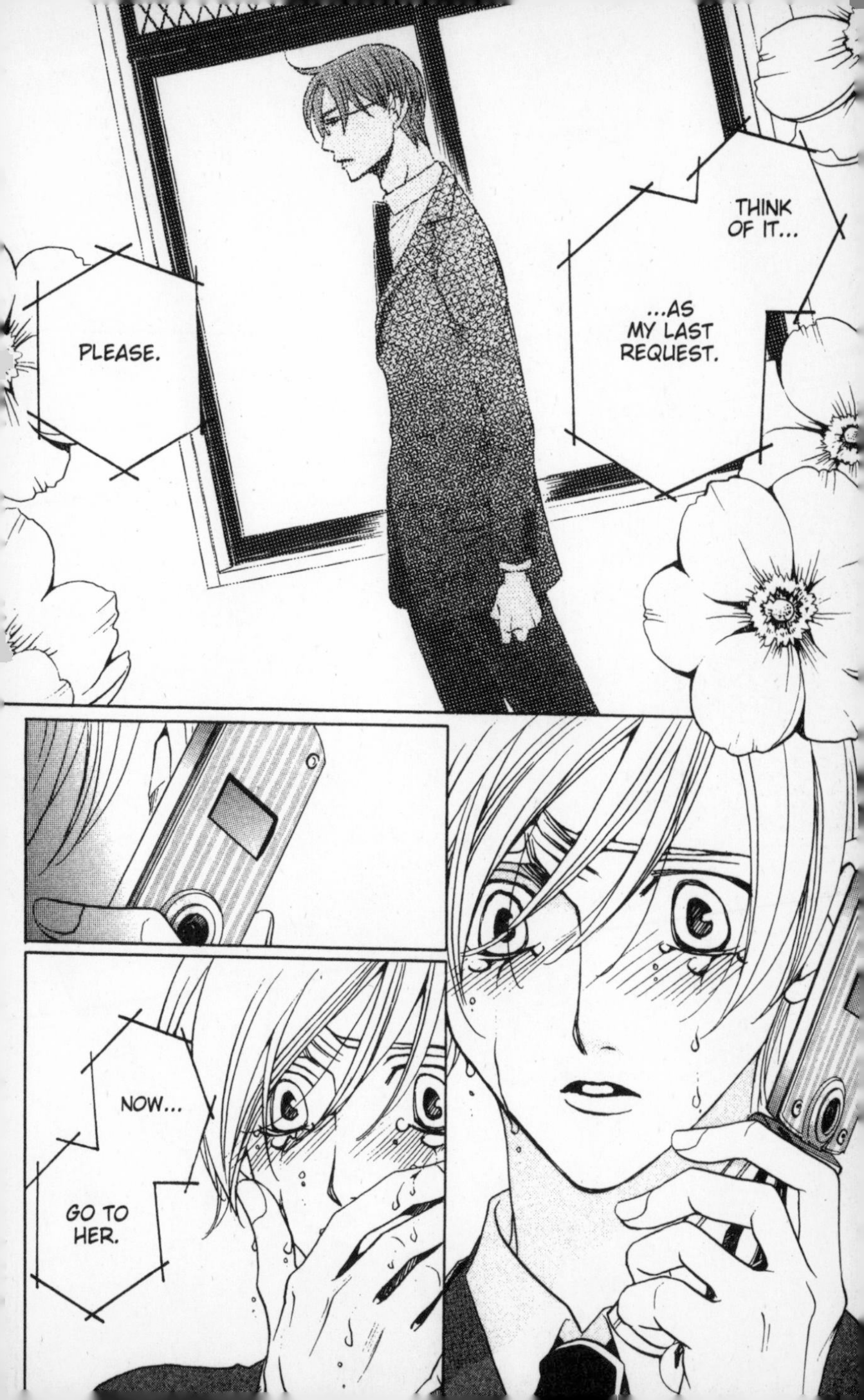
THINK OF IT...
...AS MY LAST REQUEST.
PLEASE.
NOW...
GO TO HER.

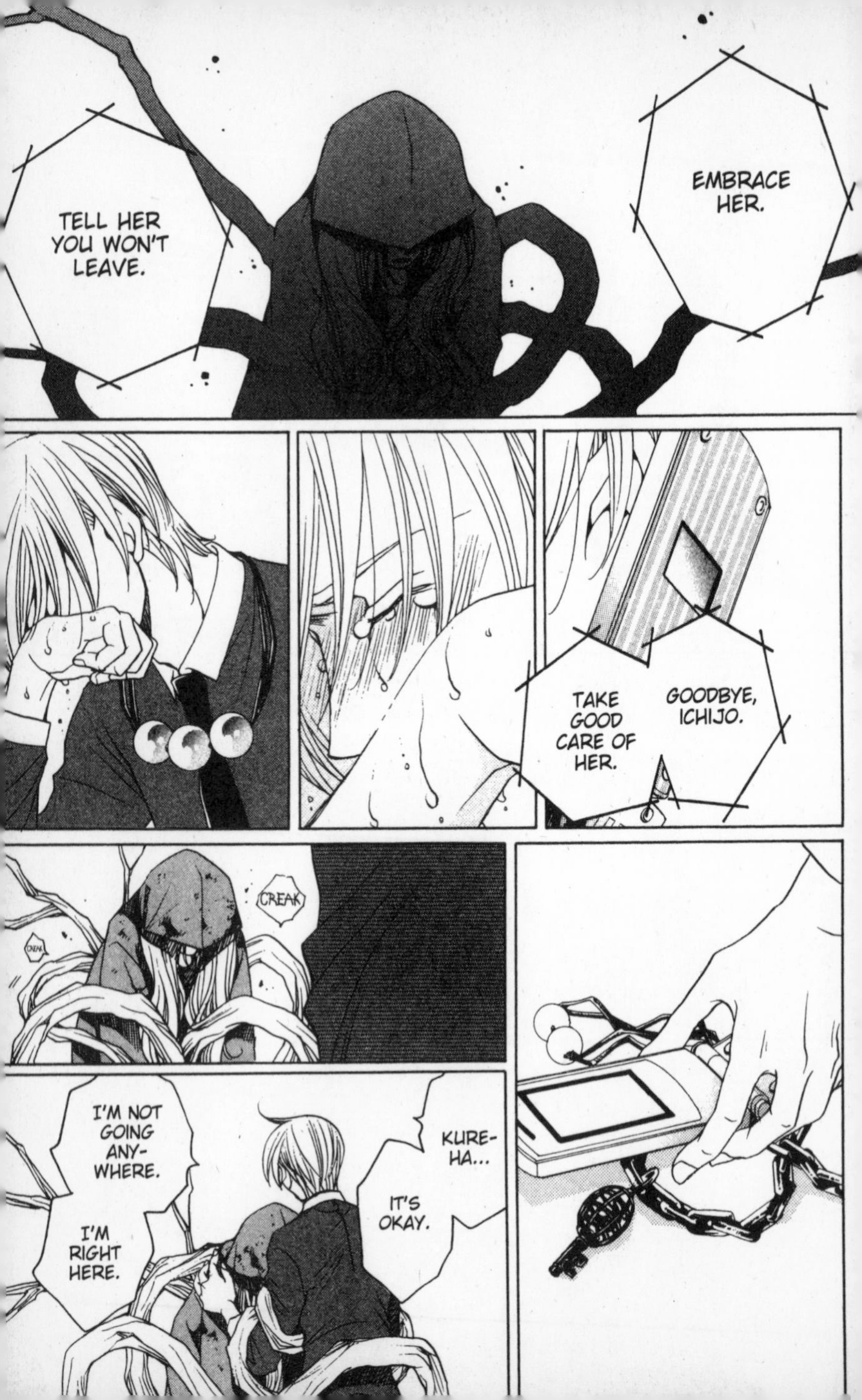
EMBRACE HER.
TELL HER YOU WON'T LEAVE.
GOODBYE, ICHIJO.
TAKE GOOD CARE OF HER.
CREAK
CREAK
KURE-HA...
IT'S OKAY.
I'M NOT GOING ANYWHERE.
I'M RIGHT HERE.

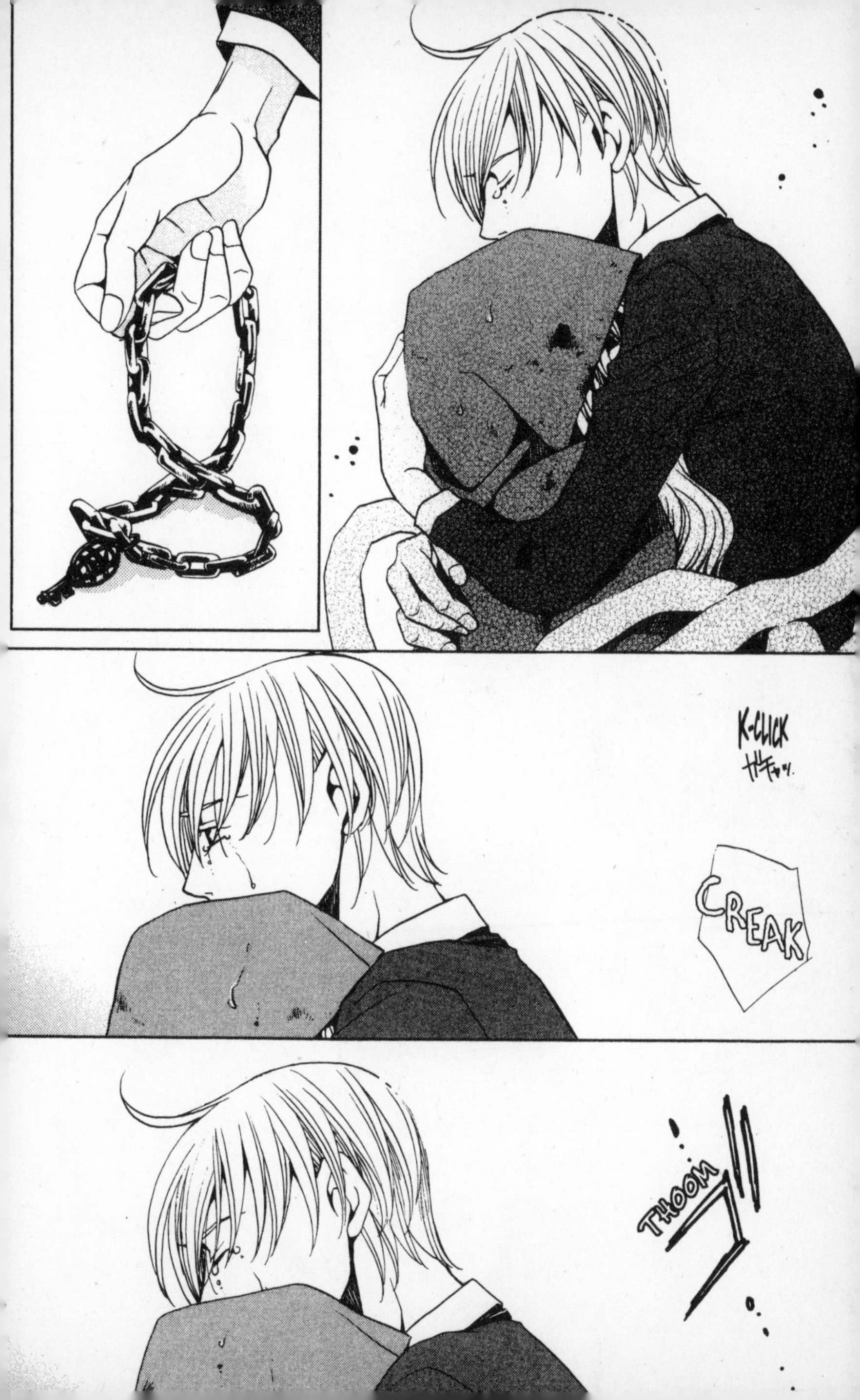
K-CLICK
ガチャッ
CREAK
THOOM

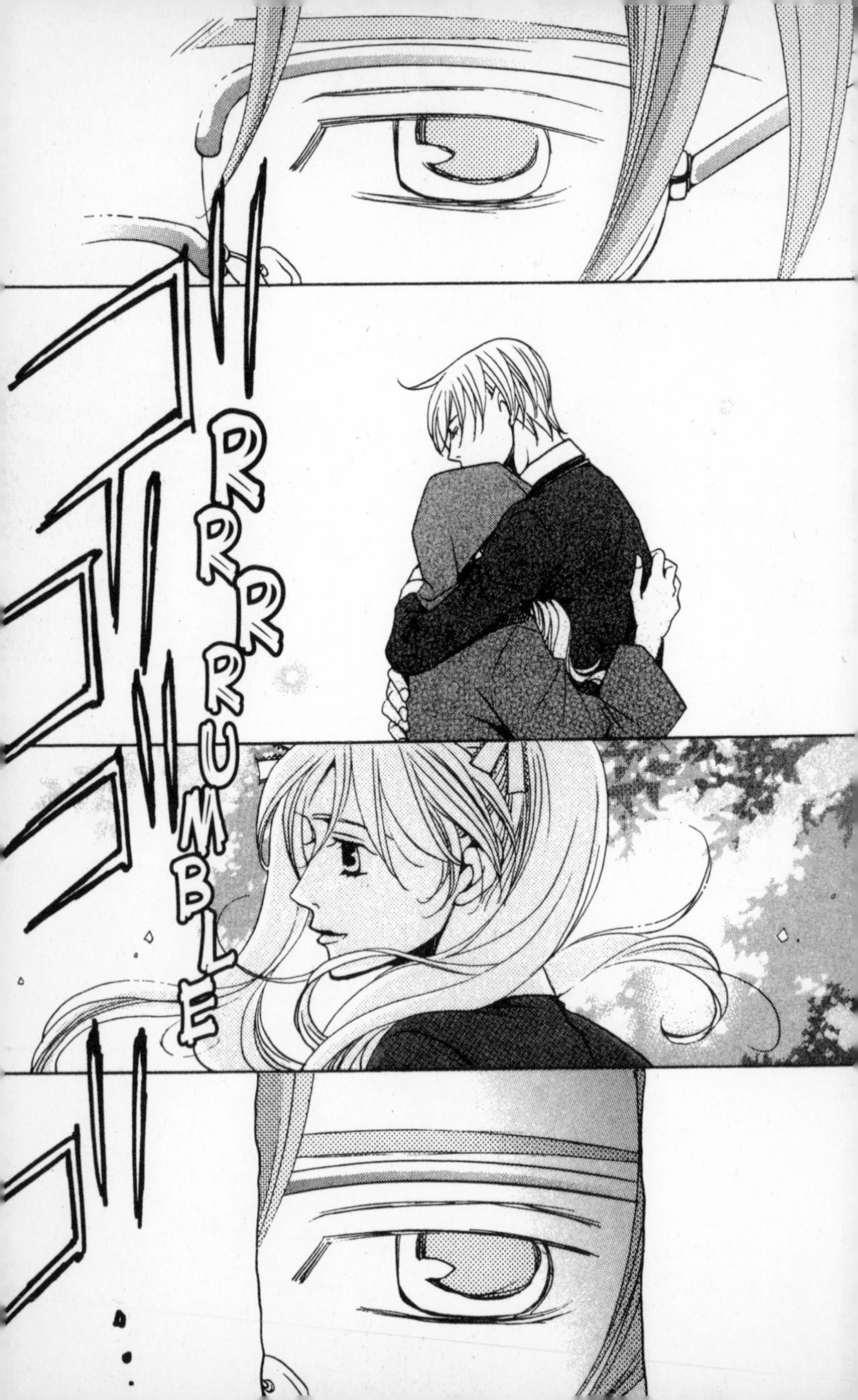
RRRRUMBLE

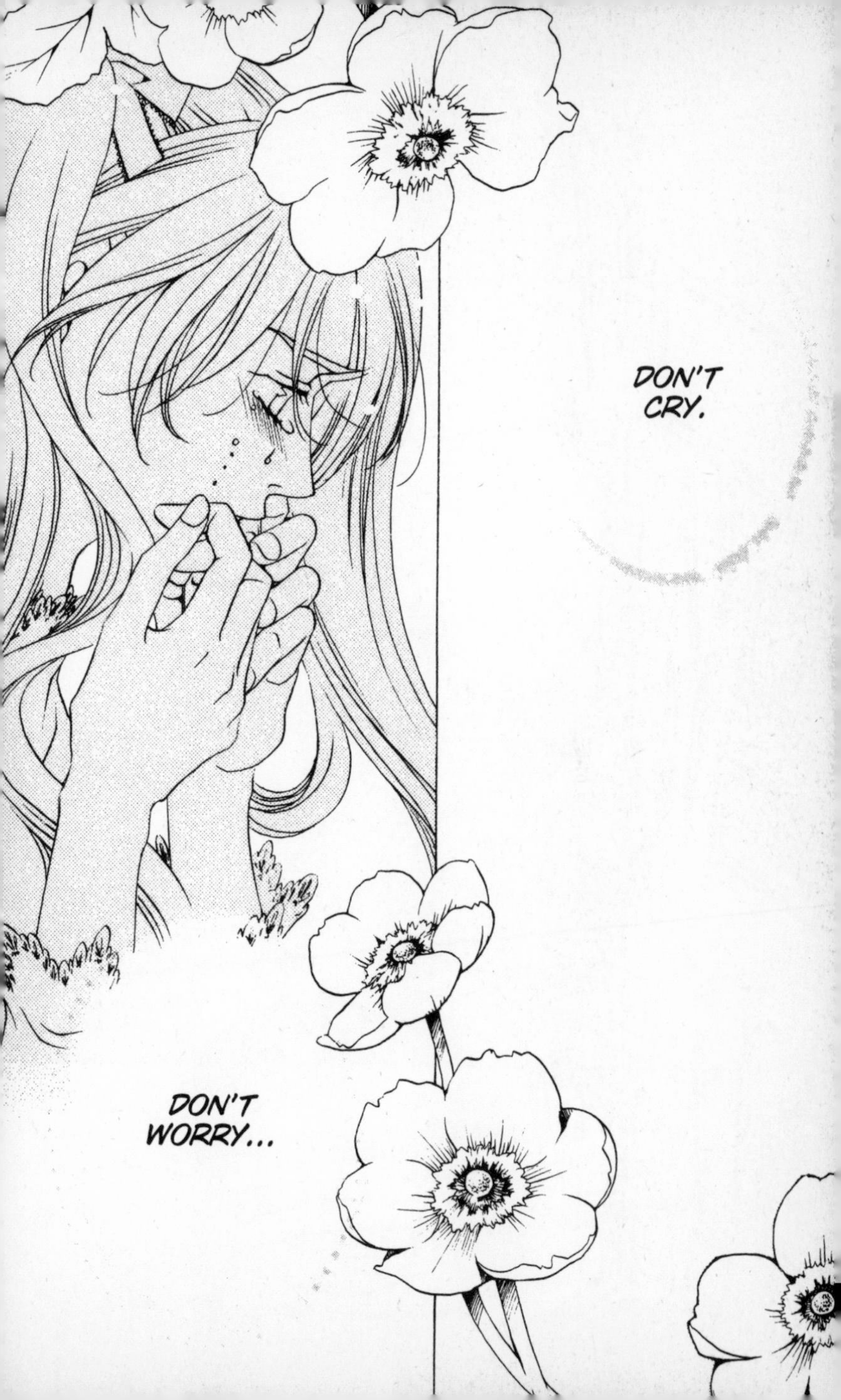
DON'T CRY.
DON'T WORRY...

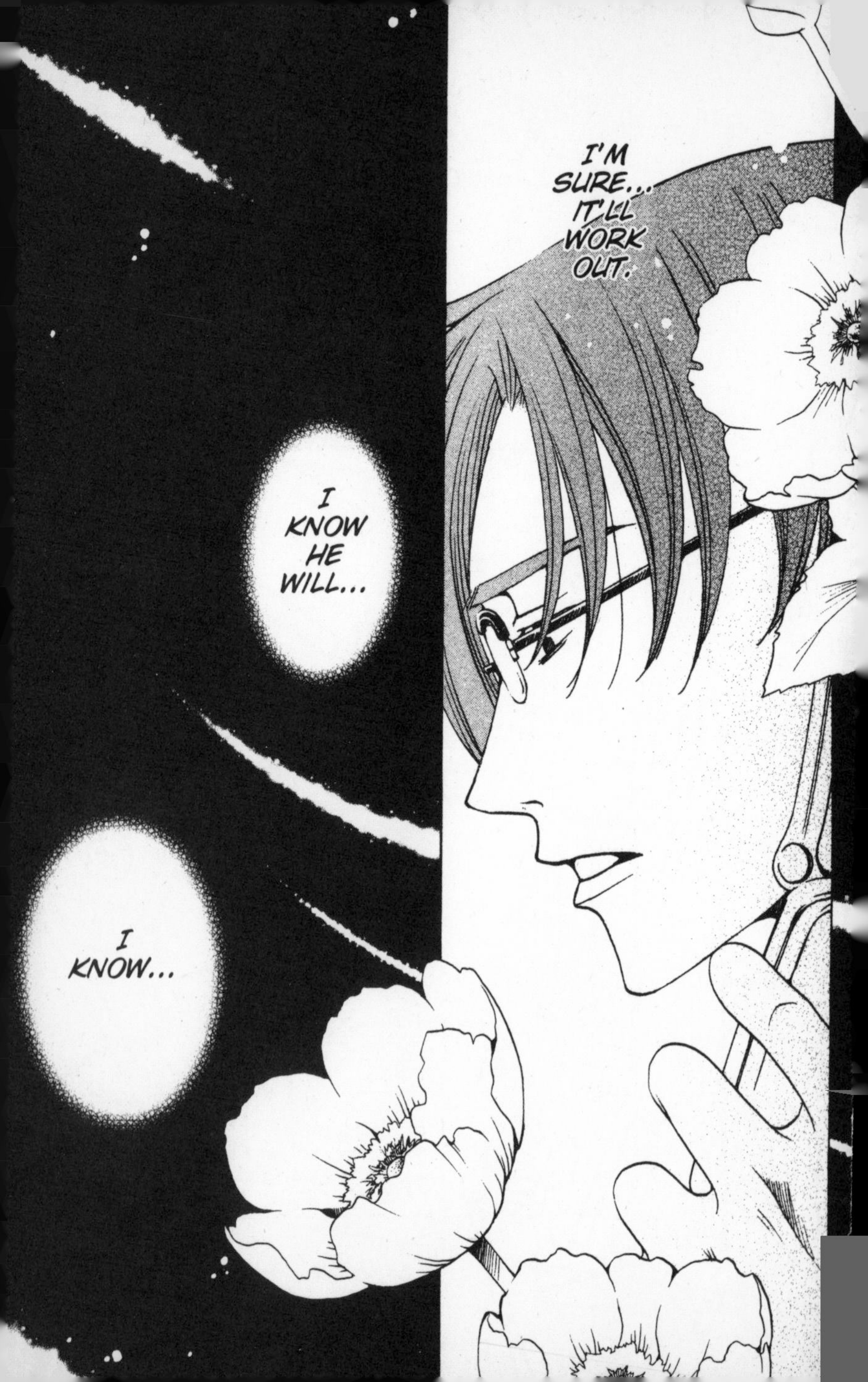
I'M SURE... IT'LL WORK OUT.
I KNOW HE WILL...
I KNOW...

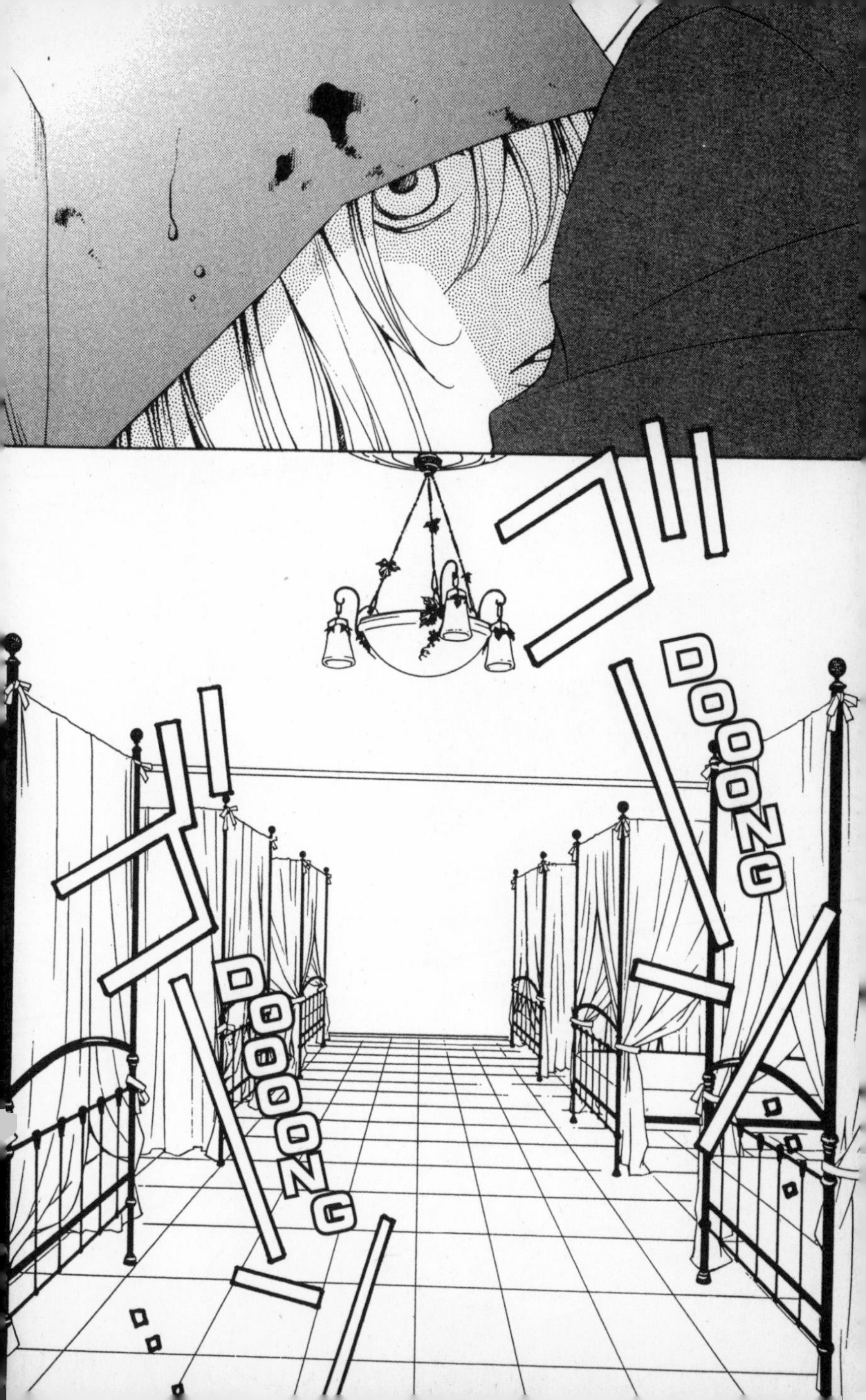
DOOONG
DOOOONG

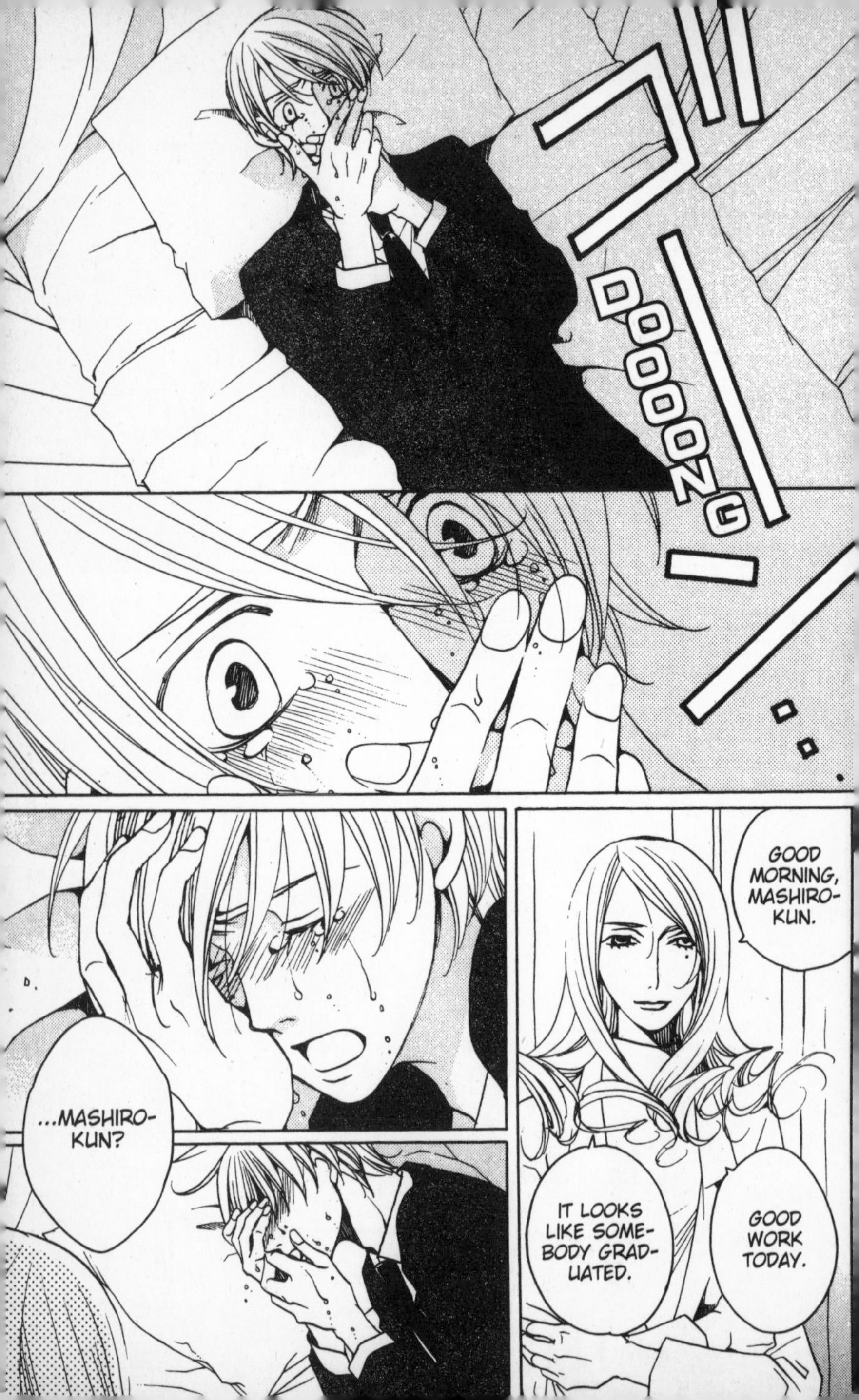
DOOOONG
...
GOOD MORNING, MASHIRO-KUN.
GOOD WORK TODAY.
IT LOOKS LIKE SOMEBODY GRADUATED.
...MASHIRO-KUN?

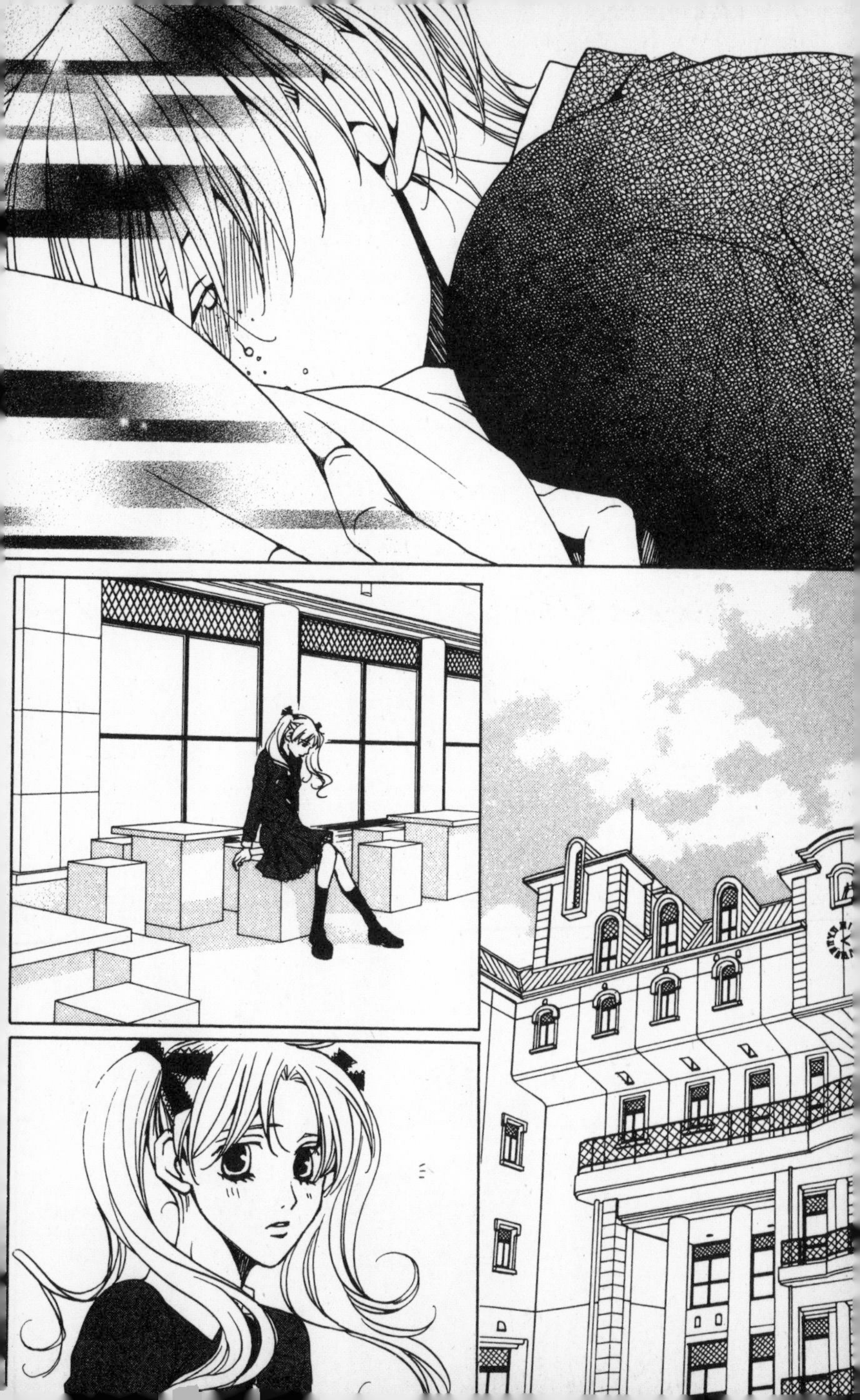

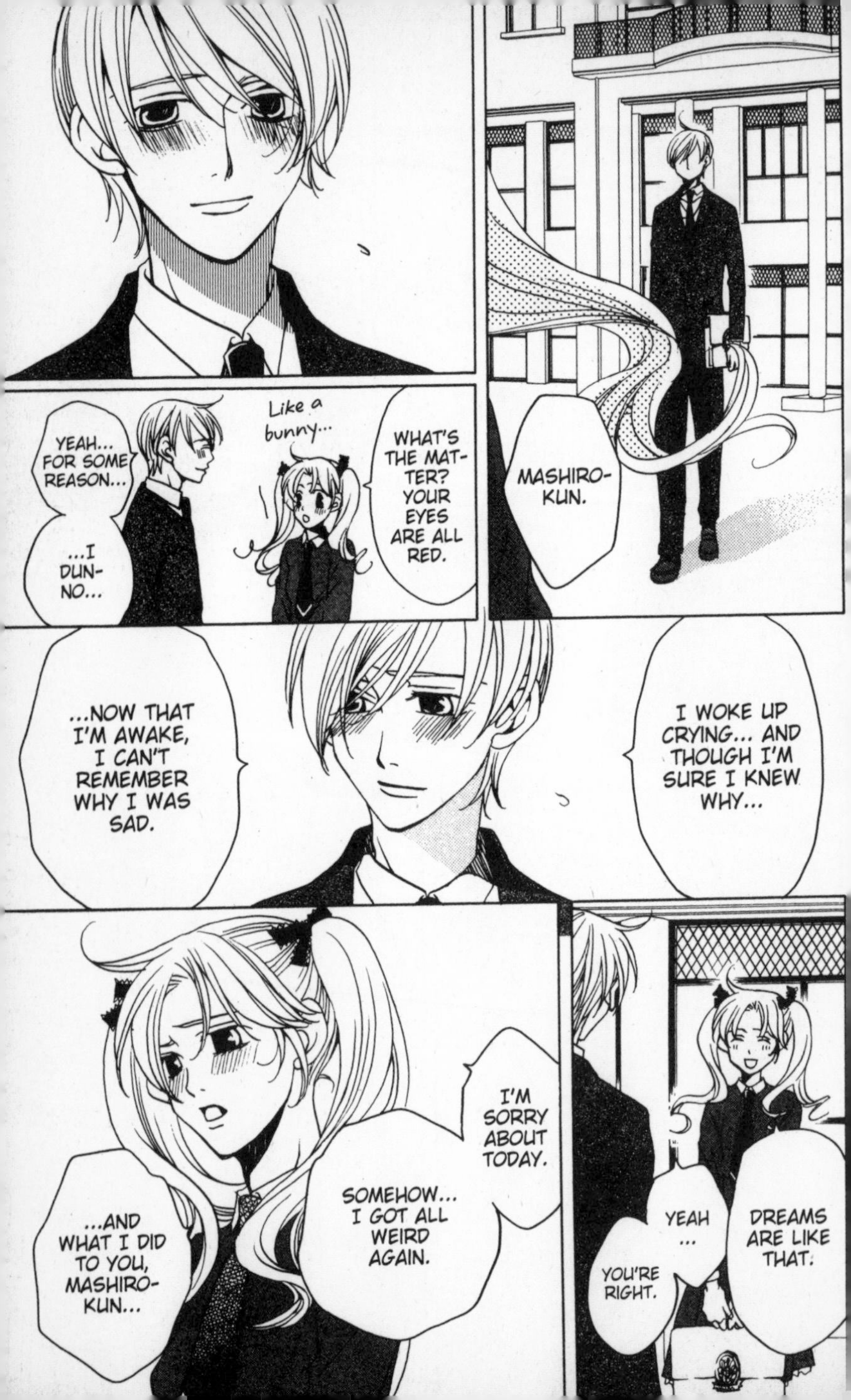
MASHIRO-KUN.
WHAT'S THE MATTER? YOUR EYES ARE ALL RED.
Like a bunny...
YEAH... FOR SOME REASON...
...I DUNNO...
I WOKE UP CRYING... AND THOUGH I'M SURE I KNEW WHY...
...NOW THAT I'M AWAKE, I CAN'T REMEMBER WHY I WAS SAD.
DREAMS ARE LIKE THAT.
YEAH... YOU'RE RIGHT.
I'M SORRY ABOUT TODAY.
SOMEHOW... I GOT ALL WEIRD AGAIN.
...AND WHAT I DID TO YOU, MASHIRO-KUN...

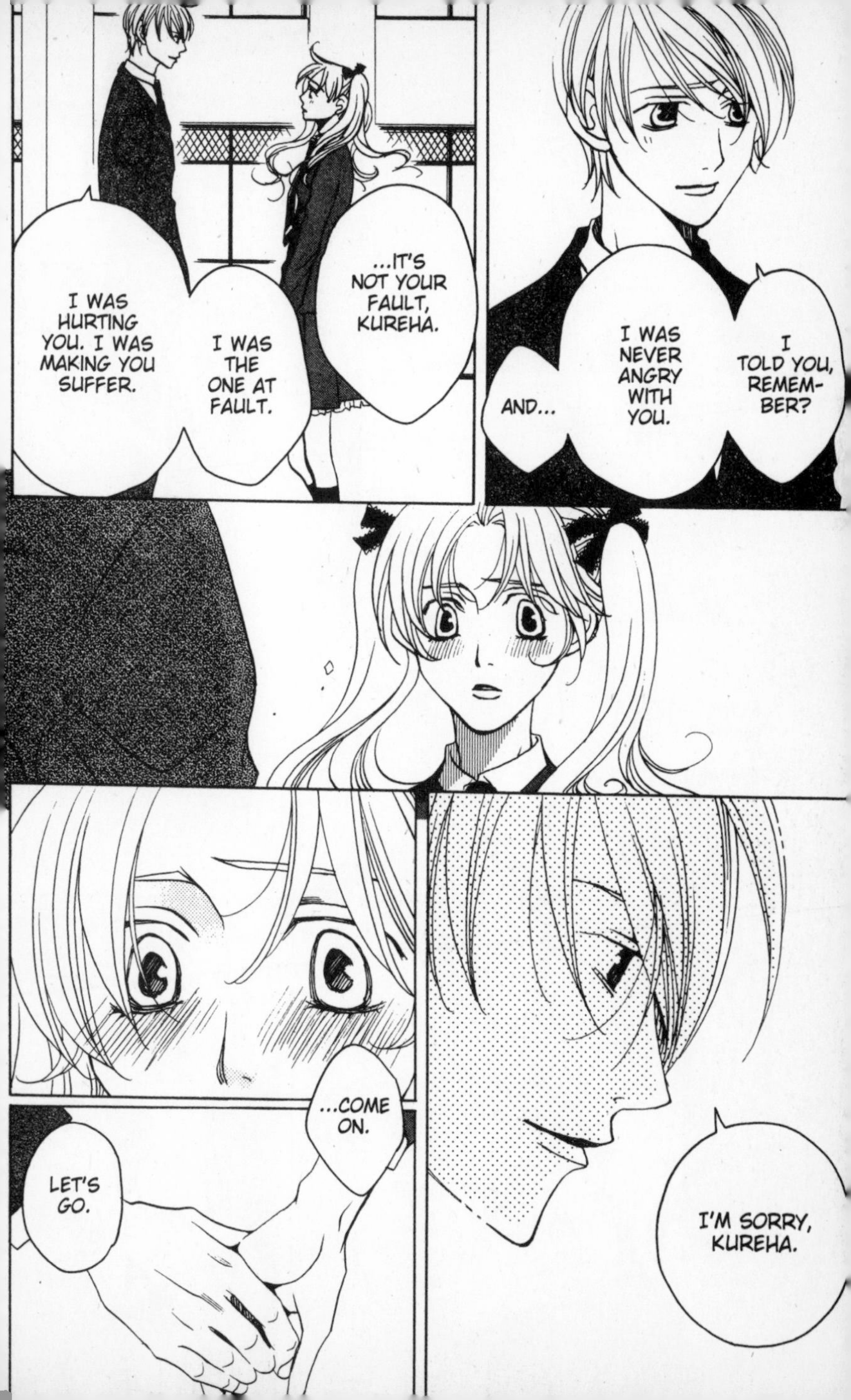
I TOLD YOU, REMEMBER?
I WAS NEVER ANGRY WITH YOU.
AND...
...IT'S NOT YOUR FAULT, KUREHA.
I WAS THE ONE AT FAULT.
I WAS HURTING YOU. I WAS MAKING YOU SUFFER.
I'M SORRY, KUREHA.
...COME ON.
LET'S GO.

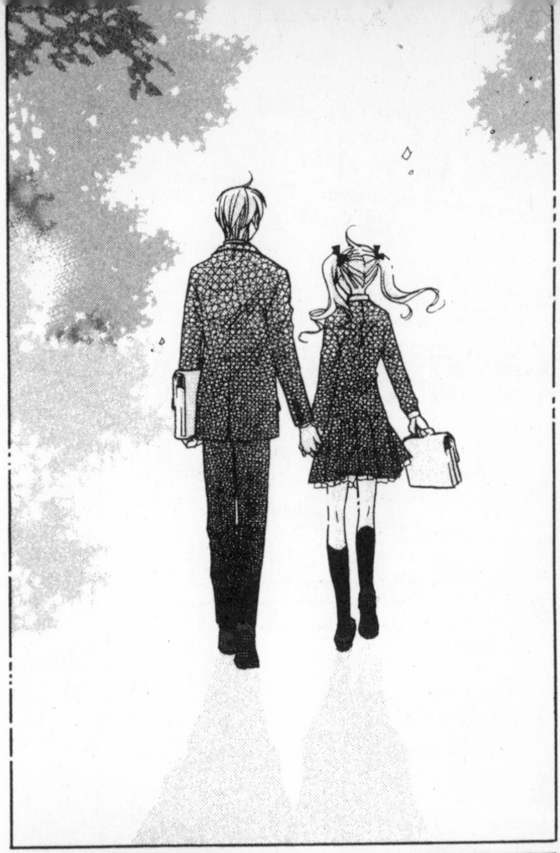

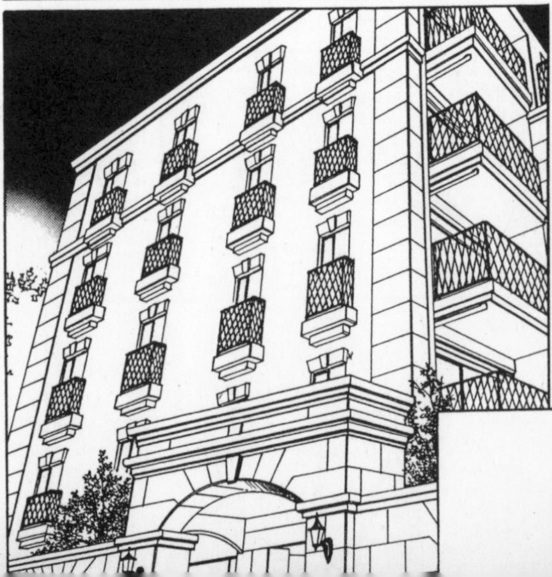

All the characters in this story have colorful names.*

They don't necessarily all have significant meanings behind them, but since I started by naming the three main characters that, I've made sure to continue naming all the other characters that way, too.

I think all the colorful names are elegant and carry some connotations to them, so I'm really very pleased with it.

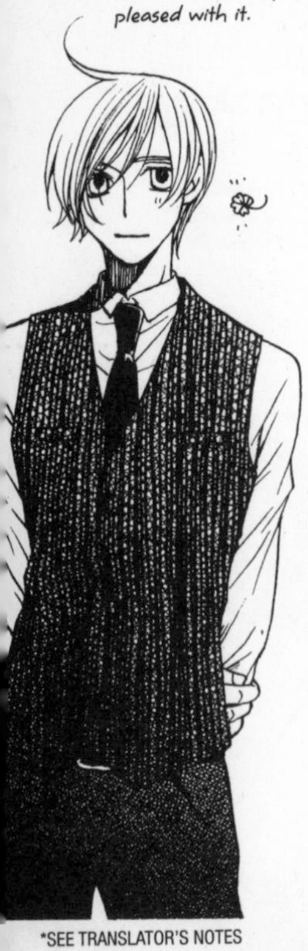

*SEE TRANSLATOR'S NOTES

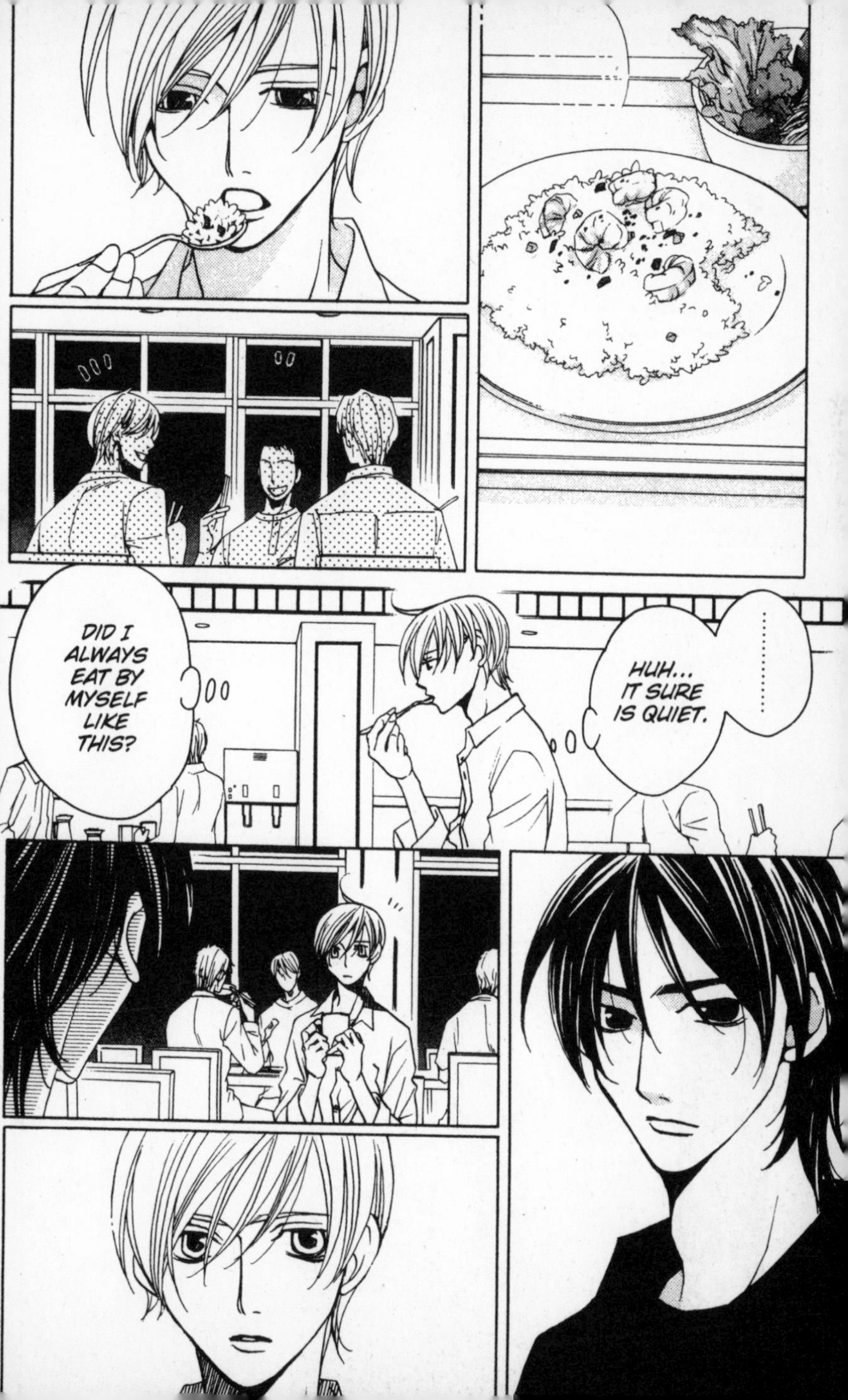
......
HUH... IT SURE IS QUIET.
DID I ALWAYS EAT BY MYSELF LIKE THIS?

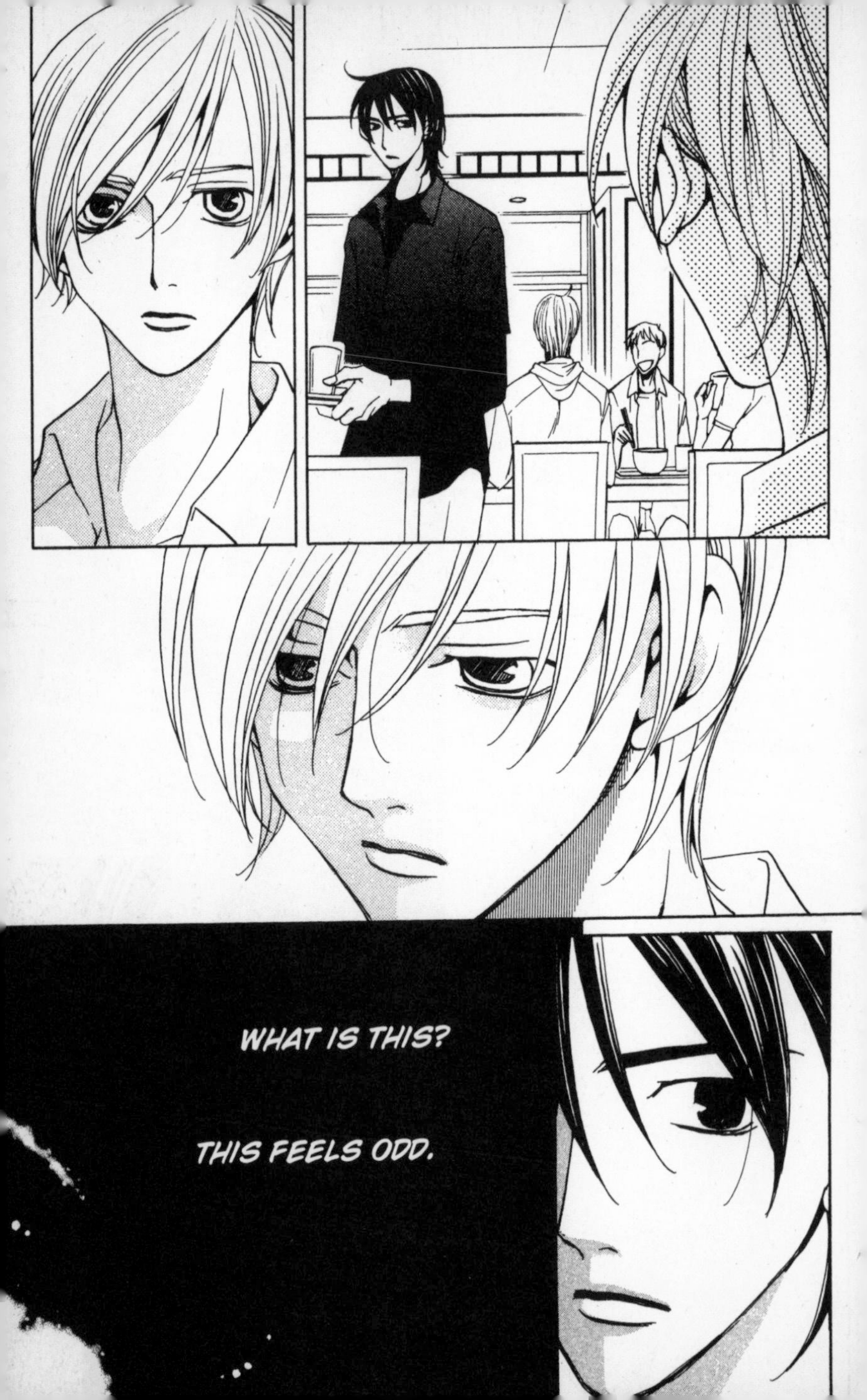
WHAT IS THIS?
THIS FEELS ODD.

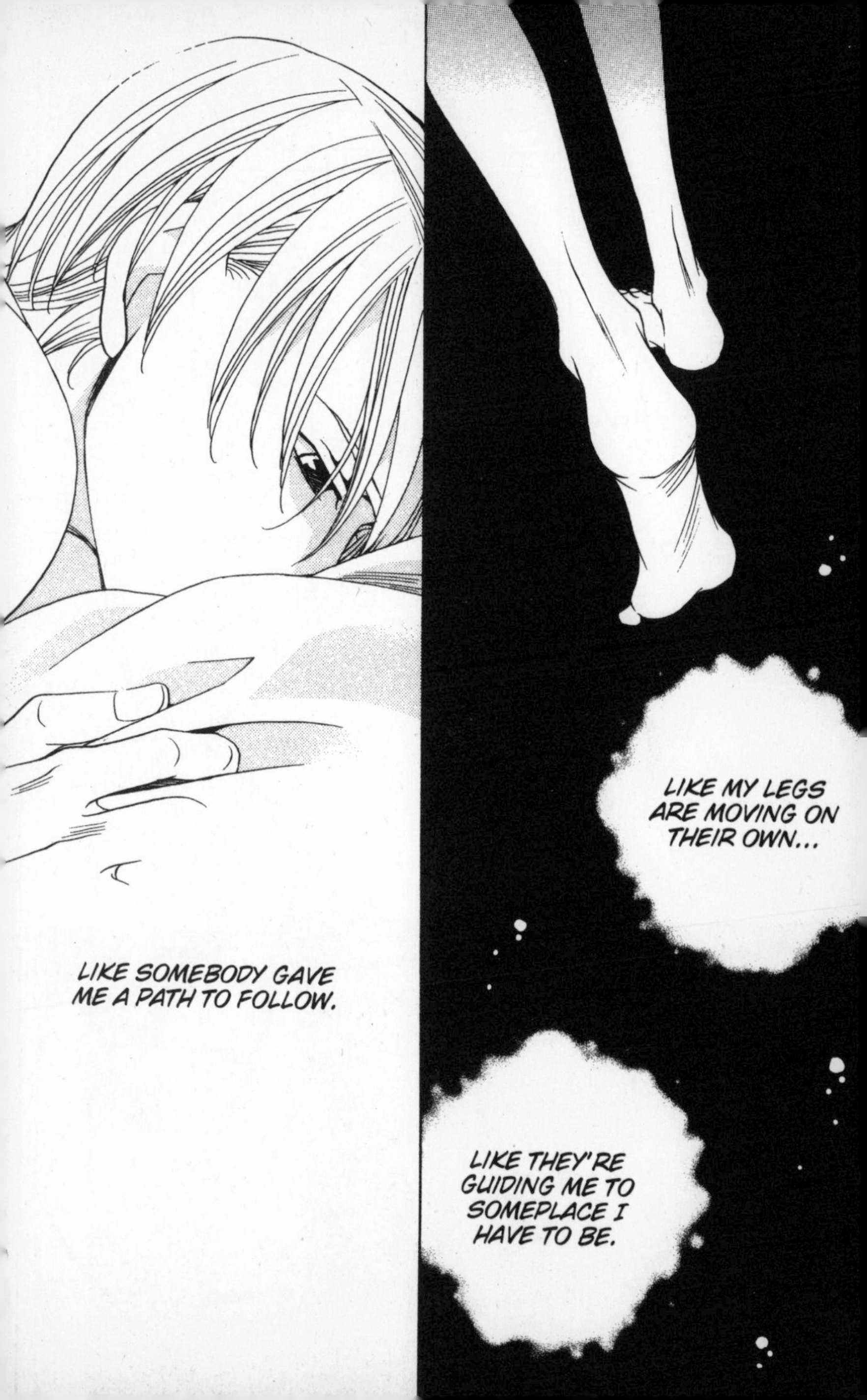
LIKE MY LEGS ARE MOVING ON THEIR OWN...
LIKE THEY'RE GUIDING ME TO SOMEPLACE I HAVE TO BE.
LIKE SOMEBODY GAVE ME A PATH TO FOLLOW.

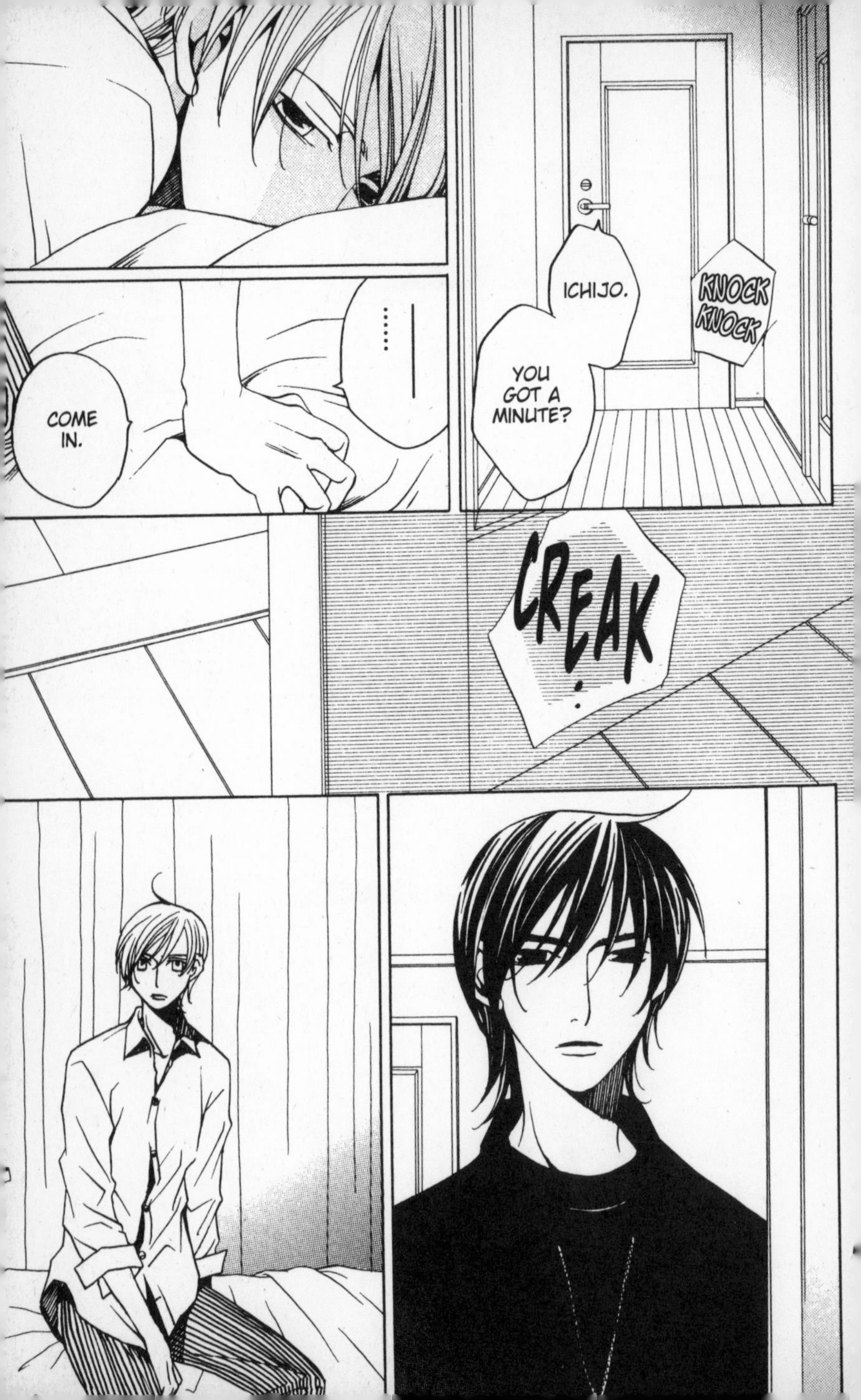
KNOCK KNOCK
ICHIJO.
YOU GOT A MINUTE?
……
COME IN.
CREAK

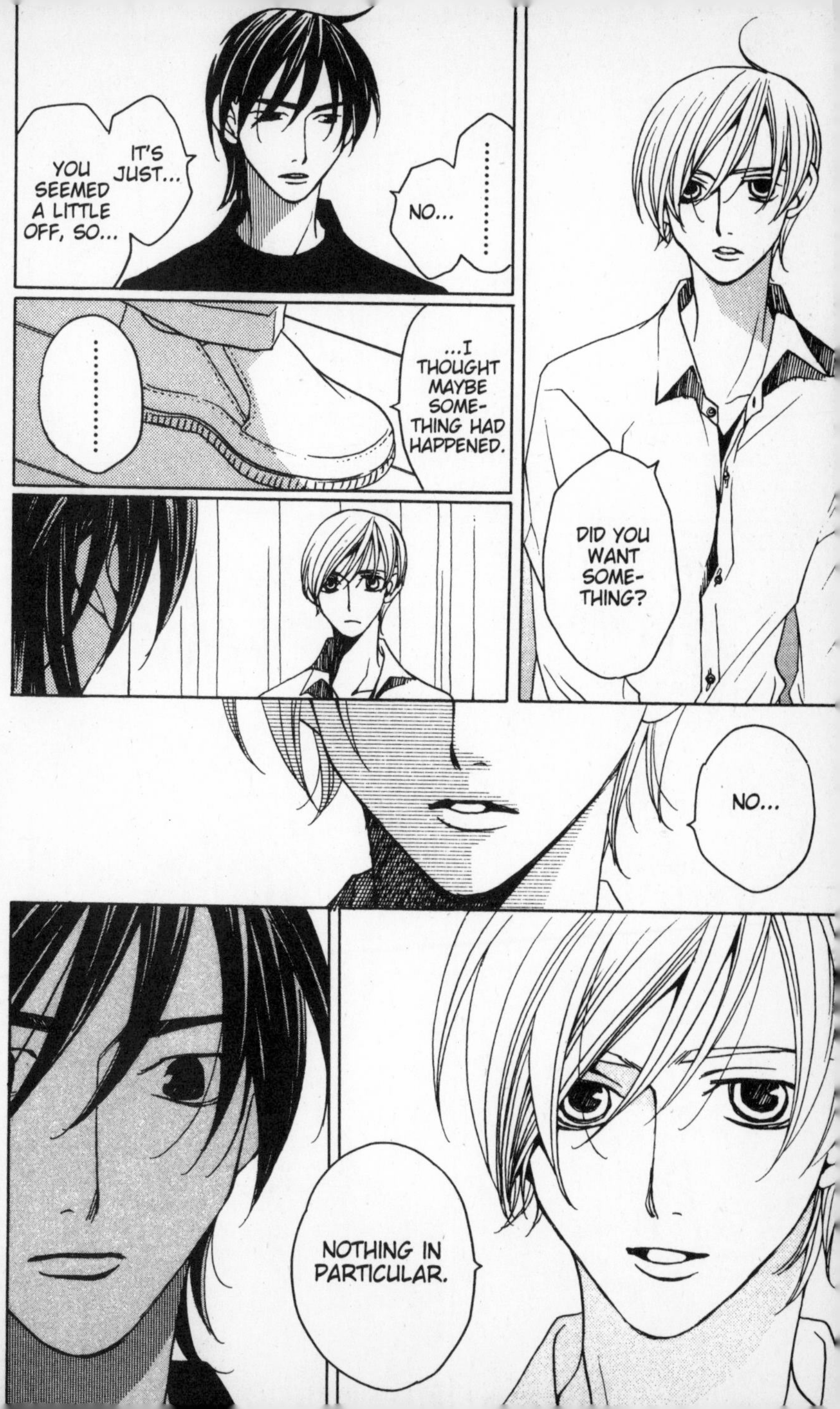
DID YOU WANT SOMETHING?
...... NO...
IT'S JUST... YOU SEEMED A LITTLE OFF, SO...
...I THOUGHT MAYBE SOMETHING HAD HAPPENED.
......
NO...
NOTHING IN PARTICULAR.

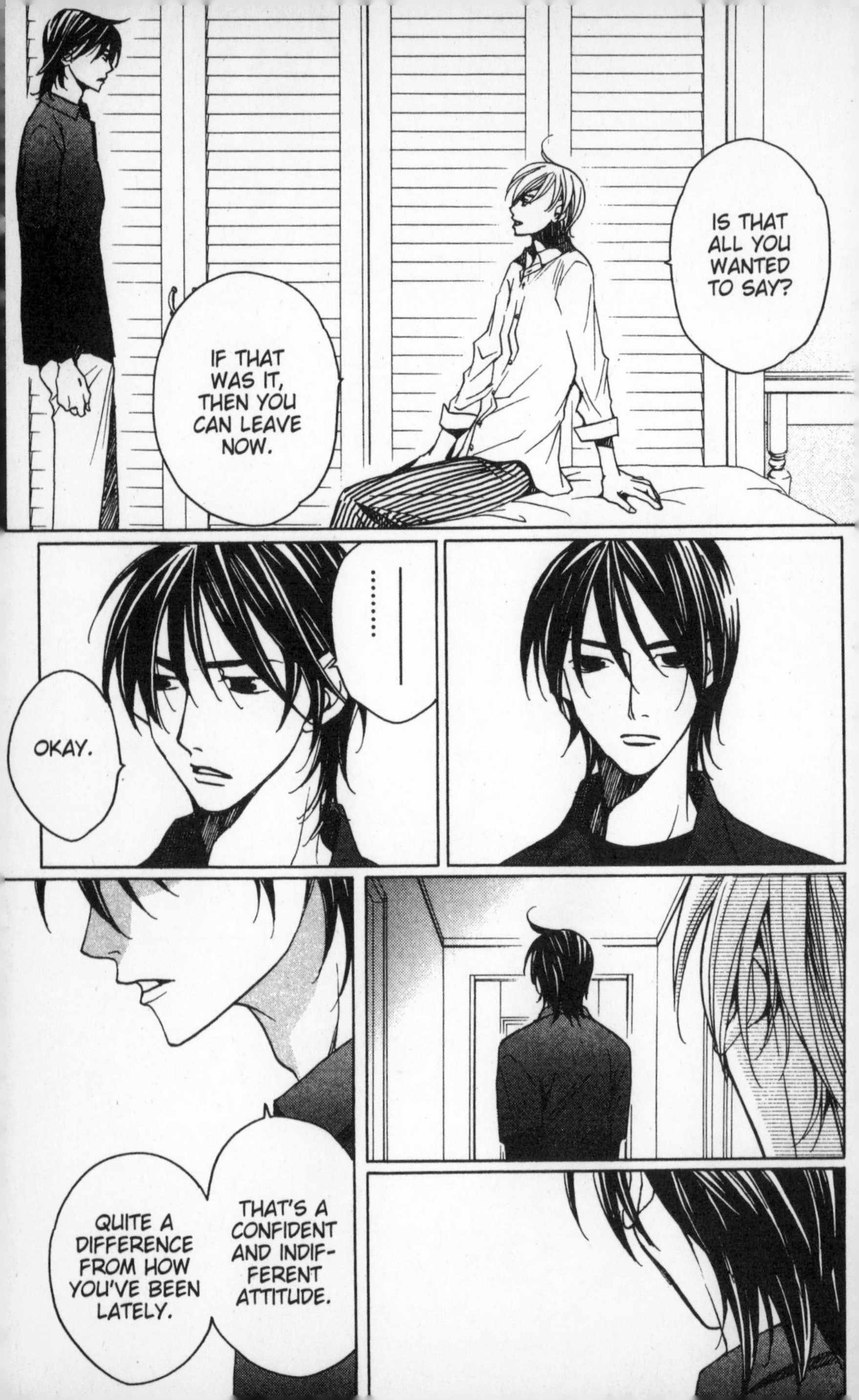
IS THAT ALL YOU WANTED TO SAY?
IF THAT WAS IT, THEN YOU CAN LEAVE NOW.
......
OKAY.
THAT'S A CONFIDENT AND INDIF-FERENT ATTITUDE.
QUITE A DIFFERENCE FROM HOW YOU'VE BEEN LATELY.

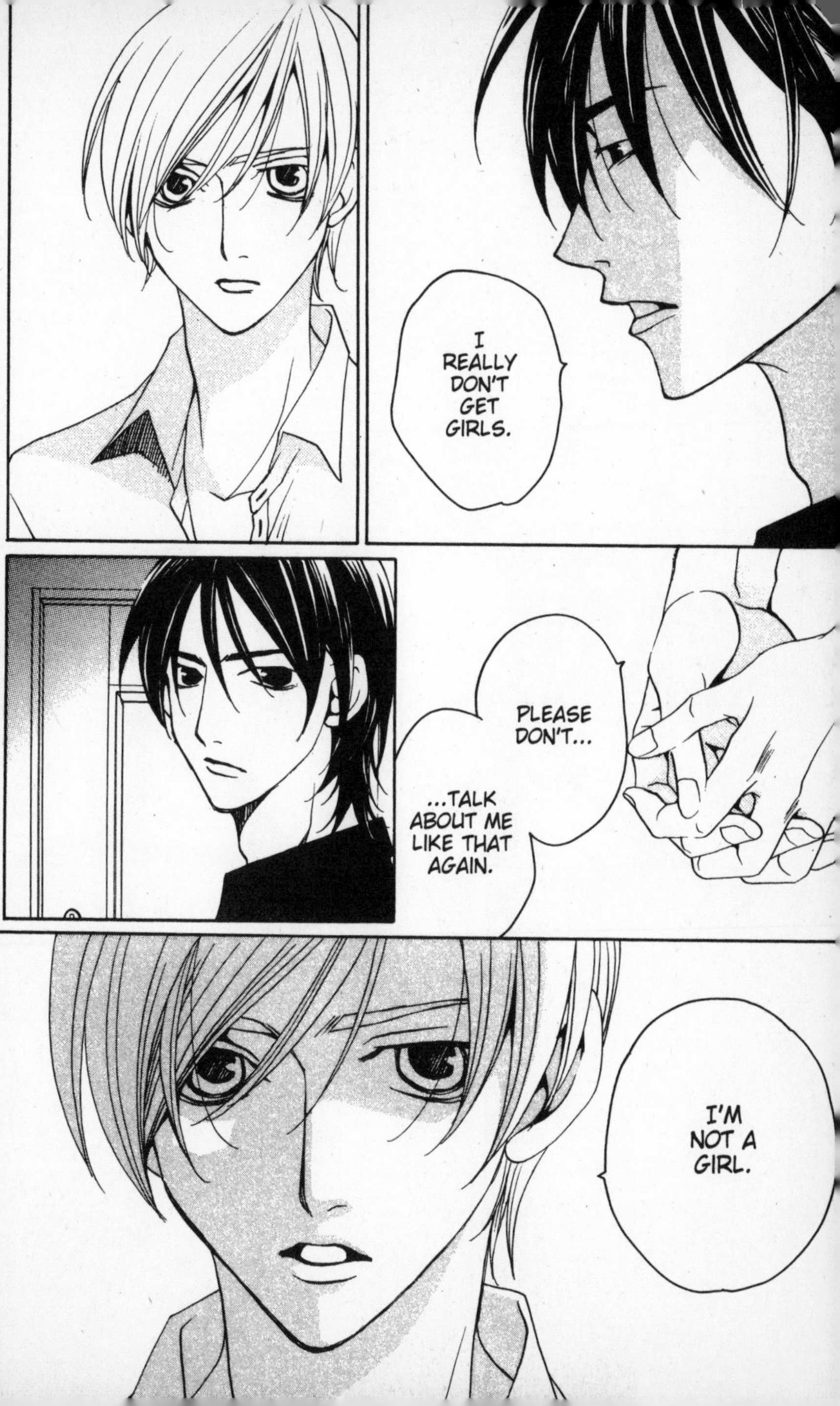
I REALLY DON'T GET GIRLS.
PLEASE DON'T...
...TALK ABOUT ME LIKE THAT AGAIN.
I'M NOT A GIRL.

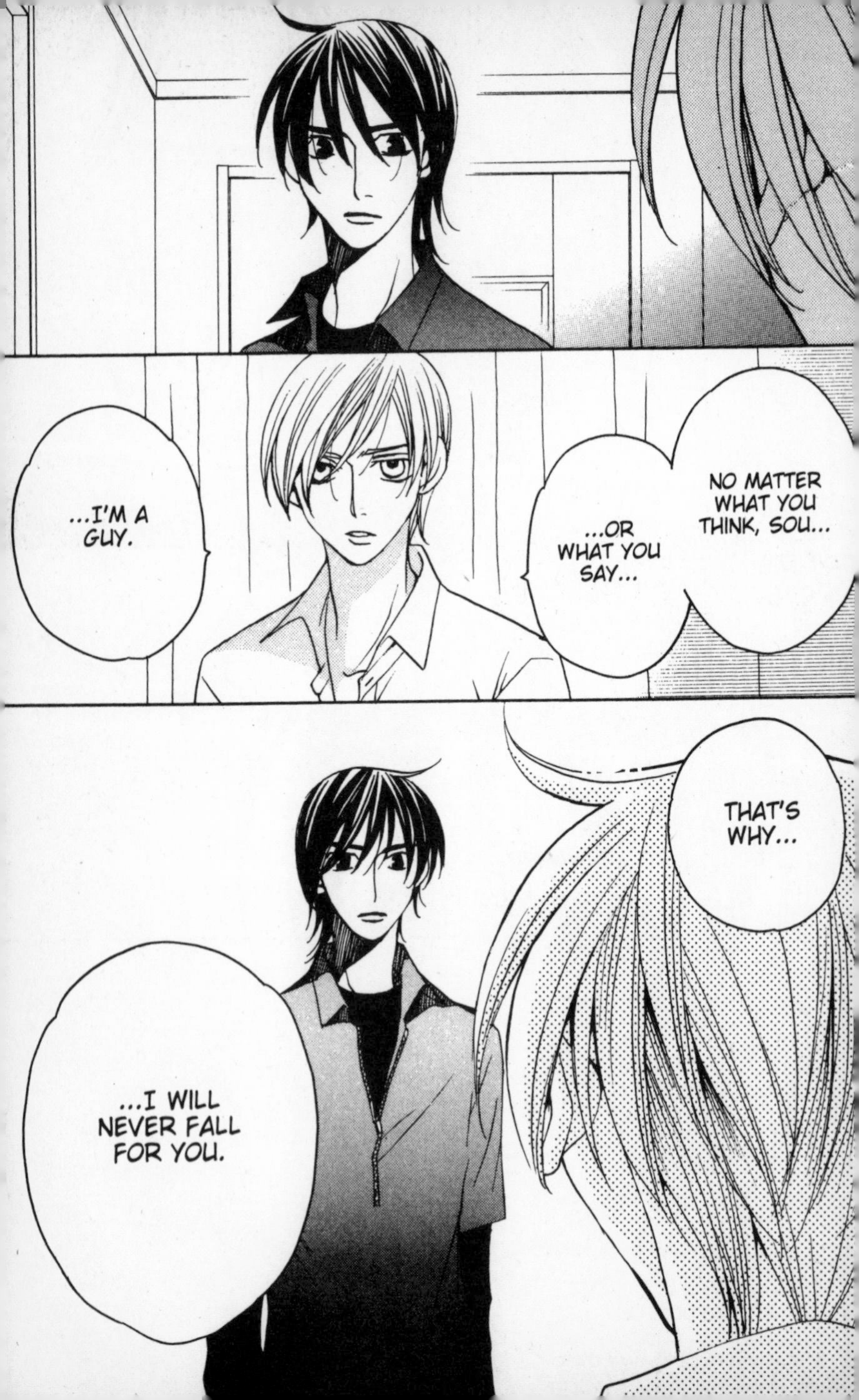
NO MATTER WHAT YOU THINK, SOU...
...OR WHAT YOU SAY...
...I'M A GUY.
THAT'S WHY...
...I WILL NEVER FALL FOR YOU.

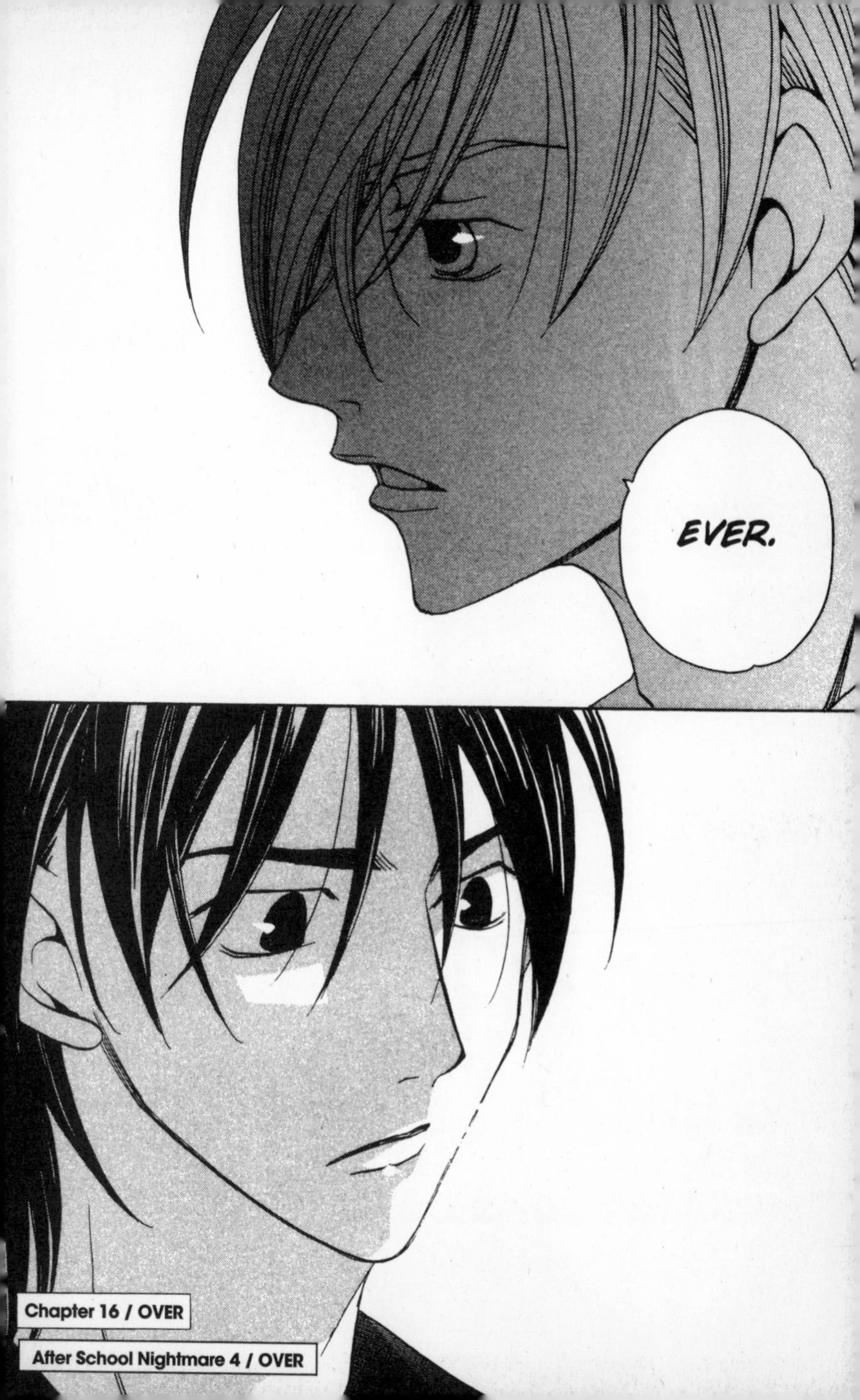
EVER.
Chapter 16 / OVER
After School Nightmare 4 / OVER

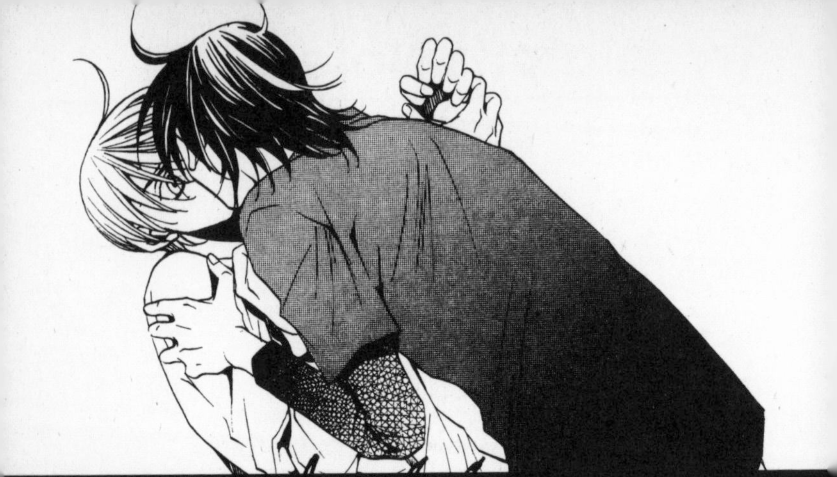

Coming Soon...

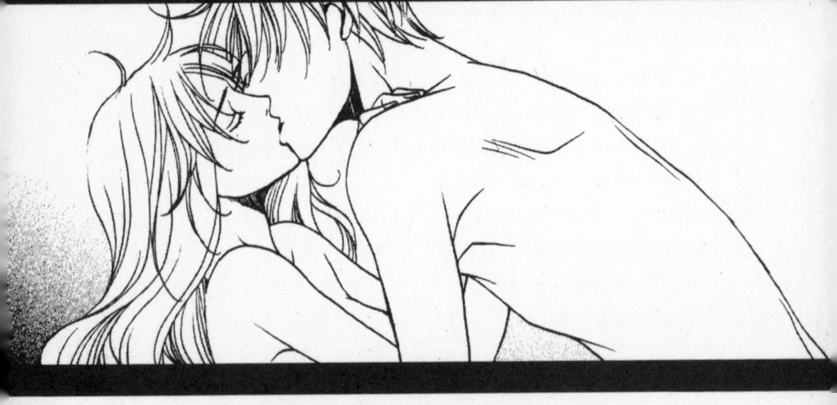

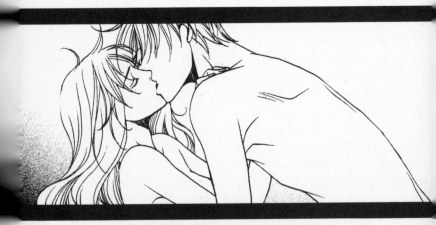

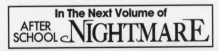

In The Next Volume of

AFTER SCHOOL NIGHTMARE

Translator's Notes:

Pg. 72 – Ai
Going along with the theme of colors in the names of the characters in this series, Sou's sister's name, Ai, means "indigo." 藍

Pg. 112 – *obento*
A boxed meal quite similar to a boxed lunch.

Pg. 119 – cherry blossoms and graduating
The Japanese school year ends in late February or early March and so come into the new year of school in April in the Spring when the cherry blossoms are in full-bloom. The graduation from junior high into high school is the most highly anticipated shift and the vivid connection between graduation and approaching cherry blossoms is memorable in the way that one's Sweet Sixteen birthday is in the States.

Pg. 179 – colors and names
Since the cast of characters from volume 1 of this series was introduced, new characters have shown up whose names have not yet been explained.
新橋 Shinbashi, Mashiro's good friend, is a very traditional color not realized by many this day to mean a dark to medium turquoise.
東雲 Itsuki Shinonome's color meaning rests in his last name. Broken down it means "eastern clouds" and is associated with the dawn. It is a light salmon color.
黒崎 Kurosaki-sempai, the head of the Judo club, contains the color black in his name
黄川田 Even "Aimi Kikawada" which is mentioned only briefly in passing in volume three, possesses the color yellow in her last name.

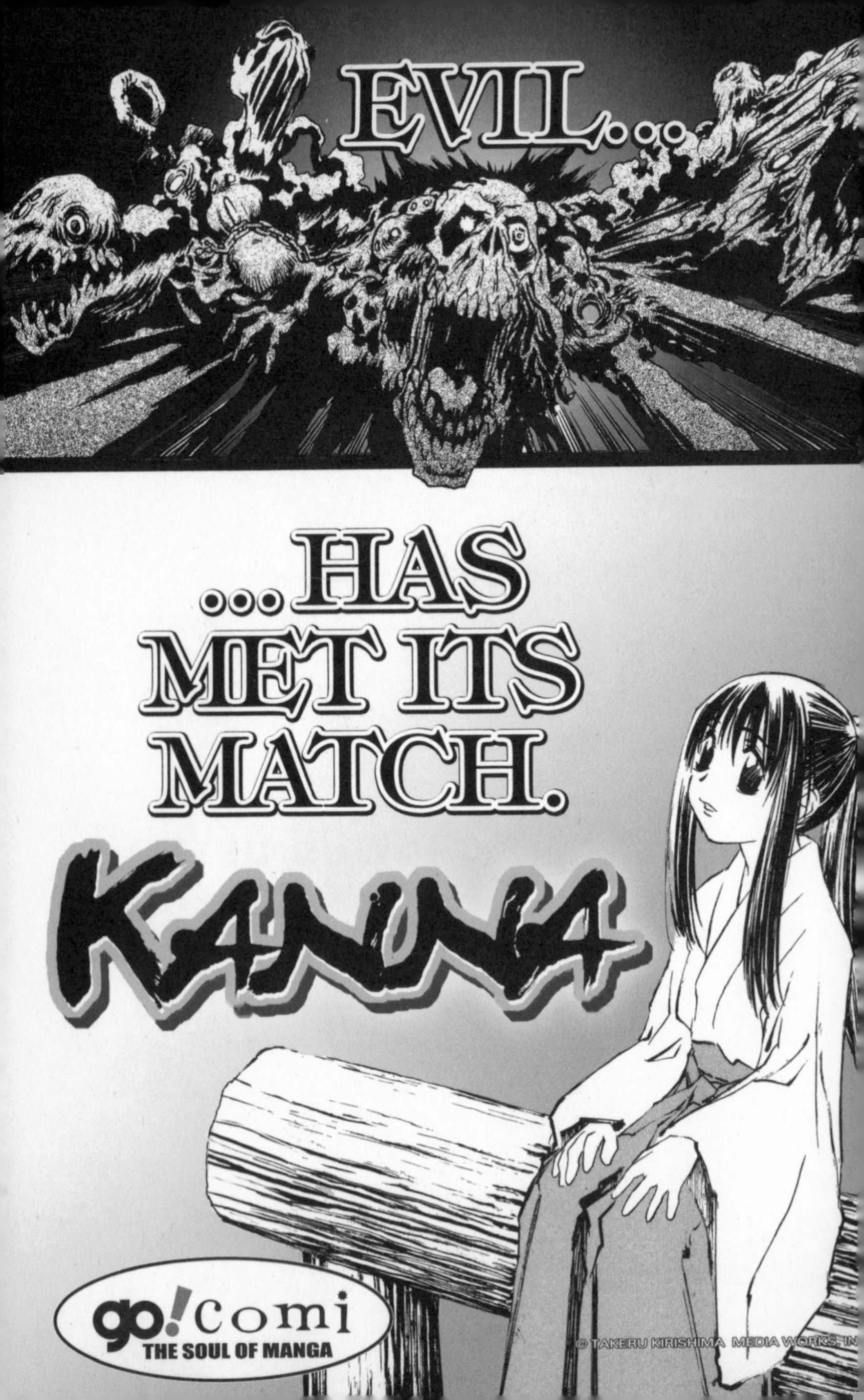
EVIL...
...HAS MET ITS MATCH.
KANNA
go! comi
THE SOUL OF MANGA
© TAKERU KIRISHIMA MEDIA WORKS, IN

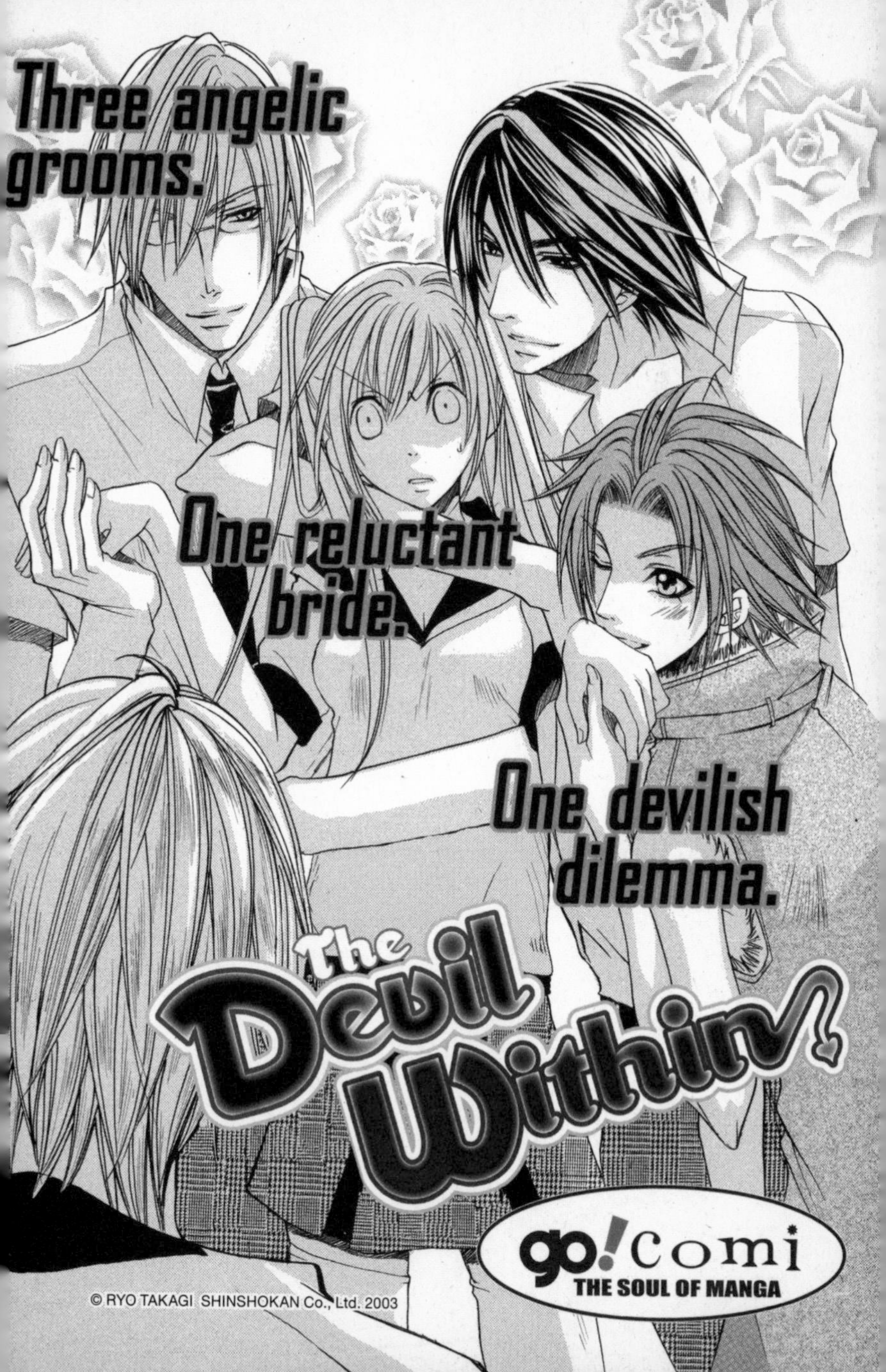
Three angelic grooms.
One reluctant bride.
One devilish dilemma.
The Devil Within!
go!comi
THE SOUL OF MANGA

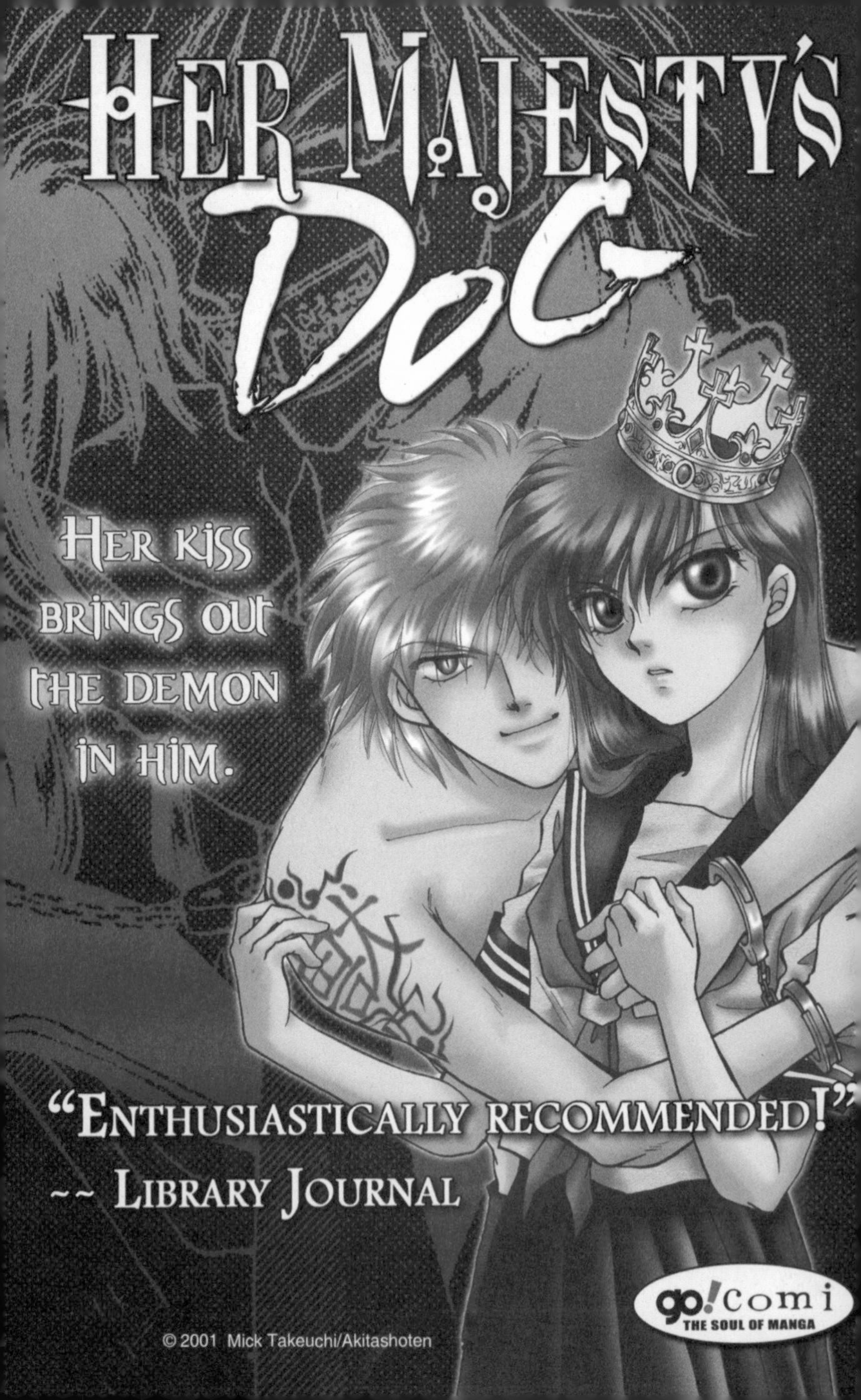
HER MAJESTY'S DOG
HER KISS BRINGS OUT THE DEMON IN HIM.
"ENTHUSIASTICALLY RECOMMENDED!"
~~ LIBRARY JOURNAL
go!comi THE SOUL OF MANGA
© 2001 Mick Takeuchi/Akitashoten

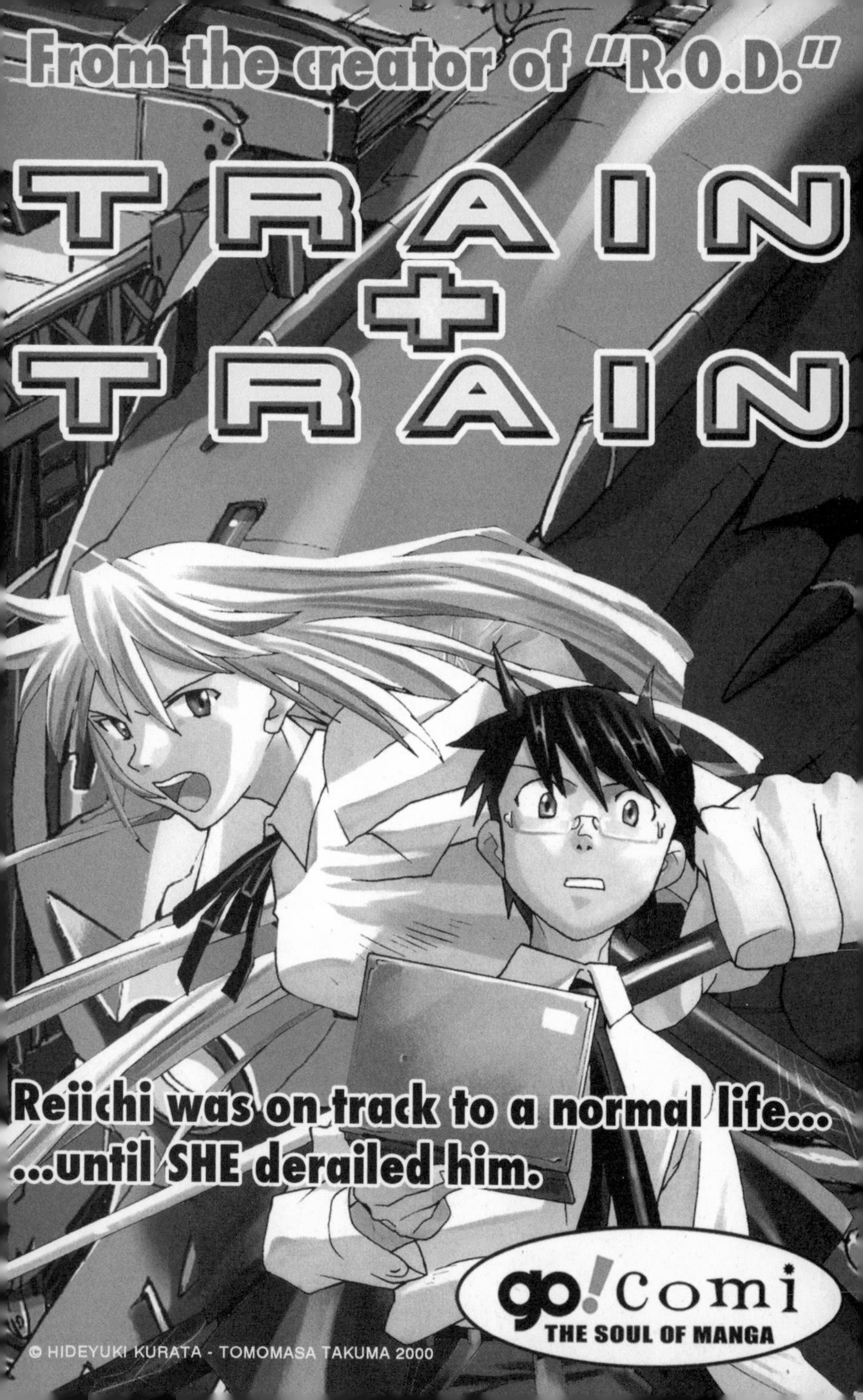
From the creator of "R.O.D."
TRAIN + TRAIN
Reiichi was on track to a normal life...
...until SHE derailed him.
go!comi
THE SOUL OF MANGA
© HIDEYUKI KURATA - TOMOMASA TAKUMA 2000

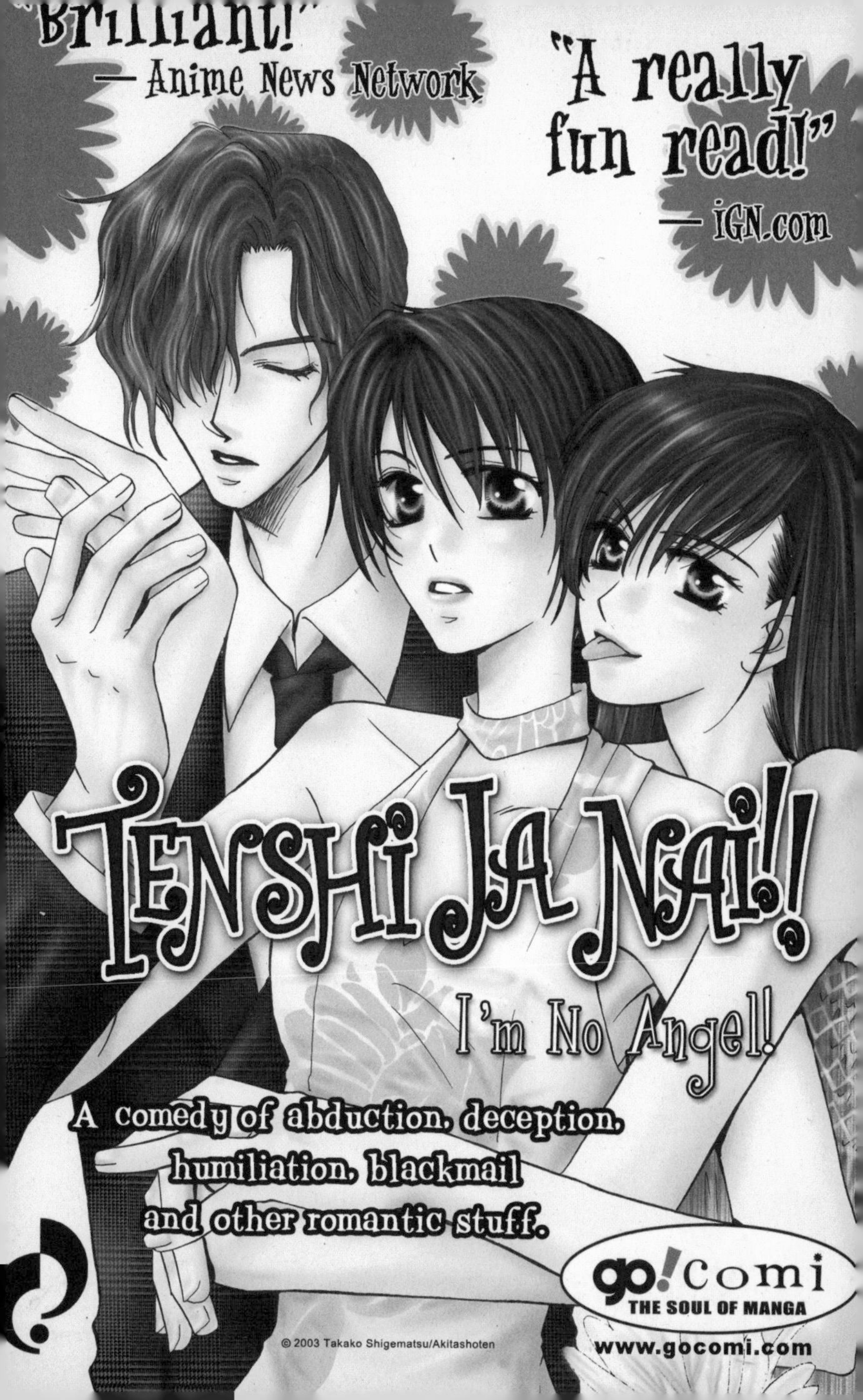
"Brilliant!"
— Anime News Network
"A really fun read!"
— IGN.com
TENSHI JA NAI!!
I'm No Angel!
A comedy of abduction, deception, humiliation, blackmail and other romantic stuff.
go!comi
THE SOUL OF MANGA
© 2003 Takako Shigematsu/Akitashoten
www.gocomi.com

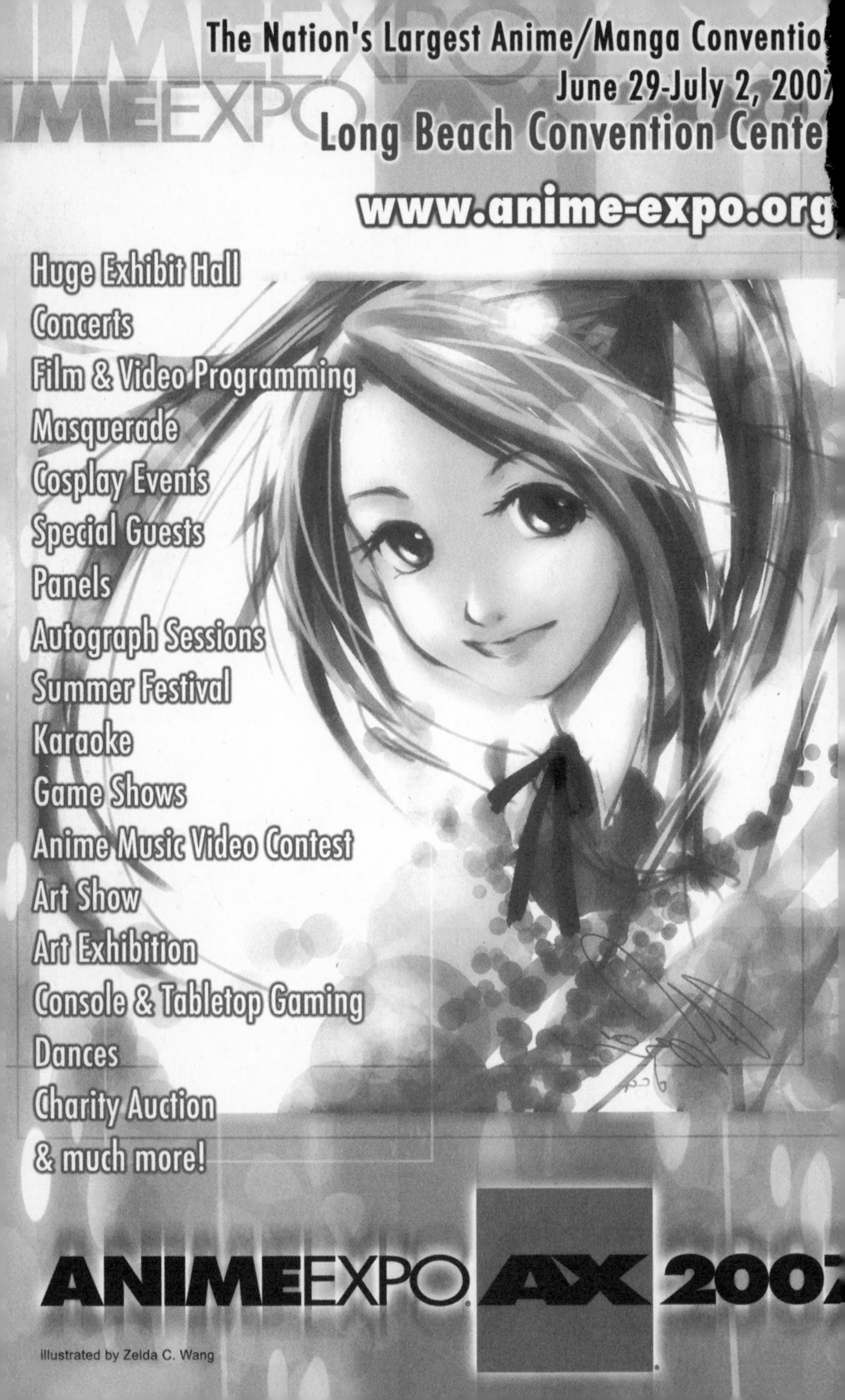
ANIME EXPO
The Nation's Largest Anime/Manga Conventio
June 29-July 2, 200
Long Beach Convention Cente
www.anime-expo.org
Huge Exhibit Hall
Concerts
Film & Video Programming
Masquerade
Cosplay Events
Special Guests
Panels
Autograph Sessions
Summer Festival
Karaoke
Game Shows
Anime Music Video Contest
Art Show
Art Exhibition
Console & Tabletop Gaming
Dances
Charity Auction
& much more!
ANIME EXPO AX 200
illustrated by Zelda C. Wang

SETONA MIZUSHIRO

Since this story's begun, I've received so many positive responses from readers, and it's made me so happy. Thank you all.

This is the first mystery story I've done that has run this long, but it's fun for me. As a creator, I've never gotten the kind of happiness I get from people reading and enjoying it.

To those who have read my stories before, and those who are just starting with this one, I promise I'll put forth as much effort as I can to draw this manga quickly so you can all enjoy it till the very end.

Please, join me on this journey for a little while.

ABOUT THE MANGA-KA

Setona Mizushiro's first real dabble in the world of creating manga was in 1985 when she participated in the publication of a dojinshi (amateur manga). She remained active in the dojinshi world until she debuted in April of 1993 with her short single *Fuyu ga Owarou Toshiteita* (Winter Was Ending) that ran in Shogakukan's *Puchi Comic* magazine. Mizushiro-sensei is well-known for her series *X-Day* in which she exhibits an outstanding ability to delve into psychological issues of every nature. Besides manga, Mizushiro-sensei has an affinity for chocolate, her two cats (Jam and Nene), and round sparkly objects.